The Era of the Individual

NEW FRENCH THOUGHT

Series Editors

Thomas Pavel and Mark Lilla

Titles in the Series

Mark Lilla, ed., *New French Thought: Political Philosophy*

Gilles Lipovetsky, *The Empire of Fashion: Dressing Modern Democracy*

Pierre Manent, *An Intellectual History of Liberalism*

Jacques Bouveresse, *Wittgenstein Reads Freud: The Myth of the Unconscious*

Blandine Kriegel, *The State and the Rule of Law*

Alain Renaut, *The Era of the Individual: A Contribution to a History of Subjectivity*

Marcel Gauchet, *The Disenchantment of the World: A Political History of Religion*

Alain Renaut

The Era of the Individual

A CONTRIBUTION TO A HISTORY OF SUBJECTIVITY

Translated by M. B. DeBevoise and Franklin Philip

With a Foreword by Alexander Nehamas

NEW FRENCH THOUGHT

PRINCETON UNIVERSITY PRESS · PRINCETON, NEW JERSEY

Published by Princeton University Press, 41 William Street,
Princeton, New Jersey 08540
In the United Kingdom: Princeton University Press, Chichester, West Sussex

Translated from the French edition of Alain Renaut, *L'ère de l'individu: Contribution à une histoire de la subjectivité* (Paris: Gallimard, © 1989)

The foreword by Alexander Nehamas previously appeared as "The Rescue of Humanism" in *The New Republic*, vol. 203 (12 November 1990): 27–34.

Library of Congress Cataloging-in-Publication Data

Renaut, Alain.
[Ere de l'individu. English]
The era of the individual : a contribution to a history of
subjectivity / Alain Renaut ; translated by Malcolm M. DeBevoise
and Franklin Philip ; with a foreword by Alexander Nehamas.
p. cm. — (New French thought)
Includes bibliographical references and index.
ISBN 0-691-00637-7 (alk. paper)
1. Individualism—History. 2. Philosophy, Modern. I. Title. II. Series.
B824.R4613 1997
141'.4—dc21 96-45263

Published with the assistance of the French Ministry of Culture

This book has been composed in Adobe Bauer Bodoni

Princeton University Press books are printed on acid-free paper and meet the guidelines for permanence and durability of the Committee on Production Guidelines for Book Longevity of the Council on Library Resources

Printed in the United States of America by Princeton Academic Press

10 9 8 7 6 5 4 3 2 1

Contents

Foreword

UNTIL RECENTLY, Martin Heidegger's philosophy attracted and repelled, with equal intensity, a large number of American readers. To his admirers, Heidegger was one of the great philosophers in history, the thinker who understood most clearly the impasse that Western technological civilization is supposed to have reached, who may have had a glimpse, if only dimly, of another world. To his detractors, Heidegger was an obscurantist with an odious political past, with a talent for coining impenetrable neologisms that appear to display deep understanding but really serve only as a barrier to systematic, rational criticism.

Was he a genius? Was he a fraud? This debate has finally been left behind. Though Heidegger is still a suspicious figure to a number of American philosophers, his reputation has gradually become firm and his authority broad. Now his admirers seem to outnumber his detractors. The fact is that Heidegger has arrived in America. This is due partly to some connections between his thought and American pragmatism, particularly his view that practice precedes theory. It is a central thesis of *Being and Time* (1927) that our fundamental interactions with the world are practical and essentially unreflective, as long as everything functions as expected; we become reflective, theoretical, when things begin to break down, and we need to understand them in order to fix them. More important, Heidegger's increasing respectability is due to the dissemination of postwar French thought, on which his influence has been seminal. As Michel Foucault, Jacques Derrida, Pierre Bourdieu, Louis Althusser, and Jacques Lacan have come to be studied seriously, Heidegger, whose disgust with modernity lurks behind their own adversarial thinking, has come to be read more positively by American readers than ever before.

In France, however, the fate of Heidegger's reputation has been changing. The tables have been turned. As a result of a general change in the philosophical atmosphere, and in the wake of a number of revelations about Heidegger's politics in Nazi Germany, the question in France is now whether one should be allied with him at all, philosophically or politically. In the aftermath of the 1960s, Foucault and the other authors of his generation became almost canonical figures in Paris, but by the early 1980s an intellectual and political backlash against them began to emerge. As the Socialists gained control of the government, the intellectuals moved away from the left, toward the center and the right. Luc Ferry and Alain Renaut are important figures in this new movement. Their *French Philosophy of the Sixties* appeared in 1985. It contains a spirited defense of the accomplishments of liberal democracy in the West and a sustained attack against "the thought of '68," whose distrust of liberalism Ferry and Renaut attribute to the influence of an "antihumanism" inherited from Heidegger and, to a lesser extent, from Marx.

Ferry and Renaut believe that the wholesale rejection of modernity and democracy that Heidegger advocated is profoundly mistaken. They argue, as we shall see, that "antihumanism," in eliminating the very idea of the human subject, also eliminates the possibility of the existence of basic rights, which belong to human beings precisely because they are human. They are firm believers in such rights, which they describe as one of the great "promises of modernity." But they are not simply defenders of democracy, they are also its critics. They claim that "the democratic world endlessly makes promises that it does not keep," and they propose to criticize that world in the name of those very promises. Their criticism, however, unlike the rejectionism of the Heideggerians, is meant to be internal: it upholds the goals of democracy, but it demonstrates how far we still are from meeting them.

The contemporary recoil from Heidegger and his influence has not been only conceptual. Heidegger had never been known as an admirer of democracy, but it was not until 1987, when Victor Farias's *Heidegger and Nazism* appeared, that the issue of the extent and the systematic nature of his involvement with National Socialism took center stage. Farias's book established beyond any doubt that Heidegger's involvement with the Nazis was far deeper and longer than the notorious ten months when he was the rector of the University of Freiburg. He remained a dues-paying member of the party, and maintained ties, political and ideological, with a number of leading Nazi figures. Worse, perhaps, he never really saw his attitude or his behavior as a serious error.

The main thesis of Ferry and Renaut's *Heidegger and Modernity*, which appeared in France in 1988, is that Heidegger's criticism of modernity—indeed, his criticism of the whole history of "the West"—is rooted in his authoritarian, nostalgic, right-wing politics. Such a politics, they argue, was extraordinarily ill-suited to the radical, left-wing, and utopian uses to which Heidegger's French followers put it: "We cannot overestimate the amount of political purification that went into the translation of Heidegger's philosophy into a leftist intellectual context. . . . Until a few months ago [they wrote in 1988] Heideggerianism made it possible to hang onto . . . the crepuscular task of salvaging thought from the general collapse of humanity into American-style businessism."

Heidegger believed that democracy and technology, the two central institutions of modernity, correspond closely to one another. Technology turns what had been prerogatives of the few into the necessities for the many. The power over nature that technology gives each individual is translated, in political terms, into the power within society that democracy allows us. Both technology and democracy place individual human beings in the center of the world. They are, in that sense, "humanist." (For Heidegger, their "humanism" was precisely the problem.)

Ferry and Renaut's own attitude toward technology and mass culture is not at all unlike Heidegger's. They wish to drive a wedge, however, between the contempt for technology and mass culture and the denial of democratic politics. They consider it part of "the tragic side of modernity" that it is associated with "the emergence of the world of pure technology and its consequent transformation of culture into industrial mass culture." They believe that their criticism and Heidegger's can share the same "object," that is, technology and mass culture, but they insist that their "purpose" and his do not overlap.

Heidegger's main philosophical weapon in his criticism of modernity and democracy, they argue, was his "antihumanism," his conviction that human beings neither know nor control their basic nature and desires. In *L'ère de l'individu*, Renaut offers a philosophical diagnosis of the origins and the nature of antihumanism. The book develops in great detail some ideas only briefly alluded to in *French Philosophy of the Sixties*. It traces the notion of the individual back to Leibniz, and charts its progressive liberation from all constraint from Berkeley to Nietzsche. And it supports the controversial view that the continued growth of individualism ends in nothing short of the dissolution of the idea of the subject: when no limits are anywhere acknowledged, the notion of autonomy, which always places one in relation to people or to norms, also disappears. Thus Renaut concludes that two of the main features of modern philosophical thought, usually considered to be part of a single strain, finally cancel each other out. Modernity does not only give rise to the idea of the subject, as Heidegger believed. It also, paradoxically, leads to its disappearance. To some extent, then, antihumanism is part of the modern tradition itself.

Ferry and Renaut's philosophical project is to preserve the most valuable aspect of modernity, the idea of human rights, which are shared by all simply by virtue of the fact that we are human, whatever our particular circumstances. They argue for a new faith in our sovereignty over ourselves, a view that they characterize as a "modest" and "nonmetaphysical" humanism. The articulation of that humanism is the central aim of their many works. Their aim is admirable. And their idea that criticism should only be "internal" or piecemeal, that grand rejections are often nothing more than grand illusions, is deeply right.

French Philosophy of the Sixties, however, is a thoroughly polemical work, which simplifies the position of its adversaries and overstates its own case. Its central argument is that with the exception of Marx, whose influence in France (though still obvious in Bourdieu, Althusser, and some of Foucault) had already begun to wane by the 1970s, Heidegger has been the single most important influence on the movement represented by the thought of '68, on Foucault, Derrida, and Lacan. Why was Heidegger so important to postwar French thought? And what exactly is the "antihumanism" that underwrites his criticism of modernity?

For a start, it is important to recall that in *An Introduction to Metaphysics*, which appeared in 1935, after Heidegger's supposed break with Nazism, he still felt free to write that "from a metaphysical point of view, Russia and America are the same: the same dreary technological frenzy, the same unrestricted organization of the average man." And he concluded: "We are caught in a pincers. Situated in the center, our nation incurs the severest pressure. It is the nation with the most neighbors and hence the most endangered. With all this, it is the most metaphysical of nations. . . . All this implies that this nation . . . must move itself and thereby the history of the West beyond the center of their future 'happening' and into the primordial realm of the powers of being."

Now if one were to forget that the political structure of the nation whose "metaphysical" nature Heidegger is praising was National Socialism, his thought might appear to provide a way of criticizing both great postwar powers at the same time. As a result of such a feat of intellectual acrobatics, one might even think that to reject the individualist and the consumerist madness of the West would not have to imply an endorsement of the totalitarian and bureaucratic insanity of the East. Heidegger, in sum, seemed to offer the devoutly desired middle way: both powers could now be seen as products of the "spiritual decline of the earth" brought about by "the reign of technology." Adversarial intellectuals could use such a purified version of Heidegger to avoid a direct political stand in favor either of the United States or of the Soviet Union.

For Heidegger, moreover, the reign of technology is in its "essence" identical with the essence of "Western metaphysics." And this metaphysics, in turn, is centrally characterized by "humanism." The humanism that Heidegger attacks is the belief that human beings are the ultimate "subjects" of the world, in reference to which all things, or "objects," are thought and classified. It involves two main ideas. First, it holds that the world conforms to the principles that govern our own intellectual life, especially the principles of reason; like the self, therefore, the world contains no irresoluble mysteries. Second, it maintains that, again, like our own self, the world is fully consonant with our desires and will; the objects of which it consists are thought to derive what reality they possess from their amenability to our use and exploitation. Things are what we can make of them.

Heidegger was not willing (perhaps he was never able) fully to articulate this alternative attitude, which considers nature as a system with its own order and integrity, and the best human life as a harmonious contemplative relationship with it. But he wrote at length against the victory of "metaphysics," the long line of thought that leads from Plato through Aristotle, Descartes, and Kant to Nietzsche. That tradition, in Heidegger's account, conceived of nature only in relation to its usefulness, only as an object of exploitation and mastery. In Descartes, Heidegger conceded, technology and science still aimed at the mastery of nature in order to secure greater freedom and happiness for people, but in Nietzsche mastery became a goal in itself, serving no further purpose. Nietzsche's "will to power," according to Heidegger's controversial but influential interpretation, is a self-perpetuating activity: it is a will that aims at nothing beyond itself, a will to will, no matter its object. "Nature" has ceased to be something in its own right altogether; it is simply raw material to be shaped, a source of resistances whose only function is to provide new opportunities for domination.

Heidegger's high criticisms were easily adaptable to the lower phenomena of modern life. The language of advertising, for example, provides a vulgar but accurate emblem of what Heidegger finds distasteful in modernity. All we are now concerned with is the search for "new and improved" versions of whatever means are already available for attaining whatever goals such means make possible. The value of the goals themselves is irrelevant; the only valuable goal is the endless proliferation of means. What counts is doing things better than before. Whether such things are worth doing in the first place is no longer a question.

According to Heidegger, the blind desire for manipulation came about because modernity turned reason—which was, for the ancients, and even for the medievals, a source of valuable goals—into a purely instrumental faculty. And here, as it turns out, we have a crucial point of contact between Heidegger and the left. The war of the members of the Frankfurt School, especially Max Horkheimer and Theodor Adorno, against "instrumental reason" was as vicious as the war against it that Heidegger waged. And though the changes that the critical theorists advocated led exactly away from Heidegger's nostalgic desire for a return to an earlier, most authentic relationship to nature, both they and he were united in their distaste for what they saw as the crudeness and the vulgarity of technological progress and mass culture.

According to Ferry and Renaut, Heidegger and his followers unleashed an uncompromising attack on modernity on the grounds of its humanism, of its thinking of "Man" as the ultimate subject, as "lord and master of the earth." Subjectivity, which is closely connected to humanism, involves personal autonomy on the practical level and self-knowledge on the theoretical. The two levels are connected: that is, a subject knows itself through and through; it contains no opaque or inaccessible parts of the operation of which it remains unaware. The subject is also the absolute master of its decisions, able to make them on its own without interference from any factors over which it has less than perfect control. In view of the fact that external objects obey the same theoretical and practical principles, nature, the totality of things, is completely open to human understanding and manipulation. As the subject is "present" to itself, in knowledge and control, so what is, is "present" to the subject. Indeed, "being present," in this not always intuitive sense, is the mark of what it is to be.

To attack humanism is to deny that a subject conceived in such terms exists, to deny that human beings are fully self-aware and autonomous. According to Ferry and Renaut, Heidegger and his followers dispute, in just this way, the sovereignty of human beings. Permeated or even fully constructed by lines of impersonal power, domination, and normalization (Foucault), by codes whose ability to communicate fully is undermined by their own structure (Derrida), by unconscious forces and desires (Lacan), or by economic and social factors (Bourdieu, Althusser), the human subject is held to be anything but transparent to itself. And what the subject does not know, it cannot control. Autonomy disappears, since apparently free decisions turn out to be effects of these unknown and independent lines of force.

And if the subject is not, in this sense, "present" to itself, there is even less reason to believe that the world is present to it. What things are, therefore, is not necessarily exhausted by their availability for human use and consumption. "Metaphysics"—the dominant mode of thought in the West, according to which to be is to be available for use, and which is therefore in its "essence" identical with "technology," with the systematic manipulation of the world—represents only one possible path of human history.

In the incantatory, almost hieratic language of his late works, Heidegger attempted to evoke what some other relationship to the world might look, feel, or be like. He tried to develop a vocabulary that would embody a "nonmetaphysical" attitude to the world, though he was also aware that any effort to leave metaphysics behind might always appear as just one more metaphysical system. Can an effort to escape the totality of one's tradition avoid being a desire to know and control the totality of one's history, of one's world? This is, famously, the charge that he himself made against Nietzsche, "the first of the last metaphysicians"; it is the charge that Derrida eventually made against him; and it is the charge that others are now making against Derrida. No doubt they will have it made against them in the future.

I believe that this charge is correct. An attempt to leave one's history and tradition behind, combined with the view that this history is unitary, is bound to fail. For it will necessarily have to preserve some parts of the old tradition as building blocks for the new. And since "metaphysics" permeates the old tradition through and through, it will also infect its successor. Heidegger was haunted by this problem. To solve it, he developed the strange poetic vocabulary of his late works. His hope was that individual words could be liberated, as it were, from their earlier subjection to metaphysics, and that the story they could be used to tell would be free of that subjection. His urging us to turn away from metaphysics as the study of "the being of beings" toward "the question of Being," his calling language "the house of Being" and man "Being's poem," were all parts of his effort to construct a nonmetaphysical language and a nonmetaphysical attitude—an attitude that would place us "at home" on the earth and not at odds with it.

But Heidegger's effort was a failure. Even a home is something we use. It was a failure, moreover, that sometimes seemed designed to terrorize those who perceive it as such. For qualifications like "the essential nature of . . . ," "metaphysically," or "the inner truth and greatness of . . . " (in this case, "the inner truth and greatness of" National Socialism, which turns out to be "the encounter between global technology and modern man") suggest that Heidegger is always concerned with a deeper level of whatever he is addressing, and that one's lack of agreement only betrays a lack of understanding and sensitivity.

Heidegger's effort to leave metaphysics behind was based on serious philosophical misreadings, beginning with his tendentious interpretations of the pre-Socratics and culminating in his massive, if brilliant, deformation of Nietzsche. The continuity between the pre-Socratics and Plato is much greater than he ever imagined. And Nietzsche was too canny, too prolific and protean, too aware of the complexity of the tradition that he attacked, to be pinned down as a metaphysician on the basis of a few passages from *The Will to Power*, a haphazard collection of notes edited posthumously by his sister and doggedly interpreted by Heidegger as the skeleton of his major and unfinished work. Heidegger's tendency to consider "Modernity" and "the West" as monolithic structures with a single essence, whether it is "technology" or "metaphysics," also presents a great problem; I doubt that even "technology" designates a single phenomenon.

And I believe that the wholesale rejection of one's time, brave and brilliant as it may sometimes be, is bound to lead to nothing. Nothing is left when everything is left behind.

I share, in sum, many of Ferry and Renaut's criticisms of Heidegger, as well as their positive goal of an internal criticism of democracy that does not reject it completely. Still, I cannot escape the feeling that their own positive approach remains too deeply indebted to Heidegger's analysis of modernity. For surely "humanism" is itself as complex and ambiguous a concept as "the West" or "metaphysics" or the others. To characterize oneself as a humanist is not necessarily to be a friend of the human; and to be antihumanist is not necessarily to be its foe. Heidegger's antihumanism, in fact, springs from precisely his sense that it is humanism that has made us slaves of the technology that it fostered and engendered.

Humanism, at its most extreme, is a position that attributes to human beings absolute importance in the universe, absolute freedom from any outside forces in the world, absolute knowledge and control of themselves. It is a little like attributing God's features to his erstwhile creatures (and some of this extreme humanism originated in such a heaven-storming impulse). Antihumanism, at its own extreme, holds that individual human beings are of no consequence in the universe, that they are totally controlled, even constituted, by outside forces (economic, social, sexual) that are the real subjects of history, that they are essentially incapable of seeing themselves for what they are. The two extremes, of course, are at the opposite ends of the continuum of the history of philosophy, which contains a large number of positions, differing in the degree of importance, freedom, and self-knowledge they attribute to us. Toward the middle, where individual and social factors begin to merge and to influence one another, it becomes difficult to say exactly to which side a particular position belongs. It could even be that a proper mixture of these factors might constitute a position to which neither label could be correctly applied.

Now Ferry and Renaut believe, again, that Heidegger's main objections to modernity proceed from his particular brand of antihumanism, his belief that technology and democracy have given the individual more power in the world and in society than is appropriate. They agree with him that modernity possesses what they call a "tragic side." This has two aspects. The first is constituted by the erosion of the authority of tradition during modern times. Generally accepted answers to serious questions no longer exist; individuals, however ill-equipped, must answer such questions by themselves. The second aspect, again, is "the emergence of the world of pure technology and its consequent transformation of culture into industrial mass culture."

Ferry and Renaut conclude that these features of modernity explain "how appealing and persuasive Heidegger's criticism" can be. Still, they want a subtler and more complex approach than Heidegger's total rejection of the modern. They insist that some form of humanism is necessary for the preservation of human rights, the nature of which they leave generally unspecified, but which, they believe, the thought of '68 was intent on abandoning: "Whether conducted in the name of a radiant future [Marx] or a traditionalist reaction [Heidegger], the total critique of the modern world, because it is necessarily an antihumanism that leads inevitably to seeing in the democratic project, for example, in human rights, the prototype of ideology or of the metaphysical illusion, is structurally incapable of taking up, except insincerely and in spite of itself, the promises that are also those of modernity."

Ferry and Renaut insist that "it would be absurd today . . . to attempt philosophically to restore figures of subjectivity whose deconstruction dates . . . at least as far back as Kant." Traditional humanism, the optimistic Enlightenment view that human beings can become complete masters of the world, cannot be recaptured. But its virtues can be preserved. A more modern criticism is possible. "Between 'collaboration' and external criticism," they ask, "is there really no place for an internal critique?" And they answer that because "the democratic world endlessly makes promises that it does not keep," it is "in the name of these promises . . . that one should perhaps criticize it, in the name of the present."

These are all commendable sentiments. Ferry and Renaut refuse to take a stand outside modernity as a whole. (That is an impossible task, in any case.) They wish to vindicate a moderate humanism, a view that attributes significant but not "absolute" or "metaphysical" autonomy and self-knowledge to human subjects, a view that supplies a solid foundation for human rights.

Humanism is a flexible concept. Ferry and Renaut present their own "modest" version of it—rather surprisingly—on the basis of the famous definition that Sartre offered in "Existentialism is Humanism," the definition "which he was unfortunately to recant." In that essay, Sartre explicates his famous formula, "Existence precedes essence," by contrasting artifacts with human beings. An artifact, he writes, is produced according to a conception of the function that it will serve, and therefore "its essence—that is to say the sum of the formulae and the qualities which made its production and its definition possible—precedes its existence." Religion, Sartre continues, thinks of human beings as God's artifacts. But since, according to him, God does not exist, "There is one being whose existence comes before its essence": "Man first of all exists, encounters himself, surges up in the world—and defines himself afterwards. . . . To begin with he is nothing. . . . Man simply is . . . what he wills, and as he conceives himself after already existing. . . . Man is nothing else but that which he makes of himself." This is how Ferry and Renaut gloss Sartre's account:

> The authentic subject is "nothingness" since it escapes any attempt to capture it in a definition. This is the freedom by which he distinguishes himself from manufactured objects, which in order to exist had to be conceived, thus defined, from the start by the mind of the artisan. If, therefore, objects are "something" (definite), the true, properly human subject is *nothing* determined, is *not* identifiable; in other words, he breaks with himself since he is always beyond everything that might define him, even in his own eyes.

In their view, Sartre's humanism belongs to a "tradition going back to Rousseau." In such a tradition, "the distinguishing feature of man is to be indefinable; his essence is to have no essence." According to this conception, we can deny ourselves the freedom that such humanism grants us by acting in "bad faith." This is to identify ourselves with a single one of our roles or features, to act "as though one were a creature, as though nature or history could become our codes."

That nature or history is our "code," that we are completely determined by forces exterior to us, is precisely the view that Ferry and Renaut attribute to the "thought of '68." I could argue with this attribution, at least in regard to Foucault's later work on the history of sexuality, but a general question concerning the "moderate" nature of their brand of humanism seems more urgent.

Sartre's humanism may well hark back to the Enlightenment, and even to Fichte, on whose exquisitely obscure thought Ferry relies for his conception of rights in the first volume of his *Political Philosophy*, but it is anything but "moderate." Appealing to Sartre, with his absolute distinction between human beings ("beings for themselves") and everything else in the world ("beings in themselves") and to Rousseau, who in his *Discourse on Inequality* envisages that an unbridgeable gap separates us from every other living thing, seems to me to lead Ferry and Renaut right back to the "undeconstructed figures of subjectivity" to which they believe we cannot return. And why can't we? Their reason seems to be that what we are and what we can do is at least partly a function of our history, that what we are and what we can do differ according to our historical period, our social and cultural situation—the forces, in short, that partly constitute both ourselves and the world we live in.

Ferry and Renaut want to deny that we are totally subject to such forces. This, I think, is right. But Sartre believed that we are totally independent of such forces, perfectly sovereign over ourselves and our choices: this is precisely what he means when he writes that "man . . . is not definable . . . because he is at first nothing." For Sartre, we could be free agents only if we were something over and above *everything* that could be said of us, something beyond *every* situation in which we happened to be found. This, I think, is wrong.

All that is necessary in order to avoid reducing human beings to their situations, to forces over which they have no control, is to think that we are able to distance ourselves from any specific situation in which we happen to be. Our ability, our need, to occupy various roles, to belong to various groups, to accept various standards of description and evaluation, to be, in a word, complex, is sufficient to allow us to criticize and to "transcend" particular roles, groups, or standards. All that we need in order not to be defined by one role is our ability to occupy another role. What we cannot do is criticize them, and thus abandon them, all together and concurrently. We can indeed pull ourselves up by our own bootstraps—but only one boot at a time. And this view that individuals are a combination of strands as complex as the world to which each is related owes something to Nietzsche and Foucault; it is not antihumanist in any objectionable sense. It is still too early, therefore, to declare that "the French philosophy of the '60s," which criticized humanism, is dead. Some of its strands may be, others may not.

In the end, for all the admirably un-Heideggerian motive of their campaign for a theory of human rights, Ferry and Renaut are still under Heidegger's spell. They claim to pursue "an internal criticism of the world of democracy," but they actually share his contempt for the world of technology: "Who doesn't deplore chopping up movies with commercials?" they ask in an irresponsible aside—irresponsible, because the technology that broke new ground in cultural vulgarity also brought us indoor plumbing, mass inoculations, and the increased availability of information. By their own account, the world of technology is the world of modernity; and the humanism to which they appeal does not belong to that world.

It is impossible, in the end, to speak in disapproval of technology, of the world of "mass" culture, without speaking also in disapproval of democracy, as if the two were independent of one another in the modern world, as if one could be "against" technology and "for" democracy. Technology and democracy cannot be easily separated from each other. The idea that they can be separated is an error as grave as it is common, and we must guard against it. "Mass culture" may just be the price at which democracy comes. To find it distasteful is also to find the people whose culture it is (and whose culture isn't it?) themselves distasteful. And further reflection on "mass culture" may reveal it to be less objectionable than it seems.

It is their insistence on dissociating technology from democracy that forces Ferry and Renaut to subscribe to a conception of human beings that belongs, by their own definition, to a "premodern" world. They characterize such a conception, which they correctly attribute to Heidegger, as a "traditionalist reaction." Those are harsh words, especially since Ferry and Renaut are not above traditionalism themselves. It would be kinder and more accurate to say that though Ferry and Renaut are engaged in what they consider a revival of traditional liberalism, they are also at the same time traditional conservatives. They are respectful of the ideals of a free society, but they are suspicious of some of the means for achieving them, and they might appear disdainful of the people for whom these ideas are to be secured.

Alexander Nehamas

Translator's Note

THE TRANSLATION of this impressively learned, closely argued, and highly individual work was begun several years ago by Franklin Philip, who had previously translated books by Alain Renaut (and by Luc Ferry) for the University of Chicago Press. It subsequently fell to me to complete and thoroughly revise Philip's draft manuscript. My aim, in keeping with the policy of the series editors, has been to produce a readable version that carries over as far as possible the letter and sense of the original French text while adapting it where necessary to the somewhat different conventions and style that characterize philosophical exposition in English. Where English translations of works cited by the author exist, reference has been made to these; where they do not, I have made fresh translations. Additionally, I have taken the liberty of including a certain amount of bibliographic material not found in the French edition, both in the text and in the notes, particularly in connection with works of German philosophy whose original titles are likely to be more familiar to readers than their French versions.

I am grateful to Thomas Pavel for his useful comments on a preliminary version of the revised draft, and to Michelle McKenna, Heidi Sheehan, and Licia Wise at Princeton University Press for their careful work in helping prepare the final manuscript for publication. My greatest debt is to Joshua Landy, without whose meticulous research the present edition could not have been brought before the scholarly public at this time.

M. B. DeBevoise

Preface

AT LAST the moment has come for someone to find the time and the means to work through the question of the subject in its full extent and difficulty. I propose to do this by inquiring into its history. My inquiry takes the form of a philosophical history of modernity, particularly of modern philosophy.

Academic tradition has too often accustomed us to regarding—even practicing—the history of philosophy as a respectable but rather uncreative discipline, inspired solely by a concern for philological accuracy, which makes it possible to appreciate and preserve great ideas. For this reason a profound cleavage has developed between the philosophy of historians of philosophy, who are apt to be demoted (often by themselves) to the rank of mere professors, and the philosophy of philosophers, who are typically elevated (here again, often by themselves) to the supreme dignity of thinkers.[1] This is to forget that at least since Kant the history of philosophy has been itself a philosophical problem: witness the brilliant "History of Pure Reason" that concludes the first *Critique*. Kant's efforts in this direction have been extended in the meantime, notably by Hegel and Heidegger, each in his own way helping to give the history of philosophy an authentically philosophical dimension. Most such attempts at writing a philosophical history of philosophy seem certain not to withstand the test of time, nor to resist the assault of a truly historical history of philosophy, which is incomparably better equipped to meet the standards of scholarly adequacy. Thus a history of philosophy still remains to be written that is both philosophical and at the same time more historical than any that has been attempted until now. The philosophical history of subjectivity I am proposing here dares to claim to be such a history.

The kind of daring I have in mind should be understood in the following way. Though for fifteen years I have devoted a large part of my philosophical work to what is called the "history of philosophy," I have done so in the full and undeceived awareness that the history of philosophy as such held no interest for me whatsoever. (By this I mean a purely historical, or historicising, history that has the goal—perfectly laudable in itself—of reconstructing as faithfully as possible the philosophies of the past, which are to be admired for their monumental grandeur and educational value.) At bottom, what has always kept me from doing history of philosophy in this way is that the question of truth is put aside: from this perspective, the point is not to scrutinize philosophical doctrines with an eye to their possible intellectual fruitfulness but merely to revisit their origins or to analyze their internal coherence. On this view, all ideas are seen to have the same claim on the historian's attention: whether one is considering Malebranche's theory of vortices or Nietzsche's notion of the Eternal Return, one's work will contribute to the unfinished reconstruction of the past. Choosing the object of attention becomes an aesthetic matter, so to speak, a question of taste: one may, for example, prefer the austere architecture of Spinoza's *Ethics* to the fragmented and symbolic writing of Pascal's *Pensées* just as one may attach greater value to the suggestive power of Nietzsche's aphorisms than to the demonstrative rigor of Hegelian systematizing. While I agree that this very broadly dominant way of writing the history of philosophy has occasioned many admirable works, it seems to me to suffer from three main drawbacks.

First, it redirects philosophical work toward the mere reconstruction of what has been thought in the past, leaving to (unnamed) others the trouble of conceiving the world as it is. This shift, trivial though it is to note, deserves to be emphasized because of the more or less conscious assumption on the part of the historicizing historian that philosophy has run its course, that its fate is settled, and that from now on the only imaginable task left for philosophy is to review its history, the better to appropriate it. This historical sort of history of philosophy makes the death of philosophy a self-fulfilling prophesy, treating philosophy as a kind of unoccupied palace open to the public in which no new treasures can any longer be expected to be found. I do not dispute that this notion of the end of philosophy, which may be philosophically justified in various ways, contains a certain truth, nor that the possibility of its coming to an end must now be taken seriously as a legitimate question for philosophy; but it is nonetheless still the case that it is a *question*, which cannot be fully answered without its having been posed and worked through. In this sense the philosopher, in doing history, must not behave as though this question were settled or pretend not to see that this falling back on history, as it were, would mean that philosophy had effectively been made into a sort of closed book. In short, because it appears by no means impossible to go on thinking of philosophy as a living thing, capable yet of assuming new forms,[2] it seems to me important to be wary of anything that assumes its death.

Second, insofar as a truly historical history is prompted only by a wish to reconstruct the past, it fails to account for the evolution of philosophy, which becomes instead a gallery of great books that are all equally estimable, differentiated in the mind of the historian only by the greater or lesser enjoyment that reading them brings: this aestheticization of *our* relation to philosophical systems thus tends to sidestep the question of *their* relation to the issues that concern us. It might be accurate to say that while some previous systems continue to be useful for us, not all systems are equally useful. In removing the question of truth from the analysis of philosophical systems, historical histories miss what permits certain ideas (not all ideas—and not always the same ones) to acquire far more value than they would ordinarily if we were content merely to regard them as so many testimonies to the human capacity of understanding—as certainly they all are, more or less (rather more than less, in fact). If we are to profit from whatever advantage the history of philosophy can confer, philosophically or even intellectually, it must be investigated on the basis of the issues that presently command our attention. Since current problems call for more or less attention to be paid to one philosophical tradition or another, the philosophical consideration of historical issues involves quite different stakes than mere historicizing reconstruction. Having said this, I am of course aware of a rather predictable objection that can be brought against philosophical history: is it really possible to guarantee that in bringing present-day concerns to bear upon works of the past we do not distort these works, and that in "exploiting" the ideas they contain for our own purposes we do not place them in the service of intellectual interests very different than those of their original authors? Does not the integrity of the historian of philosophy consist in an ability to neutralize one's own interests, to remain philosophically uninvolved, so to speak—that is, to be a philosopher to the least degree possible, as little engaged in a personal philosophical quest as one can be? This is one of the deep paradoxes of the history of philosophy: the very condition of historical objectivity seems to mandate a division of labor between the mere historian and the true philosopher, with all the awkward consequences this split implies—the historian being cut off from the philosophical creativity and demands of his time, and the philosopher being obliged to stand above (or in any case at some distance from) the great systems of the past, which are taken to be external to his work as a thinker. Beyond noting such a preverse result, which contributes in some measure to the discredit of both parties, I wish to point out that the insistence on philosophical detachment conceals yet another shortcoming, this time an epistemological one, of any history of philosophy exclusively cast as a historical history.

This third, and final, drawback of traditional history of philosophy is that it requires the very naive assumption that the works of the past can be approached without any presuppositions, as though the history of philosophy were the last among the various historical disciplines to have completed its epistemological revolution; it remains oddly attached to a *positivist* conception of cognitive activity, based on the belief that the historian can reconstruct the facts of a case (in this case the intellectual facts contained in books) "as they took place." In the context of historical knowledge in general, this belief betrays an illusion that has been exposed by critical philosophers of history from Dilthey to Raymond Aron: the historian, by virtue of the fact that he himself is a historical being, cannot escape seeing the past from the viewpoint of his own historically determined present. This act of putting the past into perspective, far from needing to be criticized and rejected as a source of distortion, constitutes the very condition of historical study. The question of objectivity is inevitably complex, and the historian of philosophy has no choice but to face up to it. Rather than continue to succumb to the mirages of the positivist illusion, he is obliged to admit that when he focuses on one particular moment rather than another in the history of philosophy, he does so at least partly on the basis of where he stands regarding present-day philosophy—more exactly, on the basis of how he understands this present. The moments of the past that seem the most in need of exploration are not always the same; their interest to the historian depends on the evolution of his own philosophical concerns. That is why the history of philosophy has an exciting history of its own: not just because of its methods, but also because of its objects and content. Though noteworthy books are still being written about Hegel, the era of the great disquisitions on Hegelianism, so characteristic of previous generations, now seems past; analogously, the reason Fichte has recently enjoyed a revival in France is surely that shifts in philosophical concerns have made it necessary to reread his works, which are now approached in very different ways than during earlier waves of interest in Fichtean ideas. The fact that problems and approaches change should not provoke skepticism about the seriousness and fruitfulness of the work of historians of philosophy. Just as recognition of the role that personal perspective plays in historical research does not deny it some measure of objectivity, the ceaseless reexamination and reinterpretation that characterizes the history of philosophy shows the value of all the work done in its name—which I am inclined to see as an encouraging sign of philosophical vitality, a sign that philosophy continues to transform itself in relation to its own history. Rather than engage in a futile attempt to resist the orientation of current historical work toward the philosophical present, we should welcome this as a proof of life—life that the purely historicizing ideal, by contrast, only works to destroy.

All of this leads me to endorse the idea of a philosophical history of philosophy that, while scrupulously historical, is at the same time candid about its presuppositions. If I say that history of philosophy *as such* does not interest me, this means that I cannot study a work on Spinoza or Victor Cousin (or even Fichte) a priori, that is, without noting the intellectual motivation of the author and trying to see how his or her analysis fits in with what I take to be the current state of philosophical debate. For my part, undertaking here to reflect upon the logic of the philosophical history of modernity, I cannot separate this task from a certain number of convictions I hold concerning the place—the central place, in my view—of the problem of subjectivity in the intellectual life of our time. The importance of this topic, and the present state of disagreement about it, seem to me therefore to require a historical inquiry in the sense I have just described.

Luc Ferry and I concluded our study of certain figures who have been particularly representative of contemporary antihumanism, *La Pensée 68*, by suggesting that the assault mounted against the idea of the subject, at least since Nietzsche or Heidegger (and more recently by French thinkers of the 1960s), was based on unusually simplistic premises—as though any mention of subjectivity inevitably implied the notion of the subject as entirely transparent to itself, sovereign, master of itself and the universe; as though the undeniable collapse of this older model of the subject had to translate into a complete abandonment of any reference whatever to subjectivity. Given the persistence of such naivete, and the ritual identification of a "metaphysical subject" with the "Cartesian *cogito*," it seemed to us fruitful to review the history of the modern concept of subjectivity. Our aim was to oppose the supposed homogeneity of the various faces of the subject, which were treated as totalizable in a single concept, as constituting so many steps along the way that, starting with Descartes, led to and culminated in the absolute Hegelian Subject. By positing the contrary hypothesis of the subject as a *plural* entity having many different faces, we attempted primarily to point out the unnoticed discrepancies or cleavages among them, and therefore to contribute to a more differentiated appreciation of modernity. Above all, however, it seemed to us that reconstructing the often oversimplified history of subjectivity, in all its diversity and complexity, would help bring out unexplored potentialities inherent in the idea of the subject that were irreducible to those underlying the evolution of modern metaphysics—to bring out unexploited possibilities which, because they lay dormant during this evolution, were now perhaps capable of being revived. While naturally we did not assume that this project of revitalization would require a complete conceptual reorganization of the subject, we did imagine that among those potentialities that had been abandoned in favor of other more historically privileged ones, some might be made to serve as starting points for a new philosophy of subjectivity, even though they could not be fully exploited without fundamental redefinition and profound rearrangement.

The debates sparked by the publication of *La Pensée 68* have only confirmed the need to carry out this program. Beyond the quite understandable mistrust shown by some critics towards a book that challenged the main assumptions of an entire intellectual generation, sketched the contours of an alternative, nonmetaphysical humanism, and called for a rethinking of the conventional wisdom that for many people meant a genuine transmutation of all their values, there were a great many misunderstandings. It may be useful here to describe the most common ones, and to explain how they strengthened my conviction that the debate Ferry and I had launched about subjectivity could make progress only by being set in historical context.

Without attempting a fresh justification I should like to remind the reader of the main thesis we defended in *La Pensée 68* (and in some earlier publications as well). We argued that philosophy—indeed society—was faced with the imperative task of reexamining the familiar condemnation of the subject (and the values accompanying it), which had provided most currents of contemporary thought with their most conspicuous leitmotif. To call this sort of attack *antihumanist* was hardly disconcerting in itself: ever since the emergence of modernity, humanism had after all consisted in valorizing humanity's twofold capacity to be conscious of itself (self-reflection) and to determine its own destiny (freedom as self-determination). Historically, these two dimensions have defined the classic idea of *subjectivity* as consisting in the capacity—the quintessentially human capacity—to be the conscious, responsible author of one's thoughts and acts: in short, to be their foundation or *sub-jectum*. It is also easy to understand why this assault on the subject, which was sometimes explicitly antihumanist, should have expressed two central themes of contemporary thinking:

- On the one hand, the theme of the *unconscious* in its various forms: whether asserting the existence of a level of mental life that lies irretrievably outside consciousness (the mental unconscious), or stressing the manipulation or conditioning of consciousness by collective forces outside its control (the social unconscious), or designating a dimension of the real as an irreducible "*différence*" (or "*différance*") that is ungraspable by the identitarian representations of consciousness (the ontological unconscious)—in every case the assumption of *transparency to itself* used to define the modern subject as a form of consciousness is attacked as intrinsically naive; and the insistence on the breakup of the subject, and its inability ever to coincide with itself, reduces the wish for *identity with oneself* to a mere metaphysical illusion unmasked by the discovery of the unconscious.
- On the other hand, the theme of *finitude* (so characteristic of post-Hegelian philosophy) also profoundly undermines the notion and values of subjectivity:

> as against the Cartesian aim of making the human subject "the master and possessor of nature," against the claim of Hegelian reason to have access to absolute knowledge, contemporary thinking originates—as Foucault (following many others, particularly Heidegger) stressed[3]—in an intrinsically antimetaphysical recognition of the radical and insuperable limits to our knowledge of and power over the real. In this sense, if one means by humanism—as did, for example, Heidegger—a conception of man that valorizes his capacity to affirm his sovereignty over himself and the world (thus making himself "the Lord of Being"), the successive reminders of finitude conveyed by philosophers since Hegel may indeed appear to constitute so many overthrows of humanism and of the representation of man as subject. Thus it was that Heidegger—who, more (and better) than anyone, made the recognition of finitude the starting point of philosophy—thought that the resolute acknowledgement of this finitude called for a program of thinking "against humanism" and "against subjectivity" to go forward in parallel with the project of "going beyond metaphysics."

These arguments, based on finitude and the unconscious, constitute the two main intellectual underpinnings of modern criticisms of the idea of the subject.[4] Opaque with regard to itself, and finding itself thrown into a world founded on other principles, the subject—thought by early modern philosophy to be the foundation both of itself and of reality—was shattered. With it were shattered the values of humanism: consciousness, mastery, will, self-foundation, and autonomy. These values have been all the more easily criticized to the extent that arguments from the unconscious and from finitude have been a source, in the domain of political philosophy, of rich and nuanced analyses that have contributed to the poor reputation of the subjectivist tradition. For a whole other tradition of thought, beginning with Heidegger and leading on as much to Hannah Arendt as to Claude Lefort, the totalitarian phenomenon has been interpreted as a consequence of the reign of subjectivity. This approach is not without its attractions. Defining totalitarianism as an attempt at total domination, however, depends entirely on the assumption that the sociohistorical existence of humanity is susceptible to complete control by a power capable of rendering it transparent and rationalizing every aspect of it—in short, by a power that could make itself "master and possessor." On this view, therefore, the fantasy of total domination is to be seen merely as the ultimate and most monstrous face of the modern ("Cartesian") promotion of subjectivity, with the splendid ideals of humanism and of the *philosophes*, who believed they were freeing man by affirming his sovereignty over the real and by clearing away the darkness of unknowing, having been converted into their opposites: humanism is thus shown to amount to an unleashing of the inhuman, and the *Aufklärung*—the dream of a totally "enlightened" society, wholly transparent to the light of reason—as a dream that can only be realized in a totalitarian universe in the form of an utterly administered society.[5]

The argument's strength flows from its simplicity. It asserts that democracy, by contrast, "establishes and maintains itself by dissolving the standards of certitude"—that antitotalitarian society refuses the temptation of mastery, whose intellectual origins had been traced to the advent of the Cartesian subject. Now safely beyond the reach of any unleashed will to power, that distant heir of the wish for certitude, the age of democracy would begin with the inauguration of "a society in which [the foundation of] power, law, and knowledge [is] exposed to a radical indetermination"—this "foundation" that man, trapped by his finitude, could no longer claim to embody.[6] The frequently brilliant and suggestive application of such ideas to political thought did much to reinforce the persuasiveness of the philosophical criticisms of subjectivity, and helped make them appear self-evident.

If Ferry and I were to succeed in overthrowing what was by now a commonplace, clearly it was going to take some doing on our part just to prevent the trial of the subject from being prematurely declared at an end. Why did the case need to be reopened in the first place? Did we take it for granted, as our critics charged, "that the subject had to be reenthroned," and that, instead of going to the "trouble of saying how it would be more justifiable to believe in this divinity . . . rather than seeing it as a form whose advent can be identified and dated," we contented ourselves with some "extremely trivial digressions about the dangers of antihumanism"?[7] Allowance has to be made for the hasty and often unjust things that are said in the first reviews of a book, of course, and in any case it would be vain and cowardly to think of protesting the initial response to ours. Nonetheless it may now be possible to explain more clearly what we were trying to do.

Though we have often insisted on rigorously examining the problem of subjectivity with reference to human rights, we did not mean to judge all possible philosophies by a sort of "litmus test" that would measure their compatibility with the 1789 Declaration of the Rights of Man—posing, as it were, as intellectual magistrates awarding certificates of civic responsibility to some undertakings while denying them to others. We had serious reasons for questioning the criticisms of subjectivity, and deliberately chose to do battle on the very ground on which, as I have just mentioned, our critics had staked one of their most powerful claims to allegiance: namely, the analysis of the intellectual conditions of totalitarianism and, corresponding to this, an internally consistent defense of antitotalitarianism. This choice in no way implied that the ultimate problems posed by the various attacks on subjectivity were reducible to their political "effects." Our point was simply that such "effects" were symptoms of far deeper theoretical difficulties. Our aim was therefore not at all to speak out in the name of human rights against any and all writers, great and less great, who from Nietzsche to Foucault, from Heidegger to Derrida, from Marx to Bourdieu, and from Freud to Lacan had helped demolish the idea of the subject: such an enterprise would have been just as ridiculous as failing to recall that other thinkers, among them Bechelard, Cavaillès, Canguilhem, Braudel, Lévi-Strauss, and Dumézil—all of whom also played a role in the "demolition" of subjectivist philosophies—actively defended democratic values with more genuine heroism than many theoreticians of human freedom and responsibility.

The problem to which we wished to call attention was this: how are we to make sense of the presence in our intellectual universe of the assault on subjectivity as the root of totalitarian or technocratic enslavement, and the simultaneous appeal to subjectivity in describing and denouncing this enslavement as underlying a certain conception of humanity that is alien to the totalitarian world—a world in which human beings are denied any possibility (and thus any right) of being the source of their own thoughts and acts, of being *subjects* rather than *objects* (that is, the reified basis of an infinite manipulation)? The claims of such an appeal—notably (but not exclusively) symbolized by the discourse of human rights,[8] despite all its confusion—could not be ignored. At the very least, it invited a skeptical reconsideration of so unsubtle an assault, and the question: *how can the subject serve as a source both of ultimately dangerous illusions and as an unsurpassable value?* The difficulty of the problem becomes clear when we consider that each of these rival perceptions of subjectivity is, in its own way and on its own level, profoundly true.

If this formulation of the problem is honestly faced up to,[9] it must be granted that there was some misunderstanding—and, let it be said, some injustice—in attributing to us without further qualification the highly naive, indeed crude intention of exploiting the discovery of the gulags and the intellectual persecution of the Soviet system simply for the purpose of promoting a philosophical resurrection of the "thinking, responsible, voluntaristic, moral, and free subject in each of us"—in short, of the "Cartesian *cogito*" as "sovereign consciousness," as "a rehabilitated subject, a mature *cogito*" that would miraculously emerge, now "cleansed and matured by the ordeal."[10] In retrospect, it is clear where the misunderstanding lay in the eyes of our critics: our daring to question the pertinence of the criticisms of subjectivity that had been worked out principally by French philosophers during the 1960s could only be taken to indicate that we wished to reanimate utterly discredited forms of thought, that we failed to grasp that these forms *had* in fact been discredited by the previous generation of philosophers—the proof of which, to name only the most striking example, was that we took no account whatever of the challenge posed to the whole philosophy of the subject by the discovery of the unconscious. Painful though it may be for these critics to accept, such a "misunderstanding" represents a threat to reason only if its underlying logic is not grasped. The logic is perfectly clear: because subjectivity remains a value and a term of reference once the illusions surrounding it have been dispelled, the problem (in that book as in this one) is to determine how the subject can be investigated in light of the discovery of the unconscious and of finitude—that is, by taking these things into account rather than dismissing them. But this flew in the face of a solidly entrenched prejudice: namely, that the philosophy of the subject is at bottom mere "metaphysics," and thus captive to the illusions that had already been identified by contemporary philosophy and the human sciences; and moreover that, despite minor differences, the various possible representations of the subject constitute variations on a single theme—the sovereignty of the human being (understood as autonomous, free, towering over history, the undisputed source of his own action and representation). That Ferry and I, in the final pages of our book, should thus have called for a "return to the subject" and suggested the need for a *new* model of subjectivity[11] was not taken seriously by our critics since, in their view, subjectivity means by definition that one is always to one degree or another a prisoner of the Cartesian *cogito*—proof that we had not caught up with the decisive advances of contemporary thinking. Under these circumstances, our critics claimed, the "return *to* the subject" could be only a "return *of* the subject"—a sterile phenomenon of revival and repetition rather than a creative program of research that would have to invent itself as it went along.

This is why I believe that it is now more imperative than ever to examine the concept of subjectivity in historical context. Rather than assume it to be a single homogeneous idea that is necessarily metaphysical in character (the term "metaphysics" will have to be clarified, by the way), we need to distinguish several models of subjectivity that have developed over time, not all of which are "metaphysical" in the same sense, for the same reason, or to the same degree. The "metaphysics of subjectivity" forged by Heidegger, which his disciples took to be the major intellectual system of modernity, can now be seen to constitute the main epistemological obstacle to understanding the subject. In suggesting that all subjectivity is mere "metaphysics," that a leap beyond "metaphysics" is possible only with the evaporation of the idea of the subject, and that the only means of escape from the perverse effects of humanism lies in the resolute search for access to some "postmodernity," the Heideggerian legacy threatens to bog down debate about subjectivity in polemics and accusations. It can only be overcome through a careful analysis of the various forms that subjectivity has taken throughout the history of modern philosophy, combined with a fresh inquiry into the meaning of this history, which is too readily construed as the unobstructed march—from Descartes to Hegel, or to Nietzsche—of a single image of humanity. Such an analysis invites us not only to admit just how complex the notion of the subject is (making wholesale condemnation a harder thing), but also to rethink the logic, if any, of a history of modernity so closely tied to the history of subjectivity.

I propose to begin this study by examining two major reconstructions of the logic of modernity, due to Heidegger and Louis Dumont. Why these two, when so many other interpretations of modernity could be selected instead? In *La Pensée 68*, Ferry and I tried to relate the theoretical attack on subjectivity to a certain campaign (extending far beyond the field of philosophy) on behalf of the values of individuality: with the advent of the individual, we suggested, the subject dies. Of course we did not date this overthrow of the subject in favor of the individual (and the corresponding eradication of the values of humanism in favor of those of individualism) from the 1960s, even though May 1968 surely gave a rare impetus to the tendency to exalt individuality; in many respects, at least since the French Revolution, modernity can be interpreted (as we ourselves have proposed) as a succession of various images of the individual.[12] The main problem posed by a philosophical history of modernity, so far as the subject is concerned, is understanding how the values of subjectivity are expressed in relation to those of individuality. Is the outstanding feature of the increasingly triumphal installation of the subject as the "Lord of Being" (here one recognizes the influence of Heidegger, for whom individualism represented merely an inessential aspect of a destiny in which man constantly is—and "*remains*"—subject)?[13] Or is the relationship between the subject (and therefore humanism) and the individual (and therefore individualism) more subtle, so that the individual succeeds in asserting himself only "where he is already essentially a subject," while undermining—to the point eventually of destroying—the subject, from which however he nonetheless derives? Given this much, is it necessary to exchange a reading of the history of modernity in terms of subjectivity for one that sees it as the result of the progressive spread of individualism? Surely no one has pushed the individualistic reading of modernity further than Louis Dumont, not only in *Homo Aequalis* but also in the *Essais sur l'individualisme*. Because the question of the subject can scarcely be posed now without confronting the possibility of its withering away in what might be called the era of the individual, I think it makes sense to begin by comparing Heidegger's interpretation of modernity, which is formulated exclusively in terms of subjectivity, with Dumont's, which takes the rise of individuality as its sole guiding principle.[14] An examination of the difficulties inherent in each of these two "monist" readings will yield a more complex hypothesis whose adequacy as a history of subjectivity will need then to be tested against the logic of the modern evolution of philosophy.

PART ONE

Readings of Modernity

CHAPTER I

Heidegger: The Reign of the Subject

The contemporary interpretation of the history of modernity, which sees this as a perpetually consolidated reign of subjectivity, is profoundly marked by the Heideggerian deconstruction of the modern history of philosophy and, more generally, of modern culture. We find direct or indirect traces of this influence in thinkers as different as Hannah Arendt, Leo Strauss, Michel Foucault, and Claude Lefort. Yet the history of subjectivity as Heidegger has accustomed us to reading it creates more problems than it solves, and introduces a number of ambiguities that seriously jeopardize the chance of finding a new role for the subject. I want to discuss first the principal difficulties that seem to me to be inherent in this analysis of the logic of modernity, stemming mainly from a deliberate bias toward homogenization, in order to develop a rival interpretation of the history of subjectivity.

Homogeneous Modernity

In the Heideggerian interpretation of modernity, the overarching (and, indeed, overriding) principle is that the *modern* consists in a relation to the world according to which mankind posits itself as capable of providing the foundation for its own acts and representations, as well as for history, of truth, and the law. This foundational capacity, or power, defines subjectivity: in becoming a subject, man claims his place as the *sub-jectum*, the "under-lying" reality on which everything else depends. Though this rather trivial characterization of the subjectivity of the Moderns is basically correct, Heidegger's treatment of the topic is notable mostly for its extraordinary levelling effect.

Modernity is interpreted as being fully identical with the epoch of subjectivity—fully, because Heidegger tries to show that *all* the faces of modernity are in fact "consequences" (*Folgen*) of the advent of man in the position of subject. I shall not dwell on this first aspect of the tendency toward homogenization, which relates every feature of the modern world to the emergence of subjectivity:[1] everything from the aestheticization of art to the rise of the diesel motor, from the emergence of the consumer society to the globalization of wars and totalitarianism, is attributed to the reign of subjectivity or, what amounts to the same thing, to the rise of humanism, which represents merely the *cultural* expression of the *philosophical* inauguration of man as subject.[2] I shall cite just one example: Heidegger (and he is not alone here) sees one of the chief cultural characteristics of modernity as what he calls the loss of gods (*Entgötterung*),[3] or dedivinization—the death of God, if you prefer, or the disenchantment of the world. The linking of this phenomenon, via humanism, with the appearance of man as subject comes as no surprise: what in classical antiquity, and even more in the Middle Ages, was the "place of God" becomes in the modern era the "place of man,"[4] with the values of modernity being defined by man's claiming for himself the two traditional attributes of God, omniscience (thus the view of modern culture as *scientistic*, nothing in principle being beyond the grasp of science)[5] and omnipotence (thus the insistence on the *technical* dimension of culture).

This style of analysis is now well known. One qualification, however, needs to be made on account of certain misleading formulas. Heidegger obviously did not establish purely mechanical cause-and-effect relations between the history of philosophy and the other levels of evolution. Simply put, since the metaphysics of an age makes explicit the "determined relation to being in its totality," which in turn defines the way of being-in-the-world, "every era, every human epoch, is sustained by some metaphysics."[6] Metaphysics may thus be said to "ground an epoch insofar it establishes and *maintains* humankind in a truth concerning beings and as a whole this way retains it."[7] In short, inasmuch as any human attitude toward the whole of reality is sustained by a certain way of understanding the realness of this reality, and as philosophical systems since the time of the Greeks have given expression to these successive understandings, philosophy "basically determines the most intimate course of our history"[8]—not because it produces this course, but because the deepest meaning of "what later occurs" is expressed and lets itself be grasped by it.[9] It is from this perspective that behind all the manifestations of a perfectly homogeneous modernity we can see the deployment of the metaphysics of subjectivity as well as the process, which defines humanism, "through which man places himself at the center of being."[10]

Leibniz and the Metaphysics of Modern Times

Heidegger's first homogenization is duplicated by a second one that directly concerns the history of subjectivity, and seems to me therefore to warrant closer examination. "The metaphysics of modern times," we read in Heidegger's *Nietzsche*, "is characterized by the special role which the human 'subject' and the appeal to the subjectivity of man play in it,"[11] and this in a way that reduces every image of subjectivity to a prototypical model of the subject whose philosophical identity goes back to Leibniz, or rather to the way in which the emergence of the Cartesian subject found its true impact only in Leibniz. "[. . .] Descartes and Leibniz . . . give essential shape to the first explicit metaphysical founding of modern history," he says,[12] meaning that Leibniz's clarification of Descartes' discovery truly establishes subjectivity as the essential foundation of modernity. In this sense, "The thinking of Leibniz supports and molds the chief tendency of what, thought broadly enough, we can call the metaphysics of the modern age"—by virtue of which, Heidegger insists, "for us the name of Leibniz does not stand as a tag for a bygone system of philosophy. The name names the presence of a thinking, whose strength has not yet been experienced, a presence that still awaits to encounter us."[13] If every manifestation of modernity is thus "deduced" from the advent of subjectivity, all the moments in the history of subjectivity could in turn be reduced to the Leibnizian moment, insofar as it determined "the more radical interpretation of the subjectivity of the subject within the philosophy of German idealism and its subsequent scions"—to the point that "only through looking back on what Leibniz thought can we characterize the present age," whether the atomic age or any other designation expressing the technical essence of modernity.[14]

The point is important, and should be examined all the more carefully because Heidegger's version of the history of subjectivity is most often read as reducing all its moments to the Cartesian *cogito*—which can be true only if one adds that, for Heidegger, the truth of the Cartesian subject was found in the Leibnizian subject. Leibniz's project was to reinterpret subjectivity as a monad, the *monadological cogito* demonstrating the truth of the *rationalist cogito*—as the second volume of *Nietzsche* clearly attests, arguing that with the monadological perspective "the new essence of reality begins to permeate everywhere and explicitly the totality of beings," and that "the beginning of that metaphysics develops which will remain the ground of history of the modern period."[15] Thus, in this reading of the history of subjectivity, the inaugural and truly decisive moment to which everything is reduced can be unambiguously located in the Leibnizian monadology. Homogenization, in this history, works entirely to the benefit of Leibniz.

Having identified the principle of this interpretation, we now have to understand it before we can discuss and evaluate it. Why was this formidable privilege accorded to Leibniz? The well-versed reader of Heidegger will have no trouble thinking up possible explanations, the likeliest perhaps being that Leibniz (to whom Heidegger devoted a whole book)[16] was the thinker who "could discover the principle of reason," who could see the "the principle of reason [as] the fundamental principle of rendering reasons,"[17] whose power gives to the "spirit" of the age its distinctive tonality and motifs.[18] In addition, the *Système nouveau de la nature et de la communication des substances* (New System of Nature and the Communication of Substances, 1695) was the first philosophical work whose title, for reasons specific to Leibniz's philosophy, expressed that "necessity of the system" seen by Heidegger as one of the "characteristics of modern metaphysics' essential completion."[19] Finally, redefining substance as force, Leibniz posited the dynamization of essence as characteristic of all modern philosophy "up to the completion of the modern essence of Being as the will to power."[20] In this idea it was possible to see "the turning point in the history of Being."[21]

All these things converged, leading Heidegger to organize his history of subjectivity around Leibniz. To understand fully the primacy he granted Leibniz, however, we have to understand the reasons for this convergence in Heidegger's thought. This means that we need to see how, in his eyes, *the structure of subjectivity, once it had emerged with Descartes (as both self-consciousness and consciousness of the object), could undergo only two essential modifications for whose actualization Leibniz's contribution seemed decisive*:[22]

- On the one hand, the subsequent metaphysics of subjectivity was to make explicit the dimension of activity potentially present in the *cogitatio*: for Descartes, *cogitare* was already *co-agere*, that is, to bring the real close to oneself in order to subject it to rational examination—and only then to bring out its truth (as certainty).[23] According to Heidegger, Leibniz's contribution consisted in emphasizing subjectivity as activity, making its representation (*perceptio*) one of the two modalities (the other being *appetitus*) of what essentially defines the monad, that is, force (*vis*).[24] Representation, in the modern sense, was held to be based on an unfolding of activity, for the Leibnizian explanation of the essence of representation rested on subjectivity as the intrinsically active condition of any attempt to submit the real to human mastery and possession. For this reason Heidegger believed he could treat the Kantian, Fichtean, and Nietzschean moments as mere extensions of Leibniz's deepening of the dynamic, willing essence of subjectivity: Kant having extended Leibniz by redefining the concept as the *activity* of synthesis,[25] and not as receptacle; Fichte by regarding the ego as spontaneity;[26] and Nietzsche by conceiving life as the will to power.
- A second and, in Heidegger's opinion, even more decisive change in the structure of subjectivity took place after Descartes, and here too Leibniz was seen to have played a decisive role as the first thinker to realize fully the spirit of modern metaphysics by applying the structure defining the human subject to

all reality. This mechanism, which Heidegger calls "anthropomorphy"[27] and which consists in conceiving substance itself as a subject (that is, as monad), radicalizes the spirit of metaphysical modernity, expressed only incompletely by Descartes. If indeed the spirit of the metaphysics of subjectivity (or, culturally, of humanism) lies in the attempt to conceive of reality exclusively in relation to man, posited as foundation (as subject), this spirit was already present in Descartes. The same spirit is realized more fully still when being is itself conceived as a subject, that is, when subjectivity defines the very structure of reality. Thus, in Leibniz, force (*vis*) as *perceptio* and *appetitus*—the essential property of human subjectivity (understood as activity, as self-production)—became the essence of every being (thought of as a monad): "With Leibniz, the thought arises that every being which is somehow self-contained as a being must have the true character of Being which makes itself known after Descartes in man's experience of himself as *ego cogito sum*, that is, as subject, as I think, I represent."[28] And insofar as Leibniz reinterpreted representation in the sense of activity, will, or force, "the essence of force is the original essence of the beingness of beings."[29] In this sense, because every being becomes owing to its "subjective nature," that is, aspires to represent and thus becomes effective ("because each being is subiectum, monad"), "the metaphysics of subjectivity had its decisive beginning in the metaphysics of Leibniz."[30] Thus Hegel's and Nietzsche's contributions to the metaphysics of subjectivity are in fact a twofold exploitation of Leibnizian anthropomorphy: with Hegel's proclamation in the preface to the *Phenomenology of Mind* that "everything turns on grasping and expressing the True, not only as *Substance*, but equally as *Subject*,[31] the "True"—also called the "Whole"—therefore acquires the very structure of subjectivity as the self-deployment of the identity of identity and difference; and in Nietzsche we find the equivalence asserted of being with life ("we have no other representation of being than the fact of living") and of life with the will to power ("everywhere I have encountered the living, I have encountered the will to power").[32]

Heidegger's major thesis about the history of subjectivity consists in the decision to make this whole history (and, with it, the whole history of modernity) hinge on the *monadological cogito* as the twofold deepening of the Cartesian subject, both in the sense of the *activist* reinterpretation of the *cogitatio* and in that of the *monadological* (meaning anthropomorphic) reinterpretation of substance: Every *subiectum* is determined in its *esse* by *vis* (*perceptio—appetitus*). Every *substantia* is monad. Thus the essence of the reality of the *res cogitans* developing in the light of truth as certainty attains its scope in which it rules everything real"[33]—and since the principle was to have the effect of consolidating the reign of the subject at its height, "it is only in this way of understanding that the initial positing of the metaphysics of modern times is reached."[34]

Heidegger drew on this thesis to show how the logic of this history needed to be reconstructed in relation to the Leibnizian perspective. We can identify three distinct insights.

First, the Hegelian reduction of the real to the rational was already foreshadowed in Leibniz. Such a reduction was not conceivable in Descartes, owing to the Cartesian emphasis (the exploitation of which by Heidegger's followers can now be understood) on the creation of eternal truths: the idea that God could have created a world that was inconsistent with the principles of our rationality profoundly relativized the identification of the real with the rational.[35] Leibniz, on the other hand, reduced the real to the possible, using a well-known line of argument,[36] whose application is strongly underscored by Heidegger:[37] If the real is only the possible (meaning the noncontradictory, and hence the rational) actualizing itself (solely on condition of its compatibility with other possibles), we can already have an inkling of the absolute identification of the real with the rational that in Hegel was the culmination of the campaign to assert subjectivity as imposing its law on the real and subjecting reality to reason, both literally and figuratively.

Second, a result also (on Heidegger's reading) due to Leibniz, the notion of a system is seen to play a major role in carrying out the program for a metaphysics of subjectivity developed by German idealism.[38] Following in the steps of Leibniz, rather than Descartes, the real—now virtually reduced to the rational—came typically to be represented as totally governed by principles of order that make the whole of being into a totality, and hence a system.[39] But the emergence of the system was also, and perhaps more profoundly, required by the monadological interpretation of substance as *force*: "The necessity of the system . . . lies in the essential constitutents of the will understood in this way."[40] If the basis of all being is substance as subject (that is, in Leibniz's sense, as a monad having the force to generate everything that happens to it—its history), it became indispensable—unless one accepted the possibility of a wholly chaotic universe (a hypothesis incompatible with God's choice of this world from among the infinity of possible worlds)—to assume the existence of a preestablished harmony, a prior ordering of the monads by God, acting as the monad of monads. The idea of preestablished harmony thus anticipated the notion of system, whose development in German idealism was required by its dynamic conception of substance as subject.

Third, beyond Hegelian system and German idealism, Heidegger's interpretation of the history of subjectivity made it possible to see Nietzsche as carrying out the program of modern metaphysics through the extension of Leibniz's monadology. The monadological idea did indeed imply Nietzschean perspectivism, which Heidegger compares to Leibniz's idea of a "point of view"[41] by recalling the correspondence with Clarke, in which each substance was regarded as being "by its [monadic] nature . . . a concentration and a living mirror of the whole universe; according to its point of view"[42]—that is, as putting the universe into perspective through representation. The comparison makes sense since Leibniz, in insisting that monads differ in their perspectives and thus express the world from multiple points of view, argued further that there are as many representations of the world as there are monads, as many perspectives as there are subjectivities. Recall the well-known passage in the *Monadology*: "As the same city looked at from different sides appears entirely different, and is as if multiplied *perspectively*; so also it happens that, as a result of the infinite multitude of simple substances, there are as it were so many different universes, which are nevertheless only the perspectives of a single one, according to the different *points of view* of each monad."[43] To arrive at Nietzsche's conviction that "there are no facts, only interpretations" (or, according to *The Gay Science*: "Rather has the world become infinite for us all over again, inasmuch as we cannot reject the possibility that *it may include infinite interpretations*"),[44] the Leibnizian position must be modified in certain crucial respects—chief among them the death of God as "the monad of monads," which implied a change from preestablished harmony (hence system) to chaos (and hence the proclamation that "today every kind of dogmatism stands sad and discouraged").[45] Here a profound, "historically essential inner connection"[46] can be detected between the beginning and the end of the history of subjectivity: a paradoxical cohesiveness between Leibniz's analysis of the Cartesian *cogito* and Nietzsche's well-known strong critique of the Cartesian position, which suggests that this critique was no more than a trick played by subjectivity to fortify its own position in the face of a potential threat.[47]

I will limit my remarks here to the Heideggerian history of subjectivity, which remains an impressive achievement for the exceptional skill it displayed in restoring the logic underlying the various philosophical positions that have been adopted over time and detecting a meaning in their succession: an inevitable tendency toward the triumph of "absolute subjectivity."[48] I belong to a philosophical generation for whom reading Heidegger's *Nietzsche*—especially the second volume, at the end of the 1960s[49]—was a genuine revelation: suddenly the history of modern philosophy (which had been taught to us—after a fashion—in the academic exegetical tradition as something to be acquainted with but not actually understood) began to make sense. In the monadological interpretation of substance, in the Hegelian dialectization of logic, Heidegger discovered the same destiny of modernity that in our time had produced the technologization of the real—what appeared to us as evidence of an advancing "Americanism." Thus the old texts took on a new life for us, and our attempts to make them familiar no longer seemed absurd. This experience was unforgettable: even though we found serious flaws in Heidegger's reconstruction, it is still true that the *style* of his approach, which contrasted so markedly and so enigmatically with "historical" approaches to the history of philosophy, defined for us a new standard of philosophical technique.

Having said this, it is nonetheless necessary to point out the weaknesses of Heidegger's history of subjectivity, which present both the historian and the philosopher with several problems that are hard to circumvent.

The Status of Empiricism and Criticism

The first problem is a familiar one, and arises precisely from what made Heidegger's work so attractive—the one-dimensionality of his history of subjectivity (or, what amounts to the same thing, his interpretation of modernity as humanism), which accounts for a great deal of the extraordinary "effect of meaning" that Heidegger's writings convey. But the desire to compress all philosophy from Descartes to Nietzsche into a single history that hinges on the monadological *cogito*, understood as the confirmation of the Cartesian *cogito* and prefiguration of the Hegelian absolute subject, runs into a number of difficulties. Here I cite only the two most typical.

First, it is not easy to locate the empiricist *cogito*, as defined by Locke, Berkeley, and Hume, in Heidegger's account. In fact, he barely touches on this rival image of subjectivity. His few references to Berkeley are mainly devoted to suggesting that the principle of the *esse est percipi* furnishes a particularly clear sign of the reduction of "beingness" to representability, a reduction that is claimed to define all modern metaphysics.[50] Surely this approach to empiricism is singularly thin, even simplistic. For there is an essential difference between the Cartesian *cogito* (more generally: the rationalist *cogito*) and the empiricist *cogito*, namely, that the former is defined and constituted by the mind's closure on itself while the latter operates only by virtue of openness of the mind to sense impressions. Where the Cartesian model of subjectivity proceeds by "detaching the mind from the senses" in order to discover the innate ideas of the self and, by reflecting about them, to reconstruct what had first been doubted, such closure with regard to the external world is by definition alien to the empiricist model (or models) of subjectivity, since "all our simple ideas in their first appearance are deriv'd from simple impressions, which are correspondent to them, and which they exactly represent."[51] It thus seems a bold thing to assign to empiricism, without further ado, a place in the constitutive movement of absolute subjectivity: if the empiricist subject is to be located in the logical context of the history of subjectivity, this cannot be done by simply identifying this history with an affirmation of the modern subject's undivided sovereignty over what is other than itself. In this connection it would be especially interesting to revisit the debate between Locke and Leibniz, who in the *Nouveaux essais sur l'entendement humain* (New Essays on Human Understanding, 1704) pitted a nascent form of the empiricist *cogito* against a monadological *cogito* which, being sufficient unto itself and "without doors or windows," made explicit the Cartesian closure with regard to exteriority and radicalized it *against empiricism*. A vast chasm thus opened up between these two moments in the history of the modern subject.[52] If we are to be able to claim to have narrowed this chasm, thereby demonstrating some measure of continuity between the two, we have at least to take it into account rather than pretend to be unaware of it.

A similar problem concerning the treatment of empiricism in Heidegger's history of subjectivity arises in connection with the Kantian and Fichtean moment—in connection, that is, with what might be called the criticist *cogito*. For in the *Critique of Pure Reason* the idea was introduced, surely for the first time with such acuity,[53] that representation and consciousness are enigmas: Kant, in inquiring into the conditions under which consciousness is possible, discovered problems with subjectivity that up to then, and particularly among the Cartesians, had gone undetected. As we know, these problems were to foreshadow the concern with finitude, since to have representations, the subject must be finite: thus the inquiry into subjectivity took on the form of an inquiry into the nature of finitude. With Fichte's extension of Kant's argument on this point, a model of subjectivity emerged that, to the extent it was defined by the radicality of its finitism, was devoted to criticizing all those who clung on to metaphysical illusions about the subject, whether rationalists (Descartes, Leibniz, and—for Fichte—Spinoza) or empiricists (Berkeley and Hume). In the chapter on the "paralogisms of pure reason" in the first *Critique* and, even more systematically, in the *Metaphysische Anfangsgründe der Naturwissenschaft* (Metaphysical Foundations of Natural Science, 1786), the criticist *cogito* is explicitly developed against both rationalist doctrines of closure and self-sufficiency on the one hand, and, on the other, the empiricist attack on these doctrines. Thus Kant and Fichte managed to work out a critique of the metaphysics of subjectivity within a philosophical framework that remains a philosophy of subjectivity to the extent that the problem of objectivity is posed on the basis of the subject and analyzed in terms of it.[54]

How, then, can any rethinking of the history of subjectivity ignore the stubbornly obvious fact that *in this history* the criticist *cogito* represents the first attempt to conceive subjectivity as a function of the illusions that the subject is liable to generate about itself by forgetting its finitude, its being-in-the-world? Consequently if one holds, *with Heidegger*, that the metaphysics of subjectivity culminated—through the radicalization of this forgetting—in the reduction of all reality to subjectivity in the manner of German idealism, it also becomes necessary to maintain, as *against Heidegger*, that in the history of subjectivity the criticist moment (and notably the critique of rational psychology) set a limit to how far reality could be reduced to subjectivity.

"Against Heidegger"—one should not be misled by such an abrupt formula. I obviously do not mean to deny that the early Heidegger, especially the author of *Kant und das Problem der Metaphysik* (Kant and the Problem of Metaphysics, 1929)—who indeed saw Kantianism as a source of resistance to the logic of the metaphysics of subjectivity—attached great importance to Kant's idea of radical finitude. In this sense, Heidegger does not consider Kant quite "modern," stressing that "in spite of all differences and the extent of the historical interval, Kant had something in common with the great Greek beginning, which at the same time distinguished him from all Greek thinkers before and after him."[55] It is just as clear that as early as 1929[56] Heidegger was also insisting that this Kantian resistance would in fact fail, and claimed to show that by the time of the second edition of the *Critique* Kant had already reverted to metaphysics. In short—and here again, as so often, Heidegger's *Nietzsche* best expresses his position—if "Kant's metaphysics resists this essential thrust of Being" (by which "the essence of subjectivity of itself necessarily surges toward absolute subjectivity"), it is not, however, without "at the same time laying the ground for its fulfillment"[57]—so much so that when all is said and done, and despite everything that relates it to the Greeks, "Kant's philosophy shifts for the first time the whole of modern thought and being (*Dasein*) into the clarity and transparency of a foundation (*Begründung*)."[58] Hence the appearance in 1963 of Heidegger's brief study of Kant's thesis about being squarely set Kantianism for the first time in a theoretical framework—the metaphysics of subjectivity—in which the relation between thought and being "has its roots in thought, that is, in an act of the human subject."[59]

However great the daring of the "*Kantbuch*" may be, Heidegger's reading of Kant (to say nothing of Fichte)[60] profoundly *relativized* the specificity of the criticist moment, reducing it to a critique of subjectivity that (unlike Heidegger's own) does not completely eliminate the subject, but merely deconstructs its illusions about itself. In examining the specificity of the Kantian moment, it cannot be excluded that these illusions are not inherent in the very notion of the subject; indeed it might be supposed that since criticist philosophy denounces metaphysical illusions about the subject, its own reference to subjectivity would escape such illusion. In short, to blur the source of the originality of the Kantian moment is to ignore the possibility (which may be concealed in it) of separating the affirmation of the subject from the risk of illusion entailed by this affirmation: the only alternative to a metaphysics of subjectivity would therefore be a philosophy that rejects subjectivity and its values, and so humanism as well. But in view of the dead end at which contemporary philosophy now finds itself as a result of the rejection of subjectivity, Heidegger's stubbornness in reading Kant's and Fichte's critique as a triumph of the metaphysical subject bears a heavy responsibility for having denied present-day thinkers on this topic a rare opportunity to explore one of its most promising paths.[61]

Given the profound difficulty of integrating the empiricist and criticist moments in a linear history of subjectivity centered on the monadological *cogito*, this history must be read instead, I believe, as a pluralistic one involving a number of different *cogito*s: a rationalistic *cogito*, an empiricist *cogito*—and, above all, the metaphysical *cogito* and the criticist *cogito*. In this way it becomes possible to write not only a *plural* history of subjectivity (and hence a history of subjectivities), but also a *discontinuous* history. For one of the most formidable paradoxes presented by the history of the subject, and surely the one least avoidable by contemporary thought, is that its development was interrupted by the *Critique of Pure Reason* (and by the *Metaphysical Foundations of Natural Science*)—only to be linked up again later with its metaphysical past. How was it possible for German idealism after Kant and Fichte to return to Leibniz, repeating (as if, I am tempted to say, nothing had happened) and completing the forward march toward the absolute subject, thus making new ruptures inevitable, not only those of Nietzsche and Heidegger but also the various "returns to Kant" that have punctuated the course of philosophy since 1850? Once its plurality and discontinuity have been restored, the history of subjectivity permits a variety of questions to be answered that cannot even be posed in Heidegger's reconstruction. The one-dimensionality that accounts for much of its attractiveness thus makes Heidegger's history of the subject vulnerable to objections that suggest the need for a thorough reconsideration of the topic.

Metaphysics of Subjectivity or Philosophical Foundation of Individualism?

A second problem renders this reconsideration indispensable. Perhaps the best way of getting at it is to ask not what Heidegger was aiming at, but what he really managed to contribute to the history of subjectivity by calling the Leibnizian monadology the true philosophical beginning of modernity, and making the course of all modern philosophy hinge on the monadological idea. Not that granting Leibniz the importance Heidegger assigns to him seems to me exaggerated: on the contrary, I believe Heidegger was correct in seeing the Leibnizian system as the locus of something essential in the modern history of the subject. Yet the real question has to do with determining exactly what is at stake when one endorses or attacks this system as a starting point.

Heidegger believed himself to be attacking, in Leibniz, the source of the strengthening hold in the modern period of the subject on the conception of the real: but he succeeded merely in objecting to *the emergence of a particular model of the subject*, a model he never examined in detail and which he simply identified with the truth of the subject *as such*. Where Heidegger's reading of Leibniz sees only an explanation and consolidation of what had first appeared with Descartes, one should see instead a radical change, *in the history of the subject*, that leads from the subject to the *individual*—a change so radical that it would be tempting to conclude that Leibniz's thought belongs less to the history of subjectivity than to the history of individuality.

I begin with the uninteresting observation that the Leibnizian subject is the monad construed as an individual. The monads that create the texture of reality are essentially unique, and so every being is different in every respect from every other one. Thus it is that the Leibnizian understanding of reality (or as Heidegger would say, of beingness) emphasizes *individuality*—and this in two senses: first, as indivisibility or simplicity; second, as irreducibility. To some extent the possibility of overturning the concept of "human nature" already appears in the assertion that there are only individuals: in this light, rather than marking a decisive moment in modern humanism, the emergence of the monadological perspective might better be regarded as one of the first prefigurations of the "death of man."

This ontological individualism was already expressed in Leibniz's argument concerning individuation. Here, as against the dominant scholastic orientation of his time, he rejected the principle of individuation by matter and thus denied that individuality is a dimension external to essence.[62] But the foundation for individualism finds fullest scope in Leibniz's doctrine of the identity of indiscernibles. For the principle that "there are in nature no two real absolute beings that are indiscernible"[63] is not only, as Bertrand Russell observed,[64] set up as a premise of philosophical discourse; it is actually *deduced* from the principles of contradiction and sufficient reason. Thus:

- Since each thing has its own reason for being, there cannot exist two perfectly similar or indiscernible things in nature, as there would indeed be no reason for both of them to exist.

- For two realities to be exactly similar, they would necessarily share not only the same definition, but also the same spatial and temporal location—which would obviously contradict the assertion that there are *two* of them.

Beyond its formal structure, the importance of this twofold deduction of the identity of indiscernibles cannot be overestimated. In fact, Leibniz supplies a truly individualistic reinterpretation of rationality by giving ontologically individualistic weight to his two great constitutive principles. The demonstration that reason thus demands—that the reality of the real must be conceived as rooted in monadic individualities—is so important to the overall structure of Leibnizian thought that it governs the logic of the whole system, and in at least two essential directions:

- On the one hand, if, as the principle of the identity of indiscernibles requires, substance has the property of individuality in the sense of irreducibility and indivisibility or simplicity (the monad having no parts),[65] then it cannot be modified from outside, since such a modification would entail the modification by an external influence of a part of the substance, which would be then divided between itself and the accidents produced in it by something other than itself. Hence, beginning with §7 of the *Monadology*, Leibniz can posit that since no monad "can be altered or changed in its inner being by any other creature, . . . the monads have no windows": individuality is thus made explicit in the *independence* of the monads vis-à-vis the action of other monads.[66] Yet while a change in one monad cannot be explained by the influence of some other monad, we nonetheless observe, at the level of aggregates of monads, modifications that must be explained on the basis of changes which occur in simple substances. One must therefore admit, in an absolutely simple reality, a modification that does not affect its simplicity. It happens nonetheless that we all have the experience of such a modification in our awareness of ourselves: although our representations do indeed succeed each other, consciousness is not divided by the multiplicity of its representations—it always remains absolutely simple. Thus, subjectivity provides the model of a modification not affecting the simplicity of a substrate: the monad must then be conceived on the model of the subject, as producing the totality of changes it undergoes while yet remaining identical with itself. Thus monadic reality in all its generality can be described as similar to *mind*: monads being determined by the *representative* and *appetitive* capacities, which are conceived by analogy with consciousness and will, the distinctive faculties of the subject. The anthropomorphic move interpreted by Heidegger as a sign of the increasingly powerful hold of subjective values over the conception of the real is in fact made necessary by the prior interpretation of substantiality as *individuality*.
- On the other hand, ontological individualism constitutes one of the most characteristic aspects of Leibnizian and post-Leibnizian thinking. The

representation of reality as a collection of differentiated and independent substances does indeed challenge the idea that the real is intelligible or obeys some order: if the coexistence of these *independent* substances, not exercising any influence on each other, does not lead to pure chaos, if the world can still appear as the site of some meaning, the only account possible of this astounding rationality of the real must assume a kind of preexisting adjustment of the monads to each other that harmonizes the diversity of individual substances. Here, of course, one recognizes the theory of preestablished harmony, by virtue of which the order of the real can be thought of as resulting from the particular wills of the monads, each seeking to fulfill its being and, in doing this, creating the internal coherence of the "best of all possible worlds." Embedded in the very logic of a monadological—that is, individualistic—ontology, therefore, is a scheme of thought that following Leibniz was to leave as its legacy the various versions of the "ruse of reason."[67] This simple observation about the intrinsic connection between ontological individualism and preestablished harmony has important consequences. It suggests the possibility that the notion of the "ruse of reason"—an unmistakable feature of a completed metaphysics,[68] and as such, according to Heidegger, the supreme manifestation of the reign of the subject—might be much more closely connected with the *individualistic* conception of the subject. This notion in fact presupposes that the real is made up of individualities that are unable to establish an order among themselves without the help of a preestablished mechanism of adjustment, an immanent logic. From this perspective, which entails a genuine principle of independence among individualities as the ultimate law of the real, it remains to find a way to produce order out of disorder (i.e., meaning out of chaos, good out of evil). All such dialectical reversals lead back to the theory of preestablished harmony, and will later be extended and systematized by the theory of the "ruse of reason."

If one considers how insistently critics of modern humanism have called into question the values of subjectivity, pointing out the many perverse theoretical and practical effects inherent in the notion of the "ruse of reason,"[69] one begins to realize that some of the best-established commonplaces of contemporary thinking are based on a confusion. In seeing from Descartes to Leibniz, and then from Leibniz to Hegel (even Nietzsche), only the progressive triumph of subjectivity conceived in an unequivocal way, one is liable to miss the close interdependence between certain schemes of thought characteristic of the endgame of the modern history of metaphysics, and so fail to appreciate how influential the individualistic drift has been in the history of subjectivity. By not being attentive to this profound caesura, and to the many philosophical problems that it poses, we run the risk of hunting down the wrong beast—the subject—in a field where, for a long time, the values of subjectivity have not really been in question at all.

Humanism and Individualism

To identify the errors implicit in the Heideggerian reading of modernity is not enough: one must also trace the consequences of these errors if the history of subjectivity is to be properly grasped. This requires distinguishing between subject and individual (between humanism and individualism) and stating precisely what justification there is for speaking of an individualistic drift in modern humanism. The success or failure of this attempt at clarification and justification could indeed be decisive: it may prove that, despite what Heidegger and his French followers have believed, there is no simple, constraining connection between the advent of humanism (that is, the philosophical emergence of subjectivity) and the systematic completion of rationality; in other words, that there is no direct link from Leibniz to Hegel leading from the reign of technoscience to the negation of the marginal, passing along the way through all the well-known variations on the theme of Reason repressing its Other. It could be instead that the idea, so common to various contemporary criticisms of modernity, of a "dialectic of the Enlightenment" (directly entailing the condemnation of both subjectivity and modernity, and encouraging either a return to the ancients or access to some "postmodernity") stems in fact from an inability to perceive and reflect upon the great divide of modernity—this caesura that separates humanism and individualism. If, beginning with Leibniz, one *possible* philosophy of the subject, namely individualism, had developed on the basis of subjectivity, it would nonetheless have represented only one *possible* path of development among others, and not the *sole* possible path. The unfolding of this possibility would not have carried with it the whole conceivable destiny of modern philosophy and the values of modernity.

How is it that the actual Leibnizian path (that is, modern individualism founded on the philosophy of monads rather than an early version of the theory of the subject) came to diverge from humanism—twice, in fact, having originated from it and then split off from it? This is a complex question, one that in my view should guide any attempt to identify the philosophical logic of modernity. At this point, and at the risk of appearing schematic, I must say a few very elementary things about these two concepts, humanism and individualism:

- *Humanism* is basically the valorization of humanity in its capacity for *autonomy*. What I mean by this—without, of course, claiming any originality in the matter—is that what constitutes modernity is the fact that man thinks of himself as the source of his acts and representations, as their foundation (read: subject) or author. (This is why, by the way, the antihumanistic passion common to various genealogical practices of the 1960s so often involved criticizing the idea of the author.)[70] The humanistic man is one who does not receive his norms and laws either from the nature of things (as per Aristotle) or from God, but who establishes them himself, on the basis of his own reason and will. Thus modern natural right is a subjective right, posited and defined by human reason (as per juridical rationalism) or by the human will (as per juridical voluntarism).[71] Thus modern societies conceive of themselves politically as self-established political systems based on a contractualist scheme, in contrast to societies where authority is established through tradition by means of the deeply antimodern notion of "privilege."[72]

- *Individualism*, on the other hand, carries a different emphasis. Tocqueville accurately predicted that at the level of sociopolitical phenomena it constituted a dangerous, but not irresistible, tendency in modernity.[73] The best definition no doubt follows from Benjamin Constant's deceptively simple formula of the "freedom of the moderns." Constant placed less stress on the valorization of *autonomy* that on *independence*: among the ancients, he explained in a famous speech delivered at the Athénée royal in Paris in 1819,[74] freedom was defined in terms of participation in public affairs and the direct exercise of sovereignty, by this "collective freedom" was held to be "compatible with . . . the complete subjection of the individual to the authority of the community," to the point that "[n]o importance was given to individual *independence*, neither in relation to opinions, nor to labor, nor, above all, to religion";[75] in contrast, among the moderns, for whom the sovereignty of the individual was profoundly restricted, being publicly exercised only "at fixed and rare intervals," the individual nonetheless thinks of himself as free because he is "*independent* in his private life."[76] "Our own freedom must consist of peaceful enjoyment and private *independence*,"[77] Constant added; and in an age where, "[l]ost in the multitude, the individual can almost never perceive the influence he exercises, . . . we must be far more attached than the ancients to our individual *independence*."[78]

These well-known (and henceforth frequently cited) passages are actually rather complex: the ancient/modern pair, as Constant uses it (subjugation to the city/independence of the individual relative to the "collective body"), highlights independence as a key value of modern individualism only by masking another modern value that it paradoxically presupposes (the whole difficulty inherent in the modern history of the subject arises from this paradox, by the way): the value of autonomy, by virtue of which the limits imposed on freedom must be founded on an awareness of their necessity and on the subject's wish to impose them on himself. On this view, subjectivity is the source and principle of all norms and laws. The valorization of independence presupposes the valorization of autonomy: in order for an individual to consider the ability to choose with complete independence how one is to live as the essence of freedom, it is necessary first—as Constant notes without, however, clearly distinguishing the *two* modern moments of freedom—that society recognize for each person "the right to be subjected only to the laws, and to be neither arrested, detained, put to death or maltreated in any way by the arbitrary will of one or more individuals."[79] In other words the value of autonomy must already be established, and the principle accepted that men determine the powers to which they subject themselves. We thus understand why the ancients, for whom the very idea of autonomy made no sense (the authority establishing itself not in the *concursus* of wills, but in the nature of things or the order of the world), could not valorize individual independence or even feel the need for it.[80]

We therefore need to make Constant's suggestion explicit and, in order to guard against possible misunderstanding stemming from the binary contrast between (modern) independence and (ancient) subjugation, restore the third term that this contrast presupposes while at the same time concealing it: the autonomy onto which the valorization of independence must be grafted. One might as well say that it is equally necessary not just to link autonomy and independence in their joint opposition to the freedom of the ancients, but also—since there are three terms (individual subjugation, autonomy, and independence)—to differentiate the moment of autonomy from that of independence. While the notion of autonomy is perfectly compatible with the idea of persons submitting to laws or norms as long as these are freely accepted (the contractualist scheme precisely expresses this notion of submission to a law that one has given to oneself), the ideal of independence can no longer tolerate such a limitation of the self; on the contrary, it aims at the pure and simple affirmation of the self as a value. The self-establishing normativity of autonomy thus tends to give way to simple "self-regard." Correspondingly, consensus based on shared norms tends to be replaced by a split between the public and the private, with the valorization of private happiness and the parallel desertion of the public space so well described by Tocqueville.

Having distinguished in this way between humanism (understood as the valorization of autonomy) and individualism (as the valorization of independence), it now becomes possible to formulate a new hypothesis about the historical development of subjectivity as a philosophical concept.

Humanism's Individualistic Drift: The Era of the Individual

Culturally, modernity was born with the advent of humanism; philosophically, with the advent of subjectivity. This dimension of the Heideggerian interpretation has not been challenged. In the literature on modernity it has attained the status of a commonplace, in the strict sense of the term, since it unites thinkers as diverse as, for example, Heidegger and Cassirer. Throughout his admirable *Individuum und Kosmos in der Philosophie der Renaissance* (The Individual and the Cosmos in Renaissance Philosophy, 1927), Cassirer attempts to show how the Cartesian revolution (ratified by the custom of dating "the beginning of modern philosophy from Descartes's principle of the *Cogito*")[81] was prepared by the various champions of humanistic philosophy who emerged during the Renaissance: Giordano Bruno, Pico della Mirandola—and the surprising Charles de Bovelles whose *De Sapiente* (1509) was translated with commentary by Cassirer. He found already formulated in this work "the new, specifically modern view of the relationship of "subject" and "object,"[82] according to which the dignity of the self does not lie in the *objective* situation that was assigned to it "once and for all in the cosmic order,"[83] but in its capacity to oppose its own value ("a value completely *sui* generis")[84] to the objective universe. The self-determination of this value wrenched man from his ancient status as a mere part of the whole, and for the first time revealed in all its depth the polarity of subject and object. The "opposition between 'substantiality' and 'subjectivity' "[85] served moreover to isolate freedom as a form of creativity capable of helping man navigate his way through an unpredetermined future: thus, given "this purely humanistic faith" in human creativity,[86] the "ideal of humanity includes the ideal of *autonomy*."[87] (Witness, among a thousand other proofs, these lines quoted by Cassirer, in which Pico della Mirandola has the demiurge describe the condition that is uniquely that of human beings: "We have given you, Adam, no definite place, no form proper only to you, no special inheritance, so that you may have as your own whatever place, whatever form, whatever gifts you may choose, according to your wish and your judgement. All other beings have received a rigidly determined nature, and will be compelled by us to follow strictly determined laws. You alone are bound by no limit, unless it be one prescribed by your will, which I have given you.")[88] The humanistic affirmation of man's distinctive value, defined as the Promethean capacity to be the subject of one's being,[89] and the explanation of subjectivity in terms of autonomy clearly mark the emergence of a modern sensibility and the decisive break it represented with the ancient picture of the *cosmos*.

It could be that, within the framework created by the emergence of these new values of subjectivity and autonomy, the logic of modernity (if indeed there is one) was first sketched as a gradual substitution of *individuality* for *subjectivity*, with an associated shift from an ethics of autonomy to an ethics of independence. Certainly the individual remains an instance of the subject. In this sense, it must be insisted, the conditions required for individualism to develop are indeed those of modernity. At bottom, these amount to postulating man as a "distinctive value" in a world that is not intrinsically hierarchical: thus individualism also unquestionably constitutes an instance, or "moment," of modern humanism. There is a peculiarity, however, which goes completely unnoticed in Heidegger's reading and in the thinking it has since inspired: that the individual is perhaps ultimately only a transient instance of the subject, and individualism an ephemeral moment of humanism—*whose very substance it causes to disappear*. That humanism should be threatened by that to which it gave birth appears all the more striking when we appreciate the subtle transformation by which the logic of individualism goes from being a principle of autonomy to a principle of independence, and so dissolves the valorization—in which humanism has consisted since the Renaissance—of a sphere of supraindividual normativity around which humanity constitutes itself and intersubjectively recognizes itself. More precisely, given the ideas of normativity and intersubjectivity (as agreement around common norms: as *culture*), what undermines individualism—by eliminating all values other than that of the affirmation of the self—is the fundamental and paradoxical (for being prior) idea of autonomy: submission to laws that one has set *for oneself* presupposes the possibility of distinguishing between what might be called the lawgiving self and that other part of the self that submits to it. The idea of autonomy that defines humanism thus calls for the definition of a share of one's *common* humanity that is irreducible to the affirmation of one's singularity alone—which individualism denies, by definition, in positing only irreducible differences. To the extent that the Leibnizian monadology provided a true philosophical (read: ontological) foundation for individualism, it could be argued that this monadology produced a crucial rupture in the modern history of the subject that went above and beyond even the break represented by the *Leibnizian monadological cogito*. If this argument—which constitutes the second part of the present book—is granted, one would have to accept that the individualistic drift of modern philosophy proceeded by at least three major stages after its Leibnizian origin:

- A first stage comprised of the *empiricist* versions of the monadological idea, from Berkeley to Hume;
- A second marked by *Hegelian historicism*, with the theory of the "ruse of reason" constituting a joint repetition of the Leibnizian doctrine of preestablished harmony and the liberal notion of the "invisible hand," which came out of the empiricist tradition;
- A third stage consisting in the advent of that truly philosophical expression of contemporary individualism epitomized by *Nietzschean perspectivism*, in which the infinite diversity of individuality is randomly affirmed by the elimination of any logic immanent in development: *individualism without a*

subject, as one might say, alluding both to the Nietzschean critique of the illusions of the *cogito* and to the denial of any surreptitious organization of the real by a providential subject.

If in fact the history of the subject evolved from Descartes to Nietzsche in this plural and nonlinear (rather than continuous) way, it is unsurprising that it favored the evaporation, or eclipse, of subjectivity in favor of individuality (rather than the opposite). The Heideggerian misinterpretation of the situation had important consequences for what was to be called into question in this history, and what not. As a logical matter, what needs to be critically examined is less subjectivity itself than the drift of subjectivity toward individualism—assuming of course that, as a theoretical matter, this drift created intellectual structures whose possible perverse effects can be analyzed—here I am thinking primarily of the problem raised by the "ruse of reason"—and that, as a practical matter, it gave rise to phenomena as historically important as the atomization of social life and the destruction of public space in modern democratic societies. In short, if a genuine critique of subjectivity is still possible, this is first and foremost a consequence of the fact that subjectivity and humanism were susceptible to such a drift in the first place.

I should add that a critical history of subjectivity would no longer necessarily carry with it an *antimodern* bias against subjectivity (whether premodern or postmodern), apart from establishing that the individualistic drift of subjectivity was unavoidable and irresistable, and that humanism already contained the seeds of this drift. But this much remains to be demonstrated.

Immanent Transcendence: The Philosophical Problem of Postmodernity

To get clear about what ultimately is at stake in proposing this hypothesis, one must realize that it takes as its central philosophical problem one that is quite different from the problem identified by the Heideggerian reading. The resolution of the latter problem consists in the constantly repeated attempt to "make the leap" in the hope that it might lead out of subjectivity. But where exactly would it land us?

What may be *the* philosophical problem of our age, an age that has witnessed the hyperindividualistic consummation of modernity—and hence the problem of a real postmodernity—can be best expressed in the following terms: how, given the immanence that defines subjectivity, are we to conceive of the transcendence of the norms that could limit individuality? The basic challenge facing modern society is to reconcile the "freedom of the moderns"—that is, the demand for independence *implied by the modern idea of autonomy as independence from a radical otherness, or exteriority that prescribes the subject's course of action*—with the necessary existence of norms, which in constituting an unavoidable demand for intersubjectivity therefore presupposes a limitation upon monadological individualism—and so a limitation upon individuality. All of this is summed up by Husserl's famous question: How can transcendence within immanence be conceived?[90] I interpret this question to indicate two equally indispensable requirements:

- First, as against individualism, we need to salvage the idea that without common norms there is no conceivable "republic" of intersubjectivity, but only the absurd program of that "self-regard" which resists "giving way on (its) desires." To guard against the development of such a culture (cult, actually), it is necessary to rethink the transcendence of values, which is to say their transcendence in relation to individuality.
- Second, in defending against all attempts to "return to the ancients," we need to emphasize with equal vigor that transcendence will not consist in somehow getting free of subjectivity, in breaking out of the circle of immanence in order to revive some normativity conceived in the archaic, premodern context of the otherness of divine Law or the exteriority of Tradition. The notion of a return to such models of transcendence suffers from the same weakness as all reactions against a cultural and ideological context in which (whether we like it or not) we think and act: an infinite, open world which, if it is to have meaning, values, and norms, can have them only through—and for—the subject. In an age of disenchantment with the world that, as Marcel Gauchet has shown,[91] is inherent in the democratic process of modern society, it makes no sense to try to re-create from scratch a theological and religious vision whose revival is surely neither possible nor, owing to its incompatibility with the democratic idea of a self-imposed order, desirable.

If a more informed view of the history of subjectivity must take into account the question of "immanent transcendence," attention to three main points will help us to formulate more precisely the question that the Heideggerian interpretation of modernity allows to be posed:

Nonmetaphysical Humanism v. Nonindividualistic Humanism: This question suggests another way to reconsider the aforementioned problem of what a nonmetaphysical humanism might look like.[92] Unlike the Heideggerian identification of metaphysics (subjectivity) and humanism, a nonmetaphysical humanism must take care to avoid seeming to be nothing more than that multiform individualism set forth by Leibniz, the British empiricists, and Hegel and Nietzsche.

Faced with a metaphysics whose history is best summed up by the phrase "the age of monadologies," a nonmetaphysical humanism must discover a way both to preserve whatever meaning the idea of the subject has left after the critique of the illusions of metaphysics mounted by rational psychology and to determine how within the framework of autonomy a limited form of individuality could be conceived as a ground for communication and intersubjectivity. In this sense, nonmetaphysical humanism must *also* (not: only) be understood as a nonindividualistic humanism.

Subjectivity, Objectivity, Intersubjectivity: The question of transcendence in immanence (around which the problem of subjectivity will inevitably turn in the future) obviously also overlaps with the problem of objectivity. How, within a framework of the immanence of the subject with respect to itself, can I posit norms that, though they limit *my* individuality, are valid not just *for me* (as an individual) but *for everyone*? Since I posit them, these norms will certainly be subjective; but they will also be intersubjective (because transindividual). In this sense, it is necessary to understand how the subject can posit the *objective* ("objective" referring here to the supraindividual validity of what is, at least in principle, valid for everyone—for example, the validity of a maxim proscribing anti-Semitism, in contrast to the simple subjective assertion that blue is the most beautiful of all colors, or red).

This question thus is closely tied up with the question how objectivity is constituted as a function of subjectivity. Here we recognize a particular instance of the classic problem of *truth*. But the problem of grounding objectivity on a subjective assertion arises in the same way with regard to practical matters, such as the determination of good ends which, being absolutely valid, are thus objectively—and not merely subjectively—practical. In this case we encounter a formulation of the classic problem of the *good*. The same question may be asked, finally, in connection with aesthetic objectivity, on condition of granting—what only a devout admirer of Pierre Bourdieu would dispute—that judgments of taste differ from judgments about what is pleasing in that the former also depict a sphere of objectivity that at least has a claim to universality. Here we find ourselves faced with the no less classic problem of the *beautiful*.

Three models of immanent transcendence can thus be identified, corresponding to a three-dimensional problem of objectivity that is inseparable from the problem of a non-antimodern limitation on individuality. What has gone unnoticed is that contemporary individualism has tended to dissolve objectivity into pure relativism—pure nihilism, in fact, which could be summed up by the brief formula: to each his own opinions, ends, and tastes.

On Criticism: The Impossible "Return to Kant": If the possibility of transcendence in immanence is connected with the classic questions of the true, the good, and the beautiful, it should be added that it is connected with them only insofar as these questions are formulated in a very specific philosophical way, that is, *critically*: the peculiarity of the criticist approach to the problem of objectivity, as Kant posed it, is that it replaced the dogmatic conception of truth in terms of the relation between representation and the thing-in-itself, with an inquiry into the conditions under which intersubjective agreement can be valid for all subjects. The criticist reformulation thus already clearly ushered in the problem of immanent transcendence: how can the subject posit the objective in itself—that is, a theoretical, practical, or aesthetic representation that is irreducible to the subject's individuality? In this sense, "the age of monadologies" (which is what the metaphysical history of the subject boils down to) obliges us to reexplore the route by which the Kantian (and, in part, the Fichtean) moments escaped the drift toward individualism that characterized it. To deconstruct the monadological era and to construct the Kantian moment would amount, then, to following two different routes to the same place—a place where a plural dimension has been restored to the history of subjectivity.

I am obviously not one to resist such an approach. In fact, as we shall see in Part Three, various problems with the Heideggerian history of subjectivity will lead us back to a searching reexamination of the criticist position. For the moment, however, it needs to be asked whether a pure and simple "return to Kant" is possible. Such a return is a dream: it would amount to the negation of the sum of philosophical reflection for the past two centuries, as though all the enigmas we presently face could be resolved by prudent management of the magnificent inheritance constituted by three *Critiques*. Such a dream is absurd on several counts. The complexity of the problem of subjectivity (or of nonmetaphysical humanism) has greatly increased since Kant, the problem having been enriched and complicated by a whole history that cannot now be rewound in any simple, literal way:

- On the one hand, the history of post-Kantian philosophy is marked by a decomposition of the criticist conception of the subject. This is the case with German idealism, where Schelling and Hegel in some sense revived rational psychology against Kant; it is also the case with Nietzsche, whose scathing criticism of the Kantian subject opened the way to absolute individualism. This process of decomposition cannot be ignored. If we wish to reconstruct the criticist subject, we must take into account the reasons why it should have been liable to decompose so quickly and easily.
- On the other hand, if there can no longer be any question of a simple "return to Kant," this is also because today the problem of the subject is set in a radically different context. First of all, the philosophical context has changed: in Kant, the criticist subject is built up by means of a twofold critique of

empiricism and Leibnizian dogmatism; if the criticist subject were to be reconstructed today, by contrast, this would need to be done on the basis of a twofold critique of Hegelianism (as "the height of metaphysics") and of Heideggerian irrationalism (as itself a relentless critique of such a metaphysics).[93] In both cases, the criticist discourse intervenes to resolve an antinomy between two philosophically dominant discourses, but the antinomy has undergone a basic shift—it no longer consists of an opposition between two models of the metaphysics of subjectivity, but rather between metaphysics in its highest form and its most radical negation. This shift introduces further difficulties, even in the very statement of the problem, that remain to be investigated. For the context of thinking about the subject has been transformed not only just philosophically, but also culturally or intellectually: today the problem of the subject must also respond to the needs of the social sciences, which have posed questions that could not have been raised within the framework of the original Kantian moment.

Two examples will suffice to show that if there is to be a new Kantian moment, it cannot take the form of an academic repetition of critical philosophy:

- The social sciences have, on the one hand, cast the problem of scientific objectivity in radical terms. If, for example, the subject of historical knowledge is itself a historical being whose discourse expresses an entire era, what can be said about the objectivity of the discourse thus produced? Here we encounter the problem of historicism in the form that critical philosophies of history—from Dilthey to Weber and Aron—tried to deal with it. While they certainly made reference to Kant's contribution (think, for instance, of Dilthey's project of a "critique of historical reason"), they were obliged to develop original lines of argument since the problem of historical objectivity was not really tackled in the *Critiques*.[94] I do not claim that these critical philosophies of history fully succeeded; I merely suggest that their attempts, though they certainly belong to a tradition, did not on that account take the form of a "return."
- On the other hand, the social sciences have widely exploited the notion of the "ruse of reason," whether in psychoanalysis or a certain functionalist sociology that naturalizes society and dissolves the causality of human agents, who are held to be resolutely unaware of what they are doing and unresponsible for an evolution that would occur without them. No one (or almost no one) any longer denies that such a strategy poses many problems, if only from an ethical or politico-juridical standpoint, since it seems neither easy nor desirable to do without the idea of responsibility; but, more importantly, it raises the question, clearly stated in France by Boudon, whether social facts cannot in fact be better explained by assuming that social agents are conscious and responsible for what they do. This counter-hypothesis relies on the principle of "methodological individualism" (to use Schumpeter's rather unfortunate expression—

> unfortunate since if one takes the social agent to be conscious and responsible, the author or subject of his acts, it would be more natural to call such a state of affairs methodological "subjectivism" or "humanism" rather than individualism). But it makes little difference what name is adopted: the question is whether it would not be methodologically more productive to reintroduce, as a sort of guiding thread, the idea (read: the regulative Idea) of *subjectivity* or *autonomy* among social actors. Note that this carries a very important implication for philosophers, who would have to leave off talking about the death of the subject and the end of man. What we need is at least a methodical thinking through of this problem and of the host of others that follow in its train: in what cases, for example, should social facts be interpreted using an explanatory schema of the "ruse of reason" type (which, quite obviously, is often legitimate and even necessary); in what cases should one proceed differently and assume responsibility on the part of social actors? Because considerations of mere efficiency (in the economist's sense) cannot furnish an adequate criterion, what is called for here is an enterprise of legitimation. On the (surely distant) day when philosophers cease to regard social science as the embodiment of radical evil, for having so often extended its domination at the expense of philosophy, they may perhaps notice that the disciplines that study society have given birth to a real philosophical problem concerning the status and function of the idea of subjectivity as a regulative principle. They will then have to admit that this problem also belongs to a tradition, since it clearly requires a critical approach to the general problem of transcendental deduction, which is to say, the search for the conditions under which concepts can be applied to experience. But in this kind of deduction, the inquiry shifts from categories to Ideas. It will be granted that where it is a question of a transcendental deduction of Ideas, in this case the Idea of the subject, a literal reading of the *Critique of Pure Reason* is of no great help.

That philosophers today should find themselves faced with the challenge from the social sciences to reinvest the acquired knowledge of a particular tradition in new philosophical activities strongly suggests that drawing upon tradition is likely to be productive only if it does not take the lazy form of a regression or repetition. Assuming that it does not in this case, a new field seems ready now to be opened up on which certain philosophical options of modernity can be played out again. For this to come about, it will remain necessary to prevent novel and potentially fruitful possibilities from being foreclosed by a homogenizing reading that reduces them, as it has at other moments in the past history of subjectivity, to mere variations on a single theme. In this connection, the insistence on the way in which the cleavage between humanism and individualism works to block the sort of homogenization practiced by Heidegger and his followers could prove useful in helping us pay more sustained attention to what differentiates the successive moments in the history of the subject. First, however, we need to work out the logic of individualism, the other guiding thread in our attempt to make sense of modernity. The virtues, and, in my view, the limits of this tradition are well expressed in the work of Louis Dumont, to which I now turn.

CHAPTER II

Dumont: The Triumph of the Individual

THE ATTEMPT to bring an individualistic approach to bear upon a philosophical history of modernity runs into major methodological difficulties.

First, the term "individualism" is notoriously imprecise. Max Weber was correct to say that it "includes the most heterogeneous things imaginable." To get some idea of its multiplicity, think of the various terms with which it can be paired as an opposite: universalism, totalism, holism, altruism, traditionalism, and socialism. All these notions can function in various ways as opposites of individualism, leading one to wonder whether the term exists solely because of its capacity for contrast, without having any determinate meaning of its own. The difficulty may be merely one of fact rather than of principle: at the least we can agree with Weber that, in view of the term's vast conceptual range, "a thorough analysis of these concepts in historical terms would at the present time be highly valuable to science";[1] and we can agree that, if individualism is to be used as a guiding thread for understanding modernity, this can only be done by making a serious effort to construct a clear and distinct notion of what our aim is.

A second difficulty—this time clearly one of principle—may be even more awkward, however. To speak of individualism is to speak in a *political* key. In his important reconstruction of the term's history, Marcel Gauchet traces its first public mention to 1826, when an anonymous writer for the Saint-Simonean newspaper *Le Producteur* used it to denounce the reduction of economy "to the most narrow individualism."[2] In 1829 the term was repeated by Prosper Enfantin in his *Doctrine of Saint-Simon* to refer to the dissolute state of a society profoundly in need of major reforms.[3] From 1830 on, the term had the connotation familiar to us from socialist writers who attacked bourgeois society as something to be overcome as soon as possible in order for the blissful reign of the general interest to begin.

I do not mean to lay too much stress on these historical facts, which are complex.[4] But as Tocqueville's and Max Stirner's use of the term seems to indicate, its original semantic register was unambiguous: the work designated, pejoratively or not, a number of sociopolitical phenomena commonly taken to be characteristic of the modern age. How is it then that this original meaning came to mark indelibly all subsequent uses of the term and so to limit its range of application? Can the term be incorporated in a philosophical history of philosophy that is primarily concerned with the analysis of problems as alien and seemingly irreducible to the political sphere as, for example, ontology? Here again I do not claim that the difficulty is necessarily insurmountable, but we will at least need to be aware of the transposition and what it entails—namely, that in some sense the political horizon cannot be held to be completely external to the meaning (or to one of the possible meanings) of the fate of modern metaphysics. Certainly there is no justification for using political history as a proof of the truth of the philosophical history of subjectivity, or regarding it as the "infrastructure" of such a history; rather it is a matter of forging links, in a way that remains to be spelled out, between what has been done politically in the modern era and what has been played out philosophically, so that the same history can be seen unfolding in different ways.

A clear view of these two difficulties, and the precautions they call for, can be had by examining Louis Dumont's studies of what he calls "the modern ideology." Taking individualism as the key element of this ideology, he has worked out a reading of modernity that compels our attention, and warrants discussion here in view of our hypothesis that at the core of the modern history of the subject is to be found a decisive turn toward individualism—a turn that Heidegger missed.

Holism and Individualism

Dumont's work is rich and also surprisingly diverse, running from a narrow monograph like *La Tarasque* to the lengthy socioethnological descriptions of *Homo Hierarchicus* on the social and mental structure of India, and, beyond these, to the profound history of modern ideas developed in *Homo aequalis*[5] and *Essais sur l'individualisme*.[6] My discussion obviously bears only on this final moment of his career when, having returned home from India, the magisterial comparativist set himself the task of showing how original and problematic our own values in the West—and, more generally, those of modernity—actually are. To try to bring out what is distinctive about this "return to Ithaca," the end of an extraordinary intellectual odyssey, I should like to begin by considering the questions that Dumont's contribution to an understanding of modern individualism seems to me to raise. Let us look first at the connection between Dumont's claims and the questions being asked here, in order to establish the coherence, as I see it, of an individualistic interpretation of the mental system of modernity.

In linking up his study of the hierarchical society of India with a set of reflections on a modern society that, by contrast, is seen as egalitarian, Dumont constructs two ideologies[7] that he believes correspond to these two types of societies. On the one hand there is a holistic ideology, which "valorizes the social whole and disregards or subordinates the human individual." The society that corresponds to this ideology is a hierarchical one in which, as with the Indian caste system, order results from "putting value into play"—the value of the whole—with the parts or elements (notably individuals) thus appearing by definition as subordinate to the whole or what stands for the whole. Individualist ideology, on the other hand, valorizes the individual—"the independent, autonomous . . . and thus essentially nonsocial moral being"—and accordingly "disregards or subordinates the social whole." The society that logically corresponds to this ideology is egalitarian, for if the individual as such is the supreme value, he cannot be subjected to anyone other than himself: thus the principle of hierarchy is thereby excluded in favor of the principle of equality. Such an individualism is the "cardinal value of modern societies,"[8] notably in the economic-political sphere, where the principle of equality takes the form of "liberalism."

It should be noted that defined in this way, as ideologies with mutually contradictory principles, the two are radically incompatible, and no compromise is possible between them. Hence one of Dumont's most famous theses, warning against what is bound to be fictitious and dangerous in any putative return to holism within the framework of modern societies: once the splendid whole formed by hierarchical society is broken, the desire for unity can be reintroduced on individualistic foundations only in the form of a fanatical determination to put an end to the division or atomization of society. As a result, because the society cannot find any *consensus*—anything that is commonly accepted—on which to base itself, it ends up becoming either totalitarian or terroristic.[9]

A Genesis of Modern Individualism

Given this much, Dumont's whole project (at least the one that concerns me here) can be seen as an exciting reconstruction of individualist ideology and the way in which it gives birth to modernity. This genesis raises a particularly complicated problem, which basically involves understanding how it could happen that "starting from the common type of holistic societies, a new type has evolved that *fundamentally contradicts* the common conception": in short, how can we "conceive a transition between those two *antithetic* universes of thought, those two *mutually irreconcilable* ideologies?"[10] Set up in this way, as a matter of understanding not simply a cultural shift but the actual transformation of a society into its absolute opposite, the problem predetermines the kind of solution that can be found: if a "direct transition" from one opposite to the other is not only "improbable" but "impossible,"[11] it remains to find some "mediation," some face or form of traditional society that, while forming an essential part of it, could give rise to a kind of individualistic reinterpretation and thus serve as a pivot between the two systems—the individualistic reinterpretation of this ingredient of the traditional culture constituting the point around which the cultural universe turns and pushes hierarchical societies over the edge, flattening them into the form of modern egalitarian society. Dumont finds the model for this pivot in an institution of traditional Indian society: the doctrine of the "renunciation of the world."[12]

His argument proceeds from the observation that Indian society, being fundamentally holistic, creates an extremely close interdependence among its members by means of the caste system. This system imposes collective obligations on all members (with regard for example, to marriage), connecting them hereditarily: constraining group relations thus occupy the place that in our individualistic societies we grant to free individual initiatives. Nevertheless, within a system where "the individual does not exist," the institution of worldly renunciation enables certain individuals to achieve "full independence": in the figure of the "renouncer," the notion that "the individual does exist" began to emerge.[13] While this figure is not a source of tension or contradiction within holistic society, being an integral part of it, another meaning can be attached to the act of renunciation in which individualism drops out. In short, as a religion in which the believer finds his faith *in the world* by submitting to a network of constrained relations expressing the hierarchical order of nature, Hinduism *also* encourages a tendency toward otherworldliness, and with it the conception of faith modeled on the ascetic who tears himself away from the world and its burdens. For someone who becomes a *sannyasi*, Hinduism is not a religion of individual self-renunciation, of losing oneself in the world; on the contrary, the renouncer renounces the world "to devote himself to his own liberation."

Describing how an entirely different "mentality" comes into play, Dumont says:

> He submits himself to his chosen master, or he may even enter a monastic community, but essentially he depends upon no one but himself: he is alone. In leaving the world he finds himself invested with an individuality which

> evidently he finds uncomfortable, since all his efforts tend to its extinction of this transcendence. He thinks as an individual—the distinctive trait that opposes him to the man-in-the-world and brings him closer to the western thinker. But while for us the individual is in the world, here he is found only outside the world, at least in principle.[14]

Thus we easily see what Dumont thinks determined the genesis of modernity. Within the traditional society, "the religion of the group is overlaid by an individual religion based on a choice" that allows "the full independence of the man who chooses it";[15] but if in this regard the idea of the renouncer "is similar to that of the modern individual,"[16] two differences set limits to the analogy, which must be abolished for modernity to be born:

- While the modern individual "lives in the social world," the renouncer "lives outside it." In order to go beyond the simple superimposition of an individual mentality upon a fundamental group mentality, a culture truly pervaded by the values of individualism must emerge; for this to occur, it would be necessary to substitute the model of the "individual-outside-the-world" for that of the "individual-in-the-world."
- In the holistic universe, renunciation corresponds to "a social state apart from society proper."[17] For in the eyes of the law, not every man can become a renouncer and thus cease to exist as a member of his caste: the option is limited to a few by the very logic of the group, which depends on a person belonging to one caste rather than another. In this sense, then, the option also refers to the collective order and its constraints. The birth of modern individualism occurred, in effect, through the extension of the opportunity for exercising such an option to every man, each one then being able to think of himself as an independent individual, self-sufficient, and concerned chiefly with his own destiny.

Having identified the conditions under which the transition to individualism can be made, we must look to discover in the premodern West a model comparable to the Indian "individual-outside-the-world" who posits himself, within a holistic society, as a "kind of supplement to it" (and, in this sense, as its "principle of dissolution")[18]—and to show how what in Indian society basically remained an unexplored possibility could come to be traced out in all its consequences in the West. Dumont finds the Western counterpart to the Indian renouncer in early Christianity, arguing that a "dualism" or "tension" developed that would "permeate throughout history" in Christian culture:[19] the teachings of Christ and Saint Paul indeed made the Christian an "individual-outside-the-world," on a level (i.e., in relation to God) that "transcends the world of man and of social institutions"; by the terms of this relation, which affirms "the infinite worth of the individual," the world of human society—hierarchical, "holistic"—is lowered and devalued. What is distinctive *ab origine* about the Christian version of the "individual-outside-the-world," however, is the universalistic perspective in which the otherworldly relation to God is cast: the absolute value enjoyed by the individual soul by virtue of its filial relation to God is shared by all humanity, whose fellowship it thus grounds.[20] There follows a principle that was "given from the start in Christianity" and that "no Indian religion has ever fully attained": that of "the equality of all . . . in the presence of God."[21] It can easily be seen that this principle contained the seeds of modern individualism: because the principle of equality operated in relation to God (that is, outside the world) it could thus coexist with a principle of hierarchy (operating within the world). Medieval Christianity carried on this ancient dualism, superimposing an otherworldly value of equality on the worldly, holistic value of hierarchy that structured all social relations. For modern individualism to be born, it was necessary for the individualistic and universalistic element in Christianity to "contaminate" worldly life, so to speak, to the point that the worldly and the unworldly came to be gradually unified—with the result that the initial dualism was obliterated and "life in the world . . . thought of as entirely comformable to the supreme value": at the conclusion of this process, "the outwordly individual will have become the modern, inworldly individual."[22]

In both *Homo aequalis* and his *Essays*, Dumont explores what he takes to be the most important moments of this "contamination": the appearance at the beginning of the fourth century of a "Christian state," owing to the emperor Constantine's conversion to Christianity, which for the first time raised the problem of compatibility between otherworldly values (equality) and worldly values (hierarchy); the Reformation, primarily in its final stage, marked by the advent of Calvin, the disappearance of the church as a "holistic institution," and its transformation into an "association made up of individuals";[23] the birth of political individualism—the result of the transformation of the concepts of politics and of the state since the thirteenth century, which affected the whole history of modern natural law;[24] the "triumph of the individual" in the Declaration of the Rights of Man of 1789, which, in consecrating the individualistic breakup of the old "hierarchical Christian community," finally elevated equality and liberty—the "implications of individualism"—to the rank of supreme values (equality supplanting hierarchy, the keystone of the holistic universe; and liberty in the sense of independence, held to constitute citizenship insofar as individuals are not members of a whole but simply elements of an atomized society).[25] While these analyses are certainly suggestive, I shall not dwell on them, for everyone by now is well aware that they represent decisive discoveries in the archeology of our mental universe. On the other hand, I think that attention can and should be paid to the contribution Dumont's studies make to our understanding of modernity.

A Unilateral Reading of Modernity

At the outset, an observation: beyond the incontestable "effects of meaning" this perspective has on "modern ideology" (a sure sign that it must indeed have some point of contact with our destiny), the reconstruction Dumont proposes has a drawback that is symmetrical with—and the converse of—that of Heidegger's reconstruction. Heidegger read the history of modernity unilaterally as a story of subjectivity ever more fully affirming its domination over reality. Dumont unilaterally reads modernity as a story of individuality in which the values of individualism do not cease being ever more completely deployed. In each case—the reign of the subject, on the one hand, the triumph of the individual on the other—the interpreter seems convinced beforehand that modernity is homogeneous and that, where a movement goes against the current, it nonetheless does not prevent the overall tendency from fulfilling itself. In this sense there is more than an analogy between the way in which Heidegger interprets the moments of resistance to the fulfillment of the metaphysics of subjectivity (in Kant, Nietzsche, and the early Husserl) as having ultimately only contributed to the irresistible advance of what they seemingly tried to hold back, and the way in which Dumont sees the anti-individualistic reaction attempted by certain modern thinkers (Herder and Fichte, or Hegel and Marx) with a view to achieving a rebirth of the community (*universitas*) that finally grows up within the tradition of individualism and causes it to bear its ultimate and most perverse consequences.[26] This kind of interpretive move is so characteristic of unilateral readings of modernity that it warrants some discussion.

In his analysis of the natural law tradition, Dumont emphasizes that all champions of political individualism (from Althusius to Rousseau) harbor a kind of nostalgia for the unity guaranteed by the holistic conception: once *universitas* is replaced by *societas*, the whole problem of modern political philosophy becomes how to construct a social order and to preserve the possibility of social unity among a humanity made up of individual atoms. Rousseau's *Social Contract* exemplifies the difficulties, and also the risks, to which individualism exposes modernity: the abandonment of individual rights by the particular wills that constitute a general will which is presupposed always to be right is seen by Dumont to amount to nothing less than "a prefiguration of the Jacobin dictatorship, of the

Moscow trials, or even of the Nazis' *Volksseele*."[27] More generally, modern despotism and totalitarianism are merely the result of a desperate desire to recreate by force a sociopolitical organism in the place where the spontaneous cohesion of the social body constituted by tradition had been undermined. Totalitarianism thus only apparently introduced a breach in the logic of individualism: in reality, "no more than anyone else" could Hitler escape the "cardinal value of modern societies," and in fact a "deep individualism underlies his racist rationalization of anti-Semitism."[28] Thus we find in Dumont, as in Heidegger but with a different twist, the conviction that the safety catches supposedly set to protect against the logic of modernity are ultimately only tricks of the logic itself.

The implication of this belief is clear: the possibility is *by definition* and a priori excluded that modernity might not be homogeneous, that not everything in it is somehow determined from the outset—that something indeed might have happened. This bias in Heidegger in favor of homogenizing modernity so absolutely that its history is made basically devoid of real *events* corresponds directly, in Dumont, to the principled decision to consider holism and individualism as two opposites that exclude any third or middle term: if nothing intermediate between the valorization of the whole and that of the individual can be imagined, neither could anything occur between the holism of traditional society and individualism as we know it through which another pole of valorization might be formed. The understanding of history here obviously derives from the construction of the concepts used for approaching it.

Heidegger, who saw in individualism only one genre among others of the "humanistic" kind (collectivism, nationalism, internationalism, and so forth), perceived only the reign of the subject beyond the ruin of the Greek cosmos, and missed the problem posed by the *becoming-individual of this subject*. Dumont, who conceives of individualism only as the opposite of holism, sees the collapse of traditional values followed only by the triumph of the individual, and leaves aside the question of what left only individualism as a possibility (perhaps, more precisely, as a mere possibility): the humanistic valorization of man as *subject*. Similarly, and no less than Heidegger, he sidesteps any question about the *individualization of the subject*, that might well provide the logic of modernity with an essential principle of intelligibility. *Humanism could be located between holism and individualism, and the subject between the whole and the individual*—but only by a complex set of moves still to be worked out: making humanism either a compromise between the two other terms or a third term located equidistant from them will in any case *not* do. Dumont's work, whatever its interest in other respects may be, has little to contribute in this regard. His thinking about "modern ideology" seems never to have considered the possibility that modernity was pervaded by a conflict internal *to itself.* Instead it is as if, once the holistic universe of tradition and hierarchy was destroyed, no other alternative existed to that of the indivisible triumph of the individual—as if everything that might appear to be an obstacle to the reign of the individual had to be interpreted as an impossible return to holism, which would ultimately turn out to bring more calamity than benefit.

An Unnoticed Conflict between Modern Values: Autonomy and Independence

The confusion between the subject and the individual is remarkably consistent in Dumont's works. I shall confine myself here to providing some evidence that the problems which arise from failing to distinguish between them went unnoticed.

Dumont makes the individual the central value of the modern world, calling him an "independent, autonomous, and thus (essentially) nonsocial moral being."[29] Can independence and autonomy be equated in this way? One can accept this only by allowing a highly imprecise notion of autonomy, one very far from the way in which modern philosophy has dealt with it—which is to say, in terms that are hard to square with the logic of individualism. Dumont correctly says that the logic of individualism is that of independence, the "liberation from fetters," which points the way toward the modern individual who, like the Hindu renouncer who had already prefigured him, is "concerned only with himself."[30] Taken to an extreme, the valorization of independence or "self-sufficiency"[31] leads undeniably to the gesture of the man who "foregoes social life and its constraints"—who, in any case, does not see them as essential to his fulfillment—"to devote himself to his own progress and destiny."[32] In exploring this dimension of modern ideology and its perverse effects, Dumont places himself within the great tradition initiated by Benjamin Constant and Alexis de Tocqueville: when de Tocqueville, in *Democracy in America*, described the risks incurred by a society in which men "turn restlessly on themselves to obtain small and vulgar pleasures with which they fill up their soul" and where "each of them, withdrawn to a distance, is like a stranger to all the others," he was measuring the effects of this "freedom of the moderns" that Constant had explicitly defined in terms of "independence." When Dumont, on the other hand, radicalizes certain ambiguities inherent in his theory, abruptly assimilating autonomy and independence, his definition of individualism (and thereby his interpretation of modernity) becomes very imprecise.

Thus the *Essays* hold that in the modern conception of law and politics the supreme value—from which "first principles regarding the constitution of the state (and of society) have to be extracted or deduced"—is "man taken as an autonomous being independently of any social or political attachment."[33] By virtue of this, autonomy would have to imply absolute independence: the need of the human being (as in the case of substance for Descartes) only for itself in order to exist. Hence in various places Dumont is apt to liken autonomy-as-independence to self-sufficiency—for example, in regarding modern society as having "asserted the self-sufficiency of the particular human being on the moral and political level."[34] Hence too, if autonomy is equivalent to independence, and independence equivalent to self-sufficiency, it follows that modern societies can conceive of freedom as the "unchartered freedom" that Rousseau made the characteristic feature of the state of nature:[35] for does not absolute independence—pure self-sufficiency—coincide with the rejection of any rule that would limit the "spontaneous or arbitrary will"?[36] Such a rule might involve, for example, taking account of the problem of relations with the other and the conditions necessary for coexistence, a problem that implies the individual is not sufficient unto himself and needs more than just himself in order to exist. From autonomy as independence we thus drift, by a chain of equivalences taken as self-evident, to an exclusive concern with the self—to pure narcissism and hedonism.

I readily concede that this linking up of independence, self-sufficiency, and rule-less freedom fairly well characterizes the trend of modern individualism, and even more so of contemporary individualism. But can *autonomy* legitimately be inserted as a link in this chain of values? Dumont tells us that modern ideology is the valorization of the "autonomous, independent being," and that independence is self-sufficiency: that is, freedom with no rules. But is freedom without rules the same as autonomy? If the answer is negative (and I shall come back to the reasons why this seems a reasonable answer), then approval of Dumont's characterization of modern ideology must be profoundly qualified: *while it may be agreed that modernity has valorized autonomy and independence, it does not follow that this twofold valorization is unitary*. In other words, if modernity, with its logic of individualism, did indeed place independence (as freedom without rules) above everything, it also valorized autonomy (which has nothing to do with freedom without rules—and hence nothing to do with independence). Modernity has not been homogeneous; rather, it has involved the whole history of modern values, serving primarily, perhaps, as a battleground between the values of autonomy and those of independence. In this sense, to read modernity as having wholly valorized an individualistic independence that is indistinguishable from the values of autonomy is to refrain from posing a decisive problem, surely *the* decisive problem for the interpretation of modernity: *how did the valorization of autonomy come to be eclipsed by that of independence?*

In the name of what principle can we assert, as against Dumont, the irreducibility of the values of autonomy to those of independence? One thinks of Rousseau, whom Dumont incorrectly cites in constructing the individualistic concept of freedom: when the *Social Contract* talks of natural freedom and freedom without rules (i.e., of perfect independence), it is clear that this is far from true freedom for Rousseau—who located "civil liberty" much more in the individual's submission to rules freely accepted, in what Kant (seeing himself in this regard as the heir to Rousseau as the "Newton of the moral world") was later to call the "autonomy of the will." Therefore, with respect to a whole dimension of modernity expressed in the works of Rousseau, Kant, and Fichte as well, the supreme value is not at all that of independence as freedom-without-rules: it is "auto-nomy," or self-rule, which is contrasted not with dependence (i.e., submission to rules) but with heteronomy.

For autonomy is indeed in a sense a form of dependence—but in the sense that its valorization consists in making humanity itself the foundation of source of its norms and laws, since these are received neither from the nature of things, as the ancients supposed, nor from God, as in the Judeo-Christian tradition. It is no less true that autonomy in the sense of *dependence with regard to self-grounded human laws* is a *form* of independence (on account of which it is unsurprising that it should be confused with independence), but *only in relation to some radical Otherness that seeks to impose Law*. As a form of independence, autonomy (literally, the self-establishing of law) is not to be identified with *every* conceivable instance of it: the autonomous individual remains dependent on norms and law, on the condition of his free acceptance of them. This is to say that the valorization of autonomy is perfectly compatible with the principle of a *limitation of the Self*, through *submission* to a common law. It is also to say that the value of autonomy is constitutive of the democratic idea. On the other hand, the valorization of independence can lead to the "perfect independence" cultivated by individualism: the pure and simple affirmation of egoism as a fundamental, indefeasible value, *not in essence limitable*, shielded from any normativity whatsoever. As soon as one admits—with Dumont—that modern individualism (modernity in its individualistic aspect) has led to the valorization of independence *as such*, it follows that such a valorization was possible only through the breakdown of this more limited notion of independence as autonomy. Clarifying the relation between these two incongruent registers of value, which cannot (except at the risk of inexactness and superficiality) be *superimposed* upon one another, may well be the key problem for the interpretation of modernity.

What Dumont misses is that although modernity was unquestionably the site where individualism developed (via the valorization of man as individual), it was also where a conception of man as the foundation of his laws and norms emerged (via the valorization of man as an *auto-nomous subject*). *This emergence of the subject can scarcely be treated as a mere moment in the development of individualism.* Dumont thus confounds subjectivity and individuality: by reducing the emergence of subjectivity to the logic of individuality, he explicitly links the project of mastery that is constitutive of the modern subject to the advent of the individual—and so he reads the Cartesian theme of the mastery and possession of nature as proceeding from an "identification of our will with the will of God" in which he sees the freedom of the individual affirmed as the supreme value.[37] What is more, if man thinks of himself as a free agent (subject) by contrast with nature (object), this is because in the individualist scheme the man/world relation (nature) takes precedence over the man/man relation, since nature is what the individual has to master in order to ensure his independence.[38] Thus the advent of the subject fits naturally with the logic of individualism, according to which the history of subjectivity coincides with the history of individuality. If this is true, the irreducibility of the values of autonomy to those of independence is inconceivable. The confusion of Dumont's interpretation of modernity is therefore worth bringing out, and not merely as an exercise in conceptual clarification. At issue is something that extends far beyond an attempt at definition; it represents an attempt to preserve *the possibility of developing a critical analysis of modernity in some of its more absurd manifestations that remains fully modern in spirit and resists the temptation to strike up the familiar anthem of antimodernism.*

"Moderns" and "Antimoderns"

To reduce the destiny of modern societies solely to the playing out of individualism, without seeing that this destiny is characterized by a conflict between the values of humanism and those of individualism, is to expose oneself to two symmetrically dangerous risks: unqualified approval of modernity on the one hand, and wholesale condemnation of it on the other—each of which, after all, gives rise to the other.

If we privilege the way in which the logic of individualism replaces the principles of hierarchy and tradition with those of equality and freedom, we only make it harder to explain the advent of the democratic age. For then it becomes necessary to highlight the dimension of *progress* inherent in the transition from a holistic to an individualistic culture by showing that while the emergence (and, to a still greater degree, the contemporary radicalization) of individualism are liable to be accompanied by negative phenomena (the atomization of society, an indifference to politics, obsession with consumption, and the like), the rise of "democratic individualism" is nonetheless a generally positive process.

In this regard, Gilles Lipovetsky's remarkable book about fashion[39] is apt to meet with some misunderstanding: to see fashion, the logic of which today structures our societies from top to bottom, as the driving force behind the "spiraling movement toward individualism" and the consolidation of the democratic universe,[40] amounts to promoting the "fashion form" and accepting fashion's social consequences, from the global invasion of advertising to the gadgetization of existence and the subjection of cultural activity itself to the imperatives of consumption. We should keep in mind that Lipovetsky does note, among the effects of the "formidable thrust of individualist existences and aspirations," a "relational impasse, an unparalleled crisis in communication"; that he calls attention to the "increasing breakdown of the community" and the "deficit in intersubjective communication," and worries about "anemic social relations."[41] He concludes:

> The lesson is a harsh one: the progress of enlightenment and the progress of happiness do not go hand in hand. The euphoria of fashion has its counterparts in dereliction, depression, and existential anguish. We encounter more stimulations of all sorts, but also more anxiety; we have more personal autonomy, but also more personal crises. Such is the greatness of fashion, which always refers us, as individuals, back to ourselves; such is the misery of fashion, which renders us increasingly problematic to ourselves and others.[42]

One can hardly complain, therefore, that his book expresses unqualified approval of the age and a naive optimism devoid of critical acumen.[43] It remains true, however, that if his reading of modernity is de facto a differentiated reading, it will be necessary to give it true conceptual foundations if misunderstandings are to be avoided. In taking the "logic of modern cultural values" as his guiding thread, Lipovetsky does not sufficiently emphasize what otherwise he observes with great lucidity, namely, that this complex and multivalent logic brings antagonistic principles into conflict with each other in the wake of the rupture with holistic values. Witness his marked tendency to repeat the confusion between autonomy and independence that characterizes Dumont's works:[44] the exercise of choice (and even "overchoice") constantly invited by fashion may certainly be considered as a sign that a new area of freedom has opened up in place of the pure and simple renewal of an age-old practice inherited from tradition. But does it really make sense to attribute to fashion the development of "the autonomy of consciousness," or an increase in "personal autonomy?"[45] Locating this phenomenon wholly within the domain of autonomy leaves one unable to distinguish between *liberation* from the authority of traditions and authentic *freedom*, whereby the subject furnishes itself with the principle of its own action. Surely there is no doubt that progress has occurred in the direction of individual independence, in the sense that we have passed into the sphere of choice in vast areas of behavior that in traditional societies were decided in advance in obedience to a collective order. Whether there has been progress toward the "ideal of subjective autonomy in the sphere of opinion" is a far more dubious thing, however, as Lipovetsky knows perfectly well since he is obliged to wonder whether one can "really speak of individual freedom where the life of the mind resonates to the rhythm of changing moods in fashion."[46] Confronting the question of what ultimately will come of "personal sovereignty or self-determination in the order of thought" (the democratic purpose *par excellence*—for which I propose reserving the term "autonomy"), Lipovetsky is forced to appeal to Tocqueville and his analysis of the strengthening in democratic society of the power of "ordinary opinion" and the influence it exerts on minds.[47] Given that he reaffirms that "[c]onsummate fashion is not an obstacle to the autonomy of human consciousness" and that "the mimetic reign of fashion" makes the operation of "personal autonomy" possible "at the level of the majority of human beings,"[48] would his analysis not gain in force and clarity if it distinguished—as two possible outcomes of modernity, or as two possible horizons toward which the separation from traditional societies points—between a humanistic culture of autonomy and an individualistic culture of independence, both capable of coexisting with each other, and so of acquiring the force of a metapersonal domination?[49] By showing that the disintegration of the holistic universe could lead to one or the other of these two cultures, it would then become possible to investigate a phenomenon like fashion by asking to which of these two dimensions of modernity it made a greater contribution. Doing this would not at all exclude the possibility that, in the course of the history so masterfully reconstructed by Lipovetsky, fashion might have successively—perhaps even simultaneously—nourished each of these two cultures. Many misunderstandings could have been avoided by this strategy, and the nuances of this view of the universe of fashion and advertising as "neither the best nor the worst of worlds" could be protected against simplistic interpretation.

The implications of a thoughtful distinction between autonomy and independence appear even more clearly when we consider the hyperbolical way in which the misdeeds of modernity are denounced today. Lipovetsky cleverly notes the irony of the fact that we are now witnessing the reappearance of a hypercritical discourse aimed at revealing the "immense wretchedness of modernity"—the crusades of "lofty intellectual souls" once again unearthing "the hatchet of apocalyptic war" to fulminate against modern "barbarianism" and denounce "the soft totalitarianism" that "has infiltrated our democracies."[50] On various counts this description can easily be seen to apply to recent books by Allan Bloom, Alain Finkielkraut, and Michel Henry.[51] What Lipovetsky may have overlooked, however, is that the antimodern *lamento* will periodically gain in vigor, all the more as its reevaluations of modernity are liable to *appear*—

owing, let me repeat, to a misunderstanding—able to qualify its support for contemporary culture only with difficulty. For want of a clear vision of this internal conflict between independence and autonomy—internal to modernity—that led to the break with tradition, there is no other alternative to excessive praise of modernity than allowing oneself to be seduced by the confused charms of a radical condemnation.

In support of this claim, Dumont's whole work can be cited. By confusing autonomy and independence, it ends up revalorizing (as against the modern principles of individuality and equality) the traditional principle of hierarchy—for which Dumont unhesitatingly admits his preference.[52] Curiously, like Heidegger (but for other reasons) Dumont attributes the worst of modernity's evils—totalitarianism,[53] even racism[54]—to its very logic. Because he cannot use *modern values* (least of all autonomy) to defend modernity against itself (particularly against the perverse effects of the cult of independence), Dumont's work can only take its place among those apocalyptic visions of modernity that contemporary thinkers have so often preferred to a less dramatic but more nuanced inquiry into what in the modern condition has helped promote totalitarian and racist frenzies.[55] Thus, notwithstanding a few rare denials,[56] Dumont hardly hesitates to disclose his preferences and to embrace the holistic view "according to which society . . . is sociologically prior to its particular members"[57]—by virtue of which it appears to him, for example, that by insisting on "the necessity of sovereignty and subjection" Hobbes "was more right than the adherents of egalitarianism."[58] His antimodern approval of the values of holism proceeds, after all, by highlighting what he takes to be a particularly negative dimension of individualism, to wit the valorization of man as an "essentially nonsocial being."[59] Linked to an antihierarchical cult of independence, this "nonsociability" finds expression in the famous primacy of the man-things relation (i.e., mastery, production, consumption) over the man-man relation to which hierarchical society assigns cardinal importance, locating each person in relation to the others who together form the community. Here we see particularly clearly how the primary confusion of autonomy and independence engenders a secondary one that decisively skews the argument in an antimodern direction.

Modernity and Sociability

Certainly the view of man as a desocialized being follows from Dumont's assumption that man *qua* individual is capable of constituting himself independently of any relation to society, as a subject without intersubjectivity. But the valorization of autonomy, that other possible outcome of modernity, in no way implies such a desocialization.

To suppose it does would require understanding the term "autonomy" in a superficially literal way: namely, that to be autonomous, I must obey only the law that I have laid down for myself, which amounts (through the reduction of ipseity to its most particular instance) to not recognizing any rule that opposes—that imposes itself upon—the arbitrariness of pure personal caprice. If one grants this much, then autonomy can be understood to carry with it a desocializing individualism. Modernity, however, expressly did not understand autonomy in this trivial sense: Kant's whole purpose was to define autonomy in a fundamentally anti-individualistic way. Like Rousseau, he made the "law of desires and inclinations" (the law that a human subject would give itself) a "natural law" that concerns man insofar as man is "part of the world of sense" and, as such, refers back to the "heteronomy of nature."[60] Kant states further that this law of desire takes the "principle of happiness" as a guide: hedonism, an obvious dimension of contemporary individualism (and even, according to Dumont, a constitutive element of individualism as such)[61] thus refers back to this heteronomy—in contrast to true autonomy, where it is not *nature* in me that dictates the law of my actions, but practical reason in the form of free will. As an autonomous subject guided by practical reason, I am obviously not nonsocial in any essential way since (as Alexis Philonenko insisted apropos of Kant)[62] ethics is one of the three modes of communication, along with knowledge and aesthetics. In the ethical sphere, communication between men and other men, as reasonable beings, occurs as a matter of definition: by submitting to law, and the requirement of universalizing the maxim of his action, the moral subject ideally agrees with other possible subjects with whom he conceives himself in solidarity as a fellow member of the realm of ends. In short, when the modern subject—as an ethical subject—considers himself in terms of autonomy (rather than of independence), he cannot relegate the perspective of the men-men relation to the second level; to the contrary, it is in thinking of himself against the backdrop of such an ethical intersubjectivity that the moral subject can conceive his will as being autonomous.

The diagnosis underpinning Dumont's antimodernism thus turns out to be mistaken: the men-men relation was not wholly obliterated by modernity in favor of a mere men/things relation, whose triumph meant that man could henceforth think of himself in these terms without thinking of his relation to other men within a community. The desocialization of man, while consistent with the logic of individualism,[63] does not follow from the overall logic of a modernity (supposing that such a logic is imaginable) which, while it cared more for the subject than for the individual, thought of subjectivity primarily in terms of intersubjectivity.[64] Here, in fact, antimodernism suffers from a grave illusion, which consists in supposing that the only way to conceive the men-men relation is from the hierarchical perspective of holism. Dumont, now manifestly confusing *intersubjectivity* with *interdependence*, can conceive of the former only on the model of the latter: where democratic modernity has taken root—where hierarchical interdependence is not the organizing principle of society—he can only see society as atomized. Thus he can summarize the difference between modern Western societies and caste societies as "liberty and equality on the one hand, interdependence and hierarchy on the other"[65]—with the consequence for modern societies that when man's regard for other men is eclipsed by regard for his relation to things, the other suddenly looms as a mere pole in a possible conflict over the possession of property. Hence the mind-boggling conclusion: "We should then say, speaking roughly, that there are two ways of somehow recognizing *alter*: hierarchy and conflict."[66]

On this account, it is easy to understand why Dumont declares his "irenic preference" for hierarchy, feeling a certain repugnance toward individualistic/modern desocialization, which would necessarily lead to the emergence of the other as enemy, or at least as rival in the appropriation of material things. But must we share his certainty that the only form of intersubjectivity, the only imaginable modality for recognizing the other, is hierarchical interdependence? Modernity has bet all along that the opposite will turn out to be the case—that the recognition of the other involves the recognition of an *other myself*, of an alter ego (whose otherness is seen in terms of identity and not, as in the hierarchical perspective, in the form of an absolute otherness.)[67] From what position of authority could one maintain that modernity has completely lost this wager?

Because he has not really been able to detect the terms of such a wager in modern culture, Dumont's only option has been to cast his venture in different terms—if not of *restoring*, then at least of *deploring*: the only truly positive values having been irretrievably lost,[68] it remains to separate out (in a manner more *tragic* than simply *pessimistic*) the "gap beyond return" (in Paul Valéry's lovely expression) that has formed our destiny.[69] Because of its tragic dimension, this reading of modernity definitely has the peculiarity, among all the variants of antimodernism, of sparing itself the aporias (and occasional absurdities) of a return to the ancients. Nevertheless, it has the profound difficulty of being able to understand modernity only as a universe from which Value has retreated: that is, as the locus of radical Evil. In this sense, even when no *practical* restoration of the ancient principles of evaluation is contemplated, modern culture is nonetheless understood *from the point of view of these principles*, in the name of values whose retreat is constantly noted, together with the more or less disastrous (and in any case negative) effects that accompany it. Is it really possible to adopt this point of view, which calls for an *intellectual restoration* of the values of hierarchy (on the basis of which modernity is to be sized up and judged)? Can we truly revalorize, if only as a thought-experiment, the ideas of *natural* hierarchy and subordination? Can we accept, even merely as an idea, considering the other not as an alter ego but "as an other"—and this "insofar as it would be superior or inferior to us"? Can we really? This last question obviously is meant not only, or even primarily, in the psychological sense (as Dumont himself grants, subordination cannot easily be made part of our mental universe), but in the *moral* sense: ought we to do so?

The argument so far assumes that the change from (natural) hierarchy to equality (of rights) is a *loss*. In this regard Dumont parts company with Tocqueville, whom he often cites as his inspiration: for even though Tocqueville called attention to the potentially perverse effects of equalizing conditions, he saw modern individualism as unmistakably representing progress, and, in criticizing its shortcomings, proposed remedies that remained modern in spirit. The shift from Tocqueville to Dumont is quite clear: from an *internal* criticism, or, if you will, a *self-criticism of modernity*, all within the framework of modernity and its values (that is, of equality and freedom), one arrives at an external criticism, mounted upon the premises of the ancients. Not only does the renunciation of democratic values seem a prohibitive sacrifice, but under these conditions we must wonder whether Dumont's interpretation, constructed on the basis of the lost ideals of hierarchy and natural subordination, is not also strictly *dependent* on the adoption of such ideals.

In other words, should not the very problem of what modernity means be posed on a completely new basis, again using individualism as a guiding thread, but without *straight away* ruling out the possibility that modernity contains within itself the resources needed for conceiving of (and putting into practice) a limitation of individuality? This is a possibility that needs to be examined. I should note that Dumont's writings point to a major exception to this overall devalorization of the values of modernity, one that is particularly tantalizing and stimulating when we realize it has its origins in the philosophy of Leibniz.

The Leibnizian Monadology: Holism or Individualism?

According to Dumont, it is fitting to assign to Leibniz (whom he mentions several times in his *Essays*)[70] an exceptional status in the intellectual history of modernity. He credits the Leibnizian "genius" with the "one serious attempt to reconcile holism and individualism": the working out of the monadological structure. For, as Dumont explains, "Leibniz's monad is at the same time both a whole in itself and an individual in a system that is unified in its very differences—let us call it a universal Whole. The closing off of the monad externally—an often misunderstood point—expresses this double requirement."[71] More precisely, the monadological idea provides a model for solving "our fundamental problem," posed today by the demand (which Dumont interprets as "holistic") for "human solidarity on a world scale"—in other words, for "justice" among states or peoples that aspire (and here the aspiration is characteristic of individualism) to be treated as individual entities. Put this way, the task for our time is to discover the terms of a synthesis between "universalism and individualism," which until now have seemed utterly incompatible.

Is it merely a matter, to Dumont's way of thinking, of reconciling opposites? If this were the case, the very process of reconciliation at this level would suddenly change, in style and overall tone: rather than having to massively (and tragically—since there is no hope of return) place the values of holism in tension with those of individualism, it would become possible, in accordance with the Leibnizian model, to adapt the (holistic) tradition within a modern (individualistic) framework. This move would permit the development of a "modified universalism"[72] that would integrate the modern individualistic/particularistic conviction that each culture is a "particular form of humanity" with the conviction (reasonable enough) that the very possibility of a dialogue between cultures (a possibility attested to by the very existence of anthropology) requires some form of "universal reference." As an aid in finding the formula for this "rather subtle blend of modernity and tradition, universalism and particularism," the Leibnizian monadology is indispensable—so much so that Dumont here unhesitatingly recognizes the importance of his debt: "It is actually the study of [Leibniz's] thought that enabled me to clearly conceive the thesis I am proposing."[73]

Just how clearly Dumont conceived his thesis may be questioned, however, if we consider what the *Essays* suggest about the heritage of the monadology in the German tradition. Leibniz's successors, from Herder to Hegel and Marx,[74] who wanted to go on giving a meaning to the holistic component, were "often less precise than he himself was on one essential point: in their philosophy, the incompatibility of individualism and holism is more often forgotten than recognized."[75] The reasoning here is singularly hard to follow: while Leibniz is credited with having made "the only serious attempt to reconcile individualism and holism," he is now criticized for the failure to recognize "the *incompatibility* of individualism and holism." In his attempt to find a ground for reconciliation between these two principles, Leibniz can stand as a model only to the extent that he records and preserves their fundamental incompatibility!

What Dumont is in fact trying to say is that while Leibniz's successors *effectively* tried to reconcile individualism and holism (resorting to a strategy that could be interpreted as one of the sources of totalitarianism), "we [can] . . . avoid the inherent danger [of this] by taking Leibniz's model not as justification for an imaginary identification, but as an ideal to guide our work"—in short, as a "regulating idea" in the Kantian sense.[76] The originality of "the Leibnizian model" as an incomparable exemplar, as a "unitarian scheme,"[77] would thus stem from the way in which, while clearly seeing the incompatibility of holistic and individualistic values,[78] he insisted on the simple requirement of reconciliation—whereas Hegel, the "Great Conciliator,"[79] would have thought of such a reconciliation as real. What does Leibniz contribute to all this? For the first time in modern individualism, in Dumont's view, a new model of humanity was set forth, conceived as "the integral sum of all those social particularities—a sum that we postulate to be real and coherent." It is in this sense, then, that we are to construe "the Germans' ambition," as showing that "our humanity is like Herder's garden"—that is to say, a Leibnizian garden "in which each plant—each society—has its own beauty to offer because it expresses the universal in its own way."[80] The reason why, after Leibniz, the requirement of reconciliation came to be asserted as a thesis (as in Hegel and Marx)—why the individualist principle came to be reaffirmed in its absoluteness (in its entirely "Voltairean" inability to see things otherwise than "locally")—is that the opportunity offered by the monadological perspective was lost and, with it, the possibility of escaping the perverse effects of individualism without yielding to the illusion of a return to the traditional viewpoint: "Leibniz's world should not simply be identified with the traditional world. Perhaps theodicies are an index of individualistic questioning and an effort, more or less successful, to reassert the holistic view."[81]

What are we to think of this interpretation of the philosophy of monads? I fear that it runs into a series of insurmountable objections, which serve to indicate how hard it is to work out a sufficiently comprehensive interpretation of modernity using individualism as a guiding thread.

The first objection is this: if Dumont is using Leibniz as a model to elaborate the proper way to look at sociopolitical reality, how exactly do things appear from this point of view? How do we relate the antinomy between traditional society and modern society to the antinomy between holism and individualism? As we have just seen, the viewpoint attributed (rightly or wrongly) to Leibniz is characterized only by reference to the *aim* of reconciling intrinsically incompatible principles. It presupposes the basically Weberian thesis of an irreducible conflict between value systems, and so necessarily forces one to take sides, *in favor of one of the two opposing systems*[82]—in this case, since it is a matter of warding off the perverse effects of individualism, of imagining things "globally" and not "locally" (that is, from the viewpoint of Leibniz, rather than of Voltaire). More precisely, the position that Dumont adopts (while attributing it to Leibniz) is, in effect, *a viewpoint of a viewpoint*: a holistic viewpoint of the reconciliation between holism and individualism that is in itself only a viewpoint (of the "required" or "postulated" reconciliation). Under these conditions, however, would not the monadology be only an apparent exception to the holism-individualism pair? Thus understood, the Leibnizian model in fact falls on the side of holism, of which it would amount to no more than a particularly subtle variant. Dumont makes this explicit when he says, in connection with Leibniz: "Here the modern model itself becomes a particular case of the nonmodern model."[83] The peculiarity of *Leibnizian holism* stems from the way in which the Whole that is prior to individuality is realized in it through the single (finite) reality—the monadic individualities. And, continues Dumont, it is thus (I would even say: only thus) that "we overcome—ideally[84]—the incompatibility we have recognized and respected": this, when all is said and done, *to the benefit of holism*, even if it is in a mode that gives its "relative value to the two principles"—a clear confirmation, if one were needed, that Dumont's whole analysis is worked out from an essentially antimodern viewpoint, even though the antimodern viewpoint is backed up by reference to Leibniz.

Now—and this is really the crux of the problem—is it really reasonable to give Leibniz this status, making him the most "ancient" of the "moderns" or the most "modern" of the "ancients"? Can we imagine isolating Leibniz this way within modernity, particularly by accusing his successors (including, as is the case with Herder, his disciples) of immediately letting go of what he alone had been able to recognize (the elements of which were incompatible, however, and needed to be reconciled)?[85] Certainly theodicy consists in privileging the Whole, while monadology favors the element—with the crucial qualification (by virtue of which, according to Dumont, the preeminence of the Whole is assured and the holist legacy of the Leibnizian schema thus affirmed) that the element (the monad) is what it is only insofar as it expresses the Whole: as a mirror of the universe, monadic individuality exists only on the basis of its relation into the Whole, only insofar as it is pervaded by the universal—on which it affords only a limited perspective. But does this distance that Dumont believes he detects between Leibniz and his successors (notably Hegel and theorists of "economies" such as Quesnay or Mandeville) really exist? The essential difference, the one that gives Leibniz's thought its unique seriousness, would thus lie in the fact that in Leibniz the Whole is only a point of view, something arbitrary. I am fully aware of what in the Leibnizian system attracts one's attention on this point, and even can even prompt one to contrast the status assigned by Leibniz to the Whole with the way in which Hegel—reifying what would have been only a viewpoint—wished to conceive an effective reconciliation between the individual and the universal: namely, that Leibniz—whose metaphor of the city that "looked at from different sides appears entirely different"[86] is well known—makes each monad a "point of view" or a "perspective" on the world, and that his vision of the universe as a totality, of God as the sum of these "perspectives," is imputed to what is after all itself only a monad, albeit a "primitive monad"—the "monad of monads."

To conclude from this that the Whole (the universe as the totality of perspectives) is also just a point of view, represents nevertheless a huge step—and the very one that historically distinguishes the Leibnizian monadology from the Nietzschean outlook. In the Leibnizian system, as a consequence of the doctrine of the perfection of the primitive monad, the divine sum of the individual perspectives defines a moment of objectivity that functions as a limitation of perspectivism and makes it possible to elevate the totality from a simple point of view to a dimension of the real as such. It thus seems very hard to agree with Dumont that the holistic component of Leibniz's philosophy (theodicy, in effect) differs profoundly in status from its Mandevillean or Hegelian analogue (the theory of the "ruse of reason"): in both cases, reference to the Whole is made as a sign of Truth, not as the sign of a "regulating ideal." Kant needed to devote every effort (this time a genuinely insular effort) to assuring that the thesis affirming the individual as a moment in the self-deployment of the Whole had been rid of its ontological pretensions (as against Leibniz, and in anticipation of the Hegelian return to theodicy), and that, having become "ideal," "regulative," or "methodological," it now served as a mere guiding thread for reflection.[87]

If Leibniz's originality by comparison with his successors regarding the holistic component therefore seems less clear than Dumont believes, does not this very fact mean that the relations between monadology and individualism must be understood quite differently? Far from being the source of a unique unhinging of the values of individualism, does not the monadological model express—*even in the dimension of its concomitant theodicy*—the very essence of a distinctively *modern* individualism?[88] For faced with the ontological conviction, which is constitutive of philosophical individualism, that there exist only individual or individuated realities that are independent of each other (that is, without direct influence on each other, as is the case with monads in the Leibnizian system), it is necessary—*if this thesis is to remain compatible with the presupposition (required by the very demands of reason and by the project of constructing a science of reality) of an order or intelligibility at the heart of reality*—to posit that the apparently unconnected (or even contradictory) initiatives of individuals (meaning the activities of the monads: their respective series of states) are nonetheless organized (if not for individuals, then at least in themselves, unbeknownst to them) according to a preestablished harmony that is immanent in the monadological reality. In other words, ontological individualism could be integrated into the framework of modern rationalism only by introducing an element of overall rationality immanent in the interplay of particular wills. Theodicy therefore stands at the very core of monadology, at the very core of philosophical individualism. Monadology as such—monado-logy—rests on a project of rationality, and so requires theodicy: *monadology is, in essence, theodicy*. Thus there is for Leibniz no corrective to individualism, no search for a reconciliation between holism and individualism: on the contrary, what is involved for him in squaring the monadology with the theodicy is building a real philosophical foundation for modern individualism—a foundation that gives full reign to individualism by bringing out what the individualistic perspective and modern rationality have in common.

In this sense, Leibniz did not invent a model that was misconstrued by his successors: he provided a model for them to use, and the many uses to which it was put (whose differences should be identified and analyzed) coincide with the philosophical history of modern individualism. From this point of view, what is striking is that it is really only with Nietzsche (who called into question the project of modern rationality, denouncing reason as an "error") that philosophical individualism (monadology, if you will) first comes to be separated from the perspective of theodicy: when reason disappears as a value, when the very project of discovering a rationality (intelligibility) in reality appears as a falsification of reality, God dies as the "monad of monads"—and with Him the idea of theodicy and preestablished harmony. There then remains only a monadology that renounces its monado-*logical* calling: only the series of states of the various monads, intersecting with each other without regard for any principle of order, a chaotic interplay of monadical perspectives—the world seen as chaos.[89] Thus arises contemporary individualism. By integrating the perspective of a theodicy into an intrinsically individualistic (monadological) ontology, Leibniz in no way resisted an individualism that was already affirmed before him, and that would be reaffirmed after him; to the contrary, *monadology-as-theodicy*—a formula of ontological individualism (according to which individuality as a structure of being is compatible with the thesis of an ordered reality) that needs to be precisely described—represented *the only possible philosophical option for assimilating the demands of individualism within the framework of modern rationality*. It is for furnishing a decisive and lasting foundation for modern individualism, and not as the site of its temporary upheaval, that the Leibnizian monadology is original by comparison with what preceded it, particularly with the emergence of the Cartesian values (also modern in their way) of subjectivity.

The Cartesian Headwaters: Subject or Individual?

To read the Leibnizian monadology as the search for a way to reintegrate the demand for holism within the very framework of individualism, it would be necessary to show that the philosophical affirmation of modern individualism had already been accomplished before Leibniz. What in fact was the state of individualism before Leibniz?

It is certainly possible to trace its genesis back very far, even as far back as medieval philosophy (one thinks, for example, of the nominalism defended in the fourteenth century by William of Ockham).[90] Granting that we are not dealing here with models of *modern* individualism, I think it is worth observing that "prefigurations" of individualism are to be found side by side with conceptions of the world in which the conditions of modernity are not fulfilled. If we are to be able to maintain that modernity really begins with the emergence of subjectivity—that is, with the conviction that meaning, truth, and value can exist in the world only on the basis of man and for man—it is plain that something stronger than either Ockham's doctrine or, more generally, medieval philosophy, is required. The disintegration of the ancient image of the *cosmos* as constituting an order by itself had not yet been completed by this point: for medieval philosophy in general, there is meaning in reality without its existing through man; and even though, after the Fall, this meaning that exists *through itself* (rather than *through me*) no longer gives itself *for me*, a fallen creature, at least it exists *for another*, whether it is God, Adam before sin, or Adam after redemption. The presence here and there in medieval thought—in Ockham's nominalism, for example—of a definition of reality in terms of individuality thus cannot have the same meaning, or pose the same problems, as a similar definition appearing within the framework of the modern conception of the world.

Here we touch on a new possible source of error or confusion about individualism: for *modern* individualism to exist, it is not enough for reality to be conceived as a collection of individualities.[91] Individuality must be posited as *princeps*, and the totality, conceived only on the basis of (or through) individuality, as subordinate to it. In other words, if individualism in the modern sense (with all the problematic aspects this implies) predated Leibniz, this could only have been on the philosophical terrain where subjectivity first emerged—namely, in Descartes' thought, even though it incorporated elements of prior thought about individuality.[92] What is the status and value of individuality in Descartes? Can Cartesian thinking be interpreted as strongly affirming the individual, which the Leibnizian monadology would attempt to rebalance (subject to all the qualifications such an attempt would require) in the direction of holism? It is a cause for some regret that Dumont did not think it worthwhile to examine this possibly "exceptional" situation in connection with Leibniz's place in the logic of modern ideology, thus missing a chance to construct a truly persuasive argument. At the very least, the Cartesian moment can be said to exhibit an extraordinary ambiguity in this regard.[93]

Let us first consider the theoretical thrust of Descartes' work, chiefly the question of whether in the *Regulae ad directionem ingenii* (1628–1629) and the *Discours de la méthode* (1637)—even the *Meditationes de prima philosophiae* (1641)—the subject fails to be individuated: *method* gives everyone the same power of knowing the same objects with certainty, and everyone is subject to the same limits to knowledge, which define the same ignorance. In this sense, the epistemological subject of the *Regulae*, or the "ego" that in the *Meditationes* is the subject of the *cogito*, appears primarily as a *universal*—the *mathesis universalis* presenting itself as a universal as much through its subject as through its objects.[94] From this fact an empirical intersubjectivity can clearly be inferred (consider the theory of natural language sketched in the famous letter to Newcastle of 23 November 1646), yet intersubjectivity has no real status at the epistemological level, where the subject needs no being other than itself to provide support for the *mathesis universalis*; and if good sense is "of all things in the world the most equally distributed," it is so insofar as reason is one and the same in all men. "The question of more or less," Descartes stressed, "occurs only in the sphere of *accident* and does not affect the *forms* or natures of the *individuals* in the same *species*."[95]

In this whole aspect of his work, Descartes granted only inessential differences between individuals: individualities are distinguished from each other only according to what Aristotle called an arithmetical difference—by "number" rather than by essence. The knowing subject is both identical with itself (the continuity of the *cogito* establishing this identity) and with all "other" subjects (whose "otherness" seems at this level, where the unity of reason prevails, to reflect little more than an imprecision of language). Descartes thus appears as the faithful heir of a Thomistic scholasticism that, through a reductive reading of Aristotle, conceived the individuation of substances as proceeding not from their form (essence) but from the particular assumptions of this form (the assumption of form being contingently related to it) by matter.[96] Consequently, if it is agreed that individuality connotes both indivisibility (which makes the individual an indissoluble *unity*) and differentiation (which, by contrasting the individual with other members of the same species, makes individuality a *unicity*), it must be granted that this register of individualist values did not in any way derive from Descartes.

If, however, we consider certain other texts, centered less on questions of knowledge than on ones of salvation or morality (along the axis, if you will, of practical philosophy), matters suddenly seem very different. We now find a surprising ambiguity attaching to the ontological status of individuality. The often-analyzed letter to Mesland of 9 February 1645 on the Eucharist[97] indeed explicitly defends the thesis of individuation *by form*—and thus, in the case of man, by the soul—arguing that the numerical unity of the human body does not depend on that of its matter, but of its form (which is to say its soul). In this letter, as in a whole series of writings,[98] the relations are reversed, and bodies are numerically identical, beyond the changes that occur to them, only because they are informed by the same soul. Thus, in Descartes's eyes, even the mystery of the Eucharist ("How can one conceive the body of Jesus Christ to be in the Eucharist?") can be fathomed: the numerical identity of Christ's body does not require "that all its parts must be there with their same quantity and shape, and with *numerically* the same matter as they were composed of when he ascended into heaven"; it is sufficient that Christ's soul inform a fragment of the Host for the body to be "whole and entire . . . because all the matter, however large or small, which as a whole is informed by the same human soul, is taken for a whole and entire human body."[99]

Beyond the aridity of theological debate, what is being played out here is nothing less than the ontological status of individuality: if it is the soul that, by informing the body, makes it possible to differentiate individuals, individual differences are established at the very level of essence where, according to the first line of argument about individuality, these differences were only accidental in relation to an essence defined in terms of undifferentiated identity. Hence, in a letter to Mersenne for Hobbes (21 April 1641), Descartes can defend (as against Hobbes) a position that we may join Frédéric de Buzon in characterizing as being finally very close to what Leibniz's position was to be: "no individual differentiating characteristic of Socrates could perish—for example his knowledge of philosophy—without his simultaneously ceasing to be a man."[100] This is a really extraordinary passage, which we should make an effort to understand. It obviously does not mean that all the most superficial aspects of Socrates, from the color of his eyes to the length of his beard, are intrinsic to his person: in fact, these characteristics are not what Descartes calls here "individual differentiating characteristics" since other men can have Socrates's eyes or beard without having anything in common with the true Socrates, who could perfectly well exist as such by regretfully consenting, for example, to the sacrifice of his beard. In this important sentence, Descartes is talking about the specific characteristics that are constitutive of the person in his ipseity, in his irreducible difference: about that which makes

Socrates Socrates, and not Glaucon or Callias. The decisive point being made here is that essence appears to integrate fully these individual differences (one thinks of Leibniz and his identification of the monadic substance with the totality of its predicates or accidents), and that the purely formal determinations of substance ensure the irreducibility, and hence the individuality, of each person—who has no need of a body to be individuated. Unlike what we found in considering the Cartesian subject in relation to knowledge, we now encounter the subject as an individual: *the subject, as such, is now essentially individuated.*

With regard to the status of individuality (and the relation between the subject and the individual), Descartes's work thus combines two perspectives that are hard to square with each other: as the subject of knowledge, the Cartesian subject is identical with itself and all others, and individuality remains extrinsic to subjectivity; on the other hand—and here the Thomistic legacy is less important than the Scotistic and Suarezian influences[101]—the Cartesian subject as the subject of its passions and its salvation becomes (by its identity with itself) essentially different from all others, and individuality (in the dual sense of unity and unicity) becomes intrinsic to subjectivity. How then can it be doubted that we are dealing here with two nonsuperimposable perspectives? The one makes the "person" the secondarily individuated exemplar of an essentially common species; the other defines the "person" as an individual essentially determined by its irreducible ecceity or presence. The result, as Buzon has emphasized, is that there are two possible logics underlying the Cartesian moment. The first is an impersonal logic of interpretation, meaning the *cogito* in the sense of a *cogitatur*[102] and leading, for example, to Brunschvicg's designation of the "thought itself" as "the true subject of the 'I think.'"[103] The second logic highlights what is internal about the *cogito*, in the sense that permits Maine de Biran to credit Descartes with having to some extent proceeded on the basis of an intimate, private sense.[104]

Three points will summarize the conclusions that can be drawn from these analyses of the ambiguity inherent in the Cartesian moment:

First, and unfortunately for his reconstruction of the history of modern philosophy, Heidegger—though he grasped that if modern philosophy truly began with Leibniz it was through his radicalization of what Descartes had first introduced—misinterpreted the nature of Leibniz's Cartesian inheritance.

Second, by clearing up the ambiguity of the Cartesian moment, the Leibnizian legacy was to consist in privileging a potential aspect of Cartesian discourse and exploiting the *individualistic stream* that, in Descartes, remained concurrent with a *universalistic stream* that another tradition—the Kantian one—could also legitimately claim to descend from.

Third, it is therefore rash to argue that the Leibnizian monadology represents a reconciliation between a well-tempered holism, on the one hand, and an individualism against whose excessive claims Leibniz's genius rose up in protest, on the other. In reality, the *philosophical* uses to which modern individualism has been put, against which (if Dumont is to be believed) the *Monadology* reacted, are exactly as old as the *Monadology* itself—in the sense that it was by ridding the Cartesian moment of its ambiguities that Leibniz, radicalizing the idea (which in Descartes was only a *possibility*) of an individuality intrinsic to subjectivity, laid the first true philosophical foundation for modern individualism.

What then is to be concluded from this rather casual discussion of Louis Dumont's thought? We should certainly retain the guiding thread of his work, the very one that Heidegger could not grasp, which bids us to read modernity on the basis of the logic of individualism—and which undoubtedly leads to a result quite different from seeing in it the constant and indivisible triumph of subjectivity. But if we want to follow this guiding thread to its end, to see where it will finally lead us, we should take care in unwinding it to avoid two pitfalls. These pitfalls, which I am afraid that Dumont did not manage to avoid, stem from two confusions:

- First, the confusion between the subject and the individual makes it impossible to say what is specific to the criticist moment, which is now hard to identify as a stage in the affirmation of individuality, and at the same time to preserve the initial ambiguity of the Cartesian moment. More generally, this confusion leads Dumont to see everywhere in modernity the triumph of the individual and nothing else: one should *also* take note of the defeats and victories experienced by the subject.
- Second, the confusion of individualism and its later, degraded forms (that is, the narcissism that is at least partially characteristic of contemporary individualism) leads to a generally *pejorative* reading of modernity. In order to form a better idea of the nature and different faces of individualism, one must consider the possibility that modernity could have been protected—on its own terms, without renouncing its own values—against a drift toward individualism.

The point that needs to be carefully explored, if the guiding thread of individualism is to be unwound without mishap, is obviously the Leibnizian moment: recognized by Heidegger as inaugurating the metaphysics of subjectivity (though it represents more a decisive turning point in the history of this metaphysics), and upheld by Dumont as the locus of an inspired exception to the logic of individualism (though Leibniz does much more, philosophically, to ground its development), the monadological moment is, in any case, the moment that must be reconstructed in detail if these symmetrical and converse errors regarding modernity are to be avoided. It is also the moment on the basis of which it should be possible to detect, within modernity itself, the philosophical logic of the history of the subject.

PART TWO

Logic of Philosophy

CHAPTER III

Leibniz: The Monadological Idea and the Birth of the Individual

By setting this philosophical history of subjectivity in the context of a "logic of philosophy," I mean both to indicate the sort of usefulness it might have and also to expose it straight away to the kind of objections that it cannot help but invite. To my mind, it is clear that the logic of philosophy brings out the interpretative dimension of history: that is to say, the *meaning* of history over and above its purely archaeological dimension, which aims, sometimes naively, only at accurately restoring some particular *corpus*. Need I add that I neither scorn nor neglect to concern myself with exactness? Some of my foregoing objections to Heidegger stem directly from this concern, in fact. I merely wish to secure for my undertaking—which is not merely to restore, but also to *understand* history—the right to go beyond what strictly distinguishes one idea from another, beyond what makes each one a unique creation, irreducible to any other, and to discover analogies, relationships, and kinships among them. The historicizing historians may always dispute such a right (which would allow me, for example, to uncover a monadological theme in Berkeley or Hegel outside the Leibnizian context) in the name of philological integrity. But their history, with its scrupulous concern for the differences between systems, is apt to amount merely to a monumental history that emphasizes the heterogeneity of ideas, but from which the meaning and logic of history will be absent: a dead history, in effect—"museum history." My hope is that historians of philosophy will accept this declaration of intent at face value, then, as scholars specializing in one work or another in the modern history of the subject—the full range of which I have set myself the task of covering. As I say, the historical history of philosophy as such does not interest me; what holds my attention throughout this survey of the logic of modern philosophy is less any particular work than the succession of works taken together. These historians need not feel too fearful of my interpretations, for I do not stake a claim to their turf: I dispute neither the validity nor the value of their work, and ask in return only that they grant me the right, alongside the right I grant them, to attempt something else.

Problems with the Monadological Idea

If it were to be asked what are the primary claims of the monadology, the claims that ground the monadological idea, we would be obliged first to note Leibniz's conviction that what we call matter—i.e., sensory realities as they are presented to us in space and time—does not really exist. In short, phenomena are merely appearances and what is real in a given phenomenon does not appear: because the reality of the real is not sensory, it will necessarily be defined in terms of mind. And it is in terms of this *spiritualization of the real* that the first constitutive thesis of the monadological idea is set up. We are familiar from Leibniz's two essays on the theory of motion with the argument against the Cartesian reduction of matter to extension: Descartes having explained the laws of motion using only the quantity of matter and speed, Leibniz showed that his calculations were in error because they eliminated the notion of force.[1] True reality was thus seen to be force, matter being merely a phenomenon; and space, consequently, was no longer a substance, as in Descartes, but a relation between forces. Hence the core claim of the Leibnizian ontology: beyond material appearance there exists energy, of which all reality is made. And if all reality is thus made up of what is not itself material, the intrinsic difference between mind and matter is abolished: in some sense and to some degree, everything has the structure of mind.

It is pointless to dwell further on the way in which this well-known thesis is expressed in Leibnizian discourse; interpreting it—that is, trying to understand what it means—is the important thing. From Heidegger's perspective there is nothing surprising in this: the spiritualization of reality and the elimination of Cartesian dualism mark a decisive stage of idealism—the reduction of being to representation,[2] that is, to subjectivity. Hegel, in his fine account of Leibniz's philosophy in the *Lectures on the History of Philosophy*, did not judge the meaning of the monadological idea any differently, apart from the fact that of course he reversed the signs: he explained the Leibnizian system as an "intellectual system" in which "everything that is material would be something representative, perceiving," in which "representation, the determination that is included in itself" becomes "the main thing." It is precisely this idealism, Hegel concluded, that is interesting in Leibniz's philosophy; for him, "the intellectuality of all things is Leibniz's great idea," since it suggests that the concept is the very structure of reality, that substance is the subject.[3] It was not until Charles Renouvier that similar terms were used to insist on the significance of this denial of the "dualism of mind and matter"—sometimes to assert that in doing this ("no doubt in a hurry to avoid Spinozism"),[4] Leibniz "went a good ways down the road toward idealism";

other times to argue that Leibniz, in his final philosophy, adopted the monadological schema as the most perfect refutation of "materialism" (this "philosophy defining thought as the product of a composition whose elements do not imply thought").[5] In all these readings, Leibnizian monadology is thus conceived as the completion of what had first emerged in Descartes, that is, in Hegelian terms, the establishment of thinking as a principle and Leibniz as the true champion of the modern reign of subjectivity.

Perhaps, as we have seen, it is time once again to call this stereotype into question. At least two points seem to me to need to be considered. First, what is the source of this peculiar spiritualization of reality? The basic problem here is how to interpret Leibniz's distancing himself from Cartesian dualism. Second, this spiritualizing of reality is not *by itself alone* enough to construct the monadological idea, for the birth of this idea requires a second constitutive thesis, namely, the *fragmentation of the mind* (that is, the definition of reality—the mind—as a set of indivisible units). What is the source of this second thesis and how is it related to the first one? It is no doubt through the joining of the two that the monadological idea acquired its most profound impact.

The Spiritualization of Reality

The monadological reduction of reality to mind is rooted in critical thinking about Cartesian dualism and the difficulties involved in expressing the relation between the mind and the body. The first of the two theses constitutive of the monadological idea is directly connected with the problem of the interaction or communication between substances.

On this point Leibniz's criticism of Descartes is well known:[6] if mind and matter are really *two* substances, it is absurd to suppose that mind acts on matter or that matter acts on mind. On this view, the Cartesian position suffers serious difficulties, at least in ethics, where the very idea of morality seems to presuppose that mental decisions have some efficacy with regard to the impulses of the body. As commentators have often noted, Leibniz's criticism is based on the principle of incommensurability, which holds that two substances without any attributes in common cannot act on each other: because matter is extended and mind is not extended, any point of contact between them—and thus any influence of one on the other—would be inconceivable.

Confronted with this classic problem, bequeathed by Descartes to his successors, post-Cartesian philosophy has proposed a variety of solutions involving as many different positions regarding the Cartesian principle of the dualism of substances. Leibniz drew upon elements of two antithetical solutions. The first of these, the solution advanced by Malebranche, endorsed the dualism and drew from it the logical conclusion that there is no causality from one substance to another one and hence no action of the mind on the body, or vice versa. To explain the apparently causal relations observed between certain bodily phenomena and what we now call "mental" phenomena, Malebranche resorted to the unparsimonious theory of occasionalism, by virtue of which God is held to bring series of phenomenal events into agreement with each other by evoking, on the occasion of a bodily event, the event that corresponds to it on the spiritual level. The second was the Spinozistic solution, which regarded radical dualism as leading to absurdities (including occasionalism) in ruling out the action of body and mind on each other; to get rid of these absurdities, Spinoza relativized dualism by making body and mind *two aspects* of one and the same reality. From this monistic perspective, mind and body, constituting two aspects of the same reality, are able to enjoy a relation that Spinoza conceived as one of interexpression. Thus ethics regained its meaning.

How is the monadological idea related to these opposed alternatives? The Leibnizian solution combined principles from each. Like Malebranche, Leibniz posited that everything that happens is regulated by God, and thus that there is no direct causality of one substance acting upon another. This divine regulation was not conceived on the relatively ludicrous model of occasionalism, but instead according to the more economical one of preestablished harmony: everything is regulated by God, but in advance, so that the series of mental events correspond to the series of bodily events—or rather what we call "the body," which is merely a lower degree of the same reality to which the mind belongs.[7]

Like Spinoza, however, albeit in another mode, Leibniz upheld a strict monism that reduces matter to mind: if the basis of matter as extension (as space) is actually a field of forces, a complex of relations between centers of energy,[8] then the structure of matter has something in common with mind as a source of activity, as spontaneity. If matter (as extension) is an appearance, reality must be thought of as unextended energy and hence as mind.[9]

Considered in isolation, there can be no doubt about the significance of the Leibnizian move within the unfolding logic of modern philosophy: this first moment of the monadological argument, tending toward an elimination of difference between the real and the rational, represents a first step in the direction of the philosophy of identity that was to culminate in absolute idealism. Not less important is the way in which Leibniz (as against Descartes and the theory of the creation of eternal truths) reduced the real to the possible. This twofold elimination of difference (between the real and the rational, and the real and the possible) definitely fits within the framework of a philosophical modernity understood as the reign of subjectivity imposing its law on reality. *Thus it is not only a matter of taking issue with Leibnizian monadology: we are dealing with an entire stage in the history of the subject.* It seems to me necessary only to inquire into the specific determinacy of this stage, by taking account of the second component of the monadological idea in order to gauge its impact more precisely.

The Fragmentation of Reality

Reality (mind) exists only insofar as it is monadically fragmented. How did Leibniz arrive at this second thesis, with which *philosophical individualism* was born? Its emergence can be illuminated from three points of view:

1. *From the viewpoint of its historical genesis*, which can be traced directly to Leibniz's argument about individuation: let us go back to the *Disputatio* of 1663,[10] where Leibniz attacked the old scholastic problem of the ontological status of the individual. Discussing the Thomistic thesis of individuation by matter, he recalls (§ 3) that Saint Thomas "established in bodies the matter designated and in the angels their entity as a principle"—statements that now seem highly cryptic. If for Aquinas "everything is individuated by matter and located in a genus or species through its form,"[11] it must be said that what individualizes a being is the "designated" or "determined matter" (*materia signata*), that is, not matter in general, but "that which is considered under determined dimensions."[12] Thus, for example, it is "*this* bone" ("designated matter") which combined with the form of "man as man," picks out the individual man called Socrates.

This theory of individuation exposed Thomism to serious difficulties concerning angels. Because they are incorporeal, and hence lacking in matter, it was not clear how they could be individualized.[13] One was thus obliged either to say that angels are not individuals,[14] or to admit an exception to the theory of material individuation by positing, as Leibniz expressed the point, that each immaterial substance considered as an "entity" is specifically and numerically one.[15] If I may, I shall leave the angels shrouded in their mystery and merely emphasize that in his *Disputatio* Leibniz ultimately posed the problem of whether, where individuation is concerned, the exception ought not become the rule since, as he explained, individuation by matter is unintelligible. This way of conceiving individuation, which clearly implies an ontological devalorization of individuality (now held to be external to essence, and hence inessential in relation to reality), runs into a serious objection: how could matter, understood in its most classical sense as a pure receptacle of form—as pure passivity or receptivity—be a principle of individuation? In other words, how could what is pure power in the Aristotelian sense—and hence pure negation—have the power in the modern sense to bring about the *existences* of individuals? Apart from the fact that the later redefinition construed what we call matter in terms of the force or power to act,[16] the decisive point in this debate was clearly reached with the objection to locating individuation outside essence: since it could not be placed on a material basis, individuality had to be reintegrated into the very essence of things, to the point that such an ontological revalorization of individuality could give rise to the monadological idea of *being* as equivalent to *being an individual.*

I will not go on to reconstruct the stages beyond the *Disputatio*, where already the argument is to be found in outline; by which Leibniz completed his account of an individualistic ontology. It is nevertheless clear that in this respect, from the time of the *Disputatio*, "it was a strictly original insight,"[17] and that when Leibniz wrote (in §5) that the numerical unity of an entity is constituted by "what makes it what it is" (*per quod est*)—that is, by its nature or the set of qualities that make it what it is, its *entitas tota*—the principle of the identity of indiscernibles had received its first statement.[18] What was thus found in embryo by 1663 was to be fully developed with the formulation of the doctrine of the spiritualization of reality—which, as we have seen, forms the first component of the monadology: for if (a) reality is mind (the spiritualization of the real) and (b) each being is individuated in essence, it directly follows that *the mind exists in an individuated way and that spiritual being is nothing other than the intrinsic difference between minds*. Thus the second thesis constitutive of the monadology: *the fragmentation of mind* into monads that are unique in essence (i.e., entirely and intrinsically different from each other). In this way an idea of difference was reintroduced within the framework of a philosophy of identity provided by the spiritualization of reality; the difference that had been reduced to nothing by the first dimension of the monadological idea (in overcoming the split between mind and nature) now reappeared at the heart of the doctrine of the identity of substances—an identity fragmented into individualities that are irreducible to each other, thus grounding a properly philosophical (i.e., ontological) individualism.

2. *From the viewpoint of the internal logic of the monadology*, the second thesis (fragmentation), which answers the individualistic calling of the system, is really determined by the first thesis (spiritualization): for if all reality is mind, the "really real" (true being) is nonspatial and, being unextended, is defined by indivisibility (since space is infinitely divisible). It is by virtue of indivisibility that the mental atomicity or simplicity of the "metaphysical atoms"—monads—becomes the very property of reality:

thus reality *must* also be conceived in a monadic way because it is spiritualized. In other words, the break with Descartes over dualism and the question of communication between substances led not only to the first, but to *both* of the theses that are constitutive of the monadological idea, the former directly implying the latter. Hence we see that ontological individualism is definitely consubstantial with the Leibnizian system—imposed, in fact, by the very logic of the whole system.

3. If individuality becomes the intrinsic property of substance, it is *from the very viewpoint of the demands of rationality* as Leibniz understood them: for him, as we have seen, the principle of reason and that of contradiction jointly imposed the principle of indiscernibles. It is now possible to state the argument that led Leibniz to the individualistic reinterpretation of the principles constitutive of rationality. This decisive move is made very clearly in §8 of the *Monadology* with the consideration of the problem of the differences between monads.

Why is it that monads cannot be identical but must differ qualitatively?[19] P. F. Strawson, in his book *Individuals*, criticizes Leibniz for not logically grounding "the character of the ontology of monads as an ontology of particulars"; in that case individuation would be a simple *fact*—a matter "of the free choice of a God who does not care for reduplication without difference"—but not "a matter of logical necessity." Everything would therefore depend on "a *theo*logical principle," on which account "the logical integrity of the system" is seriously threatened.[20] This reading seems to me not to take sufficient notice of the care with which Leibniz gives rational grounds for the claim that all monads must differ qualitatively from each other.

Leibniz's proof takes the form of a *reductio ad absurdum*. If monads were thought not to be qualitatively different, compounds could not be conceived as undergoing change. For a compound is only the product of the simple elements that make it up, the compounding of which does not by itself introduce any new quality: the combination of identical elements makes it possible to obtain quantitatively, though not qualitatively, different products. Thus if there were qualitative differences between compounds, such differences must already be present among the simple ingredients. But if compounds are not qualitatively differentiated, how could change be apprehended? To admit the identity of monads would thus be to rule out thinking of diversity and movement: if simple elements were identical, Being would be one and immobile. In short, either ontology is Parmenidean or it is not at all.

The full import of this demonstration is revealed when we look beyond the aridity of it to note that it is once again directed against Descartes—specifically, against the Cartesian thesis that reality (identified with matter in extension) exhibits only quantitative differences. Because it ignores all chemical variety, Cartesian physics does in fact contemplate only one kind of matter, diversified only by the combination of homogeneous particles: all the perceptible diversity of the universe thus derives from the movement of these identical and infinitely divisible particles. Now if the simple is identical, it follows on the Leibnizian (as against the Cartesian) view that the compound will also be identical: quantitative changes can never produce qualitative changes. Consequently, assuming a plenum, the addition and combination of identical elements imply that "each place would always receive, in any motion, only the equivalent of what it had had before, and one state of things would be indistinguishable from another." This hypothesis of the plenum is evidence that the system of reference here is indeed Cartesian physics, since in reducing matter to extension Descartes could not think of extension without matter, and concluded that a vacuum could not exist: thus, assuming the plenum, Descartes's physics had no other way to explain the observable motions of the universe than by resort to an expedient as unavailing as the theory of vortices. Recourse to such an expedient is easy to understand: if there is no vacuum, every movement of a body displaces another body, each movement of a particle pushes away other particles, and these particles, gradually displaced in this fashion, come to fill the space left empty by the first movement. Thus motion must be thought of as circular or "vorticial."

But is this a real theory of motion and variety? Leibniz emphatically denied it, noting that from this perspective each place only receives "the equivalent of what it had had before." That is, if it were to be asserted that each body that changes position displaces another body and that its former position, in the absence of a vacuum, is filled in its turn by another, the completed motion would result in a state of affairs identical to the one that obtained at the start: in short, no change would have occurred. And since everything remains as it was, no diversity or transformation would be observable. Thus it is plain that the Leibnizian foundation for the principle of indiscernibles is not only theological; its entire argument (which, as we have just seen, works to expose Cartesian physics as merely an attempt to reconstruct the variety of phenomena on the basis of quantitative differences among homogeneous objects) invites us to consider the possibility that if there existed identical elements—that is, if monads were not intrinsically differentiated (and thus individualized)—the *Parmenidean ontology could not be rejected.*[21] Now since it is the case—and this is the only genuine postulate underlying the argument—that there is change in nature, this change must therefore be explainable by ontology. Thus the foundation of philosophical individualism goes well beyond appeal to a God who is disdainful of repetition. For this postulate of the reality of change ("Every created being is subject to change" [§10]) does not recklessly reintroduce an element of "empiricism" into the system, suddenly granting something to the experience of the external world, which would be incompatible with the argument; in reality, it suffices to observe the Self in order to note that, through the succession of representations in it, change occurs.

In order to avoid being unable to think of itself and of the succession of its *cogitata*, the subject of philosophical reflection is forced to admit the fact of change and to impose upon the ontology that he is attempting to construct the task of explaining it. To avoid violating the principles constitutive of his reason—either by admitting a fact (in this case, change) *sine ratione* or by contradictorily denying this fact[22]—the philosopher must consequently posit the principle of indiscernibles: given the existence of two realities, there must be between them an "internal difference, or one founded on an intrinsic quality" (§9)—"internal" here meaning *qualitative* in contrast to a mere extrinsic difference that would not derive from the things themselves, but from their location in space. This amounts again to showing that both the principle of reason and the principle of contradiction require the principle of indiscernibles, and thus that logic itself contains an individualistic ontology. It follows, then, that in the Leibnizian system the second dimension of the monadological idea also proceeds from a profoundly individualistic reinterpretation of rationality: as such, it constitutes a turning point in modern philosophy. The individualistic fragmentation of reality—thrice required in Leibniz's eyes by the historical debates over the question of individuation, by the internal logic of the system, and by the demands of rationality—leads to a resolutely anti-Parmenidean ontology. The *Monadology* is the straightforward analytical explanation of this concept of *individuality*.

The Monadology as an Analysis of Individuality

That the idea of substance (equivalent to ontology) in Leibniz takes the form of a carefully worked-out concept of individuality (equivalent to individualism) is easily shown by deconstructing the path taken in the *Monadology*. As has often been noted,[23] the method followed there has something in common with a purely logical analysis that proceeds from the notion of a simple (individual and indivisible) element and deduces the properties that must be ascribed to the foundation of reality—that is, to those simple elements called monads.

Here I shall confine myself to indicating the main lines of that vast deduction, which lend the *Monadology* its grandeur as an analysis of individuality. Taking an approach that is purely external to monadic individuality, Leibniz establishes (as we have seen) that monads, being simple, are *qualitatively differentiated, unextended, indivisible, and without natural birth or end* (for birth would presuppose a process of compounding the monad on the basis of that from which it is born and into which, when dying, it would decompose, thus contradicting the assumption of its indivisibility). But above all: "monads have no windows" (§7). Despite the familiarity of this doctrine, I think it is important to spell out its implications, which are directly connected with the individualist import of the monadology.

The doctrine of windowless monads introduces a cardinal thesis of any monadological ontology, namely, that monads have no relation to any exteriority, and so cannot be altered or modified from the outside. Leibniz mentions two reasons for this, in a passage whose highly allusive character gives it an unusual density:

- In the first place, it is impossible to conceive of "any internal motion" in the monad, that is, a movement of some parts in relation to others or in relation to the whole, which in fact would make no sense in an absolutely simple reality. The only modifications conceivable in the monad are therefore qualitative: the monad changes only by remaining the same, without anything being quantitatively gained or lost.
- But it must be added, these qualitative transformations cannot occur to the monad *from the outside*—in short, "monads have no windows through which something can enter or depart." This is a judgment of singular importance, whose consequences for "spiritual" monads (in the restricted sense of the term) will immediately be evident. For if the mind (or soul) is a single monad, it is necessary to hold that it produces its representations without receiving any sensation from the external world, and hence that it generates them *on the basis of itself.* While this was to be an influential theory of representation in German idealism, the notion that representation is a passive "experience" (the subject having the impression—a paradoxical fact, if we *produce* our representations—of receiving sensations from some "external" source) requires comment. We need to grasp the necessity for such a theory of representation, whatever its ultimate fate may have been, and, more generally, to determine what led Leibniz to maintain that the qualitative modifications of monads could in no case result from an action arising from any external cause.

The passage intended to clarify his reasoning is particularly elliptical: "The accidents cannot detach themselves nor go about outside of substances, as did formerly the sensible species of the Scholastics."[24] What Leibniz has in mind here is a long-forgotten scholastic theory.[25] Since Descartes, modern theories of knowledge have accustomed us to conceiving the cognitive act as a three-termed process in which, between the subject and the real object, the representation constitutes the thing to which the subject has access—the whole problem therefore becoming a matter of grasping what relation the representation bears to the object. In scholastic theory, however, the mind is related to the object itself, to reality in itself, which is supposed to send the mind something like images ("sensible species") reflecting the object's ontological status. In this realistic conception of knowledge, the image basically constitutes an intermediary between the object's matter and its form: as matter, the object cannot enter the mind (an absurdity from the point of view both of common sense and of dualism), but neither can it simply transmit itself as form (for in that case we would forever grasp only the essence of things, not their sensory appearance in all its particularity). Hence, the hypothesis that only a sensible species, a mediating instance of the object that synthesizes its form and sensory appearance without adding to its matter, penetrates the mind.

Why does Leibniz refer just at this point to a theory that had become out-of-date with the Cartesian revolution? The move here is actually strategic: it "describes in its most absurd (that is, scholastic) form the conception of an interaction of realities"—it being understood that "if, as in Scholasticism, the interaction presupposes that there are images-accidents issuing from substances and entering the mind, it will not be difficult to unmask the aberration of believing that substances interact, so foreign had the theory of sensible species become to modern thought after Descartes."[26] In short, Leibniz offers a particularly caricatured account to show that the very idea of interaction is unthinkable. This strategy suggested the idea, worked out in the *Monadology*, that if the monad cannot be qualitatively modified from the outside, any modification internal to it that is not destructive of its simplicity must involve conceiving the monad on the model of a conscious mind that produces a multiplicity of representations by itself without being divided by this multiplicity. Thus, the monad (substance) is understood as a *subject*. It then becomes necessary to insist in the case of this subject on the quite specific picture that serves as a model for the monad: for here is a subject that constitutes itself as such with no relation to anything other than itself, which, though it is limited (finite), is not limited in its relation to anything else, but rather through *self-limitation, a subjectivity without intersubjectivity, a self-identity that is posited with no relation to the otherness of a world nor of another self.* It will of course be necessary to take a further look at this peculiarity of the monadic egoity, but it will be agreed that such a model of the subject entails individualism and private independence—rather than humanism with its ideal of generating a public or cultural space of intersubjectivity through mutual recognition and mutual limitation of spheres of activity.

The fact remains that after considering the monad from a purely external viewpoint (which—*because it cannot have windows*—leads to thinking of it as a Self producing the totality of its states by itself), Leibniz very logically explains the *egoic* structure of the monad through an analysis of its internal processes. At this moment in the analysis of monadic individuality (in §11), the definition of the monad as endowed with perception and appetition is introduced. Here again a few brief observations are in order, less because of the obvious intrinsic difficulty of the passage (which would call for a detailed commentary) than because of its ambiguous import. It will be recalled that Heidegger saw this account of the internal structure of the monad as an anthropomorphization of substance, and thus the sign that the elevation of subjectivity as a principle and law of reality had reached a new and decisive stage. Perhaps, if we were to consider Leibniz's pronouncements more closely, the passage may be seen to have a quite different significance.

Consider §13: Leibniz's problem there was to find a synthesis between the absolute simplicity of the monad and the multiplicity of changes it undergoes in passing through successive states. How can the unity of monadic individuality not be affected by this multiplicity of "the detail of that which changes"? If the monad is to remain simple (without parts) despite and throughout this plurality of states, the plurality must be present in its entirety in each of the states, or else it would be endlessly divided within itself. Leibniz expresses this requirement by laying down that "there must be in the simple substance a plurality of affections and of relations, although it has no parts."[27] But, on the other hand, to conceive of the multiplicity that defines monadic individuality as a unity, a fixed term must be posited: without reference to a term that itself does not change, it is impossible to think of the change occurring in "the detail of that which changes." In Leibniz's words: "Since every natural change takes place by degrees, something changes and something remains."[28] Something permanent thus has to be attributed to the monad even though this monad is the site (in fact, as we have seen, the source) of change; for the modification of states (the "accidents") cannot destroy the unity of a substance. It is only in order to accommodate such change in identity that in §14 the idea is introduced of *perception* and, by carefully distinguishing it from *apperception*, makes it an element of the internal structure of the monad.

The greatest possible precision is called for here, for so many serious confusions are possible. What Leibniz calls "apperception" is what we now call perception: in other words, conscious perception. On the other hand, what he calls "perception," which alone is constitutive of monadic individuality, includes both apperception and unconscious perceptions (or "little perceptions"): the term is thus *generic*, and makes it possible to consider plants as being endowed with perceptions *without exposing oneself to a charge of anthropomorphism*. For perception in the Leibnizian sense refers only to the presence of a multiplicity of states in the same unity. Certainly we experience the clearest example of such a unity of the multiple in the human faculty of representation (i.e., apperception, meaning conscious perception), but to make perception a property of every

[illegible]ad is less to make subjectivity the sign of being than to conceive this
[illegible]tivity as a particular case of a more inclusive structure (that of per-
[illegible]) by virtue of which everything that exists is an individual (owing
[illegible]livisible unity of a multiplicity): thus apperception is proposed as
[illegible]perception, and subjectivity as a model of monadicity (individ-
[illegible]than to a subjectivization of reality, the Leibnizian situating
[illegible]the very structure of reality thus testifies to a *relativization*
[illegible]derstood only as one species within a larger category that
[illegible] *about it*; and by dissolving more than affirming what
[illegible], this gesture locates the very same structure at the
[illegible]s, plants (which, being affected by a series of states
a [illegible]reserve their unity), and animals, as well as physica[illegible]dered with respect to the motion that they produce,
pass[illegible]s stages of a single trajectory). *It is not so much a*
matte[illegible]*ity on the model of the human subject as of con-*
ceiving [illegible]*ubject and the least "human" reality—for exam-*
ple, a fo[illegible] *model: can we be sure that this conception rep-*
resents a [illegible] *modern humanism?* Leibniz certainly was not
denying a [illegible]r to the human mind: a whole sequence in the
Monadology [illegible]§19) is in fact devoted to setting up a hierarchy
of monads an[illegible]minds (in the restricted sense) within this hierar-
chy. Yet, states of mind continue to appear against a background of structural identity: just as the law of the series that governs a mental monad contains all the conscious representations that will succeed each other during the course of its life, so a force, in advance of being exerted, contains in its mathematical formula the series of states through which it will pass in the course of producing them.

The same observations apply to the other dimension that constitutes the internal structure of every monad, namely, *appetition*. Introduced in §15, this notion is intended to explain the "transition from one perception to another." For change to occur (§12 has already shown why change is a *fact* that needs to be explained, and that cannot be denied without contradiction), there must be "a detail of that which changes"—i.e., a succession of perceptions—and a "principle of change" (this is the principle of appetition, conceived on the model of an internal dynamism that leads from one state to another). Here again, the anthropomorphism of the term is deceptive: it does not mean that every being acts in accordance with a principle corresponding to the *desire* that leads us to work out the series of states comprehended by the unity that defines us, but simply that Leibniz designates the principle of change by referring to its operation at the level at which we know it most directly: ourselves. Appetition in its most exact (and also most general—therefore least "human") sense is thus a dynamic capability for change producing ever-new states and thus revealing the multiplicity implied by the monadic unity. Thus change can be explained while preserving the unity of the monad, for the multiple is built in as a condition of self-identity and displays the whole of its content through appetition.

Let us confine ourselves for the moment to examining the analysis of individuality found in the *Monadology*. What defines the essence of monadic individuality in physical forces and the human will alike is, under the guise of perception, a multiplicity of states not affecting the unity of substances; and, under the guise of appetition, an internal dynamism producing the succession of all possible states without the intervention of any external thing (thus making it possible to think of the diversity of states, or "events," as moments in the self-deployment of identity). This observation profoundly relativizes Heidegger's criticism of the monadological process. To equate our grasp of reality, in all its generality, with the model of monadic individuality, surely amounts less—when we consider that the meaning of individuality thus extends to all reality—to asserting an absolute and unconditioned humanization of reality than to situating humanity itself in a much wider generic category that goes far beyond, and relativizes, the sphere of the human. On this account, to read the monadological development of modern ontology as a simple moment in the triumph of the values of subjectivity—of humanism—is to commit a serious error. It is to miss one of the clearest meanings of the Leibnizian inauguration of the age of monadologies, which represents, philosophically, the overthrow of the model of subjectivity, and, culturally, the advancement of the values of individualism.

Leibnizian Individualism

Let us pose once again the question in all its complexity: to what extent can the *philosophical* age of monadologies inaugurated by Leibniz be related to the emergence of modern individualism?

For the most part, the difficulty in pinpointing Leibniz's place in the history of subjectivity lies in the temptation (to which Heidegger unfortunately yielded) to draw a highly problematic conclusion from an indubitable observation. The observation is that, like the monadology, the Leibnizian ontology is antidualist and thus already *immaterialist* ("materialism" being understood as the doctrine according to which matter is utterly opposed to mind, external to it, heterogeneous). Already in this sense Leibniz's philosophy is akin to that of Berkeley: in the next chapter we shall see that the immaterialism of the monadology can be extended and enriched through an examination of the monadological aspects of Berkeley's immaterialism. In both cases, in conformity with an *idealist* view, reality has the structure of the mind—not, as Strawson correctly noticed, that monads are in any strict sense minds themselves (since "only a subclass of monads are said to be conscious," thereby qualifying as minds in the sense they are subjects of perception *and apperception*), but that "minds are the nearest and easiest model for monads of all the categories that we employ."[29]

But how are we to interpret this appeal to mind as a model of the monad? There is no doubt that the claim that the structures of mind and reality are one and the same helps eliminate the idea of an exteriority-in-itself of reality relative to rationality; it is, in this sense, part and parcel of the movement that was to culminate with Hegel and the notion of the concept as the very law of reality. *Must we then conclude, as Heidegger does, that this triumph of the concept is also a triumph of the subject?* Is thinking of substance *as subject*, in the mode of a *philosophy of the concept*, ipso facto to affirm the triumph of subjectivity over reality? Is the *philosophy of the concept a philosophy of the subject*? To answer this question, we must consider what becomes of the subject in Leibniz. Are monads really subjects? In point of fact, all the evidence goes to show that *the Leibnizian monadology brings about the destruction of the idea of the subject.*

First of all, the monadology casts doubt on the capacity for self-reflection, which since Descartes (at least symbolically its point of origin, given the Cartesian source of the *cogito, sum* as a principle of philosophy) defined subjectivity: we cannot underestimate the role played in this regard by the theory of "little perceptions," which marks the emergence of the unconscious as a philosophical idea and, as such, the first radical break with the human subject. From this point of view it is significant that in §14, the first (but still implicit) statement of the theory in the *Monadology* (it is made explicit only in §21), the Cartesians are criticized for having "failed to distinguish between a prolonged state of unconsciousness and actual death."[30] The argument is less obscure than it may seem. The Cartesians, Leibniz observed, insofar as the essence of the thinking substance is thought, identify the latter with consciousness; they cannot conceive that, where there is no conscious thought, there can be any thought at all. Fainting, then, must be considered a kind of death, which, it will be agreed, makes it particularly awkward to interpret the return to consciousness as a return to life. If, however, one applies the law of a rational universe articulated by the principle of continuity, it can be posited that between degree zero of consciousness (unconsciousness) and full consciousness are interpolated a multiplicity of degrees, among them the "little" or insensible perceptions: thus fainting (or even sleep) does not have to be interpreted as a vanishing of consciousness, and hence a kind of death; on the contrary, these can be seen as examples of the unconscious life that thought leads, a life that eludes the grasp of the subject or the mind's capacity for apperception. We know that Leibniz described these unconscious perceptions by appealing to the notion of differential summation: as infinitesimal states, the little perceptions are only perceived (apperceived) when they reach a certain degree through the summation of the infinitely small. In short, there is a whole subterranean existence of perceptions or representations that, by definition, escapes the self-reflexive grasp—the subject, understood as the capacity for self-reflection, emerges only on the surface or periphery of a representational process that for the most part unfolds in the subject's absence, as it were.

As important as it was, this first assault on the subject in the *Monadology* via the theory of little perceptions could not alone suffice to bring about the destruction of the subject as an idea. The opacity that now characterized the subject's relation to itself did not altogether exclude finding a meaningful role for the idea of a subject through conversion of the subject's classic (Cartesian) attributes (transparency to self-reflection, of course, but also self-foundation—or freedom—as autonomy) into ideals that would have to be approximated indefinitely. But this surely was not an option for Leibniz, who not only *relativized* the idea of the subject by proposing a discontinuity with it, but indeed *subverted* it by denying its most distinctive meaning.

When we consider what becomes of the second component of Cartesian subjectivity from the monadological point of view, namely, *self-foundation*, we are obliged to agree that it loses both its reality *and its meaning*: because self-foundation can neither designate the *being* of the "subject" nor ever represent its *ideal* or *horizon*, it is difficult to go on speaking of a *subject* in connection with the monad. Modernity was inaugurated through the Cartesian invitation to man to think of himself "as master and possessor of nature," and thus as at least *destined* to impose his law on reality rather than receiving the law from nature: the goal of *autonomy* was thus consubstantial with the modern assertion of rationality. How, we may ask, did the matter appear from Leibniz's point of view? Though it may seem implied by the monad's postulated power to produce by itself the totality of what happens to it, the idea of autonomy here actually loses all meaning. To see this, one has only to look at the order that governs relations among monads—an order which is, as we have seen, required from the perspective of a theodicy. If there is an order to reality (and, in a world that is necessarily "the best of all possible worlds," such an order *must* exist), it can hardly be conceived as self-established by subjects understood as the sources of their reciprocal interaction: because monads have no windows, the very idea of a horizontal causality between them is quite excluded. Ontological independence among finite monads rules out any possibility of the slightest order being introduced into reality by the *human* imposition of certain rules that limit the spontaneity of individuals: thus the establishment of an order among beings in terms of juridical or ethical regulation (regulation by law) could make sense only from a phenomenal point of view—a deluded point of view that, because of its submission to appearances, misses the fact that the truth of beings and things lies in the monads.

The viewpoint of law is the viewpoint of the phenomenon, not that of reality—a crucial observation that does not deprive Leibniz's important contributions to the juridical theory and practice of his day of their *intrinsic* interest, but which considerably relativizes the import of the juridical moment *from the viewpoint of the overall structure of the system*: far from being at the center of the philosophical system, as it was to be in Fichte, law is relativized by the system (in this case by ontology as monadology) and (given that the juridically established order is merely the phenomenal appearance of the true order of the real) actually devalorized.[31] The true foundation of the order of reality—the infrastructure, one might say, of its juridical order and truth—can be found only in the sole causality conceivable within the monadological system, namely, the vertical causality of God or—what amounts to the same thing—"preestablished harmony." This is to say that in such an order monads constitute at the very most its substrate, in that the order is built into them through the law that governs their behavior; it is also to say that the order established by such a law in a particular monad is only an instance of the order immanent in reality, an instance of a harmony which juridical "subjects" do not themselves establish but which they serve, in their own way and without their knowing it.

In this sense, Leibnizian freedom (about which Kant spoke so ironically)[32] is not in any way auto-nomy, that is, submission to a law that one has prescribed for oneself, but merely each monad's observance of the law constitutive of its being, the self-deployment of its distinctive determinacy—*not* self-determination. This law is what organizes reality and so precedes every decision; far from there being a will that lays down this law, the law is immanent in reality and actualizes itself through the sudden appearance of this or that monad and its "will."

Given this much—that the subject is not only limited in its capacity for self-reflection by the rupture introduced by the "little perceptions," but now finds its claims to self-foundation dismissed, both in fact and in principle—it is hard to see what meaning the idea of subjectivity could retain in the monadological scheme. All the more then the question deserves to be asked: *since the valorization of autonomy intrinsically connected with the idea of the subject loses all meaning in this context, does not the whole monadological mechanism invite us to see a formidable and explicit ontological advancement of the individualistic theme of independence?* For even if within this mechanism freedom cannot be conceived as autonomy, it is still true that it is (and must be) conceived as independence—as the following passage from the *Système nouveau de la nature et de la communication des substances* (New System of Nature and Communication between Substances, 1695) among many others attests. The passage is worth quoting in full:

> [I]nstead of saying that we are free only in appearance and in a manner adequate for practice, as several ingenious men have held, we must rather say that we are determined in appearance only; and that in strict metaphysical language we are perfectly *independent* as regards the influence of all other created things. This again shows up in a marvelously clear light the immortality of our soul, and the ever uniform conservation of our individual self, which is perfectly well regulated of its own nature, and is beyond the reach of all accidents from outside, whatever the appearances to the contrary. No system has ever so clearly exhibited our exalted position. Since each mind is as it were a world apart, *sufficient unto itself, independent of all other created things*, including the infinite, expressing the universe, it is as lasting, as subsistent, and as absolute as the very universe of created things itself. We must therefore conclude that it must always play its part in the way most suited to contribute to the perfection of that society of all minds which constitutes their moral union in the City of God. Here, too, is a new and wonderfully clear proof of the existence of God. For this perfect agreement all these substances, *which have no point of communication with one another*, could only come from the one common cause.[33]

This passage is extraordinary for concentrating in a few lines the main determinations and values constitutive of modern individualism. It would not be incorrect to see in it (though on another level—that of ontology) precisely the same configuration of ideas that in the sociopolitical realm Tocqueville was to designate by the term individualism, taking this to indicate:

- the definition of freedom as the "perfect independence" of beings;
- the positing of "our individuality" as entirely impervious to the influence of exteriority (notably, to that of "others") and as controlling itself only "by its own nature;" thus the control of self is seen not as the free (i.e., auto-nomous) adoption of limits imposed on nature by freedom, but as the free (i.e., independent of external constraint) operation of nature. Nothing that happens to the "individual" can befall him from the outside, compelling him to recognize another "individual" as a separate freedom limiting his own; everything that happens to him unfolds from the laws of his own "nature";
- the exaggerated valorization of "self-sufficiency" and the corresponding dissolution of the community in favor of the simple coexistence of private spheres, each of which constitutes a "world apart";
- the disintegration of intersubjectivity as "communication" between minds: the "agreement" obtaining among them proceeds not from a consensus (or contract) among wills that thereby resolve to limit themselves reciprocally,

but obtains only as a function of the internal logic of the system (in which God exists as the "common cause"—and hence the sole foundation of order in the real world).

Owing to the remarkable parallel dissolution it achieves of both subjectivity and intersubjectivity, the monadology represents the philosophical birth certificate of the individual and individualism. Beyond this (philosophically) inaugural moment, the logic of individualism was to continue working itself out and to produce other still more complete developments. But with Leibniz the essential principle legitimating individualism in the *ethical* sense of the term was now acquired (and philosophically grounded, by means of individualism in the *ontological* sense of the term): *each individual exhibits the order of the universe, the harmony and rationality of the whole, by turning in upon himself and by virtue of being concerned only with himself, with the cultivation of his independence and submission to the law of his nature (i.e., to the formula that characterizes him).* Because the preestablished rationality of the universe is expressed through the programming of each "individual" to realize his "nature," for the first time there is no insurmountable contradiction between concern for the self (that is, an exclusive concern for the preservation of "our individuality") and affirmation of the rationality of the whole. This was Leibniz's distinctive, inspired invention: *a new intellectual structure that brings forth the values of individualism (independence) by making them compatible with the idea of a rationality of the real.* In the absence of this crucial integration of the values of individualism (monadology) with those of rationality (theodicy), the former inevitably would have come into conflict with the latter, and the logic of individualism would have been powerless to find the means to develop itself *in concert with the modern valorization of reason*, to the point it would have had to end up casting doubt (as we will see with Nietzsche) on the values of rationality itself.

It is therefore true to say that through the monadology a world was born. This formula, often misapplied, is legitimate here, since it is used to refer not so much to a particular idea in Leibniz as to the way in which, in his thought as a whole, a structure emerges that reaches here its highest degree of elaboration and abstraction, although it can be identified in other contexts as well.

Monadology and Theories of the Market

This does not, of course, amount to foolishly asserting the existence of some causal relation between the monadological model developed by Leibniz (construing monadology in the strict sense as both an individualistic ontology and a theodicy) and the subsequent appearance of new thinking about the logic of social sphere and economic relations—theories of the market, as they are customarily called—that may be shown to be structurally similar to the monadological model. Nonetheless it is striking, and no doubt instructive, to note that in 1714—the same year that Leibniz wrote the *Monadology* (which was published much later)—Bernard Mandeville published a first annotated edition of his *Fable of the Bees*, which has often (and correctly) been seen as the first anticipation of market theories.[34] At first sight this may seem to be an unsettling coincidence: Mandeville, a Dutchman who spent his adult life in London, is identified more with the philosophical heirs of Hobbes and of a certain empiricism than with Continental rationalism.[35] While there is no question of any direct influence by Leibniz, and though its economic and political significance stems from its foreshadowing of the liberal theory of the "invisible hand,"[36] *The Fable of the Bees* is singularly reminiscent of Leibnizian individualism in its analysis of the logic immanent in human society.

The fable is well known: Mandeville compared society to a beehive that lived in "luxury and ease," but lacked any morality. Each bee sought only its own benefit and cared about nothing other than its own self-interest, with no regard for that of the others. "No calling was without deceit": the lawyers were "kept off hearings willfully, [t]o finger the refreshing fee," doctors "valu'd fame and wealth [a]bove the drooping patient's health"—in short, "every part was full of vice, [y]et the whole mass a paradise" for "[t]he worst of all the multitude [d]id something for the common good." Thus, Mandeville argued that "Parties directly opposite [a]ssist each other, as 'twere for spite," and that luxury

> Employ'd a million of the poor,
> And odious pride a million more:
> Envy itself, and vanity,
> Were ministers of industry;
> Their darling folly, fickleness,
> In diet, furniture, and dress,
> That strange ridic'lous vice, was made
> The very wheel that turn'd the trade.[37]

The rest of the fable constitutes a counter-proof of the initial image. Out of a nostalgic longing for virtue, the hive prayed for the return of morality. Its wish fulfilled, it saw that along with vice, happiness and prosperity disappeared: each individual having agreed henceforth to satisfy only modest, well-tempered desires, the needs for which industry had formerly served to meet were now considerably reduced, with the result that a host of jobs vanished since everyone worked harder—so that "All places manag'd first by three, . . . [a]re happily supplied by one, [b]y which some thousands more are gone." Vain expense was avoided, fashions no longer succeeded each other with delightful fickleness as before, frivolous glory was no longer cultivated, magical palaces with superb porticos were no longer built: the arts declined, all those who lived in luxury were forced to leave the hive, and "Those, that remain'd, grown temp'rate, strive [n]ot how to spend, but how to live," no longer seeking novelty nor setting their hearts on anything—ideal prey, one would suppose, since "The hundredth part they can't maintain [a]gainst th'insults of numerous foes."[38] What Mandeville provocatively presents then as the fable's "moral" is easily guessed:

> Then leave complaints: fools only strive
> To make a great an honest hive.
> T'enjoy the world's conveniences,
> Be fam'd in war, yet live in ease,
> Without great vices, is a vain
> Eutopia seated in the brain.
> Fraud, luxury, and pride must live,
> While we the benefits receive: [. . .]
> So vice is beneficial found,
> When it's by justice lopp'd and bound;
> Nay, where the people would be great,
> As necessary to the state,
> As hunger is to make 'em eat.[39]

Evoking this famous passage in *Homo aequalis*, Louis Dumont sees in it an important stage in the "transition" from "traditional morality" (the "holistic spirit" in which each subject defines his behavior by reference to the society as a whole) to the "utilitarian ethics" of an individualistic culture in which, each subject now defining his behavior only by reference to his own self-interest, "the individual is free, his last chains have fallen from him"[40]—a debatable reading of Mandeville unless one essential point is clarified, having to do with precisely these "chains" from which the individual would now be freed.

Mandeville's contribution to the genesis of modern individualism (hence his participation in the "transition" Dumont mentions) cannot be appreciated if we do not grasp how relative the "freedom" of the Mandevillean individual—like that of the Leibnizian monad—actually is: the bee in the hive is certainly free in the sense that it is not restrained in the performance of its most selfish desires, but can it be said to be free in the face of the "skillful management" owing to which, even while caring only about itself, each member "is forced to do something for the common good?"[41] Despite the scandalous reaction it provoked, the fable only makes sense on the assumption of some harmonizing mechanism by which the selfish "freedom" of every person to obey his natural impulses, so far from detracting from or harming the common happiness, in fact contributes to it, and thereby to the realization of the greatest possible good without the knowledge of the individual—just as, Mandeville stresses (using language that is surprisingly close to that of Leibniz), "in music harmony [m]ade jarrings in the main agree";[42] just as (and how can we not think here of the many statements to this effect in the *Theodicy*?) "it would be utterly impossible either to raise any multitudes into a populous, rich, and flourishing nation, or, when so raised, to keep and maintain them in that condition without the assistance of what we call Evil, both natural and moral"[43]—in short, even this evil, once put into harmony with the universe, is a good in the sense that it contributes to a greater good.

The individual for Mandeville, more than for Leibniz, is not yet freed of his "last chains." In both cases, and in nearly the same terms, the individual affirms his nature independently of any principle of *horizontal* limitation that he is obliged to impose on himself out of consideration for what is required by coexistence with others: but those chains will fall away (individualism not yet having been affirmed) only within a system of *vertical* or *immanent* harmonization ("preestablished harmony," "skillful management") beyond all human choice, which programs individual choices in such a way that, without anyone's knowing it, they contribute to the "common good." Thus in both Mandeville and Leibniz the demands of individualism are integrated with those of a rationality of the real, whose invisible help allows the individual to pursue in complete "freedom" (the freedom of the "turnspit"), the realization of his interests—even of his most private vices. While surely this represents "a step further in the emancipation of the Individual,"[44] it does not for all that enable the individual to say that "his last chains have fallen from him": these chains will fall, in fact, only well after the time of Leibniz, Mandeville, or even Adam Smith (whose notion of the "invisible hand," which, strictly speaking, marks the founding of the theory of the market, repeats in its way the same principle for integrating the values of individualism with those of rationality)[45] is passed. For the "final chains" to fall and for individualism to flourish without restriction, it will be necessary that the values of rationality itself (harmony, cunning, the invisible hand) eventually appear as unacceptable limits (as *universal* values) upon the affirmation of individuality *that they had initially seemed to favor*—a reversal that finally occurs on the road from Hegel to Nietzsche, but that at this stage is still far from appearing on the horizon.

From Mandeville to Adam Smith, of course, the gestation and birth of theories of the market involved a complete rethinking of the economic and social sphere that prefigured the history of liberalism: thought of now as a function of "skillful management" or "the invisible hand," the game of human relations was no longer seen (at least in principle) as having to be organized from the outside by the imposition of rules that the game would not produce by itself (and that human reason would therefore have to construct and then apply). On the contrary, the general good was now conceived as the spontaneous result of each person acting individually and selfishly, without concern for others or for the common good, in pursuit of his own objectives. But the parallel with what was philosophically inaugurated with Leibniz, in the analysis of the monadological evolution of ontology, inevitably suggests broadening the range of Mandeville's and Smith's schemes beyond the economic and political: *what is expressed philosophically in Leibniz is also expressed during the same period in economic-political thinking about how human society functions.* No flatly causal interpretation of these concomitant developments, according to which the intellectual origin of theories of the market is to be found in the monadology and the social truth of the monadology in these theories, is being asserted here: it is rather a matter of *two expressions of the same phenomenon—namely, the birth of individualism—which, in order to be brought into the world, required the same intellectual structures to be erected in both philosophy and political economy.* To mistake the place of the Leibnizian moment in the history of modernity (that is, either seeing it as just a stage in the affirmation of the subject or believing it to contain the seeds of an antimodern, holistic reaction) is to deprive oneself of a clear view of the conditions and forms of emergence of modern individualism; and also, by the same token, to forfeit the chance of grasping the logic by which individualism could then, through the rearrangement of certain conditions and the abandonment of certain forms, transform itself into absolute individualism.

The (Leibnizian) birth of philosophical individualism is not the same as its (Nietzschean) completion—a blatant truism, no doubt, but one that still needs to be recalled in order to prevent misunderstanding.

Manfred Frank's important study of individualism exhibits the triple merit of 1. breaking with the common tendency from Heidegger to Foucault to see the full flowering of subjectivity as the consistent aim of modern philosophy; 2. taking issue with contemporary ("postmodern") "theoretical antihumanism," according to which the sole legitimate program of philosophy is defined by the "death of the subject;" and 3. drawing attention to questions which "current French critics seem never to have seriously considered," namely: "What is the relation between the concepts of the subject and of the individual? How are these concepts related to that of the person? What is their own identity or nonidentity?"[46]

Discovering such a work, I cannot help but feel (as the reader may well guess) a great affinity for a venture that on many points matches up with the one undertaken by Luc Ferry and myself, and which, in view of the distinction it proposes between subjectivity and individuality, seems to be closely related to what I have tried to do in this book. These signs of convergence are no doubt an indication that for the first time in several decades philosophical debate is undergoing a renewal—a renewal that is all the more encouraging in that it is being carried out by means of studies that are *sui generis*, independent of each other, and yet at least to some extent parallel in their purposes. How then can this situation not be seen as reflecting an intellectual necessity of our time, irreducible to the interests and initiatives of this or that person?

Hence I am all the more perplexed to hear Manfred Frank ask: "Is the individual a Leibnizian monad?"—and to hear him answer with the categorical assertion: "There can at bottom be no question of individualism in Leibniz—nor even of the emancipation of the thought of a singular subject."[47] In view of the very theses I uphold in this book, and because some of Frank's motivations are very close to mine, I want to try to clear up what appears to be a surprising disagreement.

Frank writes that in Leibniz we find for the first time the use of the first-person singular nominative pronoun. He quotes §34 of the *Discours de métaphysique* (Discourse on Metaphysics, 1686), where it is stated that "it is the memory or knowledge of this ego which renders it [the soul] open to reward and punishment."[48] Must it be concluded, however, from the fact that the subject is thus identified as *the* self, that subjectivity assumes the aspect of individuality? There can hardly be any doubt about Frank's refusal, noted above, to attribute any individualism whatever to Leibniz. But we can understand (and discuss) Frank's argument only if we consider the distinction he makes in his various writings between the subject and the individual.

For him "subject" means the general, universal structure of the relation to self: the subject is the universal self, that is, that relation to itself (self-reflection) which characterizes everything that presents itself as an instance of consciousness. Thus defined, the subject clearly has no more individuality than does the Kantian "I think" or Fichte's "I = I": the subject is "the phenomenon that every conscious being has in common with his fellows." Individuality, on the other hand, that which distinguishes Socrates from Glaucon or Callias, refers to "the way of being of a singular subject," irreducible to that of any other singular subject. In this sense, when I refer to myself as "I," I posit myself as both *subject* and *individual*: in positing myself as subject (meaning subject in general), I delimit myself from everything that does not have the nature of a self—from the world, from things—as not-I; in positing myself as an individual, I distinguish or differentiate myself from all other beings that have the structure of subjectivity in common with me.

Having established this terminology, the question that concerns me here can be asked: "Is the individual a Leibnizian monad?" In the overall context of Frank's thinking, what prompts this question is of course the principle of indiscernibles: for while the monadological idea requires, in its first branch, that every being be conceived as a subject (as self), the principle of indiscernibles, the second branch of the monadological idea, seems to necessitate thinking of monads as "selves" that are differentiated from each other, and thus as individuals none of which is reducible to any other. Under these circumstances, why refuse to see the monad as an individual—to think of the individual on the model of the Leibnizian monad?

Frank believes that the obstacle to calling the monadology a doctrine of individualism stems from the relation of the Leibnizian monads to the whole or the universal, or, better yet, to the concept of the universe. We have seen that for Leibniz, each monad in its way expresses the universe, and that the difference that constitutes it (and makes it irreducible to any other monad) lies in the perspective not only that it *has* on the universe, but indeed that it *is*. Differences between monads are thus only differentiations based on a fundamental identity, which corresponds to the universe's identity with itself: on the basis of this identity, and hence on the basis of the concept of the world, one can in principle—God can in fact—derive the different degrees of monadic "individualities" as so many particularizations of the same universal in accordance with logical process of continuous derivation (and of particularization), smoothly and without a gap (thanks to the principle of continuity). Thus, individuality is deducible from the concept of the universe: there is no rupture implied in passing from the universal to the monad, only limitation introduced into the initial totality. Consequently, there is no true irreducibility among the various limitations of the whole that monads represent: the monads are commensurable in relation to each other and each of them in relation to the whole, and "individuals" are elements that can in principle (even if this is not the case for us in fact, owing to our finitude) be obtained on the basis of the concept of the whole, without further hermeneutic argument.

Thus the conclusion that monads are at the very most particular cases of the whole: "particulars, not individuals"—which would presuppose being able to go beyond the homogeneity of the universal to identify a level of reality that is impossible (even in principle) to derive from any universal concept. This going beyond, from mere particularity to authentic individuality, Frank sees as not having been accomplished before Schleiermacher. Let us leave aside Schleiermacher, and the various places where one might think of situating such a radicalization of particularity in absolute individuality (in the sense of an individuality that is absolutized in relation to the universal, all connections with any universal having been broken): later we will have reason to inquire into a similar attempt at radicalization in Nietzsche. For the time being, the only question that need concern us is whether Frank's analysis, which is of course fundamentally correct as far as it goes, effectively forbids us from speaking of a Leibnizian individualism. I think our whole disagreement stems from the different way in which we understand, and locate, the most decisive breaks in the logic of modernity.

Frank, influenced here by the dominant style of deconstruction in modern philosophy, tends quite obviously to situate the key rupture at that point where philosophical thought ceases to subordinate reality to concept, refusing to derive any particular (singular) instances from a universal: as long as there is "a relation of logical derivation, a perfect commensurability, between individuality and the concept of a possible world," as is the case in Leibniz, Frank believes that thought has not yet reached the critical caesura—once this has been reached, thought (i.e., metaphysics) must give up trying to discover in the real an order capable of being "collected, defined, and enclosed once and for all in a concept."[49] It is clear that the Leibnizian monadology still falls short of this breakpoint, which in effect involves the emergence of the individual as an *element that is irreducible to any order*. Altogether logically, then, one tends to situate the Leibnizian moment in relation to what precedes it, the decisive break not yet having occurred,[50] rather than in relation to what it leads up to.

The perspective changes once one gives up thinking of the logic of modern philosophy as exercising a multiform and mutilating tyranny by means of the concept of the real in its absolute singularity. On the one hand, so far as reason (i.e., concept, that which is universal) is concerned, such a view continues to cling to life through a project of radical criticism that runs the risk of recapitulating most of the Heideggerian and post-Heideggerian aporias, and so of responding only poorly to the philosophical needs of our time: how can one think of reason or the universal in the old way after their critique? On the other hand, this view of the fate of modern philosophy tends to create an unbridgeable gulf between Hegel (taken as a symbol of all philosophies of the concept) and Nietzsche (whom one can hardly, Schleiermacher notwithstanding, think of otherwise than as embodying the demand to think of ourselves as "singular beings, such that our interpretation of the world is not based on any preestablished harmony").[51] To locate the essential turning point in modern philosophy with Hegel makes good sense, certainly, but it is a traditional and familiar choice, one that is perhaps not as obvious as it has come to seem, and it risks masking a far more profound continuity, as I shall attempt to show. Finally, it is clear that to carve things up in this way is to miss the essential role nonetheless played by the Leibnizian monadology in the genesis of individualism.

For what Frank does not see is that *everything that in the monadology appears to him to be still dependent on preindividualistic schemes (the derivation of "individuality" on the basis of the universal, the idea of a conceptual order in the universe, the commensurability of elements among themselves and of the elements in relation to the whole) has in fact fulfilled an essential and decisive function in the process of introducing the values of individualism into a cultural universe—modern rationalism—which would otherwise straight away have rejected the integration of such values.* I have insisted throughout the present chapter on the role played in this regard by the fit between the monadology and the theodicy often enough not to have to repeat my position: the individuality of the monads still *quite obviously* reduces to the particularization of a universal which makes their derivation in principle possible; the Leibnizian individuals, since they are still *quite obviously* commensurable, are not yet absolute singularities about whose self-identity there can be any question. This amounts to saying—let me repeat—that Leibniz, since he falls short of absolute individualism, is not Nietzsche: nevertheless, this shortfall was the price that had to be paid for a decisive philosophical advance (which Frank seems neither to suspect nor to see the significance of) by which philosophy passed from the values of autonomy to those of independence, to an individualism whose career, while it definitely did not come to a halt with the *Monadology*, surely could not—philosophically speaking, at least—have become a possible path for modern humanism without the *Monadology*. This is why, if we are concerned to understand the genesis of individualism here (which, in this case, amounts also to understanding the dislocation that constitutes one of the enigmas of our modernity), it seems to me more fruitful—likelier to yield an increase in intelligibility—to locate the main turning point in the Leibnizian inauguration of the age of monadologies. We have only to consider, after all, the way in which the monadological structure reappears, *mutatis mutandis*, in other models that are constitutive of this philosophical modernity: far from remaining dependent on an outmoded past, Leibniz can thus be seen to have inaugurated one of the most enduring styles of philosophy.

CHAPTER IV

Berkeley and Hume: The Empiricist Monadologies and the Dissolution of the Subject

THE DISCUSSION of classical empiricism that follows is intended to sharpen my chief working hypothesis: if the decisive turning point in modern philosophy leading from the affirmation of the subject to that of the individual is found in the emergence of the monadological problem, we should find signs of this problem outside of its original setting—outside the context given it by Leibniz, in a form certainly altered by the shift of context but one that still contains the main elements and effects, perverse or otherwise, of the monadological theme.

It may seem at first disconcerting to look for a monadological echo in the empiricism of Berkeley and Hume, since the conceptual apparatus of monadology literally disappears in both of them: there is no question of either monads or any preestablished harmony. To be sure, in his *Abstract of the Treatise on Human Nature*, Hume applauds "the celebrated Monsieur Leibnitz" for introducing into logic a consideration of those "probabilities, and those other measures of evidence on which life and action intirely depend, and which are our guides even in most of our philosophical speculations."[1] But the tribute is primarily diplomatic: we are more used to thinking of empiricism and the Leibnizian monadology as antagonistic, even antinomial, than to look for some analogy between the two systems. Everything, in fact, prompts us to think that their relation is one of radical discontinuity—both in the *New Essays*, where Leibniz argues against Locke, and in Kant's reconstruction of the "history of pure reason" in which Locke and Leibniz appear as the modern protagonists of an old debate between "empiricists" and "noologists," succeeded by Hume and Wolff, the latest rivals in the conflict between the "skeptical method" and the "dogmatic method."[2] Thus there is surely at least the appearance of paradox in the attempt to detect some continuity in the development of the monadological idea among Leibnizians and empiricists.

But the paradox is only apparent, nothing more, and stems from an insufficient grasp of the monadological problem: failing to appreciate the meaning of this problem, one does not immediately realize that the monadological question has been posed in various ways, and in very different philosophical contexts, not only within the framework of Leibnizian dogmatic rationalism but also within that of philosophical empiricism. It is interesting to note that the era of monadologies was inaugurated *on the empiricist side* at almost the same time by Berkeley (the *Treatise Concerning the Principles of Human Knowledge* dates from 1710, and the *Three Dialogues between Hylas and Philonous* from 1713) as *on the side of dogmatic rationalism, or idealism* by Leibniz (the *Monadology* dates from 1714). These works, despite their many points of divergence, have a great deal in common; and their contemporaneity singularly substantiates the claim that there existed a monadological moment in the history of modern thought.

The Monadological Problem as the Problem of the World

A monadology typically posits that, even if all realities are substantially *one* (meaning that they are all, to various degrees, mind or intelligence), spiritual substance exists as *separation* or *fragmentation* into a multiplicity of irreducibly distinct minds. This is clearly expressed by Fichte in a passage where, evoking Leibniz, he identifies the quintessence of the monadological idea: "All minds are one, but separate." In short, "the whole is broken up" into a "world of monads" existing independently of each other, each producing the succession of its representations and states by itself (i.e., without referring to anything other than itself).[3] In other words, subjectivity (what I call individuality) is posited here on the basis of itself, without any relation to a *world* (idealism) or to *other people* (solipsism).

These reminders make it possible to reformulate the central problem of any monadology. Within a monadological framework, where there are only minds, closed in on themselves and separated from each other, the difficulty is to grasp how (if we wish to preserve some intelligibility of the real) a *world* can be formed on the basis of these fragments of minds that by themselves produce everything that happens to them: how indeed can we speak here of *a* world, *an* objectivity, rather than (like Nietzsche) of a world multiplied ad infinitum by the perspectives we have of it? For *one* objectivity to be possible—for "truth" not to be a vain word—a *reconciliation* must be effected between these separate minds: if there is to be *one* world (and not merely an infinity of interpretations), it must be the case that even though the representations of individuated minds are produced using their own resources, the series of representations thus produced is not irreducibly divergent, but allows for the recognition of *one* objectivity.

In other words—to further radicalize the formulation of the monadological problem as the problem of the world: how exactly on the basis of such minds, each going through the series of its states, is the *world* formed (along with everything that such a notion implies, particularly getting beyond pure disorder, the irreducible chaos of heterogeneous representations)? The emergence of a *world* presupposes that ordered *relations* arise from the intersection of the series of representations of these separate minds. Now how are we to think of these relations of order? How are we to conceive of relations between intrinsically separate realities? When Nietzsche (in §109 of the *Gay Science*) called for thinking of the totality of being as pure chaos, as not forming a totality—and thus not a *world*—the monadological idea seemed to have borne its ultimate consequence: the whole wager (and also the whole paradox) of modern monadologies prior to Nietzsche now appearing, *a contrario*, to have consisted in an attempt to preserve the *world* from its ineluctable dissolution by the work of individualism. Did the monadologies actually succeed in preserving it? Or, rather, did they only disguise and slow down this work of dissolution, which, by providing a congenial environment for the values of individualism, they also had helped to set into motion in the first place? From this standpoint it now becomes possible to question the significance of the monadologies within a logic of modern philosophy as well.

We know that Leibniz, in order to solve this monadological problem of the world, proposed the theory of preestablished harmony. Fichte perfectly set forth both the problem and the Leibnizian solution:

> How do the thoughts of monads harmonize with each other? Leibniz replies thus: if all minds are one, but separate, it is nonetheless necessary that these fragments match up with each other. Let us suppose therefore that there exists a watch whose wheels mesh with one another: if one puts the elements of the watch together, the [same] movement will once again be produced. According to Leibniz, the world of monads is such a mechanism. However what links up is not movement, but harmonized representation. No doubt the whole is broken up; [but] it does not follow that there is no affinity. Preestablished harmony, thus understood, is a good hypothesis.[4]

Further on I shall discuss to what extent (and in what sense) the Leibnizian solution was a good one from Fichte's point of view. The fact remains that this solution had a profound impact, as its subsequent application by various philosophies of history showed. The problem of history, squarely faced by the great speculative philosophies of German idealism, is in fact strictly analogous to the monadological problem, of which it supplies a particular case: in the historical (rather than ontological) scheme of things, the question became how an order based on the intersection of seemingly unrelated (monadic) individual projects could nonetheless establish itself over time since, in the absence of such order, the very attempt to define the knowledge of history with reference to intelligibility would make no sense. Leibniz's solution to the monadological problem of the world was to erect a structure within which philosophers of history would henceforth be able to think in terms of the intelligibility of historical change: we shall see, at the start of the next chapter, that it was not at all coincidental that Herder should have played a major role in the birth of the philosophies of history as a *Leibnizian*.

This solution to the monadological problem is surely not the only possible one, however. Showing how a whole other tradition of thought—namely, empiricism—contributed to the monadological perspective through which individualism emerged in modern philosophy, thus amounts not only to demonstrating that all the ingredients of the monadological problem were to be found in this alternative tradition as well, but also to trying to determine whether it succeeded in devising a solution distinct from the one proposed by Leibniz.

Berkeley's Empiricist Idealism as a Monadology

How can there be a monadology in Berkeley? We begin to see how such a thing is possible as we read the following emblematic passage in §24 of the *Philosophical Commentaries* of 1707–1708 (usually referred to as the *Commonplace Book*):

> Nothing properly but persons i.e conscious things do exist, all other things are not so much existences as manners of y[e] existence of persons.[5]

One could not ask for a purer statement of the monadological idea: there exist only persons—which is to say, the sole realities are minds (i.e., substance is subject) and consequently what we call the object, the world, or matter, corresponds in reality to simple "ways of being" of minds, and thus to representations. Accordingly, the world being made of multiple subjects and their representations, the monadological idea may be expressed by the well-known formula, *esse est percipi vel percipere*: there exist only subjects (as faculties of perceiving, *percipere*) and their representations (the perceived-being, *percipi*). There thus can be no doubt that Berkeley's philosophy is a monadology. How is it that a line of thought so unlike that of Leibniz could lead to such a similar thesis?

This question requires us to determine how Berkeley arrived at the view that *things* (what we call things) *are just ideas*—that representations refer not to things in themselves (of which they are reflections) but to minds (which are their source). On the horizon of this *reduction of things to ideas* one can now hardly fail to notice the rise of a new thesis: that there are no facts in themselves, only representations (or, in Nietzschean terms, perspectives or interpretations)—once again highlighting the ultimate impact of the monadological theme as consisting in a potentially relativistic dissolution of the object.

Deconstructing the monadological reduction of reality to ideas (and to minds as the sources of these ideas) amounts to analyzing how Berkeley manages this both in the first of the *Three Dialogues* and in §1–26 of the first part of the *Principles*. Toward the end of §26 of the latter work, what we call reality has indeed become "a continual succession of ideas," it being understood that "the cause of ideas is an incorporeal active substance or Spirit": thus, minds and their ideas. The first *Dialogue* closes with Hylas accepting, in response to Philonous's entreaties, that there is nothing in ideas that "can exist without the mind." Thus the first and founding movement of immaterialism in Berkeley's thought; a second movement, which is decisive for the present study because it corresponds to our grappling with the monadological problem, builds upon the first—things having been reduced to ideas—in order to conceive of a world, an objectivity that can be distinguished from the subject. There is no need to reconstruct the stages of the first movement, which has been adequately discussed (sometimes with great lucidity, particularly in the work of Martial Guéroult).[6] Nonetheless it seems to me important to call attention again to the historical logic behind the reduction of things to ideas, that is, to the manner in which this logic emerges in Berkeley, through a study of the various traditions of modern philosophy as these have corrected or amended each other, often in subtle ways. The empiricist version of the monadological idea can be shown to be the result of three mutually interacting traditions:

1. *The influence of the Cartesian tradition* must not be underestimated. For representation was already a criterion of being for Descartes: if something that appears to me can be thought of as real and existing, this is because of a certain quality of representation capable of being forged from it, characterized by clearness and distinctness. For Descartes, in fact—whose perspective could for this reason be called *idealist*[7]—being was already identified with a certain way in which representations present themselves to the mind (i.e., clearly and distinctly). Berkeley adopted in effect the same perspective, but modified the Cartesian position on two essential points with reference to Locke and to Malebranche.[8]

2. *The influence of Locke* served to correct the Cartesian theory of representation with respect to the *nature* of representation. For Cartesian idealism, the representation that serves as the criterion of being enjoys clear-

ness and distinctness only insofar as "the mind may be led away from the senses": only on this basis, cut off from sensory content, can the abstract idea emerge (for example, the abstract idea of a lump of wax as "something extended, flexible and changeable").[9] Breaking here with Descartes, against whom he objects that the mind can be uncoupled from the senses and abstract essences grasped, Berkeley adopted the empiricist thesis of the sensory origin of ideas. From Locke, Berkeley took the *sensualist* theme that an idea is merely an association of particular images and at the same time embraced the *nominalistic* view that essence reduces to the name by which, in fact, the particular is always designated. *Locke versus Descartes*: thus for Berkeley there is no difference in kind between perception and idea—a modification of Cartesianism that makes Berkeley's thinking alien to the tradition to which Leibniz belongs. In this process of modifying Descartes, however, the reference to Locke remains essentially instrumental and does not signal unreserved approval on Berkeley's part. Paradoxically, but profoundly, he detected *in both Descartes and Locke* a common propensity for *realism* that severely limits the *idealist* view of being as a function of the way in which representations are presented to the mind. Both Descartes and Locke, albeit in very different modes, do *in fact* assert that there exists something *in itself* apart from representation:

- In the case of Descartes, it is very clear: that even if the spirit of Cartesianism, as Berkeley understood it, resides in designating (clear and distinct) representation as the criterion of being, representation nonetheless continues to have a referent—for example, the eternal essence of the triangle, the idea of which I form independently of any sensory contribution. By virtue of this realism with respect to essences, the letter of the Cartesian theory of representation thus contradicts what Berkeley judged the spirit of it to be.
- Now in Locke we also find, though in a quite different form, the positing of a term external to representation that serves as its referent. Within a *sensualist* framework, where ideas are held to be the residue of sense-data, the sensory image is indeed conceived as the product of a thing-in-itself that continues to be assigned a realist interpretation. The image is a reflection, the mind consisting in that passivity of the tabula rasa on which are inscribed the impressions produced by the impact of the thing-in-itself.

Though the Lockean reference thus makes it possible to correct Cartesianism with regard to the *nature* of the representation that can serve as a criterion of being (*sensory* nature—not, as Descartes would have it, *intellectual* nature), the appeal to Locke with regard to the *source* of representation does not permit the correction of what in the letter of the Cartesian theory contradicted its spirit: when empiricism remains captive to realism, as in Locke, it exhibits the same limitations as the partial idealism of Descartes. Playing Locke against Descartes amounts to objecting that perceptions and ideas are intrinsically different and to reducing ideas to perceptions; but the claim that there is no absolute difference (of exteriority) between an idea or perception and the thing perceived, put forth in order to reduce things to ideas/perceptions, requires a new corrective, this time with regard to Lockean empiricism. For this purpose, a third point of reference—Malebranche—is needed, the importance of which for the genesis of the monadological idea in Berkeley can immediately be seen. The difference between idea and perception having been eliminated, appeal to Malebranche now makes it possible to cancel the difference between idea and thing, and thus to state the central thesis of the monadology, namely, that there exist only minds and their representations.

3. *The influence of Malebranche* on the new version of empiricism expounded by Berkeley requires a brief excursus. Malebranche inherited from Descartes a realist doctrine of essences that could not be integrated into Berkeley's program (and so here again, as in the case of Locke, the reference to Malebranche was not accompanied by any real enthusiasm for his philosophy on Berkeley's part). But though Malebranche (like Descartes) posited the reality-in-themselves of essences apart from representation, he did modify the Cartesian theory of representation on one important point, which Berkeley thought decisive for his purposes.

The Cartesian version of the theory can be schematically divided into three parts: essences, the human mind, and the innate ideas through which the mind becomes conscious of essences. The concordance between ideas and essences acquired a spectacular, though not unshakable, foundation in the theory of God as guarantor of truth. For complex reasons, involving among other things a principle of parsimony that Malebranche took to govern philosophical speculation,[10] he eliminated the intermediate term referring to innate ideas in the human mind and claimed that consciousness apprehends essence in God *directly*. According to this theory of "vision in God" (as odd as it is well known), the idea of a triangle, for example, does not reflect the eternal essence of a triangle in the mind: instead it is in God that the mind perceives the essential reality of the triangle.

But what good is this curious Malebranchean theory of vision in God, even if it does presuppose a realism of essences, in helping Berkeley set up a monadology that by definition repudiates realism altogether? We need to recall one of Malebranche's best known and most contrary-to-commonsense theses, occasionalism. The principle of the thesis is simple enough: if we see an essence in God, this only happens on those occasions when sensory perceptions of an existence take place. But since, philosophically, Malebranche is situated at the opposite end of the spectrum from empiricism (and also because he is concerned with grounding vision *in God*), he interprets the "occasional" dimension of the perception of existence literally—and radically. In other words, a perceived existence (say, of some particular triangle) could perfectly well not exist, or exist in a different way, and yet in spite of all this (and only with God's help) we would see the same essence of the triangle. One sees at once why this ingenious (but complex and costly) mechanism would appeal to Berkeley: it enabled him to counter the realism that in Locke made a particular idea the effect of a thing-in-itself whose existence appeared as the cause of the presence of the idea in me. According to the logic of occasionalism, knowledge really has no need of the world. Note that this already prefigures the monadological idea: since we see an essence on the occasion of a perception, whether or not the perception is real, *the vision of essences would be possible without the world existing.*

Thus Berkeley found monadological immaterialism in embryo in Malebranche's doctrine, for occasionalism made it possible to deny any *real* causality to objects: what affects my mind is God, not any thing. In this sense access to essences can be conceived without the material world being the source of our apprehension of the true. Cancelling out the causality of the thing as a source of representations, and replacing the notion of causality with that of occasion, Malebranche committed himself to such an extreme version of immaterialism that (as has often been noted) the material world for him becomes a mere object of belief:[11] while the existence of world is certainly a fact, it is a fact so seemingly inexplicable by reason[12] that only revelation—rather than philosophy—can convince us of it. The move to deny the existence of the thing-in-itself as *cause* of representation is what Berkeley borrowed from occasionalism: for him there was certainly no question of adopting the whole of a philosophy that remained rooted in a realism of essences, but Malebranche's annulling of the thing-in-itself as a cause operating on the mind appeared to Berkeley to realize more fully the spirit of Cartesianism and of modern philosophy (that is to say, the idealist reduction of being to representation) than either the letter of Descartes's own theory of representation or, *a fortiori*, Locke's realist empiricism. Such a negation of the thing-in-itself within an empiricist or sensualist framework gave Berkeley's thinking its own distinctive formula, what might be called *empiricist idealism* or, if you will, *Locke + Malebranche (in a Cartesian key)*—a formula whose impact upon the philosophical genesis of modern individualism has been considerable: by canceling out the causality of the thing-in-itself, Berkeley's empiricism shows itself to have been constructed in the spirit of a monadology.

For if ideas/perceptions cannot be thought of as caused in the mind by its encounter with things, the theory of representation must be elaborated by supplying it with minds that *in this sense*—with regard to things—are, so to speak, as windowless as Leibniz's monads. Berkeley did indeed follow the Malebranchean lead in outfitting representation with a new logic such that it could be conceived not in terms of a relation between things and minds, but (as I will insist) in terms of a relation between the mind of God and the mind of man—*between minds*. And so the structure on which all monadologies depend is set up in all its purity, affirming two propositions:

- That there is no intrinsic difference between ideas and perception: thus the Lockean contribution—short-circuiting a realist interpretation of essences, which the mind knows instead through ideas that are supposed to be cut off from the sensible world.
- That there is no difference between idea/perception and the thing perceived: thus the Malebranchean contribution—according to which the thing perceived cannot be the cause of ideas since a material body cannot act on the mind, with the result that being is now effectively reduced to representation.

In short, the truth of Cartesianism for Berkeley is this: only minds and their representations exist—or, even better: only monadological minds closed in upon their representations exist.

We thus see in what sense and in accordance with what logic Berkeley's empiricism belongs to the age of monadologies, this essential moment in the modern history of subjectivity. It yet remains to examine how Berkeley, under such circumstances, tackled the central problem of all the monadologies—the problem of the world—and the solution he proposed. And so we now turn to these questions, to determine the originality of Berkeley's contribution to the monadological problem and the influence of his role in the individualistic dissolution of subjectivity.

Berkeley and the Rescue of the Subject

Having reached the logical conclusion of this first movement in his thinking, which reduced being to representation, Berkeley found himself faced (as it has often been remarked) with the need to score a second movement that would offset any excesses contained in the first.

We must be clear here: arriving at the end of this series of corrective actions, which mobilize several of the chief modern theories of knowledge against each other, it must be admitted (if we are to insist on being rigorous) that the thesis according to which there exist only minds and their representations carries with it the danger that the true endpoint of the process—that at bottom, and *in principle*, there are only representations—will be obscured. We must see that, in Berkeley's system, it becomes extremely difficult (if not impossible) to conceive—alongside representations and what underlies them—of the existence of minds as subjects of these representations. *Esse est percipi vel percipere*: thus being is reduced to representations and the minds that represent them. To be fully grounded, this formula must assume that behind the representations it is possible to isolate the being of a representing subject that is not reducible to its representations. The logic of the argument makes this appear singularly difficult since, *at least in the case of the thinking being*, it is necessary once again to distinguish between the being *and* its representations. Thus the movement whose coherence we have been trying to restore goes very far indeed, perhaps too far: not simply as far as the formula *esse est percipi vel percipere* but, ultimately, to the *esse est percipi* to which posterity has often reduced it—no doubt unfairly, on a literal reading of the theory; but perhaps logically enough, if we consider the real impact of the empiricist monadology.

Threatened with an inability—*on its own principles*—to distinguish between the subject and its representations, this version of the monadology has no alternative but to dissolve both the idea of objectivity (the idea of an external world) and that of subjectivity: the modern notion of the subject (conceived as the foundation of its representations, irreducible to their mere succession) would thus tend to disappear in favor of the reduction of the mind (or the subject) to a mere *name* for designating aggregates of representations—a stunning confirmation, if one were still needed, that in the history of the subject the monadological structure should be connected much more with the dissolution than with the strengthening of the notion of subjectivity.

We know that Hume accepted and insisted on the dissolution of the Self as such: his radicalization of Berkeley's breakthrough in this regard will be discussed at the end of this chapter. The chief interest of Berkeley's achievement for the history of subjectivity lies in the effort to resist the logic of dissolving the subject, and to preserve a meaning and consistency for the notion of a thinking subject distinct from its representations. Berkeley tries to rescue the subject for religous reasons, as commentators have often stressed, but these are secondary by comparison with what is really at stake here—namely, that if the mind reduces to the ever-changing flux of its representations, the notion of the soul's immortality (to which Bishop Berkeley, if I may say so, was professionally attached) risks losing all foundation. While these reasons are documented only anecdotally for the most part, they have nonetheless exerted a rather felicitous philosophical influence—since on this view of the matter Berkeley attempted to distinguish within the realm of representation between a sphere of subjectivity and a sphere of objectivity, or (to put it in deliberately naive terms) between "something" seeming to refer to a Self and representations seeming to refer to a Non-Self—that is, a world.

This attempt—whose angle of approach to what I call the monadological problem (or the problem of the world) is easily gauged—must be precisely characterized: it cannot mean that after having reduced being to representation, Berkeley then thought of reintroducing a subject-in-itself and a world-in-itself. His quite different (and far more interesting) idea was to *salvage two phenomena*; to provide a foundation for two impressions that, justifiably, he took to be *facts*, the possibility and imaginability of which he attempted to demonstrate:

- On the one hand, even though everything is representation, we perceive ourselves as distinct from our representations, according to what may be called an "effect of subjectivity." Religion, of course, has an interest in the making of such a distinction, but this is merely grafted onto an irrefutable (and so to speak, phenomenological) experience—namely, that we do not feel ourselves to be reducible to the succession of our representations. This fact is what distinguishes the state of consciousness in which we perceive ourselves as *having* representations (and hence as not being reduced to them) from, for example, those states of daydreaming or of insomnia in which we dissolve into the succession of our images (in which we *are* our representations, but in which it is precisely consciousness—the person, and the subject as such—that tends to disappear).[13] In other words (those of Berkeley himself), the idea is the object of thought: "the house itself, the church itself is an Idea, that is to say an object, an immediate object, of thought," while the "thought itself, or Thinking is no Idea tis an act i.e. Volition i.e. as contradistinguish'd to effects, the Will."[14] The first phenomenon needing to be salvaged, as a consequence of subjectivity, is expressed by the question: how can we perceive ourselves as distinct from our representations if everything is representation?
- On the other hand, however—and this is really the same phenomenon, differently expressed—, we perceive our representations as implying a dimension of exteriority or objectivity. This "effect of objectivity" must also be taken into account, according to which we perceive ourselves as distinct from the representations implying such an "effect." For if everything is representation, this effect of exteriority through which we see a *world* appear must be able to be given a foundation *within the representation itself.*

Accordingly the challenges to empiricist idealism stemming from these two phenomena forced Berkeley to confront the decisive problem facing all monadologies: if it is claimed that reality does not exist outside representation, *how can we distinguish between the subjective and the objective within subjectivity*? This problem has, of course, received considerable attention in critical philosophy and in Husserlian phenomenology, since these traditions are concerned with thinking of *transcendence* (in relation to the subject) *within the framework of immanence*—the framework adopted by philosophies of subjectivity once they noticed in Berkeley the insuperable aporias of realism.[15]

All the ingredients of the monadological problem are therefore to be found here combined. Not only is it a matter of grounding the distinction between subject and object (between the Self and the world) but also, along with the rescue of the subject, of providing a foundation for the idea of *a* world, of an objectivity that is truly *one* and that can be valid not just for me, but for everyone: if we can distinguish between the subjective and the objective *in representation*, the objective element of my representation will correspond to what in my representation is not reduced to the fact that it is *my* representation, to what can also be shared by other subjects—and thus constitute an objectivity for them by supplying a sense of intersubjectivity. Once more one perceives how indissolubly linked the destinies of subjectivity and intersubjectivity are: *to save subjectivity from its dissolution in the interplay of representations is also to save objectivity, by enabling the individual to get outside of himself, to escape his monadic individuality and thereby gain access to representations shareable by the multiplicity of subjectivities.*

Berkeley and Fichte: Two Solutions to the Monadological Problem

To conduct an exhaustive examination of how Berkeley went about this double rescue mission would entail the analysis of a series of solutions found not only in the *Principles* or *Dialogues*, but also in some paragraphs of the *Siris* in which he returned, more than thirty years after the main texts on immaterialism appeared, to the problem of knowledge.[16] It would then be necessary to study Berkeley's philosophy for its own sake, following its winding course from the earliest to the final works, which is clearly not what I propose to do here.[17] I shall limit myself instead to indicating Berkeley's mature thinking on the subject (notably in §27–33 of the *Principles*) and to comparing its significance with a wholly different kind of solution that would call into question the principles of monadological individualism.

The problem is to explain why things seem to be external to the subject and thus to establish a distinction between subjectivity and objectivity. This calls for understanding how the object of the representation is both *internal to the mind* (since there is nothing external to the representation) and yet, in a sense, *external to it* (since it is opposed to the subject as its object). To ground this exteriority in the interiority of the mind (transcendence in immanence), Berkeley defines the mind as a *simple* being, capable of *perceptions*, intrinsically *active*, and whose essence is the *will* (here, we may note in passing, all the features of the Leibnizian monad are to be found, notably the reference to the internal activity that produces representations).[18] How could it be otherwise, given that the logic of idealism implied a rupture with any theory of the mind as the passive receptacle of impressions emanating from an in-itself? On the basis of a definition such as this—of the mind as activity—any attempt to ground an exteriority corresponding to the emergence of a world must exploit the notion of a *limitation* upon this activity.

It is easy to grasp the principle behind Berkeley's solution: the representation of an exteriority and the effect of objectivity will express the consciousness that the mind forges of a limitation on its activity. In other words (to cite a formula that was later adopted by German idealism), the passivity of the representation (which accompanies the appearance of a world) in fact signals a limitation intervening in the mind's activity. To unpack the meaning of such a formula, it is legitimate to ask how the limitation of a mind defined as activity or will is to be understood. For it could well be that the difficulty has merely been shifted: if it is held that the mind contains an involuntary dimension, we would apparently have to suppose an external cause—which would land us back in a realism incompatible with the whole enterprise.

This problem was to be discussed in great detail by representatives of German idealism, notably Maimon,[19] who advanced the hypothesis that the mind becomes passive: what we perceive as passivity would in reality (note, by the way, that the structure of this solution is taken directly from Leibniz) be merely the summation of small activities. Berkeley's solution is different and *indicative of the most profound difficulty of monadologies: once reality is thought of monadically, how can the mind be imagined to step outside of itself, as the constitution of a world demands*? The reasoning in the *Principles* is as follows: if the mind, which is active, has representations imposed upon it, this is because there exists a cause external to these representations; but this cause, as we have seen, cannot possibly be matter, since no material thing (a Not-Self) is capable of producing representations (a faculty of the Self); but it therefore remains true that the cause of ideas is "an incorporeal active substance or Spirit"—more precisely, in this case, another mind (or, if you prefer, another Self).[20]

It is thus of the highest importance that the principle of the solution thus adopted is to *think of the emergence of the world as the limit of two wills, of two activities, based on the relation between two minds*. First of all, that Berkeley's empiricism belongs to the age of monadologies can now be clearly seen: his solution is nothing other than an application of the idea, central to monadologies, that there exist only minds and relations between minds. In Berkeley as in Leibniz, all the reality involved in imagining how a world can be perceived is based on these relations between minds. The explicit adoption of such a solution is due above all, however, to the fact that Berkeley (again, like Leibniz) found himself facing a choice between *two possible treatments of a single idea, according to which the perception of a world is only the limit of two wills*: one would have allowed the monadological perspective to escape the logic that triggered the individualistic drift of modern humanism, while the other (which Berkeley adopted, following Leibniz) was on the contrary bound up in that logic and caused it to develop.

The first treatment led to Fichte, and consisted of conceiving that limitation of the will by another will as a *horizontal and reciprocal limitation of wills*. The solution of the monadological problem would then have taken the form of a *theory of intersubjectivity as a condition of subjectivity*: it is owing to the fact that subjects (minds, consciousnesses) mutually recognize each other as such, and reciprocally limit their spheres of activity, that the consciousness of a world and the consciousness of self emerge for each one, based on the consciousness of others as a limit of its own activity—and hence the consciousness of a distinction (resolving the monadological problem) between the subject and what is not the subject. This is the path Fichte took in his *Über den Begriff der Wissenschaftslehre* (Principles of the Doctrine of Science, 1794) and in Sections I and II of his *Grundlage des Naturrechts* (Foundation of Natural Right, 1796).[21]

As we have already noted, Fichte welcomed Leibniz's statement of the monadological problem ("How do the thoughts of monads harmonize with each other?") as a good formulation of the question of objectivity, which a philosophy freed of the illusions of realism must answer *on the basis of the Self*.[22] He even regarded the Leibnizian solution—the appeal to preestablished harmony, by virtue of which separate minds can represent the same world to themselves—as satisfactory in a formal sense; what was wanting, in his view, was a more thoughtful working out of the implications of the doctrine of preestablished harmony and of the monadology. The "ordinary Leibnizians" retained just as much of the doctrine of preestablished harmony as permitted them to speak of a harmony among intelligences and matter (as well they could in that case, since harmony is what made it possible to understand why there should exist a correspondence between the states of the body and those of the soul), without, however, really understanding the motivation of the argument—namely, that since for Leibniz there are only minds (or intelligences), resolving the problem of the world (i.e., providing a foundation for agreement among monads) required "a harmony between minds and other minds."[23] Recalling that the Leibnizian solution thus involved a harmonization among minds, Fichte brought the monadological problem back to the point where Berkeley attempted to solve it—by reference to the doctrine of limitation between minds. But does this mean that Fichte's thinking, like Berkeley's, simply worked itself out within the context of monadology, without altering it?[24]

In fairness it must be said, even if Fichte was right to tax the "ordinary Leibnizians" for not understanding the true significance of the doctrine of preestablished harmony, such superior insight as he possessed was likely to be found only in a Leibnizian who was, if not "out of the ordinary," then at least highly unusual. For just after pronouncing preestablished harmony—understood as a harmony between minds—a "good hypothesis," Fichte states that it is part of the foundation of the *Wissenschaftslehre* itself; and that, since freedom is affirmed in it, it is not a question only of monads. In short, in order to be a truly fruitful hypothesis, the idea of harmony together with the monadological idea itself must be revised so that the harmonization of minds is no longer understood as itself a *monad* in the strict sense. The Fichtean correction, which amounts to a program for the practical transposition of the monadology (i.e., a program of *practical monadology*, devoted to the harmonization of *freedoms*), is very profound—so profound, in fact, that in many respects it bursts the monadological idea itself to bits.[25]

How did Fichte, working from the notion (*common to him and Berkeley*) of a limitation by and among minds as a solution to the monadological problem, arrive at the idea of a reciprocal limitation by and among freedoms of their respective spheres of activity? The question amounts to asking why Berkeley seems never to have fully envisioned this solution, despite eventually coming round to it. The question is, of course, difficult to settle in a categorical way. Still it does not seem far-fetched to see in it one consequence of the potentially individualist tribute to be paid to the monadological thesis, at least in its "ordinary" version. If we begin, as Leibniz and Berkeley did, with the idea that there exist only monads—minds closed in on themselves, whose essence consists in their *independence* from all the others—it is hard to see why or how the individual mind would somehow have to first get outside itself, as it were, and then recognize others, in order to be what it is. In other words, the Fichtean solution to the monadological problem (constructing a practical monadology by harmonizing spheres of freedom) presupposes a moment of *reciprocal recognition*, which in turn requires that the mind, to posit itself as such, must open itself to an exteriority, recognize others in it, and in so doing, conceive the necessity of their reciprocal limitation, thus grounding (in the content of the agreement about limits) a space of intersubjectivity. In short, the problem of recognition—which Fichte formulates in monadological terms: "How can my monad succeed in representing another monad?"[26]—*already assumes that a subject in the presence of another is not a monad.*

Berkeley never actually formulated this problem any more than Leibniz did—and for good reason: to formulate it, he would already have had to violate the monadological thesis (in its strict construction) by conceiving the monad as being only *illusorily* able to think of itself as a totality closed in on itself. This is exactly the monadic illusion: the illusion of solitude in the absolute independence of a self that posits a pure identity with itself ("I = I"), needing only itself in order to exist—in other words, the illusion of the Self-substance, adopted by Fichte in 1794 as the starting point and first principle of the *Science of Knowledge*. Fichte's whole way of proceeding, according to one established and well-known interpretation,[27] was to deconstruct this metaphysical illusion (the same one that defines the paralogisms of rational psychology) to make the point that there can be no consciousness of the Self without positing a world and an opening to this world, within which the problem of the recognition of others can then be posed. We thus see to what extent the practical transposition of the principle underlying the solution (now seen as a reciprocal limitation of freedoms, recognizing each other as such) that Berkeley had at his disposal required an abandonment of the *monadical* conception of subjectivity—and, hence, *a criticism of monadological individualism*.

When, in Fichte, the monadology becomes *practical* (in the twofold sense that harmonization—the assumption of which resolves the monadological problem—is henceforth conceived as a reciprocal limitation of *freedoms*, and that this reciprocal limitation, which has law as its locus, is then conceived in terms of a *system of law*), the monadology is thus enabled to escape the monadological framework. For the solution to the monadological problem to be given the form of a theory of intersubjectivity as a reciprocal limitation of freedoms, and for the solution to be found in a *philosophy of law*,[28] it was already necessary to have separated, as it were, the notion of the monad from the monadical illusion, to have freed oneself from the monad's spell—that is to say, from the spell of the *individual* as well: hence the full importance of Fichte's attempt to establish that "man ... becomes man only among men," that "if in general there must be men, there must be many of them," that "the concept of man is thus in no way the concept of an individual, for that is something unthinkable, but it is the concept of a species,"[29] and that "the concept of individuality is ... a *reciprocal concept*, that is, a concept that can be thought of only in relation to another thought."[30]

In contrast, as long as—as in Berkeley—the monadological thesis keeps its old form, the individualism implied by the thesis prevents the problem of intersubjectivity from being posed and, by excluding any solution based on the reciprocal limitation of freedoms, blocks the way to establishing a distinction between subjectivity and objectivity—thus inevitably imperiling both the notion of subjectivity and that of objectivity, neither of which makes sense in the absence of such a distinction.

Did there remain a way for Berkeley to ground this distinction and thus to resolve the monadological problem? He did in fact attempt another treatment of the same idea (in §30–33 of the *Principles*), according to which objectivity proceeds from a limitation of my will by a will external to mine: not, as with Fichte, a practical-juridical treatment, but a *theological* one. In a few words—for this well-known way out has often been described and discussed: *representation (with its resulting distinction between subject and object) was to be thought of as the limit between the will of man and that of God.* Thus sensory ideas, "more strong, lively, and distinct than those of the Imagination," do not appear "at random, as those which are the effects of human wills often are"; on the contrary they are produced "in a regular train or series—the admirable connexion whereof sufficiently testifies the wisdom and benevolence of its Author." And so it is only for want of reflection that, "having observed that when we perceive by sight a certain round luminous figure, we at the same time perceive by touch the idea or sensation called *heat*, we from thence conclude the sun to be the *cause* of heat." Berkeley judged it a naive realism which does not understand that sensory ideas, "more strong, orderly, and coherent than the creatures of the mind," depend less than the latter "on the spirit or thinking substance which perceives them" and are in fact "excited by the will of another and more powerful Spirit." What we call "real things" are therefore seen to be "ideas imprinted on the Senses by the Author of nature." Like Leibniz, then, Berkeley had recourse to a theological foundation for objectivity, on which account he mobilized a theory of preestablished harmony—a notion that his *Siris* explores further with reference to a theory of perception as that which constitutes the language of God in us: since every mind is activity, there exist in the mind of God ideas that are wills. These ideas/wills have meaning in us through our representations, which for this reason appear to bear a connotation, vis-à-vis our will, of exteriority.[31] We can now see how the question of objectivity was thereby solved: if a representation is merely the effect of my will, it is irreducibly subjective—or what Berkeley called a simple "creature of the mind"; on the other hand, if a representation is the way in which a divine will is signified in me, it is not the product of my will—and thus has a dimension of passivity, to which there corresponds an effect of objectivity.

I shall not examine this theological solution to the monadological problem further. In a sense this solution fits nicely with the monadological framework, since it resolves the problem only by taking minds as the sole reality and assuming the conjunction of two activities, that of the human Self and that of the divine Self, with the latter limiting the former: *at this limit* the world produces an effect upon me, which is simply a set of images that are the result of divine activity. *Within representation*, there can be a world—and we can have a sense of a world—only insofar as the activity of the Self comes into contact with the activity of God—an encounter that explains the impression we have of passivity (as the limit of the two activities): the feeling that there exists a non-Self, the cause of our representations, thus proceeds from the way in which the Self's activity is finitized by an infinite activity, which as such is necessarily limiting. The non-Self is thus asserted to be, *in the self*, the meeting place between the human mind and divine will—with the result that, formally speaking, Malebranche's influence bears the entire weight of the claim; representation can now be said in a quite different sense to have been born of a relation between God and the world, and not as a result of the shock of some thing-in-itself. Having said this, two difficulties in Berkeley's solution that seriously undermine his undertaking need to be noted.

First, if our sense of the world is born of the encounter between human activity and divine activity, it must be that these two activities are in some sense opposed—or in any case *external*—to each other: how is it then that human activity does not limit divine activity to just the same extent that it is limited by it? What would such a limitation of the infinite amount to? For this solution really to make sense, we would have to understand how God could limit Himself through the emergence of a human Self, and how the infinite could finitize itself. These are questions that were to occupy German idealism to a great degree, but which Berkeley left entirely unaddressed.

Second—beyond what could, after all, be regarded as only a mere gap needing to be filled in (and, as such, not therefore interfering with the consistency of the solution proposed)—there appears a rather more formidable difficulty that casts doubt on the coherence of the argument itself: at this level of theological excursus, are we not witnessing the reversion to a frankly causal schema according to which the source of my representations is now the divine *in-itself*? If this is true, why then would the critique of causality borrowed from Malebranche not apply to the *cause* that God's intention appears to constitute? It is hard to see how a divine will that is posited both as a *cause* and as a *reality external to representation* could be deployed in a manner that would be consistent with the other principles that inspire Berkeley's project. No doubt he was aware of the risks entailed by his solution, since the whole of the *Siris* is devoted to an attempt to find a way out of this schema by resort to a linguistic paradigm that would reestablish a causal relation between God and the finite mind. The elliptical remarks one finds in the *Siris* are hard to interpret. They appear to have the effect of making representations less the result of divine intention than signs of God in the sense that they would be imbued with, and governed by, structural laws in a way analogous to the operation of syntactical laws in relation to language. These structural laws would constitute the sign of God in us, by limiting the interplay of representations in something like the way syntax limits the usage of language (representations, like words, being able to be associated only according to certain rules), and so defining the *limit* that is imposed on our will—a limit that generates a whole world.

Even if it is not at all obvious that Berkeley actually succeeded by this expedient in overcoming the causal schema (for how can this syntax of representations not be conceived as having been established by God, and thus as a product of divine intention?), his subtle working out of the outlines of a linguistic paradigm must in no case be underestimated:[32] it testifies, above all, to a keen awareness of the difficulties inherent in the kind of theological solution that Berkeley found himself forced to apply to the problem of monadologies. The very acknowledgement of these difficulties (however we may ultimately judge Berkeley's success in resolving them) is perhaps what most deserves to be noted. The awkwardnesses Berkeley encountered seem emblematic of the way in which, among the different monadologies developed throughout the history of subjectivity, one finds models of the subject that are characterized by a marked tendency to make this getting out of oneself—the inescapable condition of there being any objectivity and intersubjectivity at all—seem inconceivable. Models of the subject of this sort, in both the empiricist monadologies and that of Leibniz, illustrate above all the individualistic decomposition of subjectivity. From this point of view, it is surely significant that the course of empiricism from Berkeley to Hume moves from an indisputable weakening of the idea of the subject to its complete dissolution.

The Humean Decomposition of the Subject

If we wished to imagine what a Heideggerian interpretation of Hume might look like, we could without any great risk of error point to at least two dimensions of Humean thought that seem to lend support to Heidegger's conviction that it too represented an important stage in the reduction of reality to subjectivity. On the one hand, Hume set up the science of human nature as the foundation for all other sciences.[33] Surely Heidegger could have seen in this move the unflagging work of modern humanism, replacing metaphysics with anthropology as the root of the philosophical tree? On the other hand, Hume's empiricism is defined by the complete reduction of reality to the fact of its presence to the human mind. If it is true that "whatever can be conceiv'd by a clear and distinct idea implies the possibility of existence"[34] and that ideas are only copies of impressions, any disparity between being and representation in the mind tends to disappear in favor of the view that "the world is unique in being and in the mind, and it is sensory and particular"[35]—a reduction that arises from the legacy of Berkeley, but which, more generally, it is tempting to see as yet another instance of that swallowing up of reality in the subject that has characterized all philosophy since Descartes.

Nevertheless, the legitimacy of this "Heideggerian" reading of Hume seems dubious at best. It will be enough for us to review the main achievements of Hume's "science of human nature" with regard to the status of the Humean subject. Undoubtedly the most profound shift that Hume introduced in this connection stemmed from the claim that human nature is not an *essence*. As has often been noted, the problem Hume set for himself was in a sense regressive relative to Berkeley: starting from the fact that man has representations, Hume posed the critical question of under what conditions such a fact is possible,[36] but, unlike Berkeley, he did not even think to ask how the Self is distinguished from its representations. For if man were actually to be reduced to his representations, what distinction would there be between man and the changing set of his representations? In that case, what meaning would be left for the notion of the subject? As we have seen, this was the question that prompted Berkeley's analysis. Hume's problem turned out to be a quite different one, which consisted only in asking how man could become an empirical subject constituting a self, a *human nature*—that is, a system governed by laws organizing its representations. This reduces to a simple question of *genesis*: having posited that man has representations, how do instances of representation acquire their nature (in other words, the rules that structure its activity)? Two specific theses help set up this question:

- The mind is reducible to imagination taken in the broad sense (i.e., as a collection of images of things). The mind is originally only "fantasy"—meaning the place where images associated by chance are found in random arrangement.
- Consequently, the mind is thus not a faculty in the Aristotelian (or scholastic) sense of the word: that is, a power actualizing itself. As Gilles Deleuze has stressed,[37] Hume was in no sense a psychologist of mind—someone who regarded the mind as a virtual structure in which concepts would presuppose an understanding, sensation a sensitivity, images an imagination: in short, as many faculties as there are identifiable mental operations. On this view, the mind is identical with the collection of representations present in it.

Accordingly, the problem Hume faced was precisely this: how is human nature (i.e., the empirical subject, that which is capable of having representations organized according to rules) produced in the mind (i.e., "how does the mind become a human nature,"[38] the subject of theoretical and practical activity obeying organized laws)? The genesis of human nature was held by Hume to take place according to certain principles that govern the association of representations by reference to simple criteria (of resemblance, identity, contiguity). These associations engender habits, or customary ways of behaving, such that a particular representation concludes by evoking another one, a certain kind of situation typically arouses a particular feeling, with which it becomes associated. It is this interplay of associations that gradually constructs a structured subject, thus creating the impression that the mind is active, even though originally and throughout the process it is entirely passive and devoid of any spontaneity whatsoever.

This well-known argument, which certainly displays the originality of Hume's inquiry, seems to occupy an intermediate position between the transcendental project and a pure psychological investigation: unlike Kant, Hume never wondered how there could be objects for us, and so how a representation could be produced in the first place; but if, in already assuming representations, he short-circuited the transcendental inquiry, unlike a psychologist of mind he does not assume the fully constituted subject with all its structures and faculties. In Humean terms, reflection begins with the *mind* (i.e., the whole set of representations) and constructs the *understanding* (i.e., a system organized according to the rules to which acts of knowing are subject). In this sense, human nature, since it is constructed, is not an *essence* always and already given, predetermining the development of each of its exemplars: it constitutes the horizon above which something new will rise.

It must be added that on this interpretation human nature, *precisely because it is not an essence*, cannot be intuited by means of some clear and distinct idea of the "self"—on account of which the notion of the destruction of man's "essence" acquires meaning and *bears* consequences for the Humean "subject." Hume's empiricism, internally consistent and following directly from the critique of abstract ideas and the rejection of any appeal to "essences," argues that we can know ourselves only from experience—and this *on the basis of impressions*, as so many ever-various experiences of existence. Thus there can be no question here of an intuition of the self, having the self-transparency of a *cogito*. The best Hume scholars have rightly insisted that empiricism, by asserting that human nature can know itself only on the basis of a primary experience (which, as an infinitely diverse experience of existence, is better characterized by "the absence of self" than by any sign of self-identity), puts "philosophies of the subject to the test"[39]—a severe one at that, so severe that one could celebrate in Hume, with the advent of the conception of a self "limited to a succession of perceptions connected by relations," the birth of the "self without the subject," or an "antisubject of the self."[40]

What becomes of the problem of subjectivity in Hume, then, given that the theory of a foundational subject is rejected in principle? In place of the fiction of such a subject is substituted the only experience man has of himself: not that of a fully constituted Self, but of a succession of impressions. In a philosophy for which impressions form the true, absolute principle—or, if you will, the radical origin of every representation and idea—the only task needing to be carried out in relation to the subject necessarily consists in showing how the idea of a self can be constructed on the basis of impressions. Far from it being the case that the self serves here as a principle or as a foundation (in which case it would be necessary, in keeping with Cartesian precepts, to begin with the I's presence to itself in order to construct the world and rescue its phenomena), the perspective is just reversed: the Self (the feeling of unity or identity to itself that every person experiences) is one of those phenomena that must be explained on the basis of true principles, which is to say the simple impressions from which all our ideas derive. In Hume's thinking the impression thus functions as an *atom*:[41]—a mental atom, I would say, constituting "an independent unity, subsisting in itself and complete";[42] or, if you prefer, a *monad* such that all ideas, including that of the self, bear the same relation to the impression as in the Leibnizian monadology phenomena bear to the monadic principles. If the vocabulary of the monadology seems to have been somewhat encroached upon here, one need only consider, to be convinced of its appositeness, how far the Humean impression displays all the characteristics that go to make up the monad:

- *Simplicity* or *indivisibility*: all ideas refer, directly (in the case of "simple ideas") or indirectly (in the case of "complex ideas"), to impressions that are in the final analysis "simple impressions." An example of the first type is "that impression, which strikes our eyes in sun-shine," which, like all simple impressions, "admit[s] of no distinction nor separation": to the simple impression, the undecomposable and first element of our relation to reality, correspond simple ideas that resemble them. As for complex ideas and impressions, which "may be distinguished into parts," they "are formed" of "simple ideas and impressions" (which is to say, since the idea copies the impression, of simple impressions).[43]
- *Unicity* or *individuality*: "All [our perceptions] are different, and distinguishable and separable from each other, and may be separately consider'd"[44]—to the point that, if we consider the ideas that correspond to them, "it will readily be allow'd, that the several distinct ideas of colours, which enter by the eyes, or those of sounds, which are conveyed by the hearing, are really different from each other, tho' at the same time resembling"; for "if this be true of different colours, it must be no less so of the different shades of the same colour, that each of them produces a distinct idea, independent of the rest."[45]

Like the Leibnizian monads, simple impressions thus obey a true principle of indiscernibles: they are strictly individuated, none being identical with any other.

- *Self-sufficiency* or *independence*: a complementary characteristic that follows logically from the monadicity of impressions: if each distinct idea is "independent of the rest," the simple impressions that they reflect "may exist separately"—better still, they "have no need of any thing to support their existence"[46] (as if they constituted the truth of the notion of substance, understood as monadical self-sufficiency).
- *Unity and closure on itself*: a sign of the independence that is constitutive of monadic individuality—for insofar as it is indivisible the impression is not only unique, it is unitary. Now, being immediate, the unity of the elementary impression is necessarily a unity "without relation," a unity that is not mediated by some relation to "another" or to internal components—in short, "a unity without either internal nor external opening."[47]

I shall not dwell further on Hume's transposition of the monadological model. In his hands it becomes an impressional monadology, in which the monads are impressions[48] and the science of human nature has no more impact at the level of (psychological) experience than does the Leibnizian construction of the world: in both cases, the monad is a being of reason that must be posited through the decomposition of the phenomenon into its elements, for in Hume "the impression does not correspond to anything of which we mentally have experience"[49] any more than Leibniz's "simples" did. Thus the empiricist monadology was in its way also to have a properly *ontological* impact, which is exclusively located (as it must be in an ontology that reduces being to perception) in its capacity for explaining the formation of those "compounds" that are ideas (or complex impressions), as, for example, the idea of the Self. If everything is constructed on the basis of a combination of monads that are simple impressions, the idea of the Self (what we call the subject) is in turn merely a combination of impressions governed by the general rules of association.

The deepest meaning of empiricism within the modern history of subjectivity now appears in all its clarity. Being monadological, the science of human nature makes the atomic or monadic impression the absolute of experience, and thus *the only true modality of the mind's existence*. Here we find the monadological idea in all its purity: *the mind exists only so far as it is fragmented into those monads that are simple impressions*, with all that remains beyond this being mere construction—or, if you will, phenomenon.[50] In other words, to grasp the mind's reality, one must run counter to the pseudo–evidence furnished by self-consciousness: the experience of oneself, as of every universal for Hume, is a fiction. Like causality or purposefulness, the Self is a product of the imagination whose genesis can be reconstructed on the basis of the only real datum, which is the impression as a monadical datum—here taking the place of the *cogito* as the ultimate condition of any experience. If, *like Descartes*, Hume indeed seeks a first experience as the foundation of any certitude, he locates it, *unlike Descartes*, not in the self-evidence of the subject but in the absolute immanence of the impression: that impression is indeed a form of *consciousness* insofar as a content is presented to the mind, but insofar as it is pure immediacy, devoid of self-consciousness, without reflection on itself, it is not a *subject*, a *consciousness of a Self identical to itself beyond its differences*. And it is on the basis of this *consciousness-monad that lacks subjectivity* that a self or a person is constructed, which, Hume insists, "is not any one impression" but merely "that to which our several impressions and ideas are suppos'd to have a reference." More precisely, the Self is not even an idea, since "If any impression gives rise to the idea of self, that impression must continue invariably the same, thro' the whole course of our lives; since self is suppos'd to exist after that manner. But there is no impression constant and invariable . . . and consequently there is no such idea."[51]

So what finally, for Hume, is the Self (or, if you prefer, the subject)? Section VI of the first book of the *Treatise* ("Of personal identity") is entirely devoted to working out an answer to this question: the subject is nothing but a possible product of the imagination, conceived in the context of impressional individuality. The dissolution of the Self in the interplay of monadic impressions is total: *the subject is merely an "effect" of impressional individuality*, emerging among the diversity of impressions and as a result of this diversity—one among many "connexions among distinct existences" that bring forth, though they lack a principle of unity, the form of a Self.[52] If it were to be asked what "gives us so great a propensión to ascribe an identity to these successive perceptions, and to suppose ourselves possest of an invariable and uninterrupted existence thro' the whole course of our lives," the answer would thus have to be sought uniquely in the "perpetual" nature of the "flux" and of the "movement" within which the "different perceptions" in their multiplicity "succeed each other with an inconceivable rapidity."[53] Thus the identity of the Self becomes an "effect" of that uninterruptedness that characterizes the succession of impressional individualities: for one cannot make the subject the fictitious place of an empty unity, a sort of theater of impressions—only a theater reduced to the actors who parade around in it, a theater without a stage, an illusory place that is actually no more than the flux of a passing show.

It will be agreed that this is an extraordinary transposition of the monadological model, providing impressive confirmation of its versatility in opposition to the idea and value of the *subject*. So complete is the transposition, in fact, that we find in the empiricist monadology an *analogon* of the preestablished harmony itself. The function of the hypothesis of preestablished harmony in Leibniz was clear: thanks to this it became possible to imagine, in contrast to the notion of an imposed order, an agreement (or, to use the expression from the *System* of 1695, a "communication") between substances conceived as monadic individualities; that is, a vertical, indirect communication mediated at the level of the divine, free from all intersubjectivity. Empiricism, so far as it is a monadology, must also—inevitably—run up against this problem of agreement or communication between substances. This was already true for Berkeley, in the form of the problem of the "world." The problem returns in Hume, *a fortiori*, given that the only reality of the mind is the atomicity of strictly heterogeneous impressions, devoid of any meta-empirical principle of unity: how is it possible, within the framework of some such idea of pure difference or pure individuality, for potential communication to take place among "subjects"—these streams of impressions that are as little assured of discovering among themselves an identity capable of connecting them with each other as of finding in themselves support for the self-identity of each one?

Here again, as in Leibniz, the process of individualization runs up against a limit beyond which reason finds itself confronted with the idea of pure disorder—of a chaos empty of any rule. What is more, certain points of consensus do manage despite everything to establish themselves between the fictitious places occupied by two "persons," if only for example in the aesthetic realm. It is necessary, therefore, to be able to imagine *communication without subjects* or *true intersubjectivity*—a problem whose logical solution was to be found in the formula of preestablished harmony: thus the stream of our representations expresses a "course of nature" by which different minds, operating on the basis of impressions that are, however, wholly irreducible to one another, still manage to apprehend the world with some measure of convergence—leading Hume to see in this the sign of "a kind of pre-established harmony between the course of nature and the succession of our ideas."[54] About the content of this harmony one must make no mistake: within the framework of empiricisms, it refers less to the divine choice of the world than to the existence in each of us of rules that structure the association of ideas in a similar way and thus serves to reintroduce into a pure philosophy of difference a factor of identity, without which any agreement between beings or other forms of empirically observable consensus would be unthinkable. Accordingly, aggregates of monadical impressions manage to communicate to each other only insofar as they are controlled by common structures, as in Leibniz the monads communicate among themselves only by the mediation of their

Other (that is, their divine author) at the level of the world: in both cases, and beyond what separates the two monadologies, communication is established only *indirectly*, not from subject to subject or from will to will, but by the intervention of an a priori structuring (whether a divine structuring of the universe or a natural structuring of the interplay of impressions) that precedes—and exceeds—any human choice or decision. Hence the possibility of *communication without intersubjectivity* in a world in which subjects have no need to break the circle of immanence in order to constitute themselves as subjects.

Deleuze, who in *Empiricism and Subjectivity* altogether correctly understood this Humean wish to present a subjectivity "determined as an effect"[55] and analyzed how "the subject is decomposed" into impressions,[56] concluded by noting that for empiricism the mind is not a subject but is resolved into "a given collection of impressions and separate ideas" that acquires the fictitious form of a "subject" only through the operation of the principles that govern the association of ideas.[57]

Some twenty years later, Deleuze's *Anti-Oedipus* (1972) described those "desiring-machines" that he imagined as embodying what metaphysics and humanism had thought of as the subject: on the "surface" where the "machine effects" are recorded (what folk psychology calls "actions"), "something on the order of a *subject* can be discerned on the recording surface. It is a strange subject, however, with no fixed identity, wandering about over the body without organs, but always remaining peripheral to the desiring-machines, being defined by the share of the product it takes for itself, garnering here, there, and everywhere a reward in the form of a becoming or an avatar, being born of the states that it consumes and being reborn with each new state. . . .[58] [A] spare part adjacent to the machine. . . .[59] [I]f this subject has no specific or personal identity, if it traverses the body without organs without destroying its indifference, it is because it is not only a part that is peripheral to the machine, but also a part that is itself divided into parts that correspond to the detachments from the chain . . . and the removals from the flow . . . brought about by the machine. Thus this subject consumes and consummates each of the states through which it passes, and is born of each of them anew, continuously emerging from them as a part made up of parts, each one of which completely fills up the body without organs. . . ."[60]

Hume—even Hume as read by Deleuze—is not Deleuze, and we all too easily see what differentiates these two moments in the decomposition of the subject: the "subject" in the *Anti-Oedipus* does not manage to appear to itself (even if this were only a fiction) as a nonsplintered identity, a nonpulverized unity—as if the preestablished harmony in the sense in which Hume understood it (that is, as the regularity introduced by the principles of human nature into the chaos of impression) somehow failed to carry out its function and had, as a result, exploded into pieces. With this ultimate fragmentation of a Self already decomposed by empiricist individualism into an enigmatic fiction, contemporary individualism completes a process that began long before and that first announced itself in the age that rationalist monadology and empiricist monadology had, each in its own way, opened. In order to develop a more complete picture of the logic of philosophical modernity, it remains to determine by what necessity this process became radicalized, to the point of erasing that which in the (diversified) form of the theory of preestablished harmony still limited the operation of individualism.

CHAPTER V

Hegel and Nietzsche: Development of the Monadologies

WHAT JUSTIFICATION is there for associating Hegel and Nietzsche, who in many ways—beginning with their antithetical positions on rationality—are philosophical opposites?[1] We know Heidegger's verdict: united by what separated them, Hegelianism and Nietzscheanism matched up as two indissolubly linked moments of a consummated metaphysics displaying that double absolutization of knowledge and of the will which would bring to an end the modern process of reality's submission to the subject. Or, if you prefer, in proceeding on the basis of that subjectivization of every being which follows from the Leibnizian definition of substance as the unity of representation (*perceptio*) and will (*appetitus*), "What Leibniz had in mind was to be expressed in Kant and Fichte as that reasonable will on which Hegel and Schelling would meditate, each in his own way. It was also what Schopenhauer meant, when he entitled his chief work *The World* (not Man) *as Will and Representation*. And it is also what Nietzsche had in mind, when he perceived and designated the primordial nature of being as will to power."[2]

Heidegger was partly correct: it is surely proper to locate the Hegelian and Nietzschean moments by reference to Leibniz. If, however, the real import of the Leibnizian tradition were to be restored as a philosophical foundation for individualism, the comparison between Hegel and Nietzsche would acquire a new meaning. This chapter is meant to make the consequences of such a move clear by drawing attention to the philosophical vocation that Hegelianism and Nietzscheanism have in common: each aiming in its different way to bring about the monadological development of modern ontology, and thus to provide philosophical support for a cultural movement that went far beyond philosophy and led to the advent of contemporary individualism. In this sense, neither the achievement of Hegel's philosophy in raising the project of modern rationality to its full height in the form of a system, nor Nietzsche's claim that the path of reason was the "history of a long error" and that all systems stood "sad and discouraged,"[3] would necessarily mark a decisive break in modernity. Thus I wish to lay emphasis on the continuities between these two achievements, but on the basis of a hypothesis quite different from the one that enabled Heidegger to see Hegel and Nietzsche as sharing the same destiny: *the Hegelian completion of rationality and the Nietzschean dissolution of reason are both required by the logic of modern individualism considered at two different stages of its development—and also, by the development of democratic societies.*

To support this hypothesis, I shall confine myself to identifying what in Hegel and Nietzsche exhibits this logic of individualism, that is, *what in both cases advances the monadological thesis in the sense of radicalizing its intrinsic individualism.* From this point of view, the Hegelian perfection of the system and the Nietzschean destruction of it prove to have very different but nonetheless complementary functions.

Leibniz, Hegel, Nietzsche

In a magnificent passage of the *Gay Science* (§357) in which he takes stock of the true conquests of German philosophy, Nietzsche salutes "the astonishing stroke of *Hegel*, who struck right through all our logical habits and bad habits when he dared to teach that species concepts develop *out of each other.*" This is the "Hegelian innovation" that introduced the idea of evolution into science ("without Hegel, there could have been no Darwin") and prepared the European mind for approaching the problems of science in terms of genesis and gradual change—in other words, of *history.*[4] Though Nietzsche often took issue with the way in which the Hegelian system made use of history (treating history as "veiled theology" in an attempt to justify all reality as the endpoint of a necessary process), it is nonetheless true that Hegel had revived the notion of gradual change, thus overcoming the "congenital defect of philosophers" since Plato:[5]

> What separates us from Kant, as from Plato and Leibniz, is that we believe only in becoming, even in the case of spiritual matters. We are *historians* from head to toe. This is the great change. Lamarck and Hegel—Darwin is only a substitute. The thought of Heraclitus and Empedocles is resuscitated.[6]

Leaving aside the note of reservation perceptible in this otherwise admiring appraisal of the Hegelian revelation of the "historical sense" (was it to be considered as a preparation for Darwin or a return to Heraclitus?), it needs to be emphasized that Nietzsche credited Hegel with decisive progress compared to the two other great figures for whom, in the same passage of the *Gay Science*, he reserves the epithet "German philosophers": Leibniz and Kant. If Kant's virtue (of having put a "tremendous question mark" in front of the concept of "causality") is only fleetingly mentioned (and this in connection with Hume's prior recognition of the problem), Leibniz's contribution meets with singularly labored praise for "the incomparable insight that has been vindicated not only against Descartes but against everybody who had philosophized before him—that consciousness is merely an *accidens* of experience, and *not* its necessary and essential attribute; that, in other words, what we call consciousness constitutes only one state of our spiritual and psychic world (perhaps a pathological state) and *not by any means the whole of it.*" In short, "[o]ur inner world is much richer, more comprehensive, more concealed" than that which is expressed by consciousness.[7] There is a stunning shrewdness in this: combining views he attributes to Leibniz with opinions that are strictly his own, Nietzsche put his finger on one of the most profound significances—which we have already noted in passing—of the monadology. By making apperception (perception endowed with consciousness) a simple modality of perception in general, by showing how representation is constructed on the basis of unconscious perceptions (the "little perceptions"), Leibniz effectively undermined one of the chief characteristics of the modern subject: transparency to oneself, or self-reflection. Nietzsche thus appealed altogether logically to the authority of this aspect of the monadological mechanism in order to call it an important—for him, a founding—stage in that great rupture with the values of consciousness and of the subject to which he himself meant to contribute. We find, therefore, in Nietzsche's own writings, crucial evidence in support of our hypothesis that Nietzsche succeeded in demonstrating what Leibniz had been the first to bring out—a point to which we shall return in the last part of this chapter.

For the time being, let us confine our attention to the other main implication of the *Gay Science*: namely that, despite his contribution to the dissolution of the metaphysics of the subject, Leibniz remained the captive of a still Platonistic metaphysics to the extent that he ignored the claims of that historicity which was not to receive its full due until Hegel. In fact, it is only by building in the Hegelian opening to history that the true antimetaphysical import of the Leibnizian anticipation can be appreciated to its full extent: as the road leading to *Hegelianism as historicization of the monadology*.

This, it must be admitted, would be an interesting road to follow—not least for its ability to throw light on the logic of a whole sequence of modern philosophical problems; but one which, to be profitably traveled, needs to be better marked with regard to the relation between the monadological idea and its historical development. It is not clear that Nietzsche understood this relation as fully as he believed, nor that he saw that it was the monadology itself that called for its historicized revival.

The Historicization of the Monadology

In a certain sense, as I have already suggested, the Leibnizian monadology gave the philosophies of history that followed their intellectual structure: if the monadological problem lies in the sudden emergence of order in the world based on the interaction of perceptive and appetitive series that are independent of each other (i.e., that are monadic), we can easily see how the solution to this problem can be transposed to the level of history in order to conceive of a rationality immanent in a process composed of individual initiatives and undertakings that are apparently unconnected—more precisely, *the historicization of the monadological model will be more easily accomplished to the extent that the theoretical infrastructure of the very project of a philosophy of history is at bottom wholly Leibnizian.*

It is a commonplace to note the relatively late birth of authentic philosophies of history. While it is generally agreed that there are no real examples before modern times, agreement is less universal when it comes to pinpointing the actual birthplace of philosophies of history in modern times. Thus Max Horkheimer judged initially that Machiavelli was "the first modern philosopher of history," but later changed his mind, saying Vico's *Scienza nuova* (The New Science, 1725) made him "the first real philosopher of history in the modern age."[8] His hesitation is significant in itself: no doubt it was not enough simply for a place to be made in philosophical discourse for reflection upon history, so that one could speak of a "true philosophy of history." What constitutes "the essence of all true philosophies of history," as Horkheimer put it, lies in the conviction that "behind the actual chaos of life and death" can be recognized "a hidden, beneficent intention" within which "every single, seemingly incomprehensible fact must have determinate, situated value."[9] It is, of course, by virtue of its construction of "hidden meaning" that the work of Vico (contemporary with the Leibnizian monadology) appears to be the birthplace of philosophy of history: "His intention in his major work is to show that providence is the guiding force in human history and that it realizes its goals through the actions of human beings, without their being or needing to be aware that this is the case."[10]

I do not propose to test this judgment about the foundational nature of the *Scienza nuova*, however reasonable it may be and however many interpreters may share it.[11] It is more important to ask why this application of reason to history occurred so late. Horkheimer and Cassirer—in other respects so dissimilar—were agreed in this regard, holding that the rationalization of history presupposed both Descartes and a break with Descartes:

- The project of discovering relations and laws in history is indeed part of the Cartesian legacy—the challenge to reality issued by a subject bent on establishing himself as its master and possessor: in this sense, there is no true philosophy of history without the modern emergence of subjectivity.
- Yet, although the idea of a philosophy of history requires the "Cartesian" advent of the subject, there is not the slightest hint in Descartes of a philosophy of history. The emergence of the subject is thus only a necessary, but not a sufficient, condition for the philosophy of history—as though, in Descartes, something prevented it from being conceived and carried out. Horkheimer saw this clearly. Having situated the birth of the philosophy of history with reference to Descartes, he came to realize—like Vico himself—that for the birth certificate to be notarized, as it were, it was necessary to launch a "polemic against Cartesian philosophy":[12] the very project of a philosophy of history, based on the idea of rationalizing the phenomenal, depended on it being accepted that mathematical discourse—at least in its Cartesian (i.e., geometrical) form—was not the only possible model of rationality. This observation is no doubt correct,[13] but it does not bear on the main point, namely that ontology underwent a profound change from Descartes to Leibniz, with profound repercussions for the birth of a philosophical problematization of history.

As Cassirer suggests,[14] the critical presupposition that would make a philosophy of history possible was indeed the Leibnizian conception of substance as monad. So long as it was conceived as a static substrate, substance constituted merely the indifferent ground of its accidents—which, appearing as ontologically contingent and therefore impossible to *deduce* from substance, could only be empirically *noted* or *observed*. On the other hand, conceived dynamically, the Leibnizian substance as monad (whose essence is force) is capable of generating diversity by itself, and it is through this self-diversification with respect to phenomena that it manifests its true nature. Given such a modification of the notion of substance, it became clear that philosophy could successfully pursue its ontological program only by insisting on this manufacture of identity from diversity that fundamentally defines the monad; in other words, by reinterpreting the self-identity of substance not as a function of its underlying nature as a substrate, but as the continual production of a diversity that was completely prefigured in the defining determination of the monad—in short, as *history*. It is in this sense, as ontology—more precisely, as a monadological reinterpretation of ontology—that philosophy necessarily includes as part of its own definition the search for a logic of history: philosophy becomes, intrinsically, philosophy of history.

Thus the monadology was all the more easily able to be historicized by Leibniz's successors, for it was with Leibniz that *historicity* became constitutive of *substantiality*. In formal terms, historicization could be grafted quite naturally onto the final passages of the *Monadology* (starting with §84), where the problem of the moral world is addressed. "Reasonable souls" had earlier been defined (§82–83) as those very particular monads that, in addition to constituting a perspective on the world as other monads do, have the special property of reflecting not only the world but also God as the cause of the world: for thanks to the rational principles with which they are endowed, by virtue of which they are themselves intelligences, they trace their own history back to the final cause of everything that exists. But if these monads express God, it follows that they imitate Him. This imitation of God, who makes man "a little divinity in his own domain," is described as taking two forms:

- On the one hand, what is God-like in the finite monad-as-reasonable–soul is the ability to create coherent systems of representations analogous to the systematicity that God created by bringing the world into existence in conformity with the principle of the best.
- On the other hand, however, certain monads manage to imitate God more perfectly than others by giving birth to a higher universe, the moral universe: that "society of all the minds that must make up the *City of God*, that is, the most perfect state that is possible under the most perfect of monarchs" (§85).

Displaying an ambiguity too rarely noted by interpreters,[15] the final paragraphs of the *Monadology* leave open the question of knowing exactly what to think of this moral universe. In fact, the text itself does not decide between two possibilities:

- This moral universe certainly can be interpreted, as the reference to God as "the Monarch of the divine City of Minds" (§87) suggests, as designating the other world, the beyond of the Christian religion. From this viewpoint, reflection on the moral sphere would border on a *philosophy of religion*.
- Owing to the principle of continuity, however, this moral universe can also be considered as not being radically separated from the real universe, as designating only the community of superior minds that have been elevated to a correct representation of God. Otherwise how are we to understand the suggestion (found in §86) according to which the City of God—"the society of all minds"—is "a moral world *in the natural world*" [emphasis added]. According to this alternative perspective, the horizon of ethical reflection would be

> that of a *philosophy of history*, seeing the natural world as progressing toward an ever more moral condition, in which all the seeds of perfection posited by the principle of the best finally sprout.

Perfectly consistent with this way of looking at things is Leibniz's conclusion to his short treatise *On the Ultimate Origin of Things* (1697):

> . . . there is a perpetual and a most free progress of the whole universe in fulfilment of the universal beauty and perfection of the works of God, so that it is always advancing towards a greater development. . . . To the objection that may perhaps be offered that if this were so the world would long ago have become a paradise, the answer is at hand: although many substances have already come to great perfection, yet owing to the infinite divisibility of what is continuous, there always remain in the abyss of things parts that are asleep, and these need to be awakened and to be driven forward into something greater and better—in a word, to a better development. Hence this progress does not ever come to an end.[16]

In this passage,[17] Leibniz can be seen to prefigure the profound shift that in the eighteenth century was to coincide with the birth of historical consciousness, and that is part and parcel of the logic of a system for which the principle of continuity already excluded the notion of an absolute separation between the natural and the moral worlds: the idea of progress, as an inevitable march toward perfection, was not only to acquire the meaning of passing over from this world—this "vale of tears"—to another world, but also to make its true mark within the framework of a philosophy of history. In this sense, it is not at all surprising that after Vico it was with Herder, a thinker of Leibnizian descent, that the problem of history was to truly emerge in philosophy.

Herder's Historical Monadology

It is important to avoid one error in particular in evaluating Herder's work. *Auch Eine Philosophie der Geschichte* (Another Philosophy of History, 1774) presented itself in many respects as an attack on the *philosophes* and their conception of progress.[18] It is tempting, therefore, to interpret Herder's thinking in the light of its later influence and to see in it primarily an important link in the emergence of romanticism.[19] Such a perspective surely is in keeping with the logic of the cultural history of the time when Herder was writing his philosophies of history, marked as it was by the transition from the Enlightenment to romanticism. From Isaiah Berlin,[20] however, we know how under-informed and incorrect this reading is: Herder is to be seen less as recanting his prior allegiance to the cosmopolitanism of the *philosophes*, subsequently disavowed in favor of a preromantic nationalism, than as the resolute defender of a national outlook that for him was by no means incompatible with a certain universalism he never actually abandoned. This fidelity to the "Christian humanism of the German *Aufklärung*" together with the conviction that "Patriotism was one thing, nationalism another," is clearly expressed by Berlin: "All large wars are essentially civil wars, since men are brothers, and wars are a form of abominable fratricide."[21] In short, to appreciate fully the significance of Herder's idea of nationhood we must try to understand how this unrenounced universalism yet managed to take cultural differences into account in forming a complex theory which, by modifying the tradition of the *philosophes* without radically breaking with it, enriched the heritage of the Enlightenment with a new dimension more than it squandered it.

It is not my intention here to reconstruct this feat in detail. But it seems possible at least to indicate its main outlines by showing how Herder found the guiding principle for his thinking in the Leibnizian monadology. For it was indeed Leibniz, often quoted by Herder, who supplied him with his most important theoretical categories:[22] the notion of a monad made it possible to conceive of a totality as closed on itself, completely individuated and thus original, but still as a mirror of the universe, expressing the world in its way, and capable of being analyzed in terms of identity. More precisely, the Leibnizian conception of substance as monadic individuality—transposed now to the level of nations as historical individualities—appeared to Herder to supply the means for fully legitimating the idea of national originality without giving up the cosmopolitan dream of intercultural communication. For if each culture is a monad, it contains within it the principles of its own development (one of the reasons, by the way, that a culture should be evaluated on the basis of its own principles rather than by reference to ideals it does not recognize); thus, for example, influences that—far from stimulating the internal dynamics of a nation—attempt to subject it to a foreign model, are to be judged detrimental to its interests as a culture. It is therefore the monadological model that gives the notion of national community, anchored in cultural originality and independence, its conceptual foundation. But because, for Leibniz, the monadological model is inseparable from a moment of theodicy, it also provides for communication (albeit indirect, via preestablished harmony) between monads, and thus, in the case of a historical monadology, between peoples and cultures—in the absence of which the unity of a history made up of individualities would be unthinkable. Being a monad, each culture is necessary for the cohesion of the whole (and thus for humanity), as well as for the perfection that it progressively displays—a perfect analogy for that universal order which, for Leibniz, grows out of the interaction of monads that are independent of each other but linked at the same time by a harmony that establishes for each of them in advance the function it is to fulfill in aspiring to the condition of maximum perfection.

In this sense Herder was surely the first to understand the full significance of the monadology for the construction of a philosophy of history.[23] It is true that in the *Abhandlung über den Ursprung der Sprache* (Treatise upon the Origin of Language, 1772) he seemed to reject the notion altogether: Nature created man so little like isolated stones, so little like egoistic monads, he remarked, that it provided him with an opening to other creatures through sensibility. But this passage is apt to be misread, since there can be no doubt of the close relation between Herder's *Volk* and the Leibnizian monad:[24] it sought only to denounce an understanding of the monad that, departing from Leibniz's intended meaning, would prohibit any intermonadic (even direct) communication and strip the monadology of both theodicy and preestablished harmony. In fact (as Herder recalls explicitly in describing the essence of what he found useful in Leibniz for his own undertaking), the thesis of monadicity does not mean that there is no relation between substances, but rather that "the relations between monadic units are already embedded in their being." For, were this not the case, "God himself could not introduce relations among them" and "each monad would be a world unto itself, none having any communication with any other one."[25] Thus interpreted, the kinship between Herder's *Volk* and the Leibnizian monad is once again plainly seen, and the monadological idea regains all its relevance for a philosophy that wishes, as it would come to do with Hegel, to discover the pattern of rationality in history: "The present is pregnant with the future and is filled with the past: *συμπνοία πάντα*. Everything belongs to a system, and God reads in the tiniest of substances the whole series of things that form the universe."[26] That Herder's historical monadology played an important mediating role between Leibniz and Hegel can hardly be doubted.[27]

The Hegelian Moment:
The Completion of Modern Individualism

It may appear paradoxical to see in Hegel the culmination of this process of individualization that lies at the heart of the modern history of subjectivity. Does not the very idea of a "system"—elevated by Hegelianism to its highest level—imply a primacy of the totality over its elements? If, at the level of the philosophy of history, it is a matter not of "individual situations" but of universal thought operating through the whole and being constituted by it—if the "individuality" with which "philosophical history" is concerned is "the world spirit"—and hence the "universal object" that is "all-comprehending and omnipresent,"[28]—how can we fail to detect here a thoroughly "holistic" way of proceeding (in Louis Dumont's sense of the term)? For Hegel—how can it be denied?—the truth of the historical or the social lies only in the self-activation of this "universal," such that the "individual things become progressively more authentic the more completely they enter in their totality into the universal substance and the more completely the Idea enters into them"[29]—that is, "the universal acquires a real existence and realizes its inner determinations."[30] On this view, the "worth of individuals is measured by the extent to which they reflect and represent the national spirit, and have adopted a particular station within the affairs of the state as a whole."[31] So extreme (and so successful) was this Hegelian reduction of individuality to "an essential moment within the rational order of the universe,"[32] that it would be necessary for the whole of the historical profession to rise up in opposition to it in order to redirect the historian's attention to what is unique and forever differentiated in reality.

For all that, it is not correct to think of the Hegelian system as a failed and disturbing attempt to reintroduce holistic requirements into mainstream individualist thinking. To defend such an interpretation, which views Hegel as "the great Conciliator" Dumont makes him out to be, one would have to miss the fact that, as in Leibniz, the supposedly holistic dimension of the Hegelian system (i.e., the assertion of a logic of the totality) actually constitutes the means by which individualism (i.e., the valorization of the elements of the totality) finds its most perfect expression: it was in positing that the "particulars" of the world are not "exhausted in their own particular ends"—that "everything must be part of a single enterprise"[33]—that Hegel managed to give to *all* the manifestations of individuality a meaning and impact that, considered by themselves and in isolation, they could never have obtained. The legitimation of individuality thus reached its zenith through a new speculative mechanism that extended and radicalized the principle of the Leibnizian monadology.

Hegel, after all, was himself perfectly clear about the debt his undertaking owed to Leibniz. If "the only thought that philosophy brings with it is the simple idea of reason—the idea that reason governs the world, and that world history is therefore a rational process"[34]—how could he not have been indebted to the Leibnizian proclamation of the principle of Reason as the supreme law of the real? For Hegel, the designation of Reason as the substance of all reality could claim three historical antecedents:

- The first was to be found in the ancient idea of reason, which (in Anaxagoras, for example) consisted in proclaiming that "the world is governed by a '*nous*,' i.e., by reason or understanding in general" in the sense that laws structure reality and can be extracted from it by the human mind. This version is fairly close to Hegel's "only thought that philosophy brings with it," except for a twofold difference: on the one hand, in Anaxagoras, the idea that reality is governed by unvarying universal laws was "applied . . . only to nature" and so did not yet concern history, which remained still unconnected with rationality; on the other hand, even with regard to nature, as Socrates stressed in the *Phaedo*, the principle remained abstract, without application "to concrete nature." Thus it was only in a formal way that Reason was proclaimed to govern nature—no genuine explanation of natural processes in all their diversity, "with reason as [their] cause," was given.[35] As a result, reason raised to a law of reality in this fashion appeared to be no more than an empty form.

- The Christian reference to Providence advanced to some extent the idea that Reason governs the world: if the world is governed by an infinitely powerful wisdom that realizes its purpose in it, the notion that anything in reality can be "prey to chance and external, contingent causes" becomes inconceivable; to the contrary, it must be admitted that "the world's events are controlled by a providence, indeed by divine providence," just as much in the order of history as in that of nature. Because here, however, reason is considered to be merely an object of faith, and because—God's purposes being unfathomable—there is "a difference, indeed a contradiction, between this faith in providence and our original principle," the Christian version of the idea suffers from the same formalistic defect as the ancient version, particularly with regard to universal history, where "this general faith in providence" fails to reach down to the particular and "lacks a determinate application to the whole, to the entire course of world events." Instead of giving it "[this] application [men are content] to explain history [by natural causes. They confine themselves to] human passions, the relative strengths of armies, the abilities and genius of this or that individual, or the lack of such an individual in a given state—in short, to so-called natural causes of a purely contingent nature," to which appeal must be made by virtue of the failure "to apply [this] general principle [the idea of Reason] to concrete reality."[36]
- It followed, therefore, that the idea of Reason would finally bear its mature fruit only by making it possible to understand how "history is the unfolding of God's nature in a particular, determinate element."[37] In exploiting this third, historical aspect of the idea, "the aim of human cognition is to understand that the intentions of eternal wisdom are accomplished not only in the natural world, but also in the realm of the [spirit] which is actively present in the world"—hence, in that complex interplay of "particulars" that constitutes history.[38] In this sense, "our investigation can be seen as a theodicy, a justification of the ways of God (such as Leibniz attempted in his own metaphysical manner, but using categories which were as yet abstract and indeterminate)."[39]

Hegel explicitly acknowledged that his own attempt was descended from Leibniz, while very clearly indicating both the extent and limits of Leibniz's contribution. The theodicy "should enable us to comprehend all the evils of the world, including the existence of evil . . . in the light of the absolute sovereignty of reason."[40] By connecting a monadological vision of reality with the perspective of a theodicy, Leibniz set the stage for a reconciliation of the mind with the negative. Monadologically speaking, reality is such that every event (including the moral evil for which individuals could be held responsible) must be conceived as inherent in the formula that defines each monad and that makes the series of monadic events that it generates an element of the harmony that characterizes the best of all possible worlds. The underlying principle of the monadology, together with the dimension of theodicy that, for Leibniz, is inseparable from it, must therefore now be taken up and pursued in greater detail in two directions:

- Leibniz undertook the project of constructing a theodicy using only metaphysical categories—in other words, by allowing a moment of dualism to persist in his thinking: considered monadologically, all reality is mental, but the divine mind, the monad of monads, remains transcendent and hence external to the series of monads that constitute the system of the world. Thus the rationality of the real has a basis external to itself.
- Because the rationality of the real remains rooted in transcendence, the process of concretizing the idea of Reason can only be incomplete: reason subjects itself to reality only as a principle which remains to be carried out. In fact, Leibniz did not write a philosophy of history (even though the monadological idea of substance potentially gave him the means to do so); the challenge after Leibniz was to find a way to better apply the monadological idea, in order to integrate the individual particularities inherent in its logic, which, at the historical level at least, seemed to challenge reason and its ambition to establish a theodicy: "it is in world history that we encounter the sum total of concrete evil . . . there is no department of knowledge in which such a reconciliation is more urgently required than in world history."[41]

All the more, then, did Hegel insist on the necessity of making the monadological idea function henceforth in the domain of history, which he thus meant to guard against the kinds of objections that, since the time of Leibniz, had been raised against the idea of reason. Friedrich Heinrich Jacobi had initiated the "pantheism quarrel"[42] with a wide-ranging attack on reason in his *Über die Lehre des Spinozas, in Briefen an Herrn Moses Mendelssohn* (Letters to Mendelssohn on the Doctrine of Spinoza, 1785). Quoting quite skillfully from the Leibnizian monadology, he managed to turn certain of its arguments against the rationalism of the Enlightenment and the Leibnizian-Wolffians.[43] Thus in 1787 he could explicitly cite Leibniz as his authority for extracting two antirationalist weapons from the monadology:[44]

- If "all truly real things are individuals or individuated things, and, as such, living beings,"[45] how then could individuality be ignored in favor of an empty universal, and life left to petrify into a set of dead abstractions?

- If, as the *Monadology* in some sense establishes, it is by virtue of being united with a body that the soul represents the universe "in exact conformity with nature and with the organization of this body,"[46] reason therefore cannot be seen as a faculty that by itself alone could provide us with access to any truth whatever, for "Its distinctive activity is one of simple mediation between the senses, the understanding and the heart, whose common economy it has to administer."[47] In short, the concept of reason must be broadened, as against rationalism, to include that immediate opening to existence that Jacobi calls "revelation," "sentiment," or "belief," and that presupposes the intervention not only of reason (as the capacity for proving and deducing) but of our whole being.[48]

Armed with this paradoxical interpretation of Leibniz,[49] Jacobi challenged the defenders of reason. To maintain that the universe is wholly rational, he claimed, is to miss two key components of reality: on the one hand, that which is always *individuated* (since reason makes reality into a system of universal relations in which the individual counts for nothing), and, on the other hand, the fact of *change* (since reason constructs a system, like that of mathematics, whose terms and relations are eternal and immutable).[50] Carried to its logical conclusion, rationalism would by definition be incapable of conceiving of *history*, if history is understood as the field on which individual destinies are played out. For Jacobi, who classified it under the category of "Life," history by definition could not be grasped by mere causal thinking.[51]

The prospect of Leibniz being turned against the very idea of reason largely explains why Hegel believed he had to mount his defense of the Leibnizian heritage mainly on the ground of the philosophy of history: by extending the historicization of the monadological model, already attempted by Herder, and by showing that "reason . . . is itself the infinite material of all natural and spiritual life"[52]—thus replying to Jacobi and disproving the existence of an antimony between concept and life (or history). The gist of the Hegelian answer is well known: Life is not external to concept, for the Concept shares the same structure as Life—that of a self-deployed identity that arises from its own differences and surrounds itself with them. Having an infinite power to produce its own material, the concept is not an empty form; nor is the particular external to the universal—it is merely the universal in the process of realizing itself, concretizing itself in the particular.[53] Now I am not about to expound here upon the way in which Hegel undertook to give his reply to Jacobi the speculative foundation that it deserved; but at the least it is clear that this foundation drew extensively upon the dynamic conception of substance that Leibniz had been the first to propose: substance as form that produces its own content or as force that determines its own parameters. Thus the monadic conception of substance to which the familiar formula found in the preface to the *Phenomenology of the Spirit* pays tribute in its own way: "Everything turns on grasping and expressing the True, not only as *Substance*, but equally as *Subject*,"[54] that is, as "living substance."[55]

The Hegelian historicization of the monadology, rooted in the doctrine of dynamic substance, was to be fully expressed in a philosophy of history in which individual agents are to historical rationality (which is immanent in development) what the Leibnizian monads were to harmony (preestablished by divine transcendence). This historical monadology takes the form of the well-known theory of "the ruse of reason," according to which the individual, by selfishly pursuing what he believes to be his own self-interest, contributes to the overall rationality of the historical process.[56] The "ruse of reason" constitutes a monadological theory to the extent that the individual, by obeying only himself, by acting only on the basis of his own motives and reasons—hence, in all *independence* by comparison with an "other" than himself, by obeying his own nature alone—contributes to a process whose ultimate significance eludes him. The theory is monadological, therefore, by virtue of its capacity for giving expression to the essential themes of the Leibnizian theodicy, that is, the conviction that in "the context of world history, the Idea is not equivalent to reason as encountered in the subjective will, but to the activity of God alone."[57] Indeed theodicy, the claim to "understand the role of evil in the light of the absolute sovereignty of reason,"[58] is the chief purpose of Hegel's theory—a theory showing how what appears negative in history from a finite point of view in fact contributes, from the point of view of the system, to the rationality of a world that is consistent, as in Leibniz, with the "principle of the best," and in which every event consequently has its reason for being.

In this sense, not only must the Hegelian moment not be regarded as having a "holistic" import; it must be accorded a place in the history of subjectivity for its power to liberate, to affirm—even more than did Leibniz—individuality as such. It is true, of course, that the theory of the "ruse of reason" subjects the individual to a logic external to him. But to see this subjection, which leaves individuals no other freedom than that of realizing a destiny that is fixed beforehand, as proof of a perspective that is cripplingly incompatible with individualism reflects an error of judgment that arises from the confusion between the individual and the subject. For if this confusion is avoided, it is easy to see how individualism could have developed a conceptual structure in which the "ruse of reason" is transformed into a ruse of the collective subject.

The "ruse of reason" now expresses itself through "a subject-less process" in the sense that no particular subject consciously directs the activity of the system. For a theory of this kind there can be only one true subject, in fact: the system itself. But *precisely because subjectivity and individuality must not be confused*, this disappearance of (finite) subjects (as *auton-*

omous authorities) does not in any way contradict the monadological assertion of individuality (as *independence*). Quite the contrary, since so many independent selves cannot agree (being without doors or windows) to establish an order among themselves that would be the product of a common, conscious, and voluntary plan, if such an order must nonetheless exist it can only be the result of an immanent logic, characterized by a form of preestablished harmony, the "ruse of reason"—which is to say, unconscious self-organization—that works itself out through the independence of monadic individuals. The ruse of a collective subject is thus in no way the sign of a holistic reaction against the logic of modern individualism. To the contrary, it is a matter of perceiving in the Hegelian moment an extraordinary strengthening of individual action, which, even when insignificant, or even absurd and irrational, now acquired meaning, consequence, and truth: only in this way, thanks to a speculative structure that put an end to the conflict between the particular and the universal, could individuality succeed in becoming a value.

From this standpoint, then, Hegel can be seen as having finished the work of Leibniz by radicalizing the individualistic significance of the monadological idea. In Leibniz, the joining of monadology and theodicy had already made it possible to see that the assertion of individuality did not intrinsically contradict the modern valorization of rationality—an inspired move that permitted an advancement of the values of individualism *without a general inversion of all values: now marking the end of ascetic rationalism, the monadology no longer implied a sacrifice of individuality on the altar of rationality*. By historicizing the monadology, by putting the monadological idea effectively to work in the field of history, Hegel greatly increased its individualistic import.

The apparent conflict between totality and individuality in human history revealed itself far more acutely than in the domain of nature, where an individual event contrary to physical law qualifies only as an *exception* or as a *monstrosity*; but in neither case does the divergence of individuals from the law invalidate law, nor does it cast doubt upon the rationality of the universe. In history, at first sight it seems that we are dealing only with exceptions: every manifestation of individuality, every human act is exceptional, since it reflects the freedom that gives rise to it in the first place. If ever there were a field where taking account of individuality seemed to require placing restrictions upon rationality, it is indeed history—or, more generally, what are called the "human sciences." Augmenting the original Leibnizian insight, enriching it with his own distinctive genius, Hegel was able to overcome this appearance of conflict between totality and individuality: *considered from the viewpoint of the "ruse of reason," divergence from the law (irrationality) actualizes the law (rationality), by virtue of which the law of history is merely the summation of exceptions, and the universality of reason at work in history is merely the summation of individualities*. Thus the Hegelian moment both relieves man of his role as the *subject* of history and fully integrates the values of *individuality* with the values of rationality that are constitutive of our modernity, which is to say: the subject is dismissed, the individual promoted, and the value of reason preserved. How can Hegelianism not be seen then as the summit of *modern* individualism?

This Hegelian completion of modern individualism does not, for all that, represent the end of the process of individualization displayed by the history of subjectivity since Leibniz. Leibnizian preestablished harmony limited the real independence of the individual, who, being independent of other creatures, was not free from a certain "vertical" dependence with regard to the author of the plan of the universe. The "ruse of reason" makes the principle of dependence immanent, but does not abolish it. From this moment on, once individualism had been integrated within the intellectual requirements of modernity, it began to run to counter to these very requirements, which would end up appearing as so many obstacles in the way of the individual. Individualism could now no longer adapt to the values of modernity—foremost among them the values of rationality. If it was to succeed in getting around these obstacles and continuing on its way to creating its contemporary look, individualism would demand a new philosophical project suited to its special needs: a radical transmutation of all values.

The Nietzschean Moment:
The Birth of Contemporary Individualism

As we have seen, Nietzsche pays tribute to Leibniz for his role in helping dissolve the metaphysics of the subject. The praise is nevertheless moderated by a distaste for the way in which Leibniz remained captive to certain metaphysical notions: "There are no durable ultimate units, no atoms, no monads," proclaims a fragment meant for *The Will to Power*[59]—for the notion of a monad, as Leibniz conceived it, still involved that valorization of being which ever since Socrates and Plato had led humanity to deny the process of becoming and, out of a need to preserve this primary value, to substitute for it a world of stable and self-identical things. If the monadology were to be rid of its metaphysical basis by "desubstantializing" the monad and by historicizing the Leibnizian model, three defining principles would need to be retained essentially intact:

- The identity of indiscernibles, now contributing to a philosophy of difference: while Leibniz rather irksomely conceived monads as being defined by their identity, they are all nonetheless different from each other—on which account the monadological argument, in conceiving reality as individuality, had already made the world into an infinite field of differences.

- The dynamicization of the real: thought of as a monad, the essence of reality is force; and thus the world appears as a quantum of force—which the idea of the will to power, even if it believed it had to further elaborate and deepen the Leibnizian notion of force, could only try to improve upon: "And do you know what 'the world' is to me? Shall I show it to you in my mirror? This world: a monster of energy, without beginning, without end; a firm, iron magnitude of force that does not grow bigger or smaller, that does not expend itself but only transforms itself; as a whole, of unalterable size, a household without expenses or losses, but likewise without increase or income."[60]
- The perspectivism of knowledge: Nietzsche radicalized this theme, intimately connected with the monadological idea, by virtue of which the universe (likened to a city "taken from different points of view") is nothing other than the sum of monadic perspectives. Given that a perception is a putting-into-perspective and that each monad affords such a perspective on the world (because the world is itself only the set of all the monads), the world is the totality of perspectives—beyond which there is no world. Leibniz, however, did not thoroughly enough exploit this discovery of the perspectivism of knowledge: in particular, to Nietzsche's way of thinking, he did not draw out its utterly antimetaphysical significance, since at the level of God (as the monad of monads) it reintroduced an objectivity. From Leibniz to Nietzsche, the death of God—*freeing the monadology of its limitation by theodicy*—is what drives the perspectivist ambition to break with the Platonic idea of the "true world": "*Our new 'infinite.'*—How far the perspective character of existence extends or indeed whether existence has any other character than this; [. . .] Rather has the world become 'infinite' for us all over again, inasmuch as we cannot reject the possibility that *it may include infinite interpretations.*"[61] In other words, "No, facts is precisely what there is not, only interpretations,"[62] and if the task of knowledge is to "see things as they are,"[63] then henceforth it must be a matter of "seeing the world by *the greatest number of eyes possible*"[64]—without what Leibniz's God was able to achieve, the infinite totalization of perspectives, ever being able to be completed (in which case it would itself cease to be a perspective).

The Leibnizian heritage thus lies at the very heart of Nietzsche's philosophical undertaking.[65] There are more than a few affinities, in fact, between the thinker for whom "nothing is without a reason" and the one who finds "in all eternity chaos":[66] despite all that opposed him to Leibniz as far as the status of reason was concerned, Nietzsche was not merely an opponent of Leibnizian rationalism: indeed, insofar as this rationalism was monadological, he was its champion, for he believed he could free it from its subjection to the value of reason—and so extract the truth of the monadological idea. *Nietzsche brought out the full truth of the monado-*

logical idea in all its clarity by virtue of being not only the inventor of a monadology without theodicy, but also the inventor of an individualism without a subject as well.

To consider Nietzsche as the philosophical founder of an individualism in which nothing (not even the universality of truth, for even this is denied—there being no facts, merely interpretations) limits how far the values of individuality can be asserted,[67] nevertheless initially involves certain difficulties that threaten to undermine our analysis if they cannot be understood and overcome. If we look at what Nietzsche has to say about the notions of the *individual* and *individualism*, we encounter stunningly dissonant remarks that create a certain measure of tension, or paradox. Significantly, the record of his remarks in this connection has never been made an object of serious study, or even been surveyed in any very detailed way; its complexity and richness nevertheless merit a major interpretive investment, in the absence of which no appraisal of Nietzsche's role in the genesis of contemporary individualism deserves to be taken seriously.

Examining this record, we note a striking ambiguity: throughout a whole series of fragments—and this does not come as a surprise—Nietzsche assigns absolute value to the individual, making the individual the basis of a monadological principle: "It is not a question of the species but of more powerful individuals."[68] This reformulation of the Leibnizian principle of indiscernibles led Nietzsche, in many well known passages, to denounce concepts and words (reason and language) as the instruments of the homogenization of differences, of the obliteration of individuality—as emblems of the loss of reality (reality being understood as pure differentiation"); and within the logic of this ontological individualism to erect an axiological individualism as a defense of the values of individuality against what is sometimes called "commonness"[69]—that is, the disappearance of the differentiated individual amidst the general leveling of the masses. A number of central moments in Nietzsche's work issue from this attack on commonness, of course, two of which I mention here merely as a reminder:

- The critique of the values and civilization of the herd: Nietzsche reconstructs the stages of what he takes to be a tradition of "decadence," tracing a line of descent that runs from Judaism to socialism via Socrates, Christianity, Rousseau, the French Revolution, and the advent of the democratic ideal.
- The calling into question of the formation of consciousness and of language, seen now as the contingent result of the contingent evolution of life: Nietzsche explains in a brilliant passage (in the *Gay Science*)[70] how the birth—and subsequently the social valorization—of consciousness in man was not inevitable but instead was connected with the practical requirements (themselves

not inevitable) of communication (and so of language). The argument, briefly stated, is that a certain breed of men was unable to face the realities of life without each one having need of the others, and therefore substituted the values of mutual assistance for those of independence. Now the need of each one for the other brought forth both the expression and communication of this need (for "mutual understanding"), and as a result, still more importantly, the *consciousness* of this need. In this sense, Nietzsche emphasized that consciousness—the essential component of the idea of the subject—was born at the same time as language, "under the pressure of the need for communication," and as a consequence man became conscious only of what was communicable, shareable with others and thus *common*, since whoever has access to consciousness and language cannot be irreducibly individual: he must be herdlike, ordinary. The devalorization of consciousness (and hence of the subject as well) in the name of individuality therefore seemed to Nietzsche to be logically required under such circumstances: the "thinking that rises to *consciousness* is only the smallest part of all this—the most superficial and worst part"—the part, in other words, that does not correspond to individuality: "consciousness does not really belong to man's individual existence but rather to his social or herd nature"; though "[f]undamentally, all our actions are altogether incomparably personal, unique, and infinitely individual," consciousness and language accomplish a "thorough corruption" whose result is a "generalization" and, as such, a "superficialization."[71] This theory of the origin of consciousness and language is very clearly at the heart of any revalorization of individuality: if generalizing is equivalent to falsification and superficialization, then what is true and profound must be located in the affirmation of individuality as such. In Nietzsche it led directly to a criticism of modernity as a civilization in which the values of consciousness are affirmed (if only through the philosophical fiction of "the subject") and the individual dissolves into the ordinary, herdlike man: modernity thus becomes the site of the triumph of the "genius of the species" over great individuals—individuals such as the ones the pre-Socratic Greeks knew how to protect. In a parallel way, democracy—the chief political value of modernity—deserves only to be denounced for abolishing distance among individuals, and hence for obliterating the differences that make individuality possible. It is thus against democracy that "the sovereignty of the individual"[72] must be reaffirmed.

At this point Nietzsche's treatment of the question of individuality becomes more complicated, however, for in another series of passages he develops arguments that appear to undermine individualism. He repeatedly stresses that the notion of the individual is no more useful than that of the species. For example: "The concepts 'individual' and 'species' [are] equally false and merely apparent"[73]—as though it were a matter this time of elaborating a kind of ontological anti-individualism, making the individual not the ultimate principle of all reality, but simply a reflection of it. To this there corresponds (not unparadoxically, when we think of the passages just mentioned) an axiological anti-individualism: "The 'welfare of the individual' is just as imaginary as the 'welfare of the species.'"[74]

The elucidation of the paradox requires us to understand that when Nietzsche denounces the notion of the individual, he is aiming at a certain notion of individuality: "For the individual, the 'single' man, as people and philosophers have hitherto understood him, is an error: he does not constitute a separate entity, an atom, a 'link in the chain,' something merely inherited from the past—he constitutes the entire *single* line 'man' up to and including himself." In this sense, Nietzsche contends, the value of the individual varies depending on whether he "represent[s] the ascending . . . line of life" or "the descending development, decay, chronic degeneration, sickening."[75] Neither ontologically nor axiologically can the individual be considered *in himself*: he does not exist in isolation, nor does he have value independently of the process occurring inside him. Consequently, the individual is to be valorized if he represents a tendency toward increase of the will to power, and is to be devalorized when he appears as the agent of a process tending to drain life away. And thus it becomes necessary to deny a false conception of the individual in order to see that in fact "every particular being is a purely straight-line process (not the result of this process, but the process itself)," that it represents "the whole of the life that went before, summed up in a single line, and is not the result of it."[76]

These complex passages cannot be properly interpreted without connecting them with Nietzsche's criticism of the notions of *atom* and *monad* (as he understands these terms). The notion of the subject he describes as a "false substantialization" by which the Self was artificially "pried out of becoming," posited as "something that is a being" (with the help, notably, of a "faith in individual immortality"). This invention of Self/substance Nietzsche calls "the declaration that it exists in and for itself," which was compared to that of an atom, like "the false autonomy of the 'individual' as atom."[77] Thus it is only a very particular version of the notion of the individual that appears mistaken—the version in which the individual, autonomous in relation to the world and the unfolding of it, is posited as a stable and even indestructible unit, as the ultimate source of his acts and representations. As against this view of the individual, it needs be maintained that "There are no durable ultimate units, no atoms, no monads," that "'units' are nowhere present in the nature of becoming," that there is no "will" that can be taken to be a foundation identical with what it would posit.[78] Such an autonomization of the individual "as atom" would, in Nietzsche's view, be too obviously of a piece with the static image that religion, metaphysics, and science have constructed by replacing "pure differentiation and pure succession" with a "world" of beings, causes, and unities—as for example, in physics, "a firm systemization of atoms in necessary motion, the same for all beings."[79]

When Nietzsche grapples with the notion of the individual, it is thus its metaphysical disfigurement, centered on the values of unity (the individual as atom or monad) and of autonomy, that he is trying to get at: within each individual there are many centers of force, which combine and fight each other at every instant (the unity of the self being merely a fiction); what we call the will is merely the final stage of an uncontrollable conflict between these centers of force, not a free will laying down its own laws (autonomy being an illusion). As a consequence, to give the Leibnizian monadology its full antimetaphysical due, it becomes necessary to historicize the monad: to see monadic individuality not as a pole of unity and fixity, a substrate of the changing interplay of phenomena, but as an unstable moment in a process of continual differentiation.

We are therefore now in a position to understand in what sense Nietzsche's reworking of the notion of the individual, aimed at fully freeing individuality from its subjection to the metaphysical tyranny of identity, goes together with a subtle companion discussion of individualism—a discussion that is at first somewhat disconcerting, for individualism sometimes comes in for criticism as one of the components characteristic of modern mass civilization: "[I]ndividualism is the *most modest* stage of the will to power"[80]—or, better, "My philosophy aims at an ordering of rank: not at an individualistic morality."[81] The point of such statements becomes clear when we realize that Nietzsche is imputing to Christianity the version of individualism that he denounces: "[I]t was Christianity that first invited the individual to play the judge of everything and everyone; meglomania almost became a duty: one has to enforce *eternal* rights against everything temporaral and conditioned!"—in short, the individualism that he attacks, like Christian or metaphysical individualism, is one nourished by the ideas of "the 'soul', of the 'immortal soul,' soul-monads that really are at home somewhere else," and whose being is not in the least "conditioned" by terrestrial things.[82]

From this follows a whole analysis of the ambiguities of modern individualism, the heir to Christianity: "The modern European is characterized by two apparently opposite traits: individualism and the demand for equal rights; that I have at last come to understand." What Nietzsche finally understood was that *modern* individualism is in fact inseparable from the egalitarianism through which it is expressed and carried out—a seemingly paradoxical connection for him to make (since individualism for him is the affirmation of difference, of otherness; not the valorization of identity or equality), but whose genesis can be reconstructed: in order to protect itself against the assault of difference, modern individuality ("weak and fearful") had to undertake to deny them.[83] For the modern individual, defending the value of his existence meant demanding "that every other shall count as its equal, that it should be only *inter pares*"—thus it was the "principle of the individual" that "rejects *very great* human beings and demands, among men approximately equal, the subtlest eye and the speediest recognition of a talent."[84] Modern individualism is thus prepared to cultivate small differences, but will valorize these only on the basis of a prior depersonalization and homogenization. To this modern individualism Nietzsche wished to oppose another individualism, the model for which he thought he found in the "personalism of the ancients"—for whom individuality would have been valorized as such: as *distance* and as *difference*.

Thus it was that Nietzsche's most profound contribution to the history of subjectivity came to situate itself in a conflict between individualisms, in the transition from one model of individualism to another. The terms of the conflict can now be precisely indicated:

- Modern individualism is seen as valorizing equality. In this sense, it goes hand in hand with Christianity (equality before God) and with democracy (equal rights for all men). Hence it constitutes "the lowest degree of the will to power," since in it the individual valorizes himself only to the extent he considers himself the *equal* of others—not by seeking to dominate them or by affirming his superiority or distance: "*Individualism* is a modest and still unconscious form of the 'will to power'; here it seems sufficient to the individual to get free from an overpowering domination by society (whether that of the state or of the church). He does not oppose them as a person but only as an individual; he represents all individuals against the totality. That means: he instinctively posits himself as equal to all other individuals; what he gains in this struggle he gains for himself not as a person but a representative of individuals against the totality."[85] For modern individualism, it is not so much a matter of affirming one person's individuality as distinct from another's—of affirming the individual as a person in his own right, "in his own name"—as of securing the independence of each person with regard to the whole, the emancipation of the individual from the totality: this form of individualism is an "individual egoism" in which each person is determined to consider himself in isolation from society or humanity as a whole. It is this form of individualism that the monadic notion of the individual attempted to express in its own way in speaking of the "isolated man" who posited himself "against the totality," the goal of which was not the cultivation by each person of his own individuality—the affirmation of oneself—but only a poor, embryonic anticipation of the will to power (and thus to life), which, in order to preserve itself, posits itself as "one" against the Whole. Even this sort of individualism expresses a will to power, for it refuses to allow itself to be swallowed up by the Whole, but in a *minimal* form since the deliverance from the Whole is realized only through the equalization of all the members. In positing myself as identical with all others, and in positing them as my equals, I contribute to the creation of a society (democracy) in which, through the guarantee of individual rights, a *minimal* degree of independence is ensured, enough to provide the will to power with a certain expression, albeit a very modest one: the differentiation from the whole by the equalization of all. Thus understood (which is to say in a way that at bottom is almost Toquevillean—except that all the analytical signs are reversed),[86] modern (democratic) individualism bespeaks an exhaustion of the will to power, surviving only as a symptom of decadence. "One desires *freedom*," writes Nietzsche, thinking of the freedom of the moderns (as differentiation from the whole through the equalization of all), "so long as one does not possess power. Once one does possess it, one desires to overpower."[87]

- As against this modern individualism, Nietzsche calls for another way of valorizing individuality, and thus another individualism, in which the individual has less to affirm himself as such against the whole than to posit himself as a person distinct from every other person. Such an individualism, which was prefigured by the "personalism of the ancients,"[88] would correspond not to the democratic ideal of equality but to that of an aristocracy which admires distance and hierarchy: the supreme value is not that of the autonomy of individuals with regard to the Whole, but that of the infinite affirmation of oneself as independence from others. Interestingly, what elsewhere he calls the principle of his morality—individuation[89] —Nietzsche defines in *The Will to Power* in the following way:

> To say *I* more often and in a stronger voice than the majority of men, to impose oneself upon them, to stand up against every attempt to reduce [one] to the role of an instrument or organ, to make oneself independent (if only through others submitting themselves or sacrificing themselves, if independence can be achieved only at this price), to prefer a precarious social situation to uniform, sure, comfortable arrangements, and to regard a costly, wildly extravagant, and absolutely personal way of living as necessary if man wishes to become greater, more powerful, more prolific, more daring and more rare . . .[90]

We see in this passage, which dates from 1880–1881, a stunning prefigurement more than a century ago of the individualism of our own time—down to the tiniest details: narcissism, exclusive concern for oneself, the cult of independence, the sacrifice of the social, even the consumerist ethic. In opposing modern individualism and its passion for equality, Nietzsche believed he could return civilization to its sources in premodern values, particularly those associated with the "personalism" that he thought he detected in the pre-Socratic Greeks and the great individuals of the Renaissance. Above all, he identified the peculiar mutation which, by pushing these values to their logical extremes, led from modern individualism to contemporary individualism. Additionally, by historicizing the monadological model, uncoupling it from any perspective connected with theodicy, Nietzsche thought he could also make a break with what he found still too metaphysical in the Leibnizian idea of the monad. Thus he discovered a way to bring to an end the individualistic detour of humanism that the Leibnizian monadology had inaugurated, by replacing the principle of autonomy with a principle of independence.

The history of subjectivity since Leibniz—and continuing even beyond Nietzsche—can thus be seen to have obeyed a very profound logic that was philosophically crowned by the death of the subject and the advent of the *absolute individual.*[91] Whether in Leibniz or in Hegel, Nietzsche saw the modern reign of reason as an obstacle to the recognition of reality as that "pure differentiation and pure succession"[92] in which he located the emergence of a new philosophy: rationalist monadologies surely made it possible for the needs of individualism, which this new philosophy was meant to satisfy, to be fitted into an intellectual and cultural configuration that, in the absence of such mediating formulas as "preestablished harmony" and the "ruse of reason," would have rejected them. But once they had been successfully installed, these mediating devices would indeed have appeared as hindrances to the rise of new values. Nietzsche could thus think of himself as the engineer of a decisive break with the past: yet, by leading the era of monadologies to a point beyond itself, so to speak, he had done no more than reveal its true significance—that it had accompanied the profound shift which had taken place within the heart of modernity with the exhaustion of the principle of subjectivity and the values of autonomy. The ultimate repercussion of this shift (which prevents us from conceiving of modernity as a smooth path to the future) was to be the subsequent emergence of an individual closed in upon himself, sacrificing all social concern to the affirmation of his own independence.

Perhaps today we are beginning to perceive the obstacles (and even the dangers) inherent in an individualism that has no subject, that no longer accommodates any principle of limitation imposed on self-affirmation, and that tends to dissolve the community into that "precarious social situation" Nietzsche inveighed against. In this sense, one of the few tasks that can still be assigned to philosophy—if, in spite of all that has gone before, it intends to defend the values of modernity against their antimodern critics—lies no doubt in the search for the intellectual conditions under which a way out from the multiform era of the individual can be found.

PART THREE

Transcendence and Autonomy: The End of the Monadologies

Preamble: Phenomenology and Criticism

CONTEMPORARY philosophy is full of attempts to overcome its past: one consequence of the dominant interpretation of this past has been that "overcoming metaphysics"—a move that for the great post-Hegelian philosophies has been almost obligatory (if only to the extent that, in Hegel, the completion of the system claimed to bring the history of philosophy to an end)—often gave the impression, first in Nietzsche and Heidegger, of radically calling into question the idea of the subject. If, however, it is agreed that since the Leibnizian turn, philosophical modernity has consisted more in the forgetting of subjectivity than its triumph, overcoming the past now means something different: henceforth it must consist in the recomposition of the subject in reaction against the individualistic drift of humanism, even though (as I tried to explain at the outset of this work) this recomposition is not to be thought of as a return to the metaphysics of subjectivity as it appeared at the time that the Cartesian *cogito* emerged. More precisely, it must consist in making the vanished dimension of the subject, which fell into obscurity during the era of monadologies, reappear. Thus the "overcoming of metaphysics" is to be understood as an attempt to overthrow the monadological perspective, which since Leibniz has in various ways dominated the history of subjectivity. But how can this be done? Here I explore two paths that may lead to a solution.

The first is suggested by the fact that the monadological conception of the subject makes it a totality defined by immanence to itself: the monad has no windows, and is unrelated to anything other than itself. To deconstruct the monadological idea requires investigating that *rupture of immanence* which makes it appear that subjectivity, unlike monadic individuality, can take cognizance of itself only on the basis of an opening to exteriority or otherness. In this case we encounter the problem of transcendence in immanence, which, as we have already seen, is directly connected with the problem of devising an alternative to absolute individualism.

The second path is suggested by the first, and proceeds within the very framework of self-immanence that defines subjectivity: given that a dimension of openness to an otherness—in effect, a dimension of transcendence—must be recognized as constitutive of the subject, the self-sufficiency or independence of the subject/monad turns out to be an illusion (or, more accurately, turns out to be the prototype of the metaphysical illusion concerning the Self). Once rid of this illusion, the subject could then be recomposed, with its true content, which had been obliterated by the individualistic drift of humanism, restored to it—with the result that the principle of *autonomy* would regain all its former potency. It is unclear, however, how far, and with what authority, we can go beyond a naïve idea of autonomy and yet retain some of its former meaning, given that for various reasons we can no longer think of ourselves as enjoying the same freedom as God. In other words, how are we to conceive of autonomy now that the metaphysical idea of the subject has been destroyed? Can it be recast on the basis of that radical finitude which inevitably defines the terms for all contemporary thinking about man's humanity? If, in the wake of the era of monadologies, humanism can now acquire a new meaning—individualism having at last run its course—it will only be insofar as this openness to otherness, this transcendence that defines the subject, can be thought of as having *autonomy* as its intended purpose: autonomy as the *horizon of transcendence*.

To illustrate this double approach to overcoming the monadological heritage and to estimate the chances that it might be philosophically successful, indicating also under what circumstances it could be successful—this is the sole objective I wish to set for myself in the final part of this study. Two intellectual traditions, phenomenology and criticism, appear to me to be useful in this regard: by studying the dialogue between them, and from time to time the debate in which they find themselves opposed,[1] I believe that more than one path can be shown to be worth following.

CHAPTER VI

Lévinas: The Rupture of Immanence

It is well known that the theme of otherness is central to the thinking of Emmanuel Lévinas. I shall not review all its underpinnings here, nor attempt to point out all its ramifications; instead I shall concentrate only on the antimonadological import of this theme and its relation to a possible revival of the question of the subject. Alluding to "the crisis of humanism in our age," Lévinas refuses to deal with the fact that such a crisis must inevitably open the way to "the antihumanism that will reduce man to a medium":[1] on the contrary, it seems to him once again necessary in the face of these challenges to classical humanism to inquire into what constitutes man's humanity, which he thinks that neither classical humanism nor contemporary antihumanism has really succeeded in grasping. This amounts to posing yet again the question of the subject, in asking how the subject "stands out from being."[2] And it is within the framework of such an inquiry that the "rupture of immanence"[3] is encountered: here the emergence of an authentic subjectivity in being stands opposed to the metaphysical model of a humanity in which, by endlessly reducing the Other to the Same, "man shuts himself up like a monad."[4]

The Illusion of Humanism and the Error of Antihumanism

Lévinas very shrewdly pinpoints the surprising misapprehension on which the antihumanistic slogan of the "death of man"[5] is based: through its "disgust" for man, antihumanism paradoxically reveals its dependence on classical humanism, from which it inherits a certain representation of the subject—precisely the one, in fact, in which "man shuts himself up like a monad."

What fuels the antihumanistic crusade? Primarily one observation: that the rise of the human sciences has deprived man of any hope henceforth of a "coinciding of self with self." For if "the psyche and its freedoms" are "only a detour taken by structures in order to link up into a system," if it is no longer man who possesses the truth, but a truth (of belonging to the structures, to the system) that holds man in its grip, "the inwardness of the self-identical ego is dissolved," the "whole of the human is outside"—"as though its very congruence with itself were impossible, as though the inwardness of the subject did not close from the inside." In short: "Everything comes to pass as though the ego, the identity par excellence from which every identifiable identity would derive, were wanting with regard to itself, did not succeed in coinciding with itself." Under the circumstances, one has no choice but to agree that "*I is an other*," that the "rediscoveries of self with self are missing," that inwardness "seems to be not strictly inward"—and that thus: "*Henceforth the subject is eliminated from the order of reasons.*"[6] Unfolding in parallel with the many-sided discoveries of the unconscious, this crisis is aggravated by the very history of our times: "The unburied dead in wars and extermination camps make one believe the idea of a death without a morning after and render tragic-comic the concern for oneself and illusory the pretension of the rational animal to have a privileged place in the cosmos and the power to dominate and integrate the totality of being in a self-consciousness."[7]

Whatever its suitability may be for providing apocalyptic ideas for "intellectual high society," antihumanistic reasoning reflects two inadequacies. The first takes the form of a singular inconsistency: for if consciousness of self disintegrates, how is it that "anti-humanism can still reserve for man the discovery of true knowledge"? Does not all knowledge, even that of the human sciences, involve the consciousness of self? And in this sense can the human sciences, as they "resort to the mediation of the man of science," really dispense altogether with some notion of man as consciousness?[8]

Beyond these difficulties of principle, antihumanism exposes itself to a less formal objection involving the precise content to be given to humanism, and thus to the idea of the subject: for if antihumanism in fact proceeds from the conviction that the impossibility (which has become evident) of the self coinciding with itself is equivalent to the death of the subject and the downfall of any conceivable humanism, does it not thus reproduce (showing, in the process, a surprising dependence on what it attempts to combat) the most characteristic illusion of classical humanism—if you will, a metaphysics of the subject—in the form of a mistaken idea of the subject? What defines such a metaphysics is indeed an extraordinary obsession with *immanence*: convinced that "knowledge is a relationship of the Same to the Other in which the Other is reduced to the Same and stripped of its foreignness," philosophical tradition has conceived thought (and hence the subject as a "thinking thing") as "the way in which an exteriority is found inside a consciousness that never stops identifying itself" by identifying with the other, by referring itself to another that ceases to be "other as such."[9]

The task of thought, considered to be "the very business of man to which nothing remains absolutely other," thus did not cease to be the abolition of all transcendence, the restoration of everything transcendent to the immanence of a Self identical with itself, totalizing within itself everything that is not identical with it: Self = Self, absolute Knowledge, System—whose only limiting horizon is the coincidence of unity. How can one fail to recognize in this model of the subject, in which "everything is absorbed, sucked up, and walled up in the Same,"[10] that man who "shuts himself up like a monad," depriving himself of communication with any other than himself, of any relation to a radically other otherness, left alone in the solitude of his relationship to himself? If by "humanism" we understand that classical conception of the subject for which exteriority or otherness—that of the world, like that of "itself"—"is hosted in immanence" and "the activity of reason *dissolves* any otherness,"[11] the rupture of immanence produced by the discoveries of the unconscious and structures (mental, social, and so forth) in which the Self finds itself embedded, causes such illusions to disappear and legitimates the notion of a "death of man." But is the attack on metaphysical humanism fated to reproduce the very illusions that it denounces? Can we conceive consciousness only as monadic in accordance with a logic of pure immanence?

How can one fail to see—and here Lévinas gets at the root of the worst misapprehension from which the debate on humanism suffers—that consciousness, thought of as immanence, tends to dissolve in the world of things? If the subject must stand out from being, it cannot be through either its identity with itself or its closing in upon itself: as Leibniz saw, significantly, monadicity is a structure that can to various degrees be indiscriminately ascribed to things, animals, and men. In shattering the illusions of immanence, the human sciences, far from leading to a dissolution of the idea of the subject, have created instead the conditions under which an inquiry can be launched into what is most irreducible in subjectivity—the self's noncoincidence with itself, its openness to an irreducible otherness or exteriority: it is because it does not happen to coincide with itself, because it "is an other," that the "I" stands out from being. Rimbaud's formula ("I is an other") is thus not fated to be a slogan for the elimination of the idea of the subject: by indicating that "Everything human is outside," that "Everything is outside, or everything in me is open," this formula does not necessarily mean that "in this exposedness to all winds subjectivity is lost among things or in matter"—for, contrary to what classical humanism believed (and what antihumanism continues to believe), "subjectivity signif[ies] precisely by its incapacity to shut itself up from the outside"?[12]

In this sense, the metaphysical history of subjectivity—to the extent that it had led to the monadic closing up of the Self upon itself and to the advent of a gigantic monad (which, in effect, is what the Hegelian absolute subject amounts to—by resolving everything into itself, and thus bringing about the complete abolition of exteriority) may have failed subjectivity in its intrinsic truth (as openness) more than it has served it. In Lévinas, this suspicion remains partly implicit, but it does indeed express the gist of an analysis that perfectly supports what has been attempted here: *the so-called "metaphysics of subjectivity" has been dominated less perhaps by the forgetting of Being than by the forgetting of the subject.* Correspondingly, the overthrow of such a metaphysics, and even the overcoming of it, is less a matter of thinking "against subjectivity," as Heidegger naïvely believed, than of deciding finally to pose the question of the subject—in Lévinas's words, to attempt to come to terms with the subject's openness, which breaks the monadic immanence and makes the subject the site of an exit from itself or, if you prefer, the site of a *transcendence*.[13] Here we also find, in connection with what could now be called a philosophy of the subjectivity, an inquiry into the possibility of transcendence in immanence: "The main task behind all these efforts consists in thinking of the Other-in-the-Same without thinking of the Other as another Same."[14] This is a precise and convincing statement of the problem, whose solution could give humanism new life: how to make appear in the Same (i.e., in that identity or that immanence of consciousness, absent which the idea of the subject would lose all meaning) the Other, that openness to an otherness, that transcendence which destroys the monadic illusion of self-sufficiency and truly constitutes a subject capable—through this very openness, through this noncoincidence with itself—of "*standing out from being.*" Insofar as Husserl explicitly consigned the carrying out of such a task to phenomenology, Lévinas can emphasize the opposition between Husserlian phenomenology and most of the philosophical currents that flowed from it—currents which, under the influence of Heidegger, attempted less to restore truth to the idea of the subject than to object to subjectivity in all its possible forms. And since, for Husserl, phenomenology in this sense "remains thoroughly humanist,"[15] the elaboration of "the idea of a subjectivity incapable of shutting itself up"[16] would have to bear a certain relation to the Husserlian heritage. This turns out to be a complex relation, however, when we consider how Lévinas himself believed he could deal with its implications.

The Husserlian Heritage

In taking stock of Husserl's contribution to thinking of subjectivity as transcendence in immanence, Lévinas pays unmistakeable tribute to the founder of phenomenology. For Husserl saw perfectly well that "the I lies outside of immanence, while belonging to it," that there is no consciousness without "that exteriority breaking into the intimate . . . into that otherness, which is coincidence with itself and reunion with itself."[17] This "transcendence in immanence," this "*Same* infinitely referred in its most intimate identity to the *Other*," was indeed designated by Husserl as the structure of intentionality and therefore as constituting consciousness in action; even though the "sleeping Self" is closed to exteriority and becomes rigid in its identity, the awakening consciousness "transcends its immanence" and is oriented toward the object—thus, strictly speaking, emerging as consciousness (as subject) only on the basis of this openness to otherness. Better still (i.e., more profoundly), Husserl did not mean to make intentionality the mere structure of waking consciousness, drawn out of its immanence by the shock of the object: in the posthumously published *Ehrfahrung und Urteil* (Experience and Judgment, 1948) and *Phänomenologische Psychologie* (Phenomenological Psychology, 1962), intentionality precedes any influence by the object, and literally makes such influence possible; it is because the Self is "never numbed to the point of being absent" (because, even in the passivity of sleep, it constitutes potential intentionality) that the active intentionality of attention can later appear—in short, "the possibility of awakening already makes the Self's heart beat, from the disturbed and living interior, *transcendent in immanence*."[18] Immanence is not broken into from the outside, from stimulation by the object: the rupture of immanence—and hence transcendence—is, like intentionality, subjectivity itself. It is when he reaches a vision of intentionality such as this, dooming the monadic vision of the self to the status of a pure illusion, that Husserl most closely approaches a true liberation of otherness from the metaphysical tyranny of identity. For if, in pre-reflective consciousness, a faint difference already appears between the same and the other (a transcendence), no theory of affection can explain this *foundational* rupture of immanence—an original, *originating* rupture that is forever occurring once there is a subject; a rupture that gives the subject life, and that constitutes it as such. A phenomenological account of this rupture would therefore include a description of how and in what forms otherness brings about this already-achieved/endlessly-recurring rupture of identity.

In the fifth of his *Cartesianische Meditationen* (Cartesian Meditations, 1950), Husserl sketched the outline of such a phenomenology: by showing how, on the basis of the analogy with animate bodies, one's sense of a Self other than oneself is constituted, he was able to intuit that it is only "in the eyes of others" that the Self—awakening from its egological dream, tearing itself away from its complacency (and its illusory self-sufficiency), exposing itself to the other and liberating itself from itself—authentically emerges as subjectivity.[19] This is a possibility, however, that Husserl only glimpsed. It would remain to be fully exploited by a phenomenology "pushed beyond the Husserlian letter."[20] The fifth *Cartesian Meditation*, which Lévinas admittedly finds troubling,[21] does in fact construct the other self, the alter ego, "deducing it by analogy with my bodily presence," through an association with two faces that I compare—as if, in order to compare my face to that of others, I did not need beforehand to refer to others, to "a face of others," and assume an openness to the other (as another person) that precedes the act of comparison and makes it possible. Thus Husserl also meant, in a certain way, to derive the Other on the basis of the Same—to derive the sense of an other self from the activity of the Self, reemphasizing immanence as the foundation of transcendence.

I shall not discuss further here this reading of Husserl, which I bring up only for what it tells us about Lévinas's project—which consists in enriching the Husserlian heritage by radicalizing the rupture of monadicity that follows from the attempt to constitute the subject on the basis of intersubjectivity (and not vice versa). The "humanism of the other man": this formula was to be understood as laying down—as against classical humanism, which culminates finally in the monadological determination of the self—that a redefined humanism should consist in *thinking of subjectivity as transcendence, and of transcendence as communication*. In other words, man's humanity consists in a rupture of an identity, through openness to the otherness that belongs to the "other person": "the other (is) others . . . the way out from the self (is) through the approach of one's being, proximity (is) responsibility for the other."[22] The monadologies dissolved subjectivity at the very moment they broke off all direct communication between the windowless monads, and hence dissolved any true intersubjectivity. We thus cannot find it disconcerting that the post-monadological restoration of the subject involves the rediscovery of intersubjectivity as a foundational condition of subjectivity: here again, we can adopt Lévinas's way of proceeding, and designate the "humanism of the other man" as the end of "the subject turned to itself," a "subject thus defined by care for itself which in happiness realizes its *for itself*."[23] On this view, humanism is construed as the rupture with everything that had previously been adduced in support of the valorization of the *individual*, in contrast to that of *subject*, such that the movement by which it "is borne toward others" becomes part of its very subjectivity.

Thus the Husserlian heritage is enriched by regarding the break-up of immanence as representing the advent of communication. To this I would add only that Husserl himself sometimes grasped the importance of the correlation between transcendence and communication, occasionally trying to express it in the vocabulary of monadology. Thus he explicitly averred that the monadological problem—which is indeed that of intersubjectivity (i.e., how do monads, closed in on themselves, agree on a definition of objectivity?)—is logically prior to the problem of the existence of an objective world: "the transcendental constitution of other subjects . . . is indispensable to the possibility of an Objective world for me."[24] He even went so far as to state:

> The Objective world as an *idea*—the ideal correlate of an intersubjective (intersubjectively communalized) experience, which ideally can be and is carried on as constantly harmonious—is essentially related to intersubjectivity (itself constituted as having the ideality of endless openness), whose component particular subjects are equiped [*sic*] with mutually corresponding and harmonious constitutive systems. Consequently *the constitution of the world essentially involves a "harmony" of the monads*: precisely this harmony among particular constitutions in the particular monads; and accordingly it involves also a harmonious generation that goes on in each particular monad.[25]

The allusion to the Leibnizian theme of a preestablished harmony must not be misinterpreted here: Husserl did not adopt the metaphysical hypothesis that harmony presupposes in Leibniz; he merely stressed that, intermonadic communication apart, no monad could produce the representation of a world that might be regarded as the objective correlate of its subjectivity. In Leibniz, this "communication between substances" was established vertically by a theologically based harmony, but, in principle, once the monadological structure is abandoned, nothing prevents such communication from occuring by other means.[26] In short, disencumbered of its metaphysical aspect, the theme of harmony needs to be reworked to take into account the intersubjective foundation of objectivity—and so also of subjectivity. The *Krisis* (1936) could not have more clearly insisted on this: "The Ego-community, insofar as it constitutes the world, always precedes the constituted world."[27] Certainly, Husserl did not explore this question of logical chronology any further; but he did explicitly elaborate its formula, leaving it to his successors in the phenomenological tradition to clarify the manner of its operation—thus the proper task that Lévinas set for himself: to complete finally the subversion of the monadological idea of the subject.

The best way to assess the difficulty of carrying out this task, and thus to estimate the likelihood that phenomenology can go beyond the monadological horizon, seems to me to be to analyze an experience in which Lévinas sees the emergence of "the *phenomenon* which the apparition of the other is."[28] To overcome the illusion of the subject/monad, "turned to itself" and defined by "care for itself," it seems to him that the "humanism of the other man" must above all, as he does not cease to stress, reflect "the desire for the other"—for it is in a desire "born over and beyond all that can be lacking or that can satisfy him," and prior to any reflection, that "the I is borne toward the other in such a way as to compromise the sovereign self-identification of the I."[29] Thus a phenomenology of desire (or, if one prefers, a "phenomenology of Eros")[30] is found at the heart of an attempt to show "how and where the major rupture is produced in our psyche that can accredit an *other* as irreducibly *other*."[31] It is not that, for Lévinas, postmonadological reflection about communication as a condition for the emergence of the subject is exhausted by this phenomenology of Eros: for it is owing to desire, insofar as this "is desire for the absolutely other,"[32] that this "epiphany of others" survives—this epiphany that destroys the illusion of self-sufficiency and invites one to think of subjectivity not as spontaneity of self-production but as an openness to the other, as something whose fundamental modality is the welcoming of others, or "hospitality."[33]

Fragment of a Phenomenology of Eros

The "phenomenology of Eros" that figures at the beginning of the fifth section of *Totality and Infinity* is meant to describe the experience of the erotic relationship in such a way as to distill its essence. As Lévinas himself explained in one of his earliest works,[34] phenomenological analysis, as it is defined in the first volume of Husserl's *Logische Untersuchungen* (Logical Investigations, 1900–1901),[35] consists in describing various aspects of the life of the mind by deriving "the essential structure of the object or its *eidos*" and differentiating it from "its empirical concept in which the essential and the accidental are intermingled." In the phenomenological tradition, this eidetic reduction is, as we know, performed by applying a strict criterion: the essence of a mental phenomenon is nothing more than its *sense* or, more precisely, the *intended sense* prompting it. If it be granted that consciousness is "thought," phenomenology must then consist in showing how "at all levels of mental life" (i.e., at all levels where consciousness is found), "thought is aim and intention"—that is, "intentionality" or the "act of giving sense" (*Sinngebung*), even in the case of intentions "that are wholly nonintellectual."[36]

This criterion is applied in the pages devoted to the phenomenology of Eros. I shall confine myself here to considering a fragment of this phenomenology of the erotic relationship—the analysis of the caress, the very symbol of that relationship. In a subtle discussion,[37] Lévinas investigates the caress from the standpoint of its aim and intention, of the "intentionality" that prompts it as "thought" (since "thought is aim and intention"). Though somewhat disconcerting in view of the role assigned to it, this phenomenology of the caress—and, more generally, of Eros—must nonetheless make it possible to measure the capacity for renewal contained in the Husserlian heritage. The philosophical investigation of Eros is indeed as old as philosophy itself, going back as far as the *Symposium* and the fourth book of *De natura rerum*, continuing more recently with the passages on love in Sartre's *L'Être et le néant* (Being and Nothingness, 1943).[38] To have an idea of the dislocations to which an altogether traditional approach is potentially made vulnerable by the introduction of a phenomenological method, one must therefore be able to appraise the import of an approach to subjectivity in terms of intentionality.

The eidetic approach considers the caress from the point of view of the subject before considering it from that of its object. From the subject's point of view, it weaves together positive and negative determining characteristics:

1. The first characteristic involves a network of subtle relations between the caress and sensible experience that display four aspects: while the caress "is sensibility," nevertheless it "transcends the sensible"; for all that, however, it does not feel "beyond the felt," for it is in fact a *pure movement of transcendence*, a *search* to go beyond sensible experience without grasping anything "sublime"—that is, a transcendence that does not have access to anything that goes "further than the senses," and hence not to anything suprasensible.[39] The first determining characteristic carries primarily a negative significance, considering the extent to which it aims to trump the Platonist account of the erotic relation.

- Looked at in terms of the caress, the erotic relation is seen to be erotic by virtue of exhibiting a form of sensitivity—touch—that presupposes proximity: as a caress, the erotic relation is "like contact." This choice—describing the erotic relation on the basis of an experience that is "like contact"—appears significant in itself if we consider that, in the *Symposium*, the relation to the Beloved is expressly depicted in visual terms. For Plato, the lover is first of all one who gazes on the beauty of a body: if, as Diotimus points out, Eros begins when a man "has viewed all these aspects of the beautiful,"[40] the object of love conceived as vision is very logically characterized by its beauty. On the other hand, for Lévinas, these two elements of the Platonic discourse about love disappear: the loving subject's act does not consist essentially in seeing (rather in touching), nor (as we will notice little by little) is the object of Eros described in terms of beauty—a shift that underscores what in the erotic relation is originally sensory (in Plato this is sight, which, while certainly sensory, is conceived in the most intellectualized sense) and what in it presupposes proximity (the Platonic gaze amounting to sensitivity at a distance).
- Consequently, because Eros is thus deeply rooted in sensible experience, as a caress, the transcendence that is realized in it neither aims at nor attains the suprasensible; *a contrario*, it will be recalled that for Plato, precisely to the extent that Eros involved this (as it were) nonsensual sense of vision, the

Lover's search for Beauty could easily set in motion a movement of transcendence on the basis of desire, leading from the beauty of a particular body toward the beauty of the body as such, and from there to the beauty of souls, and thence, finally, to the Idea of the Beautiful, the true *telos* of the erotic relation: suddenly "[w]hoever has been initiated so far in the mysteries of love" will find that "there bursts upon him that wondrous vision which is the very soul of the beauty he has toiled so long for . . . subsisting of itself and by itself in an external oneness"—that is, the eternal *identity* and *unicity* of the beautiful in itself.[41] From beginning to end, the Platonic Eros was a kind of "seeing," culminating in that contemplation of the suprasensible which alone gave meaning to the whole process of loving and being loved: transcendence from the sensible to the intelligible, enabling lovers to see "further than the senses," to see as far as that sublime realm of intelligible Beauty.

Lévinas says nothing of the kind. Certainly the caress, though it is "like contact," is also more than contact, insofar as its aim is not contact: more precisely, the essence of erotic contact is not exhausted by touch, for we touch many people without caressing them. In this sense, what is at stake in Eros is a *transcendence*, a going beyond mere sensory relation—but here the transcendence does not open on to anything other than itself, with everything happening as though it were itself intended as a movement of transcendence; "as though the caress would be fed by its own hunger"[42] rather than, in contrast to the platonic Eros and simple need, on what satisfies it. More need than desire, the Eros of the *Symposium* is satisfied when the demand for the beauty that animates it is fulfilled by grasping the Idea of the beautiful—a possible form of satisfaction that suggests Plato missed the essence of desire:

> [I]n need I can sink my teeth into the real and satisfy myself in assimilating the other; in Desire there is no sinking one's teeth into being, no satiety, but an uncharted future before me.[43]

In short, by a caress one grasps nothing. More precisely, the caress "consists in seizing upon nothing"—a sign that erotic intentionality does not culminate in the blossoming of any presence whatever, such as that pure presence of intelligible eternity which for Plato characterized the Idea of the Beautiful. Quite the contrary, since it is not realized in the grasping of a fullness of presence, the caress aims at something that "ceaselessly escapes its form to a future": it is directed to "what slips away" (and thus to an absence) "as though it *were not yet*"—a transcendence without a *telos*, then, without an opening to the suprasensible. These negative features of the caress, however, prepare the way for arriving at a first positive characteristic: "it *searches*, it forages"—the caress as pure quest, pure movement of transcendence, a dead end in the contemplation of any transcendent thing.[44]

2. In order to forestall any temptation to locate the essence of this quest in the attainment of some *telos*, a second negative characteristic reexpresses the insight acquired from this first approach: "It is not an intentionality of disclosure but of search: a movement unto the invisible."[45] The rupture with Plato's analysis thus becomes further radicalized: in the *Symposium*, the erotic journey was prompted by the need to gaze upon, and thus to unveil, what in itself is incomparably visible, what (in the formula of the *Republic*) is "the brightest in the material and visible world"[46]—to wit, the intelligible. For the erotic gaze that has been purified to the point of becoming the pure gaze of mind, access to the intelligible opens up the dimension of the supremely visible, for the Idea defines the level of the eternally present, independent of the generation, corruption, deformation, and alteration to which the shadows in the cave are subject.

In contrast with attainment of such a *telos*, which is incompatible with the essence of desire, the phenomenological description brings out the intrinsic incompleteness of the erotic relationship: expressing love without being capable of saying so, the caress symbolizes the way in which the effective end of the erotic relationship (the possession of the other's body) is never really an end. The caress, which is meant to be a search, "goes further than to its term"; it does not reach its *telos* by touching the other body, nor in fact by possessing it, nor by possessing anything, any "being" whatever, be it this body as such, or even beauty. Rather "it aims beyond an existent" that could be possessed, that could be grasped, if only as an intelligible reality—and even though it aims at what does not yet exist, this could not involve some future being (since it would in that case, despite everything, be aiming at "something"): the caress aims neither at a present being nor at a being to come, whose coming the caress would bring about, which is why desire is endlessly "reborn," precisely because it does not seize upon any being, nor indeed anything whose approach could satisfy it. Thus, the caress cannot be thought of as aiming to bring about the desire, and then the pleasure, of the other (i.e., to actualize the other as desire and pleasure): if this were the intention of a caress, its aim at what did not yet exist would be achieved in the approach of what, through the caress itself, would cease to be, in a blossoming of presence and in the disappearance of what did not yet exist as a "not-yet." As Lévinas stresses, the "*what is not yet*" that the caress aims at is a very strange thing—a "what is not yet" that fails to be transformed into an "existing" or "being," for desire is constantly reborn as a search for that which does not yet exist.[47]

Not aiming at a present being, not seeking to make exist what does not yet exist, the caress is aimed at a not-yet-existing *as such*—a negative feature that can in turn be formulated positively: Eros constantly brings us back "to the virginity, forever inviolate, of the feminine."[48] The principle of this formulation is clear even if it poses a problem of interpretation: aiming at a not-yet-existing that is never transformed into become-being, the caress in fact never possesses its object, the possession of the other's body not being a true possession, since in the rebirth of desire the other appears as a not-yet-existing—in fact, as a not-yet-possessed whose reappearance actually feeds desire. In this sense, desire is forever faced with the "not-yet-possessed" of the other's body (and hence with its "forever-inviolate" virginity). Eros seeks this virginity: it is the Eros of a virginity irreducible and beyond possession.

It may seem surprising that, described this way, such desire appears more precisely as desire for the virginity of the *feminine*. For all that, there is no pressing need to see any trace of phallocentrism in this.[49] More simply and more reasonably, it should be observed first that the phenomenological discourse, cast as an eidetic reduction based on a descriptive analysis of experience, can be imagined only with difficulty as having been composed by the transcendental subject—and therefore, in the framework of a phenomenological description, that it cannot be considered irrelevant that the subject of the discourse is masculine. Second, and more importantly, femininity in this context is clearly a category—not a psychological category, but (since it is a matter here of eidetic reduction) an *ontological* one; more precisely, we might say that it is a matter of the schematization, or symbolization, of an ontological category, that of the "not-yet-existing" (of not opening onto a future being) that constitutes the defining property of the object of the caress. As such, this category of the desire is naturally neither masculine nor feminine. If, however, we attempt to represent this definition of such a "not-yet-existing," an image immediately suggests itself: that idea of inviolability, and hence of irreducible virginity, of which femininity obviously furnishes a good likeness from sensible experience. Thus, in Lévinas's phenomenology of Eros, the notion of the *feminine* can play a central role without obviously precluding a symmetric analysis that would attempt to inquire into the intentionality of desire from the woman's viewpoint.

3. The fact remains that Lévinas tries to illuminate this intentionality by drawing attention to a third negative characteristic, namely, that the caress does not seek "to dominate a hostile freedom, to make of it its object or extort from it a consent."[50] Lévinas now takes aim less at the Platonic approach than at the Sartrean analysis of love. In *Being and Nothingness*, Sartre made "conflict" the "original meaning of being-for-others," seeing in this conflict a "project of unification" that would work for "the disap-

pearance of the characteristic of otherness in the Other," the "identification of myself with the Other"—the reason why my relation to the other would consist primarily in acting "upon the Other's freedom" into order to deny it as such, in order to "effect my assimilation of the *other freedom*."[51] It is in this framework that the experience of love is located—with the consequence, importantly, that love itself is "conflict" and shares in the overall project of "recovering my being," which is threatened by the other's freedom: it is by virtue of this freedom that, in love, "I get hold of this freedom" by reducing it "to being a freedom subject to my freedom." Thus, to the question "Why does the lover want to be *loved*?" Sartre replies that love is not "a pure desire for physical possession" (for then "it could in many cases be easily satisfied") but a wish to "capture a 'consciousness.'" Out of this would arise moreover the insurmountable difficulties of the love relationship, for love "wants to possess a freedom as freedom": once it is possessed, it is no longer a freedom; but if love lets it go on existing as freedom, it is not possessed—a famous analysis, from which it is at least to be inferred that erotic intentionality consists in the production of an *identity*, an identity that certainly would lay claim to "a special type of appropriation" (for the other, insofar as it is a freedom, must be possessed, must recognize itself as "possessed"), but which nonetheless testifies to an ascendancy of the Same over the Other.[52]

In this regard it is significant to turn to the Sartrean analysis of the caress, which Lévinas most likely had in mind when he wrote the pages of *Totality and Infinity* that we have been considering. For Sartre likewise denied that the caress is "simple *contact*" or "simple stroking," but for very different reasons: for him, the caress is aimed at more than contact because it is a "*shaping*" that "causes the Other to be born as flesh for me and for herself."[53] The Lévinassian phenomenology directly contradicts this interpretation. The caress does not in fact seek either the consent or the resistance of a free being; far from being a matter of "grasping" a freedom, "what the caress seeks is not situated in a perspective and in the light of the *graspable*."[54] Its object, as we have noted, does not have the status of a presence, or of any present being—not even a particular being, whose existence would be freedom—that could be apprehended. Aiming at "what is not yet" (and will not be later, in the sense of a possibility that could be anticipated), the caress neither attempts to control a presence nor to make a future presence occur—as Sartre believed, seeing the caress as a form of domination that makes the other materialize as flesh. Its object is a mysterious *absence*, which is neither a matter of nothingness (for desire is indeed a desire for something, or someone) nor a matter of pure and simple future (as possibility). Additionally, its object being only "what does not yet exist," it cannot be animated by an intention to possess: a new, strictly negative feature of the caress, but one which nevertheless forcefully underscores the telling point that, if it is indeed a profanation (in the sense that it penetrates a dimension of the real which was hitherto thought to be secret), the profanation in this case does not seek to make present, or to unveil, what it penetrates; as against any putative intention to unveil, the caress as a profanation testifies to an openness to that strange dimension of absence that defines the "not-yet-existing"—that is, the feminine.

4. A final negative characteristic can be deduced directly from the preceding one: the correlate of the caress—the carnal, the tender, the beloved—is not the *body*. Note that this claim refers to two senses in which the body enters into the philosophical analysis of love with which the phenomenology of Eros makes a break:

- The object of the caress is not the body in the sense of "the body-thing of the physiologist"—the material body whose beauty formed, for Plato, the point of departure for Eros as an initiation to the beautiful;
- Nor does the caress have as its object the body in the sense of "the lived body of the 'I can' "—the body as manifestation of a freedom that is opposed to the self, which led Sartre (rightly in my view) to regard the meaning of the conflict of love as consisting in submission to the body-as-freedom.[55]

The body that is the object of the caress—the body as "erotic nudity"—thus *exists* neither in the physical sense of being nor in the sense of constituting the visible sign of a freedom to destroy. If failing to be an existent in either of these two possible modes ("In the carnal given to tenderness, the body quits the status of existent")[56] represents everything that can be said about the erotic intention as expressed by the caress, the meaning of this combination of negative characteristics still remains to be spelled out by considering the experience from the point of view of that singular object that we have so far only glimpsed as being aimed at as "not-yet-existing," as neither being, nor possibility, nor nothing, nor presence, nor future—only as the *feminine*, as "forever-inviolate" virginity. Thus the second moment of the phenomenology of the caress thus applies the elements glimpsed earlier in the analysis of intentionality to the notion of the feminine.

The relevant passage in Lévinas—an extremely compact one—deserves a particularly careful reading: "The Beloved, at once graspable but intact in her nudity, beyond object and face and thus beyond the existent, abides in virginity." The meaning of this is that beyond any physical reality that I can grasp (i.e., the physiological body), even beyond the expression of a freedom that I might wish to master, the object of the caress is like that virginity symbolized by the Feminine: "essentially violable and inviolable, the 'Eternal Feminine' is the virgin or an incessant recommencement of virginity, the untouchable in the very contact of voluptuousity, future in the present."[57] Like the Feminine (the capital letter underscores the fact that it picks out an ontological category), the "Eternal Feminine" must not be misunderstood. Elsewhere[58] Lévinas argues that if upholding "the thesis of the exceptional position of the feminine in the economy of being" (an exceptional position indeed, since the feminine here refers to a "beyond being" that is not a nothingness, to a "not-yet-existing" that is not a simple future being) can be taken to allude to so traditional a theme, the mystery of the feminine is not to be understood "in the ethereal sense of a certain literature" (one thinks of Goethe's *Faust*)—that is, in the sense in which romanticism reduced the mystery of the feminine to that "of the mysterious, unknown, or misunderstood woman." Here the notion of the "Eternal Feminine" is taken to designate not the eternity of a psychological mystery (the unknowable), but the enigmaticity of a way of being—if you will, the *ontological* mystery of the object of desire as a "not-yet-existing" that is not a nothingness and yet refuses to be, "a mode of being that consists in slipping away from the light," that is, from presence: "It is a flight before light," writes Lévinas, with reference to the feminine; and again: "Hiding is the way of existing of the feminine, and this fact of hiding is precisely modesty,"[59] which remains modesty (i.e., withdrawal, "not being") in the most absolute nudity (presence, being). It amounts almost to nonbeing, in the sense of what eternally does not yet exist (such as the eternity of the feminine) and withdraws into a future that will never be present—thus femininity eludes the opposition between being and nothingness: "It is an event in existing" (hence it is not nothing), but remains "different from the hypostasis by which an existent arises" (and hence it is not being)—and in this sense its relation to this ontological enigma is "neither a struggle, nor a fusion, nor a knowledge" (according to the Sartrean, Romantic and Platonic interpretations of Eros):

> One must recognize its exceptional place among relationships. It is a relationship with alterity, with mystery—that is to say, with the future, with what (in a world where there is everything) is never there, with what cannot be there when everything is there—not with a being that is not there, but with the very dimension of alterity.[60]

This is to say that, in the experience of the caress, the feminine—as the *apparition of otherness*—is what escapes that grasp of the same that defines the act of consciousness as an act of giving something present its identity. In this sense *the feminine, as a symbol of the object of erotic intentionality, signifies the rupture of immanence and the emergence of transcendence*. Now we are at last in a position to better see how and why the caress transcends sensible experience: it transcends it just insofar as its object is the transcendence of otherness, the rupture of the identity and of the immanence of consciousness to itself. The intentionality of the erotic experience thus becomes more understandable on the basis of its very object, namely, that transcendence of the other by virtue of its being other. Erotic relationship is the typical experience of this transcendence—surely not the only conceivable experience, but the one that concentrates the main determining features of the caress in (so to speak) an ideal-type way. But in what sense does the emergence of a subject follow from such a revelation of otherness? This is, for Lévinas, what creates a confrontation between the experience of the caress and the quite different rupture of immanence mentioned in the cryptic lines from *Totality and Infinity* contrasting the "night of insomnia" with "the night of the erotic":

> Alongside of the night as anonymous rustling of the *there is* extends the night of the erotic, behind the night of insomnia the night of the hidden, the clandestine, the mysterious, land of the virgin, simultaneously uncovered by *Eros* and refusing *Eros*—another way of saying: profanation.[61]

The Ruptures of Immanence: Dasein *and Subject*

The contrast between the "night of the erotic" and the "night of insomnia" in fact mobilizes an entire analysis—which remains implicit here—of the relation between sleep and insomnia. In other works,[62] whose richness I have already alluded to, Lévinas succeeds in showing how the very possibility of consciousness (of subjectivity) presupposes that the "there is," the brute fact of the very existence of things, is subordinated to the "what there is" of some particular object, equipped with its own identity, with which consciousness concerns itself. For consciousness, the faculty manifested by the ability to sleep of forgetting the "there is" resembles the faculty of withdrawing not only from what one has to do or think, but also from the fact that there are things—hence the faculty of annulling all presence. The "possibility of sleep" is thus one of "stand[ing] out against the *there is*," the "ability to forget it and interrupt it."[63] Beyond even sleep, one finds that ability of consciousness to forget the "there is" which constitutes it in relation to objects that it manages to master by annulling their dimension of exteriority and by integrating them, as available instruments, into the sphere of its immanence to self. This is a precarious ability, however, one that is forever threatened: "The impossibility of rending the invading, inevitable, and anonymous rustling of existence manifests itself particularly in certain times when sleep evades our appeal."[64]

Insomnia, a Lévinassian analogue to the role played by anxiety in the Heideggerian analysis of *Dasein*, does in fact appear to be an experience in which one "watches on when there is nothing to watch and despite the absence of any reason for remaining watchful"—because the "bare fact of presence is oppressive; one is held by being, held to be." In other words, the insomniac "is detached from any object, yet there is presence"—this presence being precisely the "there is," which includes things and consciousness. And just as anxiety in Heidegger subverts subjectivity by abruptly upsetting the subject's illusions about its ability to control the real, in the same way in Lévinas "the vigilance of insomnia which keeps our eyes open has no subject": whereas consciousness as subjectivity indeed presupposes a *will* that bears on the *identity* of an object, the wakefulness of the insomniac is a pure dispersion of the Self, a pure demand made on the Self by the identity-less "anonymous being," by the "play of being" (in which "the [s]elf is swept away by the fatality of being" in the "anonymous rustling" of the undifferentiated "there is.")[65] In its confrontation with this "anonymous rustling" in which things are returned to their indistinct, pure presence, the subject itself loses its *identity*:

> Wakefulness is anonymous. It is not that there is *my* vigilance in the night; in insomnia it is the night itself that watches. It watches. In this anonymous nightwatch where I am completely exposed to being all the thoughts which occupy my insomnia are suspended on *nothing*. They have no support. I am, one might say, the object rather than the subject of an anonymous thought.[66]

If the awakening of sleeping consciousness is the "advent of the subject," insomnia is thus the dissolution of the subject or Self. This is why the night of insomnia is a painfully negative experience: indeed, it opens onto a *transcendence* in relation to the sphere of everything that consciousness can control, a dimension of exteriority that is impossible to abolish—namely, that "there is" which Heidegger also designates as one of the names of Being. In this sense, insomnia destroys the immanence of consciousness, destroys its tendency to close in on itself, to think of itself as a monad, without an outside, in the illusion of mastery and self-sufficiency. But this insomniac rupture of immanence opens onto transcendence only by dissolving subjectivity in a pure *Dasein*, the anonymous witness to the fact that presence contains a "there is," demanded and swept away by this presence.

In this sense, if indeed insomnia constitutes a Lévinassian analogue to Heideggerian anxiety, it must be admitted that in the analysis of such experiences, the signs are reversed: such openness to transcendence dissolves the subject at the same time as it destroys immanence (or, in the vocabulary proposed here: by destroying the monadological illusion of individuality, it also subverts any conceivable subjectivity). What this signifies, therefore, is an experience of dehumanization, which, as such, cannot support a deliberate attempt to avoid exchanging the illusions of "classical humanism" for the errancies of "antihumanism."

In a gesture underscoring everything that distinguishes his position from that of Heidegger, Lévinas opposes the night of insomnia, as a disastrous rupture of immanence, to the night of the erotic—the night of anonymous rustlings, of the anonymous otherness in which everything becomes un-differentiated: the "night of the hidden, the clandestine, the mysterious," in which an otherness breaks through immanence—an otherness that has a face, however: the face of the Beloved. In both cases, what is at stake is the emergence of a transcendence (and hence a dimension of exteriority) that breaks through the immanence-to-itself of consciousness, but in two very different ways:

- First, the transcendence of the "there is" breaks through the immanence of consciousness only in the name of an "anonymous thought": as witnesses of the "there is," we can all *equally* be witnesses, each one as much as another, through an experience of the Same (of the swallowing up of differences in the homogeneous and anonymous presence of the "there is"). Such a rupture of immanence thus doubly dissolves subjectivity, not only insofar as it is *ipseity* (i.e., *identity* of a Self irreducible to any other),[67] but also insofar as it is *intentionality*: while every consciousness aims at something that itself has an identity and that is differentiated from what it is not, the consciousness of "nothing" or of "the nothing" cannot be called consciousness. In short, "the rustling of the 'there is' . . . is horror. . . . To be conscious is to be torn away from the 'there is,' since the existence of a consciousness constitutes a subjectivity, a subject of existence, that is, to some extent a master of being. . . . Horror is somehow a movement which will strip consciousness of its very 'subjectivity.' "[68]
- Second, in the erotic night, by contrast, the caress is "a mode of the subject's being," in which there is intentionality, the search for something, even though here, owing to "the fact that the caress does not know what it seeks," the intentionality is very special: thus "the subject is still a subject through [e]ros"—that is, intentional consciousness; but it runs into "something slipping away" and plays "a game absolutely without project or plan, not with what can become ours or us" (unlike the everyday patterns of a consciousness mastering otherness and reducing the other to the same)—it enters into a relationship "with something other, always other, always inaccessible, and always still to come."[69] The rupture of immanence is the reason for which the subject lives, *insofar as it is and remains a subject*:[70] "What one presents as the failure of communication in love precisely constitutes the positivity of the relationship; this absence of the other is precisely its presence as other."[71]

As against the passion for immanence that from Plato's *Timaeus* (where "the circle of the same surrounds the circle of the other") to Hegelian absolute knowledge has stimulated the whole development of Western philosophy, Lévinas judges it to be the task of our time to ask "what finally is this idea that is sought—neither assimilation of the Other to the Same, nor integration of the Other with the Same—that would not reduce any transcendent to immanence and not compromise transcendence by fully including it."[72] The phenomenology of Eros makes it possible to formulate a reply by showing how *for the subject* the erotic relation constitutes the experience of such a transcendence: an experience of what neither is nor will be, the erotic aim as "will to tenderness" corresponds to the search for a "not-yet-existing" that is otherness itself. Like the "not-yet-existing," femininity is the figure of the other—but unlike the "there is," the otherness of the feminine does not require the depersonalization of the self. Eros—an experience in which I am neither anonymous nor the Beloved—creates a relationship that is both *intersubjective* and *without fusion*,[73] in which each subject continues to exist as such, but in which the illusion of immanence is destroyed and in which appears the figure of the Beloved, otherness as such. The dialectic of the Same and the Other, in which the Same absorbs the Other, is now broken. Far from being, as Plato believed, a moment in the triumph of the Same (as having ascended from the diversity of beautiful bodies to fusion in the eternal identity of the Beautiful in itself), the erotic appears as the key moment in a renewed game of the Same and the Other: "Set against the cosmos that is Plato's world, is the world of the spirit where the implications of eros are not reduced to the logic of genus, and where the ego takes the place of the same and the *Other* takes the place of the other."[74] To move from a philosophy of the cosmos toward a philosophy of mind—for which the central fact becomes "that the other be others, that the way out from the self be through the approach of one's fellow being, that proximity be responsibility for the other"[75]—involves, it will be agreed, a considerable shift: far from consigning the solution to the problem of communication between subjects/monads to a metaphysics of preestablished harmony, it requires relocating communication, given its embeddedness in the erotic, on the horizon of an ethic.

The difficulty (in truth, the only difficulty) raised by the phenomenological attempt to revive the question of the subject in this way has to do with its capacity for really imagining such a horizon.

Phenomenology and the Problem of Ethics

If the rupture of immanence emerges from this openness to the other as expressed in the erotic relationship, the phenomenological approach does not content itself with calling attention to this emergence. Lévinas, examining what the intentionality of the caress already reveals by itself (an important theme in his work, as we have seen), identifies the emergence of intersubjectivity (and hence the rupture of immanence) with the impossibility of annulling "the responsibility for the other": as openness to the "essential frailty of the Beloved produced as vulnerable and as mortal,"[76] the caress opens at the same time onto the sphere of duty and ethics. The advent of duty in this case involves a duty which realizes itself in me without my consent—"traumatically," owing to the suddenly revealed presence of the other—and which, in response to that presence, occasions my emergence as a true *I*, capable of announcing: "Here I am!" To the question of how the subject stands out from being, the final answer consists in stressing that the subject is distinguished not by "a freedom that would render it master of things," but by "a responsibility prior to every free commitment"; since it is "incapable of withdrawing from it without retaining the trace of its desertion," the subject is a "responsibility before being an intentionality"[77]—a responsibility that it did not choose, but which, "in approaching another, where the other is from the first under my responsibility, . . . has slipped into me *unbenownst to me*, thus alienating my identity."[78] By concretizing the rupture of immanence, so to speak, the openness to duty radicalizes the break with the monadic Self and the apparition of the Self "*who puts himself* in *an other's place*,"[79] a Self who, far from displaying individualistic "self-regard," is what he is only in virtue of being "for the other":

> There is a divergency between the ego and the self, an impossible recurrence, and impossible identity. No one can remain in himself: the humanity of man, subjectivity, is a responsibility for the others, an extreme vulnerability. The return to the self becomes an interminable detour. Prior to consciousness and choice, before creation is assembled into the present and into a representation and becomes an essence, man approached man. He is made of responsibilities. With them he rends the essence. It is not a question of a subject assuming or escaping responsibilities, a subject constituted, posited in itself and for itself as a free identity; it is a question of the subjectivity of the subject, its non-indifference with regard to the other in a responsibility that is unlimited for not measured by commitments, to which assumption and refusal of responsibilities refer.[80]

In short: we have here a foundational responsibility, constitutive of subjectivity, that thus does not presuppose it as ability to choose, but instead makes it appear as that Self which is "a stranger to itself, obsessed by the others, dis-quiet," designated by the figure of the "hostage."[81] From Self-monad to Self-hostage—how can we not hail such a phenomenological recomposition of the subject? How can we not also fail to notice that it joins together the best elements of the critical and phenomenological traditions? Beyond a definition of subjectivity in terms of openness to duty, the two traditions share the same insistence on the intersubjective rootedness of subjectivity: both Kant and Fichte, convinced that "man becomes man only among men," would have unhesitatingly endorsed this "idea of a subjectivity incapable of closing in upon itself," a subjectivity appearing as such only in response to the other.[82] In this respect, one should note in passing that it is not clear that whether Lévinas was always capable of doing justice to the way in which the critical tradition, isolated during the era of monadologies, had already contributed to a recomposition of the subject by opposing monadicity and positing intersubjectivity as the condition of subjectivity. One cannot ignore the originality of Kantianism as Lévinas does, nor claim that the doctrine of the "unity of transcendental apperception" represents a rescue of the "*I* immediately free of classical humanism," and so attribute to the Fichtean heritage of transcendental philosophy a theory of the Self as "an activity supremely constituting the not-self."[83] These errors of judgment would be actually of small consequence for the Lévinassian undertaking as a whole if, by closing it off to an essential dimension of criticism, they did not in a certain way alter its outcome.

For certainly Lévinas sometimes maintains that Kant glimpsed the possibility of conceiving subjectivity in terms of openness to the otherness of the other—"notably in the doctrine of the primacy of practical reason."[84] Convinced, however, that this would expose the logic of immanence to no more than mild strain, and that in fact Kantian reason "retains (despite the passivity that, as the categorical imperative, it unavoidably displays) its claim to activity, that is, its belonging, initial or final, to the category of the Same,"[85] he does not delve deeply into what contribution Kant might have made in this area. It may be wondered whether Lévinas does not thereby miss the indispensable concept of *autonomy*, which Kant made the very essence of practical subjectivity.

Lévinas tends generally to take the view that the valorization of autonomy—as the "free activity" of an "I want" that "posits itself as Self"—is a symptom of imprisonment in an idea of immanence.[86] As against this reverence for an auto-nomous reason that gives itself its own law, in the sense of a "force that comes back to itself," of an "act of identification" (or "identification in action"), overcoming "classical humanism" is taken by Lévinas to mean no longer locating human dignity in personal freedom as spontaneous activity,[87] but rather instead in *passivity*:[88] subjectivity—openness to the other as representing one's fellow human beings—now presents itself as the fact of "*not being able* to withdraw from responsibility." There is a moment of "determination by the *other*," which, "on this side of the determinism/servitude alternative," coincides with the emergence of an ethics based on "a radical passivity of the subjectivity." "Domination by the Good," "impossibility of choice," "obligation to responsibility," "obedience to an order that is carried out before it is heard": such are the fundamental responsibilities that would give real content to practical subjectivity—a subjectivity without freedom, in the sense in which "the pure passivity preceding freedom is responsibility." Much more than *autonomy*, the subject—as the subject of ethics—would be "subjection."[89] Because a phenomenology of ethical experience that is observant of the modalities of its appearance dislocates the essence and meaning of such experience—shifting it from an illusory autonomy in the direction of a subjection prior to any freedom (as to any servitude), it alone would finally manage, in breaking the circle of immanence within which Kantian practical reason remains enclosed, to transfigure the subject. In short, contrary to what Fichte would have maintained, the subject is not "its own source":[90] the responsibility for others in which the "transcendence in immanence" consists—"the Other calling the Same to its depths"—refers to a "heteronomy of freedom that the Greeks did not teach us." The definition of a humanism better equipped (by virtue of escaping the categories of classical humanism) to resist the naive attacks of antihumanism would depend on learning this freedom.[91]

Yet this attempt to shift the center of ethical gravity from autonomy to heteronomy runs into two difficulties. The first difficulty concerns the justification of the attempt to show—actually, of the conviction (shared with Heidegger)—that the Kantian analysis of the practical subject in terms of autonomy of the will is only a simple moment in the smooth development of a homogeneous "classical humanism." This "classical humanism" is sometimes defined as the "metaphysics of subjectivity" (*pace* Heidegger), sometimes as a "philosophy of immanence" (*pace* Lévinas)—but in both cases it is presented, in every modern account, as an inevitable destiny. This is why Lévinas, who sees in modernity a willingness to conceive subjectivity as monadicity, considers the doctrine of the autonomy of the will to be part of the same movement, without further ado. Since earlier in this book I have insisted on what distinguishes the monadological logic, anchored as it is in the valorization of independence, from the perspective of autonomy, I will confine myself here to criticizing the pure and simple absorption of the idea of autonomy into the notion (more *individualist* than strictly *humanist*) of immanence-to-itself as a sign of insufficiently precise categorization. How can Lévinas, who so well describes the way in which the Self, animated only by a "concern for itself," regards the "independence of happiness" as its goal, presupposing the conversion of the Other to the Same, the assimilation of the Other[92]—how can he then confound autonomy and independence, failing to see that *the idea of autonomy already contains the openness to the other*? For just as autonomy is not independence (*the proof being that Kant criticizes the morality of hap-*

piness in the name of the principle of autonomy), it presupposes that I am the "source of myself" only by raising myself, as the practical subject, above the immediacy of the empirical subject and integrating the presence of the other into my ipseity: *the subject that gives itself its own law must, in order to rise to the level of this auto-nomy, have transcended the self-identity of the desiring subject (individuality) and opened itself up to the otherness of the human species. Transcendence-in-immanence is by definition what autonomy means.* Thus it cannot be seen as a sign of that perpetual tyranny of the Same that, from the *Timaeus* to the Hegelian system, continuously dominated the history of subjectivity.

A second difficulty handicaps the phenomenological approach. In Lévinas's way of going about it, this approach leads ultimately to the notion of subjectivity as responsibility—and, given this, to subjectivity as "subjection": if subjectivity is pure subjection, how can it be responsibility? Is it really possible to think of responsibility without reference to autonomy? Here lies the clearest point of divergence between the critical tradition and the phenomenological tradition (which, in certain other respects, is so close to it):[93] once it is admitted that the distinctive human characteristic, what makes man a subject, consists in his power to break out of immanence, out of self-identity (or identity with the being-in-itself of the thing and, no doubt, of the animal)—once, in other words, man's humanity has been located in transcendence—the chance that this transcendence might bring forth a *subjectivity* or a *consciousness* (and not a simple *Dasein*) depends on our assigning it the goal (perhaps an inaccessible one, but at least one to be aimed at) of *autonomy. A rupture of immanence that would not transcend the self-identity of the narcissistic consciousness toward a higher form of identity (that of the autonomous subject, where the Same is posited, as an ethical subject, only in opening itself to the other) would inevitably lead back to the kind of rupture that occurs in waking experience—exactly the kind that dissolves subjectivity into a pure being-there.*

In other words, if overcoming the age of monadologies is to be seen as restoring the dimension of subjectivity occluded by the logic of individualism, the rupture of monadic immanence must be conceived *stricto sensu* as illuminating a transcendence *in immanence*—not *against immanence*. It is thus in terms of the self-identity that is constitutive of a subject that the openness to the otherness of others is to be conceived. This concept has a name: *autonomy—insofar as the autonomous subject would basically be one whose subjectivity, as the source of itself, is not that of any particular subject, but is identified with the intersubjective community of a humanity in agreement about the law governing it.* In this sense, reference to the idea of autonomy is not a sign that the idea of the Other would find itself recycled in the logic of the Same; on the contrary, in postmonadological space it must be regarded as being no less indispensable than the notion of the rupture of immanence, if the transcendence thus achieved is to be a transcendence of a subject.

Lévinas, in attempting to understand ethics in terms of heteronomy and subjection, does not sufficiently distinguish between two moments of ethical experience:

- First, ethical experience is a moment of openness to duty, of the emergence of law, which may indeed be described in terms of subjection: because we are finite beings and not saints, the law imposes itself upon us from the outside; and, thus, from the standpoint of a phenomenological analysis of the experienced relation to duty, it is legitimate to read this as a moment of subjection—or, if you will, of heteronomy.[94]
- Second, to be faithful to the principles that inspire it, a phenomenological approach must however also come to grips with the intentionality of ethics. Now, in ethical experience, the moment of intentionality cannot be described in terms of heteronomy: the ethical project, insofar as it involves the emergence of responsibility, must unavoidably make reference to that *horizon of autonomy* without which we cannot conceive how the moral subject could think of itself as responsible to others.

The rupture of immanence thus opens onto autonomy as a horizon of transcendence. If we are to be able to reflect upon the status of this horizon, and to inquire into its compatibility with the intellectual requirements of an idea of the subject that is finally freed of metaphysical illusions, we must resolve to bring the insights of phenomenology to fruition.

CHAPTER VII

Kant: The Horizon of Transcendence

THE NEED for the subject to think of itself as *auto-nomous* is inseparable from a modernity in which ethical, juridical, and political values are not *received* from a natural order of things already containing them, but are *self-grounded* or *self-established* as norms that humanity gives itself, constitutive of intersubjectivity and based on the idea that humanity creates for itself of its own dignity. Paradoxically, this idea (or value) of autonomy is undermined both by the logic involved in completing metaphysics and by a certain logic involved in overcoming it.

Along the road to its completion, modern metaphysics after Leibniz assumed the form of those monadologies in which, as we have seen, the principle of autonomy was profoundly discredited: in systems governed by a "preestablished harmony" or a "ruse of reason," the subject is not able, autonomously, to set for itself the rules for its own action, and its freedom (the mere "freedom of the turnspit") degenerates into mere independence of other creatures. Given such a situation, one might have thought that twentieth-century attempts to "overcome metaphysics" would have tried to restore meaning to this very principle of autonomy, notably by bringing out again its antisystematic significance. In the Heideggerian and post-Heideggerian sphere of influence, however, the idea of autonomy was identified with what had previously worked toward its dissolution; in fact, this was already true in the case of Nietzsche. In Kant, insofar as the autonomous will was one that, not being determined by any preexisting concept of good and evil, wills for itself the form of law, it appeared as a mere stage toward that "will to will"—the will whose only end is itself and its deployment as will, through which the completion of metaphysics would coincide with the birth of the age of technology. Even in a thinker as wary as Lévinas of the traps of antihumanism and the dead ends of the Heideggerian challenge to metaphysics, the legacy of this analysis has proved enduring, leading to a radical dismissal of the principle of autonomy and of its capacity to serve as a faithful expression of the distinctive dignity of man.

This slope is therefore a steep one to climb back up. The postmonadological approach must think of transcendence in terms of autonomy, or by reference to a horizon of autonomy, in order not to destroy the idea of the subject in the process of breaking through monadic immanence. It must be established, therefore, that this reference does not necessarily lead us back to those deluded models of the subject that had occasionally been cultivated by metaphysics in the past; in other words, it needs to be shown that the idea of autonomy is compatible with the deconstruction of those illusions, as with the main concerns of twentieth-century philosophy, all of which are related to the question of finitude. Doing this will make it possible to see plainly why the debate on this decisive point has so often concentrated—and rightly so—on the coherence (or lack thereof) of the Kantian theory of the subject in its theoretical dimension (as the subject of the *Critique of Pure Reason*) and practical dimension (as the subject of the *Critique of Practical Reason*).

The Kantian Theory of the Subject

A systematic exposition of this theory must account for five principal moments. Corresponding to each of these moments are specific problems, some well known (for example, in the case of the first moment, the difficulty created by the idea of the "thing-in-itself"), others less evident and more formidable (the third moment comes to mind, particularly those few passages in the *Critique of Pure Reason* where Kant argues in favor of a view of pure apperception as equivalent to the representation "I am").[1] But I shall limit myself here to trying to determine the nature of the five moments that make up this theory and give it a place of originality at the heart of the history of subjectivity.

1. The theory of radical finitude as the structure of subjectivity. This is the moment that in the main is comprised in the first *Critique* by the "Transcendental Aesthetic," where it is developed chiefly in the chapter on schematism. By defining sensibility as receptivity, as the capacity for being affected, in contrast to the spontaneity of the understanding, the "Aesthetic" includes in subjectivity a dimension of openness—in the same sense that Lévinas sees in openness the sign of subjectivity (as the very "inability to close oneself off from within"). At the same time this rupture of monadicity marks the emergence of finitude in the subject, since it presupposes an exteriority, an "outside" or "an other," and hence a limit in relation to this otherness. The originality of the Kantian approach to finitude still needs to be spelled out, emphasizing the fact that the human finitude thereby affirmed does not imply (by contrast with the classical concept of finite being) any relativism:

- Traditional doctrines of finitude—those of Descartes and Leibniz, for example—proceeded by positing the Absolute as the identity between being and thought, the coincidence of the real and the rational (that is, as a thinking being for which this coincidence exists: God), and then by showing that, in relation to the Absolute, man is in fact *limited* and hence *relativized*. Conceived against the background of an infinity posited as real, finitude was inevitably seen as a deficiency, as an evil—indeed as a downfall since sensibility, the sign of this fundamentally contingent limitation (given that *in itself* the infinite can exist), could only be regarded as a blot and belittled as an obstacle condemning human knowledge to a fall from the absolute into the relative.

- The Kantian strategy exploited a well-known reversal: it first posited finitude as a structure of knowledge (since the concept, lacking intuition, is empty), as a condition of possibility for representation. Posited a priori, as it were, through simple reflection upon the nature of the concept (which does not produce its content by itself), finitude—as the a priori passivity of sensibility—becomes that in relation to which the Absolute is relativized: precisely because of the finite structure of human knowledge, the Absolute can only be an Idea, not a reality in itself. Thus even though sensibility is now relativized in its turn, as a deplorable sign of finitude in relation to the Absolute, its passivity figures in the theory of pure intuition as a *necessary* condition of knowledge (and not an inessential, or accidental, dimension of knowledge—in relation to that which in itself would be mind, if it had not "fallen" into a body): correspondingly the Absolute, relative to our knowledge, is only a requirement that is conceivable *on the basis of this finitude* as its (by definition) inaccessible limit. From this perspective, finitude is not to be conceived in relation to an Absolute posited as the in-itself, in relation to which finitude becomes measurable; finitude becomes the Absolute, as it were—in short, finitude becomes *radical finitude*.

It is this first moment of Kant's theory of the subject that stimulated Heidegger's interest: we know how, in 1929,[2] he stressed that the radicality of finitude is decided at the very level of the notion of pure intuition, where "pure" (a priori) has a precise meaning—namely, that passivity (i.e., the capacity for being affected, or "openness") is not observed empirically (as a degenerate form of intuition), but is raised to the rank of an a priori. It is also in this sense that it has sometimes been possible, by arguing that the radicalization of finitude has the effect of depriving the Absolute of any ontological status, to see the *Critique of Pure Reason* as engineering a first retreat from the divine,[3] even a first "death of God,"[4] by means of a gesture that all contemporary philosophies were later to do no more than repeat.

Even if such readings are certainly obliged to take into account the formidable question of what becomes of the divine Absolute beyond the first *Critique*, notably *Die Religion innerhalb der Grenzen der blossen Vernunft* (Religion within the Limits of Reason Alone, 1793), that the Transcendental Aesthetic implied an ontological devalorization of the Absolute is unquestionable. Moreover, this devalorization does not involve the divine Absolute alone but also (since the three Ideas stand for so many faces of the Absolute, or the Unconditioned) the cosmological Absolute and the psychological Absolute—this last being the Idea of the soul or, if you will, the subject, now likewise relativized and deontologized by the exposure of radical finitude. Hence the second moment of the theory of the subject:

2. *The critique of rational psychology*. This second moment is found in the chapter of the "Transcendental Dialectic" devoted to "paralogisms." In examining the various illusions—in Descartes, Leibniz, and Berkeley—to which the idea of the subject had given rise, Kant takes his task to be a matter mainly of showing that these illusions are a direct result of forgetting radical finitude—in the Heideggerian sense of "forgetting" (that is, a forgetting that has some necessity about it, being part of the very structure of reason). Beyond their deconstructive import, on account of which this chapter marks a major rupture in the history of subjectivity, the sections dealing with paralogisms have the further interest that they do not lead to a pure and simple renunciation of the Idea of the subject: the distinctive characteristic of the Kantian critique of metaphysics indeed consists, as has often been noted,[5] in providing a theory of the fate of Ideas after their critique; and we know in the case of the Idea of God (as the Idea of system) that the "Appendix to the Transcendental Dialectic" shows how, once de-ontologized, it preserves a regulative usage for knowledge insofar as the Idea of a total unity of knowledge (i.e., the intelligible articulation of all possibilities) acts as a sort of imaginary focus (*focus imaginarius*) of human knowledge—thus what is valid for the Idea of God cannot help but be valid for the Idea of the soul as well. The de-ontologization of the subject of rational psychology thus makes it possible for Kant to articulate a third moment to follow this moment of deconstruction, this time bearing positive import:

3. *The transformation into an imaginary focus*. The difficulty with this third moment is simply that here Kant himself did not produce a complete and synthetic statement of its operation comparable to the treatment found in the "Appendix to the Transcendental Dialectic" of the Idea of God. What, therefore, was the result of the de-reification of the Idea of the subject? Elements of an answer can be found in connection with the four paralogisms, where Kant indicates in each instance what becomes of the notion of the subject after its critique, and what function is left to it to perform. Thus, for example, the first paralogism shows (as against Descartes)[6] that "I am" cannot be deduced from "I think," which thus remains a pure formal structure to which no (intuitive or deductive) knowledge of existence can be made to correspond. Given that by the end of the first two paralogisms the subject has been completely desubstantialized, one may have the impression that the deconstruction of metaphysical illusions about the subject boils down to nothing more than the notion of the

transcendental subject as a pure formal structure of subjectivity in general (that is, the categorical structure and the identity of the "I think"—a dereified version of the paralogism of simplicity—accompanying the diversity of representations).

The impression is probably not false, but only partly correct: if the deontologization of the metaphysical subject were reduced to the emergence of the transcendental subject, it is indisputable that the Kantian theory of subjectivity would be extremely impoverished in its positive dimension—so clearly is it the case that (contrary to what the first post-Kantians sometimes believed) the transcendental subject constitutes neither the object of some knowledge nor the *real* foundation of the diversity of representations, but merely a formal and empty structure that is reflexively extracted at the end of a regressive analysis by abstraction from the diversity of representations. In a sense, this interpretation of the transcendental subject can certainly be seen as reassuring from the point of view of the post-metaphysical development of the criticist theory of the subject: nothing in the notion or function of the transcendental subject justifies regarding it as a reincarnated version of the old metaphysical notion of the subject as foundation, as the potential object of an intellectual intuition (Descartes's *cogito me cogitare*). On the other hand, however, if one grants that this subject lacks the two major features of subjectivity (self-consciousness and the capacity to ground objectivity), can it still be said to warrant being called a subject? Rather than a "subject," we would seem here to be closer to the simple Heideggerian notion of "ontological precomprehension" that in both *Kant und das Problem der Metaphysik* (Kant and the Problem of Metaphysics, 1929) and *Sein und Zeit* (Being and Time, 1927) characterizes the *Dasein*, which plainly is no longer a subject. If the Kantian theory of the subject, in its positive aspect, were thus to be reduced to merely introducing the transcendental subject, the deconstruction of the Idea of the subject would then in fact lead to its elimination—in which case nothing here would take us beyond what either Heidegger or even Lévinas was able to do in rethinking the status of subject in the aftermath of its critique. To escape this result, the importance of a fourth moment needs to be stressed:

4. Transformation of subjectivity into activity—that is, the substitution (prefiguring the Fichtean *Tathandlung*) of the subject-act for the subject-substance. In the *Critique of Pure Reason*, this substitution is introduced in the theory of the schematism, where in fact we see in the *subject of the schematism* another notion of the subject than that of the transcendental subject: here the subject is that activity of temporalization which transforms the categories into a method.[7] This is a dimension of subjectivity (of theoretical subjectivity, in any case) that clearly goes beyond the transcendental subject, since the schematizing subject, as an opening to time, is no longer reduced to the categorical structure that it employs as a method; employing it in this way requires that there be a subject for the method or that the idea of this method should serve as *subject*, since an activity must have an *author*. In this sense the theory of the schematism represents a first answer to the question "What is man?"—namely, that man is the subject of the schematism. This answer furnishes us with a subject (as the author of the activity) that is neither monadic (by virtue of its openness to time) nor, more generally, metaphysical (since it receives rather than grounds the categorical structure). This idea of the subject as activity (being neither substance, as the metaphysical subject is, nor formal structure, as the transcendental subject is) becomes clear in a fifth and final moment:

5. The theory of the practical subject. In the second *Critique*, the subject is indeed thought of as a practical subject and, more precisely, through the idea of autonomy as an activity of self-foundation, as positing for itself the law of its own actions. In this sense, beyond the schematism, a limit to the desubstantialization of subjectivity and its transformation into pure activity is reached in locating the truth of the theoretical subject in a practical subject—much as, in a general way (as Fichte strongly emphasized) within criticism, practical philosophy constitutes the truth of theoretical philosophy. And thus it is as *autonomy* that the subject finds its postmonadic status: first prepared by that "openness" to impressions with which the transcendental aesthetic endows the theoretical subject, the dislocation of the theoretical subject is then carried out by means of the opening to humanity presupposed by the practical subject. With this return from independence to autonomy, Kant managed to open up a way along which the multiform faces of individualism could be led back to a non-naïve humanism—or, if you will, a "humanism of the other man."

The whole problem, however, is to determine whether in going beyond the subject of the schematism Kantian theory did not also retreat from the arguments of the *Critique of Pure Reason*, which gave the first moment all its density. Might not the very idea of radical finitude be imperilled by making autonomy the horizon of the subject's transcendence?

The Problem of the Practical Subject

It may indeed be wondered what happens to the theory of radical finitude in passing from the first to the second *Critique*. In the *Critique of Pure Reason*, what the transcendental dialectic was devoted to bringing out—namely, the sterility of knowledge by mere concepts—the *Aesthetic* verified negatively: in using concepts closed to intuition, thought is led astray and falls into illusion. This negative proof of the theory of finitude, it is interesting to note, took on the force of a criticism of the ontological argument as well: in claiming to deduce the existence of God on the basis of the concept of God, rational theology treats His existence as characteristic like any other (i.e., as an element of the concept), failing to see that existence is not "a real predicate" (i.e., an element of the definition of a thing) but rather "the positing of the thing with all these predicates"—in short, failing to see that existence corresponds to an extraconceptual dimension of the real and, as such, requires an opening (via intuition) to the phenomenal appearance of the thing.

The link between the refutation of the ontological argument and the theory of radical finitude is altogether essential to the understanding of the Kantian critique of metaphysics, and needs to be examined. Because the concept is a "general representation," it gives me only the property common to the objects of the same class; it does not allow me to apprehend the existence (which is always particular) of the objects of this class—which is why grasping the particular in its existence requires another source of knowledge, intuition: "All cognitions, that is, all presentations consciously referred to an object, are either *intuitions* or *concepts*. Intuition is a *singular* presentation . . ., the concept is a *general* . . . presentation."[8] To try to deduce existence on the basis of the concept is to fail to recognize this distinction (the ontological argument of rational theology being the prototypical example of such a failure). More generally, however, it is the failure of all metaphysics, which "soars far above the teachings of experience, and . . . rests on concepts alone."[9] Aiming to understand particular existence by concepts, metaphysics exhibits on a larger scale the structure of the ontological argument: for in passing directly from the concept to the real, all metaphysics is basically *idealist* in the sense that it assumes an ontology of *identity* between concept and thing, between the real (including existence) and the rational. In the face of this *generalized ontological argument* (which, as Schelling stressed in his later period, constitutes speculative philosophy), the Kantian method locates the radical finitude of human knowledge in the undeducibility of the material referent of the concept (= the existence of the object) on the basis of its form (= the universal property that it expresses). Such a philosophy of finitude is thus allied, at the theoretical level, with a *generalized critique of the ontological argument*, bringing forth a moment of *difference*, if you will, between the real and the rational—an *ontological difference*—and condemning every attempt by the subject to posit existence on the basis of the idea of itself.

As a consequence of this fundamental orientation of its theoretical philosophy, criticism finds itself faced with a formidable problem of coherence when it enters the field of practical philosophy. For, in the domain of practice, the subject no longer seems to be *openness* or *receptivity*, but, quite plainly, *self-positing*: what is it to act morally, from the perspective defined by the *Critique of Practical Reason*, if not to posit the existence of an act whose maxim is consistent with the law of reason insofar as it is practical? Are we not thus taking part in a kind of *practical ontological argument* in which the autonomous subject, on the strength of the fact that it *conceives* an end as good, realizes it through its action? In passing in this way from idea to existence, practical philosophy appears to be based on the very structure (that of the ontological argument) which theoretical philosophy made the emblem of metaphysics—in which case, what becomes in the *Critique of Practical Reason* of the theory of radical finitude laid out in the *Critique of Pure Reason*? From the theoretical subject to the practical subject, from the open subject of the transcendental aesthetic to the autonomous subject, is there not a going beyond of finitude or, to borrow Cassirer's phrase, a "breakthrough to the infinite"? If this were the case, a whole series of consequences would follow: not only would it be possible to see criticism as falling back into the "metaphysics of subjectivity," not only would finitude—radical in the first *Critique*—once again be relativized (relative to the absoluteness of the practical subject), but the idea of autonomy would allow the theory of the subject to avoid the very commitment to finitude which appears to be all but indispensable for a philosophy that has escaped the illusions of metaphysics. In short, even though its foundations may seem to have been undermined by Kant's theoretical philosophy, "classical humanism" can be seen to have forcefully reasserted itself in his practical philosophy.

We can therefore easily understand why, in their important 1929 debate on the interpretation of Kantianism,[10] Cassirer and Heidegger attached particular significance to the question of the practical subject: this is where the possibility is being put to the test (along with the coherence of the critical tradition itself) of following once more today—without having to "return to Kant"—certain of the paths taken by Kant himself, and after him by Fichte.

The Heideggerian Interpretation of Practical Finitude

In §30 of *Kant and the Problem of Metaphysics*, Heidegger attempted to provide an interpretation of the *Critique of Practical Reason* that was compatible with the project he detected in the *Critique of Pure Reason*. There, at least in the first edition, he found the metaphysics of subjectivity undermined by a theory of radical finitude.

To evaluate this interpretation, it is necessary to keep in mind what, from the standpoint of the theory of finitude, forms the essential part of the Heideggerian reading of the first *Critique*—namely, that for Kant (Heidegger is correct on this crucial point) the finitude of the theoretical subject is intrinsic: as noted earlier, finitude is a matter of structure, not of degree (as in classical theories of finitude, which consisted in *quantitatively* limiting the human capacity for knowledge, and thus did not rule out the chance that such knowledge might be marked by a lesser degree of limitation). This doctrine of structural finitude, according to which it is absolutely impossible to conceive the activity of knowledge apart from the finitude that is inherent in it, regards human knowledge—as distinct from an infinite (divine) understanding—as an *intuitus derivatus* rather than an *intuitus originarius*:

- For infinite knowledge, nothing could actually present itself as an "ob-ject," as something located in relation to infinite knowledge "in front" and "outside," since any such exteriority of a non-I would constitute a limitation; infinite knowledge must thus be thought of as a source of being, as what causes being to be, as what causes it to *be born* by the mere fact of *conceiving* it (*intuitus originarius*).
- Human understanding, on the other hand, neither engenders nor causes being: it looks at a being that is *already* present, that is thus "given" to it; and so it is on the basis of this *giving*—hence in a *derived* (*derivatus*) way—that there can be knowledge of it. The minimal instrument of such a giving is constituted by pure intuition. In other words, even if I manage to neglect the particular data of empirical intuition, I still cannot "detach the mind from the senses" in order to produce representations from my own resources like a windowless monad, for, without this faculty of a priori receptivity that corresponds to pure intuition, concepts remain empty. The structural finitude of the human mind stems from this essential *dependence* of its cognitive activity on empirical intuition—actual, or, at the very least, potential.

Working on the basis of this distinction, Heidegger's whole effort in *Kant and the Problem of Metaphysics*, as well as in his debate with Cassirer the same year, was to show that this *dependence* (i.e., the derived character of knowledge) does not disappear at any level of the theory of knowledge worked out in the *Critique of Pure Reason*. Its role at the level of intuition is clear;[11] for Heidegger, it may also manifest itself at the levels of understanding and reason:

- In connection with understanding, Heidegger's proof involves his interpretation of the theory of the schematism: if, in order to be applied to what is given, concepts must be schematized by the transcendental imagination, the reason is that even in its dimension of spontaneity, the human mind (far from creating objects) is limited in its capacity to *receive* them to sketching out an image of objectivity and placing it before itself *in anticipation*—in the expectation of perception. In this sketching out of objectivity, the understanding depends on the work of another faculty, the imagination, which, by obtaining *sensory* images for concepts of the understanding, introduces a dimension of *receptivity* precisely where the mind as understanding (as synthetic activity) is active:

thus, in the very activity of the understanding there is receptivity—and so, too, dependence.[12] Hence the expression "foundational receptivity" that Heidegger uses to designate that dimension of schematization inherent in the activity of the understanding: "foundational receptivity"—not *intuitus originarius*—is the sign of finitude. Hence too the way in which Heidegger makes the doctrine of transcendental imagination (the site of this "foundational receptivity") the center of the *Critique of Pure Reason* and also its boldest moment: by installing the work of the imagination (as "foundational receptivity") at the very core of the mind, Kant caused the ancestral privilege of reason to totter and turned the image of subjectivity upside down. Far from being the absolute foundation of objectivity, far even from monadically producing the totality of its representations, theoretical subjectivity—insofar as receptivity is a key element of spontaneity—is, so to speak, *receptive spontaneity*: to the degree, that is, that the imagination produces (implying spontaneity) sensible images (implying receptivity).

- So too at the level of reason, Heidegger argues, there is dependence in relation to the intuition, but in a mediated way: the activity of reason simply seeks, in effect, to give unity and systematicity to the knowledge that has been assembled by the understanding, which is related (to what extent we have already seen) to intuition. Theoretical reason thus cannot by itself break through the chain of finitude.

What can be said of practical reason on the other hand? And what, as a practical matter, becomes of radical finitude as "foundational receptivity"? §30 of *Kant and the Problem of Metaphysics*, in attempting to relocate the structure of this a priori receptivity (which corresponds to pure intuition) at the level of morality, devotes itself to a discussion of what Heidegger takes to be its practical equivalent, namely the *pure sentiment* of respect: just as the concept is *intrinsically* linked to intuition, possessing in the schema the structure of an a priori receptivity, so too the moral law (which, like the concept, refers to an aspect of the mind's spontaneity—in this case the spontaneity of freedom as autonomous will) is indissolubly bound up with the pure sentiment of respect (which corresponds to one of the dimensions of receptivity). In short, the moral law bears the same relation to respect as the concept to intuition; and, in each case, the relation between the two terms coincides precisely with the transcendental imagination—understood as that structure which gives receptivity its place at the heart of spontaneity.[13] An ingenious hypothesis, this; but even granting as much, it may nonetheless be asked why respect deserves to be invested with such a function.

The explanation is actually fairly simple. The subject is characterized by consciousness of itself, as pure apperception, as consciousness of the identity of the "I think" that accompanies all representations. In the case of the subject, this "practical self-consciousness" must likewise accompany all activity of the practical self. Now the practical self ("the true essence of man") Kant also calls—as Heidegger reminds us—the *person*. To attempt to identify the subjectivity of the practical subject is consequently equivalent to seeking what the essence of the person's personality consists in.[14]

The answer is found in *Religion within the Limits of Reason Alone*: "Personality itself is . . . the idea of the moral law and the respect which is inseparable from it."[15] The essence of the practical subject is thus to be located in the awareness of the moral law, which, like our theoretical concepts, refers to a dimension of spontaneity (being self-posited)—but in such a way that we can be *conscious* of this law as a moral law only if we *receive* it through respect, insofar as this is pure sentiment. Respect is determined by analogy with the definition of pure intuition: here again we are dealing with a minimal dimension of sensibility (as of a priori sensibility) since respect, unlike empirical sentiments, is a sentiment that is necessarily present in every person, not being subject to the vagaries of the sensible world.

Respect thus appears to Heidegger as that moment of receptivity with regard to the moral law that constitutes the practical subject by conferring upon it too a dimension of *openness*—and thus of *transcendence*: "Respect is 'susceptibility' to the law"; moreover, "[r]espect for the law—this specific way of making the law manifest as the basis of the determination of action—is in itself a revelation of myself as the self that acts"—meaning that consciousness (based on respect) of the law as moral also makes me conscious of myself as the subject of this law, as the one in relation to which this law functions as law: "That for which the respect is respect, the moral law, the reason as free gives it to itself. Respect for the law is respect for oneself as that self which does not let itself be determined by self-conceit and self-love."[16] Respect is, above all, respect for the person, in the sense that Kant himself insists upon: "Respect always applies to persons only, never to things."[17]

In showing that the essence of practical subjectivity lies in that sentiment by which one is conscious of the moral law, and of oneself as a person (as a moral subject), Heidegger consequently finds one dimension of receptivity in particular to be constitutive of practical subjectivity—a receptivity now located at the heart of practical spontaneity (i.e., autonomy), which thus in turn takes the form of receptive spontaneity: that is, of transcendental imagination and, on this account, of radical finitude. By locating the essence of the practical subject in the person (as consciousness of the moral law) rather than in some intelligible, atemporal (numinous) aspect of the person, Heidegger is in a position to assert that *the Kantian theory of the subject is homogeneous and coherent*; that it is through and through a theory of the subject as radically finite. From this point of view, the Kantian theory—having been developed prior to Kant's putative relapse into metaphysics—would in fact be the finest imaginable prefiguration of the project undertaken by Heidegger himself in *Being and Time* under the name "analysis of human being" (*Dasein*). Heidegger, it is true, nonetheless judged that "weakness" led Kant in the second edition of the *Critique of Pure Reason* to reestablish in certain respects the primacy of the understanding over the imagination: a shift of emphasis that following its initial expression in 1787 was to have, as we shall see, unfortunate repercussions in 1788 with the appearance of the *Critique of Practical Reason*. Overall, however, considering the part of it that is faithful to the spirit of the original edition of the first *Critique*, the analysis of the practical self cannot be regarded as nullifying the earlier analysis, by means of which the Kantian theory of the subject opened a breach in the history of subjectivity—quickly, alas, plugged up by Kant himself.

This reading is indisputably brilliant—but is it really tenable? Does the argument from respect actually constitute a practical analogue to the idea of pure intuition? And if it is a matter of practical finitude, is the argument well grounded at this level? More precisely, is the *content* of the theory of the subject in practical philosophy truly homogeneous with the content of the theory of the subject worked out in the *Critique of Pure Reason*? It is in connection with this decisive point that Cassirer's challenge to the Heideggerian reading assumes special importance.

Cassirer's Critique of Heidegger: The Status of Practical Reason

Before we examine Cassirer's objections,[18] it must first be acknowledged that, everything considered, he had a good grasp of Heidegger's motivation in taking the notion of radical finitude[19] as a starting point and guide for the interpretation of Kant. He likewise had a perfectly sound understanding of Heidegger's conception of Kantian finitude (as positing the "foundational and essential *dependence* of all derived knowledge" with respect to a "giving")[20] and of the way in which the theory of the transcendental imagination was used to show that reason and understanding are intrinsically connected with intuition, and hence with finitude.[21] He was even prepared to admit that the Kantian conception of theoretical finitude implies no relativistic consequences: he stressed that the concept of intuitive understanding, while limiting human knowledge, does not assume a real absolute in relation to which finite knowledge would be merely a sort of lesser being, but merely indicates the existence of a "problem"

(*Aufgabe*), if you will—an Idea. Rather than defining any "real limit that our knowledge would run up against," intuitive understanding is instead a "limiting concept that it itself posits, that it imposes on itself to limit the claims of sensibility" (i.e., to limit the naïvely realistic tendency of sensibility to believe that things exist as entities wholly formed outside consciousness, which I merely receive as they are).

Because Cassirer's objections to the Heideggerian interpretation rest on a thorough and reasonably faithful reading, they deserve careful examination. I mention a first objection, concerning the finitude of the understanding, only as a reminder: while admitting the general dependence of understanding upon intuition, Cassirer attempts to lessen this dependence by showing that understanding *constitutes* intuition.[22] The argument is directed at what Kant calls "formal intuition" (i.e., the *constructed* space of mathematics) which the *Critique* does indeed hold to be constituted by a synthesis of the understanding.[23] But there is nothing here that can really contradict Heidegger's reading. Heidegger had already replied beforehand in §28 of *Kant and the Problem of Metaphysics*: when Kant refers to mathematical space, he talks of the "concept of space," carefully distinguishing it from the intuition of space; the mathematical concept of space is in fact a scientific abstraction, produced on the basis of empirical intuitions of external sense objects, which already presuppose the form of space.[24] While there is no doubt that the concept of space is constituted by understanding, this in no way does away with the fact that, even when engaged in such activity, the understanding is dependent on intuition. Cassirer's attack on the Heideggerian thesis really reveals its full scope only in tackling the question of practical reason, where he mounts a double-pronged assault against the claim that here too a foundational receptivity defines the structure of subjectivity.

Cassirer objects first that, if understanding and theoretical reason are in some sense connected with sensibility, this is not the case with practical reason: "According to Kant, this situation is altered when we consider reason no longer simply from a theoretical point of view but 'from a practical point of view.' For with the 'absolute' of the *idea of liberty*, it dares finally to take the decisive step toward the pure 'intelligible,' the suprasensible and supratemporal."[25] Cassirer supports this view by reference to the following passage from the *Critique of Pure Reason*:

> Should it be granted that we may in due course discover, not in experience but in certain laws of the pure employment of reason—laws which are not merely logical rules, but which while holding *a priori* also concern our existence—ground for regarding ourselves as *legislating* completely *a priori* in regard to our own *existence*, and as determining this existence, there would therby be revealed a spontaneity through which our reality would be determinable, independently of the conditions of empirical intuition. And we

> should also become aware that in the consciousness of our existence there is contained a something *a priori*, which can serve to determine our existence—the complete determination of which is possible only in sensible terms—as being related, in respect of a certain inner faculty, to a non-sensible intelligible world.[26]

The objection being raised here may seem at first hard to appreciate; but it becomes clear enough once the reasoning has been reconstructed. Cassirer grants Heidegger that *theoretical* reason does not escape the chain of finitude, and that in the last analysis it always remains connected with time. Witness the fact that when reason believes it is going beyond experience (by transforming ideas into purported objects of knowledge), on the one hand it falls into sophisms and its conclusions have no truth whatsoever (since they have no existing object); but, on the other hand, what it concludes does not even have a *meaning* (since an Idea, no less than any other general concept, can be meaningful only with reference to sensible experience). This relation to sensible experience, which the concepts of understanding enjoy thanks to the schema, exists for Ideas only *mediately*, inasmuch as they become regulative principles governing the function of the understanding, which is related to intuition and hence to time.[27] In short, the Ideas of reason have neither truth nor meaning if they are not reconnected in a certain way to intuition, which is accomplished through their purely regulative role with respect to the operation of understanding. Thus theoretical reason is finite. It is difficult, however, for Cassirer to imagine this finitude having a counterpart in practical reason:

- Practical concepts, by virtue of being what Kant calls "categories of freedom" (and also because of the dualism of phenomena and noumena), cannot have any relation at all—not even a mediate one—to the content of an intuition.
- It would therefore appear to follow that practical reason is able to slip free of the main negative constraint of the theory of the meaning of general concepts—namely, that nothing can be thought of as being without empirical manifestation and yet nonetheless having a meaning.[28] For if practical concepts—"categories of freedom"—have no relation to intuition, how can they be applicable, which is to say representable? It is easy to see that this question amounts to asking how practical reason is capable, in Cassirer's words, of taking the decisive step toward pure intelligibility. The problem is resolved in the second *Critique* through analogy with the schematism constituted by the "Typic of pure practical judgment." And here we are obliged to say that Cassirer is right, since in the Typic the presentation of practical concepts is accounted for without assuming any intrinsic relation to intuition or any temporalization: it is by reference to pure concepts (e.g., the form of legality in nature) that moral concepts (e.g., the various possible conceptual determina-

tions of submission to the law) acquire representability. Thus no openness to temporality enters in here: if practical finitude exists, it cannot be through the presence—at the heart of practical reason—of the structure of the transcendental imagination.

Cassirer bolsters this argument by countering Heidegger's emphasis on the sentiment of respect (conceived as that dimension of receptive spontaneity that makes it possible after all to find in practical reason a finitude analogous to that of theoretical reason), pointing out, rightly again, that Kant makes a rigorous distinction between the moral law and feeling for the law. The force of this objection can be appreciated only in the context of Heidegger's strategy of isolating a dimension of receptivity in practical reason by reuniting the law with respect for it, thus identifying the production of law with consciousness of it—as if the very content of the moral law was inseparable from respect for it. Cassirer's reply was this:

> The content of the moral law is not at all founded for Kant on the feeling of respect: *this does not constitute its meaning*. This feeling indicates purely and simply the way in which the law, *absolute in itself*, is represented in finite empirical consciousness; it does not belong to the foundation of Kantian ethics, but to its application.[29]

Here again, the terms of the debate must be made explicit:

- To identify in practical reason that a priori receptivity which he sees as a sign of authentic finitude, Heidegger reduces the production of law (the work of practical reason itself) to consciousness of the law (respect): just as theoretical reason produces nothing that is not directly or indirectly related to possible experience, and therefore to some spatiotemporal given, so too the activity of practical reason (e.g., production of law) would be inconceivable without the receptivity of respect.
- In fact, Cassirer replies, the foundation of law in Kant (as an activity of practical reason) in no way involves consciousness of it: practical reason is pure spontaneity, and so in order to function does not need the receptivity of respect. This argument has the effect of installing at the level of practical reason a model of subjectivity through which a kind of "breakthrough to the infinite" could be achieved—*at least if foundational receptivity is the only conceivable finitude*.

What is at stake in this technical discussion is therefore of the highest importance for any attempt to situate the critical tradition (and particularly its reference to the principle of autonomy) in the history of subjectivity: accordingly, a careful examination of the arguments mobilized by Cassirer for separating practical reason from respect cannot be avoided. The basis for this separation he locates primarily in Kant's often misunderstood distinction between *man* and the *finite reasonable individual*, according to which man appears only as a particular instance of finite reasonable being, with the finitude of finite reasonable being understood as a purely rational, nonsensory finitude that is expressed only in the difference between being and the ought-to-be. In plain language: for an infinite being, the moral law is a being; for a finite being, it is an ought-to-be—without this ought-to-be having to take the form that it happens to adopt for the particular kind of finite being that man is (i.e., the form of a duty received by sensibility through the pure feeling of respect).

This distinction between human and finite reasonable being, missing from the first edition of the *Critique of Pure Reason*, was implicitly introduced in the second edition, in §1 of the "Transcendental Aesthetic" in which Kant added a noteworthy qualification to a key sentence cited earlier: "[I]ntuition takes place only in so far as the object is given to us. This again is only possible, to *man at least*, in so far as the mind is affected in a certain way"[30]—which is to say according to the spatiotemporal forms of the sensibility. The added phrase thus qualifies spatiotemporal (sensory) finitude as being merely the human form of finitude, allowing that there could be other finite reasonable beings whose finitude does not take the form of sensory receptivity. This distinction, created in the interval between the two editions of the *Critique of Pure Reason*, logically fits with the argument of the *Critique of Practical Reason*—all the more easily as it had already been used in support of the practical argument of the *Grundlegung zur Metaphysik der Sitten* (Grounding for the Metaphysics of Morals, 1785), where no doubt it appeared for the first time: "[W]e cannot but admit that the moral law is of such widespread significance that it must hold not merely for men but for all rational beings generally. . . ."[31]

Thus the moral law, which Kant goes on to reaffirm as "a universal precept for every rational nature" and not as a norm that is "valid only under the contingent conditions of humanity,"[32] has, *as a product of practical reason*, a meaning and a validity—and thus a consistency—*independently of its reception by the sensibility* in the form of respect. It therefore becomes possible for us to grasp what use Cassirer intends to make of the following points:

> It is there at bottom that resides the real and essential objection that I have to raise against Heidegger's interpretation of Kant: in attempting to refer, indeed to reduce all power of knowing to the transcendental imagination, Heidegger ends up with what remains for him the sole frame of reference, that of temporal existence. The distinction between phenomenon and noumenon is rubbed out, worn down: all being henceforth belongs to the dimension of time, and by virtue of just that to finitude. Thus the central pillar on which rests the whole edifice of Kantian thought is pushed away, without which it

> cannot help but fall down. Kant never upheld such a monism of the imagination: he supported a radical and pronounced dualism that distinguished between the sensible world and the intelligible world. For the question he poses is not that of being and time, but that of being and the ought-to-be. . . .[33]

In short, the finitude (if any) of practical reason would be that of any finite reasonable being who, as such a being, makes a distinction between what is and what ought to be. This finitude is in fact analytically implied by the very idea of morality, or practical reason: an infinite being does not face a choice between ends—does not even propose ends for itself, as Spinoza pointed out in criticizing the notion of divine free will. But given that the very idea of practical reason includes a lack of being, and hence presupposes a dimension of finitude, practical finitude has nothing in common with the structure of the imagination, with the foundational receptivity of theoretical reason: and so if one defines radical finitude, as Heidegger does, by sensory foundational receptivity, it must be agreed that passing from theoretical reason to practical reason involves much more a breakthrough outside finitude (thus understood) than confirmation of the imaginative structure of rationality and subjectivity. In fact, practical subjectivity, for all its limitations (recall that the practical subject, by its capacity to conceive an ought-to-be, is by definition a *finite* reasonable being), is conceived wholly in terms of spontaneity, as law-producing and self-positing: here we find precisely that structure of the autonomous subject who, in acting in accordance with the law, posits in being what it conceived as prior to being and who evokes the Absolute as self-positing. At the least, practical subjectivity does not make manifest in itself that dimension of openness the highlighting of which by the *Critique of Pure Reason* was to give Kant's thinking its original place in the history of subjectivity: in short, if Cassirer's interpretation of the Kantian theory of the subject is right, the status customarily accorded to Kantianism in this history would have to be completely reconsidered.

Kant: Humanist or "Inhumanist"?

Everything in this debate on practical reason clearly turns on how the emergence of the distinction between human and finite reasonable being is to be interpreted. Why did Kant, after the first edition of the *Critique of Pure Reason*, reduce human finitude to a mere spelling out of finite rationality? Depending on the answer to this question, the very meaning of the distinction will be completely different—which cannot help but have consequences for the general problem of how the status of the practical subject and the idea of autonomy is to be reevaluated.

A first pass at interpreting the distinction between human and reasonable finite being was made by Schopenhauer. He attempted, not unimaginatively, to relate the distinction to Kant's sudden taking into account of the "dear little angels": while angels are certainly finite beings, they do not specially manifest their finitude through the structures of their sensibility. Seemingly more serious is an argument that has become popular among certain of Heidegger's followers. In a polemical review of Luc Ferry's and my book *La Pensée* 68, Jean-François Lyotard undertook to discuss what he calls our "interpretation of Kant": "When Ferry and Renaut appeal to 'Kantian humanism' to reprove those who 'wish to make philosophy inhuman,' they understand nothing of Kant"—for "Kant's thought has nothing to do with *humanism.*" In other words, however much Kant's use of the question "What is man?" to bring together all the inquiries that make up philosophy would seem to justify a "humanistic" reading of his work, such a reading is seriously mistaken. Lyotard's reasons are summarized in a few words: "Kant constantly reverts to [this point:] the categorical imperative does not concern 'Man'—it concerns all 'finite reasonable beings.' As a pure principle of practical reason, the moral law is, in the strict sense, *inhuman.*" Thus, concludes Lyotard, what "the Ferry-Renaut humanism" does not understand is that the essential moment of practical philosophy "from Kant's perspective" consisted of "bringing out the inhuman authority of the law," in "*giving the inhuman its due.*"[34]

Carried away by our alleged desire to challenge contemporary antihumanism, we thus failed to see that Kant himself, despite a few appearances to the contrary, developed a practical philosophy located beyond the norms of the human: we did not pay enough attention to the distinction between human and finite reasonable being that Kant introduced precisely in order to show that the moral law is not addressed to human beings, that practical reason is not the expression of "humanity"—in short, a distinction introduced to define an ethics at the center of which man is nowhere to be found, an ethics that would finally escape that exclusive concentration on all that is human which since the Renaissance had been supposed to define humanism and the metaphysics of subjectivity. *Ergo*: grasping this non-obvious distinction would make it clear (as Heidegger saw very well, unlike "neo-Kantians" such as Cassirer) that critical philosophy was not merely a stage in the development of humanistic modernity, but also the place where the enthronement of the human as a norm for all action and judgment was questioned, cast in doubt, and repudiated—torn out down to its deepest roots. Heidegger, to his enormous credit, perceived the extent of this rooting out; the "neo-Kantians," on the other hand, never stopped trying to repair the damage by reconstructing a more culturally "presentable" Kant—even though Kant's thought (in itself neither humanistic nor antihumanistic) was to be located beyond this opposition between the human and the inhuman, which remained captive to the values of modernity.

What are we to think of this interpretation of Kantianism—in particular of Lyotard's use of the distinction between human and finite reasonable being? First, a simple blunder needs to be corrected, one that does not threaten his interpretation as a whole but does somewhat weaken it: no one can seriously maintain, as Lyotard does, that for Kant "the categorical imperative does not concern Man." What Lyotard actually wished to suggest (as he later admitted, by the way) was that man is not the being addressed by the *moral law*. The being addressed by the *categorical imperative* is most assuredly man (rather than any other instance of finite reasonable being)—for the imperative is precisely the moral law as this presents itself to our sensibility.[35]

Having rectified this error, we come straight away to Lyotard's main claim: that the distinction between human and finite reasonable being was introduced because the aim of Kantian ethics was to "bring out the inhuman authority of the law." This explanation, prompted by the desire (shared by Heidegger) to save Kant from the humanism of the "neo-Kantians," is actually quite paradoxical. Contrary to what Lyotard (and many of Heidegger's other French disciples) may think, it is enough to read the transcript of the Davos debate to realize that the distinction between human and finite reasonable being figures importantly only in Cassirer's argument. Heidegger, in examining what enabled the Kantian theory of radical finitude to repudiate the installation of human reason as a foundation for philosophy, pays no particular attention to the distinction; to the contrary, as we shall see, he sees in it the sign (as in everything that appeared only after the first edition of the *Critique of Pure Reason*) of Kant's retreat before the shock of what he had glimpsed—namely, the frailty of the values of humanistic rationality. In §30 of *Kant and the Problem of Metaphysics*, which argues the reverse of what Lyotard (thinking he is defending Heidegger's Kant against the Kant of the "neo-Kantians") attempts to assert, Heidegger even attempts to marginalize the distinction, to the point of sketching a reading of the *Critique of Practical Reason* from the perspective of what he takes to be the true spirit of criticism: the spirit of the first edition. For Heidegger's descendants to make an "inhumanist" reading of Kant rest on a distinction which the "*Kantbuch*" itself felt it had to disregard in order to bring out the true significance of Kantianism is clearly a dangerous move. In fact, what the move conceals is a slip that can easily be explained but which must be firmly condemned as a matter of principle. Lyotard is certainly free to maintain that, in distinguishing between human and finite reasonable being, Kant wished to remove ethics from the theory of man as a theory of *psychology*, if you will—of *empirical anthropology*: "As a pure principle of practical reason, the moral law is in the strict sense inhuman," for "what the imperative prescribes for us is to transcend our empirical 'humanity' and what Kant calls a 'pathologically affected will'; to emancipate ourselves from the limits of our historical situation, from our psychological inclinations, from our human, all-too-human values, in order to be able to unhesitatingly receive the call of the Law."[36] There is in fact nothing absurd in attributing an anti-anthropological, anti-psychological significance to the distinction: this is actually the explanation proposed—the paradox continues—by Cassirer's neo-Kantianism. But how can one not see that *the distinction, significant or not, has nothing to do with whether or not Kant is a humanist?* Separating ethical principles from the psychological, or anthropological (in the empirical sense of the word) conditions of human existence, from our "empirical humanity," can in no way be regarded as equivalent to providing a foundation for an "in-human" ethics that would evade the valorization of the human *as such*—unless, of course, Kant is assumed to have crudely identified humanity with empirical humanity, and then to have carried out this wholesale identification himself. Perhaps Lyotard, for his part, takes this line (though I doubt he does, actually); Kant, however, certainly did not. He took care to distinguish man as *causa phaenomenon* from man as *causa nuomenon*: insofar as he is "one of the appearances of the sensible world," man is subject to "empirical laws"; but he is also "in respect of certain faculties," a "purely intelligible object" whose action "cannot be attributed to the receptivity of sensibility."[37] Thus a solution to the third antinomy suggests itself, the significance of which has fallen to practical philosophy to explain: "[I]n the context of his relation to others, I actually regard every person simply in terms of his humanity, hence as *homo noumenon*"—and not as *homo phaenomenon*.[38]

Considering these passages on man, we are thus obliged to acknowledge that if Kant distinguished practical objectivity from the "human," it was merely in the sense of "human, all-too-human"—the "too human" corresponding only to *homo phaenomenon*, and leaving out "the truly human human" (i.e., *homo noumenon*): to detach empirical man from the moral law is not to dehumanize the law, except in the sense of admitting that what is human in man reduces to the empirical character of his inclinations. Kant did not believe he had to take the road leading to what would have seemed to him to be a dehumanization (or animalization) of man: thus not only did the separation between the practical sphere and human psychology not amount to the subtraction of ethics from humanism, but the setting up after 1781 of finite reasonable being as the subject of practical reason was aimed, to the contrary, at strengthening the humanism of the critical program.

Once Lyotard's method of interpretation is ruled out, it naturally remains to reinstate the distinction between man and finite reasonable being in its full scope and consequence. §31 of *Kant and the Problem of Meta-*

physics emphasizes the way in which, having appeared after the first edition of the *Critique of Pure Reason*, it reveals the spirit of the second edition—namely, the effort to relativize the role of the imagination and, correlatively, to reaffirm the primacy of the (active) intellectual faculties over the capacity for extra-rational thought and foundational receptivity which, in the 1781 edition, corresponded to the functioning of the imagination. Thus it comes as no surprise that Heidegger should have deplored the emergence of a distinction that led Kant to separate finitude from sensory receptivity, thereby assigning a secondary role to the imagination and no longer treating finitude (formerly identified with sensory receptivity) merely as a particular (human) case of a finitude that was to be conceived in a purely intellectual way, based on the difference between being and the ought-to-be. For in affirming (unfortunately, in Heidegger's view) that the moral law is valid not only for man but also for all finite reasonable being, Kant made law and practical reason independent of respect and, consequently, of the structure of the imagination: "It is indisputable," Heidegger remarked disapprovingly, "that the problem of the distinction between finite rational being in general and man as a particular realization of such being comes to the foreground in the second edition of the transcendental deduction."[39] In the transcendental deduction this distinction would now have the same role to play as it had in the ethical domain: to show that the dependence of the understanding on intuition and imagination is valid only *for us human beings*, not for *finite reasonable beings in general*; and thus to reestablish the independence of the intellectual faculties *in general* (understanding and reason) in relation to sensibility. In other words, "In the second edition, Kant *broadened* the concept of a finite rational being to the point that the concept is no longer to be confused with that of man"[40]—a broadening that in Heidegger's view did not in any way constitute (as against Cassirer) an improvement on the *Critique*, but testified instead to Kant's relapse into metaphysics: the later version of the *Critique of Pure Reason* he found oriented "exclusively in terms of pure reason as such," the values of rationality, undermined in the first edition, having regained their former preeminence.

Heidegger's account of the distinction between human and finite reasonable being, because it is so closely bound up with the interpretation he gives of the difference between the two editions of the first *Critique*, is vulnerable to a number of objections:

- First, the interpretation is flatly psychologistic. Explaining a text (in this case, the second edition) by reference to the psychological circumstances of its production (here, Kant's alleged inability to cope with the distress provoked by reflection upon the doctrine of ontological difference) fails just as all other reductive approaches do; but the attempt is particularly dubious when it is made by a thinker like Heidegger, who is obliged by consistency to eliminate values (e.g., courage/cowardice) from his hermeneutics—assuming, that is, he subscribed to his own formula (in the *Letter on Humanism*) that "every valuing . . . is a subjectivizing."[41]

- As Alexis Philonenko has stressed,[42] one cannot argue that from 1781 to 1787 Kant shrank from the audacity of his theory of the schematism, since the chapter on the transcendental schema is the only one that remained exactly the same in both editions of the *Critique*. Assuming that the purpose of the second edition was to reinstate the prerogatives of reason, it would seem to follow from the fact that these pages underwent no alteration whatsoever that Kant did not consider them to pose any very grave danger to rationality, and that he did not in 1787 feel any reason for apprehension about the theory of transcendental imagination.[43]
- In the second edition, Kant was in fact so little "frightened" by the radical finitude to which he had doomed knowledge that he was prepared to use this doctrine, as part of the general structure of his thought, to affirm the ethical absolute as "absolute idea" or "absolute need."[44] If theoretical reason were not radically finite, if it actually led to a knowledge of the unconditioned, man could view reality from the same standpoint as God—on which account, just as for God there can be no choice between possibilities, and hence no question of morality, so too the concept of absolute duty would have no meaning for human reason as the possessor of an absolute knowledge. To analyze moral experience Kant therefore needed a theory of knowledge that insisted upon the radical finitude of rational knowledge—as, *a contrario*, Hegel's linking of absolute knowledge with the critique (aimed, in fact, at Kant and the philosophies of reflection) of the "moral vision of the world" confirms.

This aspect of the Heideggerian interpretation of Kant thus must be regarded as one of the most questionable; and, as a result, the explanation proposed in the "*Kantbuch*" for the emergence of the distinction between human and finite reasonable being fails to convince. The distinction was not used by Kant to help the reason of reasonable beings to escape the ascendancy of sensibility and the imagination, for the theory of the schematism, which surely contains the most profound statement of this ascendancy, was not one he judged to be in need of modification.

The most likely explanation—the one suggested by Cassirer—is in fact less grandiose. Generally speaking, it is known and accepted that the second edition of the *Critique of Pure Reason* was meant to take into account certain objections raised against the first, notably those of Garve and Feder accusing Kant of psychologism:

> What led [Kant] to rework the first edition of the *Critique* was the experience of the Garve-Feder recension, which led him to attempt to make a clear and deliberate separation between his "transcendental" idealism and "psychological" idealism. This concern forced him to shift the center of gravity of the transcendental analysis, even more than he had earlier, from the side of sub-

> jective deduction to that of the "objective deduction"; forced him to show that the main question of the critique of reason was how and under what conditions the *object* of experience was possible and not how the "*faculty of thinking*" itself is possible. But was this not precisely the thesis that Kant already so insistently maintained in the preface to the *first* edition of the *Critique*?[45]

In fact, as Cassirer reminds us here, between 1781 and 1787 Kant reversed the order of the two chief elements constituting the "Transcendental Deduction": the objective deduction, which aims to prove a priori the objective value of the categories (i.e., the legitimacy of their application to experience), appeared in the 1781 edition after the subjective deduction, which is concerned with the internal functioning of the mind and set out to establish how the categories apply to what is given by experience (but which nevertheless, even in the preface to this first edition, was introduced as having less "cardinal" importance than the objective deduction);[46] the second edition, on the other hand, begins with the objective deduction.[47] This reversal was made expressly in response to Garve and Feder, the *Critique*'s first critics. Denouncing an approach that was later to be called "psychologism," they reproached Kant for trying to explain how the generative operations that produce representations are carried out in the mind (subjective deduction) in order to draw from them the objective value of such mental products (objective deduction)—a method that, in their view, confounded the psychological question of the genesis of mental objects with the transcendental question of their objectivity, thus threatening to bring about (no less than Hume had) the pure and simple dissolution of the idea of truth. It is easy to see why, in the face of this attack, Kant should have thought it prudent to call attention to the primacy of the objective deduction, insufficiently emphasized in the preface, and particularly its independence from the subjective deduction: hence the restructuring of the "Transcendental Deduction" remarked by Cassirer.

Now that we are clearer about Kant's motivation in making corrections to the *Critique*, we can apply what becomes a general principle for interpreting the difference between the two editions to the distinction that emerges between human and finite reasonable being. Because Kant "took great care to guard against letting the meaning of his 'transcendental' argument slip over into the psychological, and against allowing his arguments to be refuted as merely *anthropological*," as Cassirer observes, "he strongly affirms that any analysis based purely and simply on 'human nature' will completely lack the idea of liberty and, therefore, ethical foundation." It was "this concern," in Cassirer's opinion, that gave rise to the thesis of the *Grundlegung* according to which the moral law must be admitted to hold not merely for men but "for all rational beings generally."[48] In insisting upon this distinction Kant was thus not thinking of "dear little angels" or looking to plug holes opened up by the theory of finitude in the sacrosanct valorization of rationality; he simply sought to distinguish clearly and completely between the tasks of ethics and those of anthropology (the latter being understood as the psychological knowledge of man, his empirical nature, and what this nature allows him to do). In short, the distinction does not fundamentally modify the Kantian way of looking at things; rather, it sharpens the implications of the Kantian project for practical philosophy—a project which, though anti-anthropological solely in the (restricted) sense of enabling morality to escape psychologism, does not in any way annul the *humanistic* calling of a philosophy that installs man (as *homo noumenon*) in a foundational position with respect to the law (auto-nomy).

On this particular (and rather sore) point in their debate over the status of practical reason, Cassirer was indisputably correct as against Heidegger—just as beforehand he was correct in opposing the paradoxical attempts to ground an "inhumanist" interpretation of Kantian ethics on the claim that all finite reasonable beings (and not only human beings) are the parties addressed by the moral law. And so too again in the case of respect: literally construed, the Kantian theory of respect, by treating only the consciousness of the law (and not its production), does not introduce a dimension of receptivity intrinsic to practical reason; but if we consider the spirit rather than the letter of the two rival interpretations, does it follow that Cassirer was right as against Heidegger in seeing practical subjectivity (thought of as autonomy of the will) as the occasion in Kant of a breakthrough beyond finitude?

If this were the case, it would have various consequences—among them, that the idea of autonomy would emerge from the debate seriously weakened, since it would have become incompatible with the doctrine of radical finitude, which defines the condition of contemporary man. The idea of autonomy could in that case no longer serve as a bulwark against the individualistic drift of humanism. Faced with the task of reconstructing the subject under these circumstances, we would have to acknowledge that the resurgence of irreducible otherness, while triggering a rupture of monadic immanence and opening the monad to a dimension of transcendence, is not able by itself (owing to its inability to conceive the idea of autonomy as the horizon of transcendence) to reinvest the notion of the subject with meaning and consistency.

Autonomy and Finitude

While Heidegger's interpretation was undoubtedly erroneous in its literal reading of Kant, a reconsideration of the spirit that animated his approach to practical philosophy at the end of the 1920s is nonetheless warranted. At bottom it is a spirit that owes everything to a postulate of coherence: if the Kantian conception of finitude is, as everything in the *Critique of Pure Reason* suggests, a conception of radical finitude, it is hard to imagine practical philosophy (in the doctrine of the autonomy of the will) having restored subjectivity to its former infinite, or absolute, condition—if only because, as we have already observed, the finitude of the theoretical subject would then once again be relativized vis-à-vis this infinite subjectivity. We are thus obliged to admit the fundamental soundness of the Heideggerian undertaking: not just in pushing the analysis of finitude (as receptivity) to its logical conclusion in the domain of theoretical philosophy (something which Cassirer ultimately approves), but in imprinting practical philosophy itself with the mark of finitude. It is at this level that Heidegger's project—aimed at discovering in Kant the principles of an *ethics of finitude*—seems to me to be worth taking another look at, with a view to reworking it.

It is indeed to be regretted that Heidegger, for his part, later abandoned this project: having come to believe that "every valuing is a subjectivizing," he left himself no option but to regard ethics itself—which, it will be agreed, can be separated from the question of values only with difficulty—as residing at the core of modern metaphysics in the form of a metaphysics of subjectivity. Consider the way in which, in response to Jean Beaufret's question about the relation of ontology to a possible ethics, the *Letter on Humanism* replies that "the thinking that ponders the truth of Being . . . is, insofar as it is, recollection of Being and nothing else." Such thinking "has no effect" and thus can have no ethical "result" or extension.[49] Between *Kant and the Problem of Metaphysics* (1929) and the *Letter on Humanism* (1946), Heidegger's increasingly radical attacks on the subject, which as such was ultimately dismissed and reduced to its various metaphysical versions,[50] severely diminished the prospects of developing a meaningful nonmetaphysical ethics. Many of Heidegger's disciples (orthodox and dissenting alike) have long hailed his true greatness as lying in this radical condemnation of subjectivity, seeing in it the gesture that saved his thought from wandering into error and losing its way.[51] It has scarcely dawned on them that Heidegger risked being led astray at all only to the extent that, confronted by Nazism, he had no ethical point of view consistent enough to allow him to immediately condemn it: thus it was that the liquidation of the subject, by causing him to abandon his intention of developing the theory of finitude in relation to ethical inquiry, came to manifest its most pernicious consequences.

It remains for us to reconsider this project, and therefore—*because criticism is a doctrine of radical finitude*—to seek in Kant's practical philosophy the principles of an ethics of the finite subject, without, however, committing the error noticed by Cassirer (namely, of confusing respect for the moral law with its creation): in short, to attempt to give new meaning to critical philosophy through a nonregressive restatement of the possibility it was the first to glimpse. But would it really amount to that—a genuinely forward-looking act of reappropriation—or rather to a "renewal" and "transformation" of critical philosophy?[52] The whole debate, to tell the truth, comes down to just this—and the temptation to come down on the side of "transformation" is, in fact, great: not only because after two centuries certain conditions of philosophical activity have changed,[53] but also because a literal reading of Kant's practical philosophy does not readily display that dimension of finitude that Heidegger thought he had detected with the discovery of "foundational receptivity." Cassirer's interpretation does indeed seem to force recognition of the fact that the content of the second *Critique*, in not allowing a place for the dimension of time in practical subjectivity, autonomizes practical consciousness relative to theoretical consciousness and the radical finitude it expresses. On this view, assuming that for Kant the truth of the subject consisted in its practical breakthrough to the infinite, his philosophy would still have a responsibility to explain why, on the level of knowledge, this potentially infinite subject would so brutally test its finitude. Thus there emerges a really classic problem for all theories of the subject as absolute subject (i.e., as capable of positing itself and of positing objectivity): why, and how, does an infinite subject finitize itself to the point of appearing to itself, in the process of acquiring knowledge about the world, as apprehending ("receiving") objects as externalities? In short, why and how does subjectivity as an activity appear to itself, in relation to knowledge, as passivity?

These questions are not in principle insoluble. They were addressed, of course, by German idealism—by Maimon and later (in a more complicated way, it is true) by Fichte. Common to both their solutions is an instinct (typical of the epoch, but already prefigured in Berkeley's treatment of an early version of the problem) to consider passivity as a moment of activity: thus, for Maimon, the passivity of representation is a differential, a vanishingly small quantity of activity (this through application of the Leibnizian theory of "little perceptions"); and, for Fichte, theoretical consciousness (that is, knowledge as receptivity of an object as an external entity) is a moment of practical reason as freedom—the subject appears to itself as freedom only by opposing itself to an object (a Non-Self) as a limit (as theoretical subject, which is to say as receptivity) and, in eliminating it ad infinitum, causing the consciousness of freedom (in the form of the practical subject) to emerge as equivalent to consciousness of the elimination of the limit.

I shall not examine here how Fichte's solution differs from Maimon's.[54] *Structurally* and *formally* they are identical. For Kant, the structure they share goes under the name of what beginning with the *Letter to Markus*

Herz (1772) he called *idealism*: that is, the claim that the object is produced by the subject, in the form of a relation between subject and object in which the subject is pure activity (cause) and the object pure passivity (effect)—in contrast to *realism*, in which the relation is reversed (the object acting on the subject whose representation of it is the effect of its being affected by the Non-Self). Now Kant as early as 1772 rejected metaphysical idealism (which, as every reader of the *Critique of Pure Reason* knows, he carefully distinguished from his "transcendental idealism"); for this reason in particular, he was to severely (even scornfully) condemn Fichte, accusing him of attempting to prepare the way for such a dogmatic form of idealism. This condemnation was undoubtably a serious mistake on Kant's part (explainable, it is true, by the presence of a formally idealist structure in Fichte's writings), but it was a significant one: for if Kant had made the practical subject the site of a breakthrough to the infinite, he would have had to explain theoretical finitude on the basis of the practical subject. This would have required either an idealist solution (which he refused) or some other solution that in any case is nowhere to be found in his practical philosophy (after all, not even Cassirer looked for such a solution there—undoubtedly because he knew there was no chance of finding one).

Under these circumstances, only one answer seems plausible: if no solution to the puzzle of explaining theoretical subjectivity (finitude) on the basis of practical subjectivity (autonomy)—other than one, denied in advance, which would have anticipated absolute idealism—is to be found in Kant's practical philosophy, this is because there is no need to look for one at all. In other words: can one seriously imagine that Kant, if he had actually located a breakthrough to the infinite in the practical sphere, would not himself have led the search for such a solution? If, in fact, he undertook no such search, how can one not feel sure that ethics for him, far from being the place where the limits of the finite subject were breached, indeed remained a genuine *ethics of finitude*? Even if, so far as a *literal reading* is concerned, Cassirer was right and Heidegger wrong, we must agree—I repeat—that in *spirit* the Heideggerian reading touched upon a truth in Kant's ethics.

The old difficulty remains, however, in its entirety: how can Kant's practical philosophy be regarded as an ethics of finitude when, Heidegger's belief to the contrary notwithstanding, nothing in the *Critique of Practical Reason* justifies ascribing a dimension of receptivity to the spontaneity of autonomous reason? A way can be imagined, in fact, to construct an "ethics of finitude" (not restricted solely to Kant's analysis) that would not run the risks of the one sketched by Heidegger in his "*Kantbuch*": this would involve conceiving of the supreme principles of practical reason as constituting principles of reflection. In other words, it may be more promising to look for practical finitude not where Heidegger looked—in the *content* or *foundation* of Kant's ethics (where plainly it is not to be found, since respect does not form part of the foundation of the moral law)—but in the *modality* of moral judgments (i.e., in the way in which ethics is posited for, and by, a finite subject that cannot—whatever content the thought that it contemplates may have—entirely disregard its finitude). It would thus be in the very *script* and *style* of ethics, in ethical *discourse*, in its *mode of expression*—and not in its content—that we should expect to find the sign of the discourse of a finite subject; the sign, in other words, that the *Critique of Practical Reason*, like the *Critique of Pure Reason*, was written by a *reflecting* subject—and, therefore, by a finite subject. All of which is to say: the discourse on moral freedom (autonomy), as it is presented in Kant's practical philosophy, exhibits the same distinctive features as the discourse in the *Critique of Judgment* on intuitive understanding—that is, on God as an infinite being.

In §76 and §77 of the third *Critique*,[55] Kant suggests that when in *thinking* about organic beings we refer to the Idea of an infinite principle (archetypal understanding) as an organizing principle, we represent this archetypal understanding to ourselves in a *mode* such that the discourse thus instituted, or the representation thus formed, inevitably constitutes a finitization of infinity. In fact, we thereby attribute to infinity (even as Idea) a capacity for positing ends, for having intentions, which it realizes by creating organic beings; but only a finite being can have intentions—can distinguish in itself means and ends, whether possible or real. Thus the representation of archetypal understanding proves to be singularly hybrid: in this discourse, the notion of *creation* expresses the infinite very well (as power to act); but if God were truly God, if the infinite were truly infinite, it would not create out of *purposefulness* (as Spinoza stressed by bringing out everything that the very idea of finality implies about finitude). On the other hand, noting the inadequacy of the idea of intentional causality with respect to infinity, if we were to try to eliminate the fact of finitization, what could we say about the Absolute? One thinks, for example, of all the difficulties Plotinus faced in trying to express the *ineffable* relation between the One and the hypostases.

The discourse about the relation between archetypal understanding and organic beings always amounts, in fact, to a *viewpoint of a viewpoint*: it expresses the viewpoint of the finite subject on what he takes to be the viewpoint of the Creator with regard to the world—and, as such, necessarily carries out a finitization of the infinite. At the level of the *Critique of Judgment* and of the discourse (that it both employs and deconstructs) about intuitive understanding, the signs of finitude are perfectly apparent—through the *modality* of the discourse itself (as a viewpoint of a viewpoint, finitizing the infinite)—even if, by virtue of its *content*, it is a discourse about infinity. Hence the following hypothesis suggests itself: that the *Critique of Practical Reason* can be read in the same way—that is, the same *status* can be ascribed to the ethical discourse about the Absolute, conceived as hybrid and incomprehensible except insofar as it is deconstructed (i.e., analyzed as the finitization of the infinite) as to the discourse of the third *Critique* about the absoluteness of the archetypal understanding.[56] From this perspective, the task of reconciling the *Critique of Practical Reason* with the theory (first enunciated in the *Critique of Pure Reason*) of radical finitude, would consist above all in stressing the evidence to be found in the discourse on practical reason of the finitude of the subject that employs this discourse (I refer here to the finitude of the practical transcendental subject and not, of course, to that of the empirical subject). To detect such signs of *finitude* in a discourse on *autonomy*, one needs to be attentive to the fact that they are inversely symmetrical to those that finitude attributes to divine Absoluteness in the *Critique of Judgment*:

- In the third *Critique*, intuitive understanding (the divine Absolute) could in principle be thought of as a creator, but not as a purpose or final cause (since finitude lies precisely in that *incomprehensible* emergence of finality in the Idea of creation).
- In the second *Critique*, the practical reason (the ethical Absolute) of moral man could in principle be thought of as acting with a view toward ends, as the locus of a purpose (since man is finite); but in that case what one manages neither to understand nor to explain is how moral man, although finite, can create—how he can both produce by himself the principles of his action and conform to them, thus creating practical reality. The absoluteness of practical reason is literally unrepresentable for a finite being—which perhaps is what Kant had in mind when he stressed that the intelligible world is "simply thought": as such—as "simply thought"—the Absolute is already no longer the Absolute, since the formula implies some restriction or limitation.[57]

If, in the case of practical subjectivity, we thus quit temporality (finitude) in the *content* of what we state (in accordance with that breakthrough to the infinite that Cassirer speaks of)—if it is an Absolute that is affirmed—we do not thereby, however, go beyond finitude in the *form* of the affirmation—which both subtly and tragically reflects the structure of reflection as a finite viewpoint of the infinite viewpoint.

It may therefore be possible to reconcile the *Critique of Practical Reason* and the *Critique of Pure Reason*—more generally, to reconcile *radical finitude and autonomy*—by insisting on the modality of ethical discourse (i.e., the viewpoint of a viewpoint) rather that its content. Did Kant actually propose such a solution? In other words, does the hypothesis formulated here amount to a "reappropriation" of his transcendental philosophy or to a "transformation" of it? If I were to submit to the demands of narcissism, which converge here with the imperatives of seduction, I would regard this as a case of profound transformation that single-handedly renews the critical tradition. Integrity obliges me to admit, however, that this is in fact a difficult matter to settle once and for all. On the one hand, there are indications, such as the one just mentioned (the intelligible world that is "simply thought"), that Kant had thought carefully about the theory of the ethical Absolute. On the other hand, we know from studying the genesis of the *Critique of Judgment* that it was only in 1789 (thus after the second *Critique*) that Kant had the idea of integrating a teleology in his final *Critique* (the original plan for which was confined to aesthetics)—that is, of integrating a deconstruction of the discourse on ends with a critique of reflection, which to some extent depends, by definition, on ethical discourse. Consequently it is possible that, in 1788, when the *Critique of Practical Reason* appeared, Kant succeeded ("spontaneously," as it were) in linking together the theoretical subject and the practical subject in the very act of writing about ethics, and that he thought only later of looking for a basis in *principle* for this conjunction, accomplished already as a matter of *fact*. This is a problem that is certainly of interest for Kant scholarship, but which, it will be granted, at bottom concerns only the history of philosophy; finding the solution to it therefore does not bear in any decisive way on what is involved here, even if it might affect our current perspective on the Kantian moment. I leave it to the reader to decide whether the theory proposed here amounts to a case of repetition or renewal: what matters, it seems to me, is recognizing that combining the principle of autonomy with an appreciation of what a fully radicalized finitude entails does not go against the main direction of contemporary philosophical thought—that in this regard it represents no regression whatsoever.

What comes of this effort to link up autonomy with finitude? First of all let me propose (without insisting—this is, after all, only a matter of internal exegesis) a principle for reading Kant's critical philosophy: that the second *Critique* (the theory of the practical subject), which is intrinsically difficult to square with the first one (the theory of the finitude of the knowing subject), should be reinterpreted in the light of the third *Critique* (which constitutes the *theory of reflection*). The latter, insofar as it is a "critique of the faculty of reflective judgment," can only be based on the relationship between the finite and the infinite—for reflection constitutes the discourse by which the finite subject attempts to subsume an object under the two Ideas of the Absolute: the Idea of System (the theoretical Absolute) and the Idea of Freedom (the practical Absolute). Under these circumstances, it is not surprising that the last of Kant's *Critiques* should shed the most light on the problem of articulating finitude with that demand for absoluteness expressed in its own way by the valorization of autonomy.

Revealing what creates the coherence of the Kantian moment in the modern history of subjectivity obviously involves rather more than the reading of Kant. What it makes clear is that *for an ethics of reflection, the antimonadological and humanist principle of autonomy can be perfectly integrated with an idea of radical finitude, since autonomy (the practical subject) has the status of an Idea or horizon of meaning.* If this were not the case—if the practical subject were not an Idea—subjectivity would have to be conceived as pure activity (i.e., pure self-positing), as pure spontaneity devoid of any dimension of passivity or receptivity. Need we remind ourselves that it is not only the recognition of the finitude of the theoretical subject (whose activity can be understood only on the assumption that something is given by intuition) that requires this illusion to be rejected, but also the various versions of the contemporary discovery of the unconscious? Thus autonomy is only the horizon of meaning in reference to which the subject *must* think of his action: outside of this frame of reference the subject would be reduced to positing himself as a machine or a thing, which would both be absurd (since neither thing nor machine posits itself as a particular thing or a particular machine) and lead to the negation of any ethical-juridical space (for ethics and law would be meaningless without responsibility—and all the more so without that horizon of autonomy absent which the idea of responsibility loses all sense whatsoever). To maintain that the acting subject cannot think of itself as such without making reference to the idea of autonomy is not, however, in any way to affirm that it *is* autonomous: we know ourselves to be determined in most of our actions, but just the same we neither can nor ought to think of ourselves as *subjects* without including the horizon of autonomy in our representation of ourselves. If we grant this observation, in which finally no residue of the metaphysics of subjectivity is to be found, we must agree that the idea (the Idea) of autonomy retains *meaning* even after all metaphysical illusions about the subject have melted away.

It may be objected that the shift from autonomy as affirmation to autonomy as horizon of meaning (or principle of ethical reflection) is too slight not to conceal a disturbing intellectual regression. But this would be a hasty judgment, which fails to take account of three profound transformations that this simple shift imposes on the idea of practical subjectivity:[58]

First, for an ethics of reflection, which integrates finitude and autonomy, the supreme principles of practical reason do not in any constitutive way fix the determining features of practical reality: they merely lay down the conditions under which meaning can possibly be given to reality. In the domain of knowledge, we have come to accept that the principles of theoretical reason (for example, the principle of causality) are not structures of *real* objects (in the sense of knowing, on the basis of actual experience, that their content is subject to the principle of causality), but only the a priori conditions of possible experience. As such, they are principles that are only *regulative* in relation to real experience; accordingly, we know in advance that if we manage to acquire knowledge of objects, we are able to do so insofar as they can be subsumed *for us* under such principles, which thus define an *ontological precomprehension* of the object (a precomprehension of its objectivity)—that is, the horizon of knowledge within which objects can have theoretical intelligibility for us. The same is true of the practical order: ethical precomprehension corresponds to the horizon of meaning of the subject insofar as it is practical: that is, the horizon of meaning for the idea of ends rather than for the knowledge of objects. This ethical precomprehension in fact defines a *necessary* point of view about the (practical) subject, for the same reason that the notions of quantity, quality, or relation, and principles like that of causality, are indispensable to us for knowing the theoretical object.

Second, the recognition of such an ethical precomprehension in no way reintroduces a metaphysical idea of the subject—the illusion that a subject can be absolutely free of temporality, free of the structures of finitude. Ethical precomprehension is in fact not any more grounded by subjectivity than is the categorical structure that defines theoretical objectivity. In both cases, the precomprehension is *given*—a point strongly emphasized in §21 of the *Critique of Pure Reason*:

> This pecularity of our understanding, that it can produce *a priori* unity of apperception solely by means of the categories, and only by such and so many, is as little capable of further explanation as why we have just these and no other functions of judgment, or why space and time are the only forms of our possible intuition.[59]

Kant thereby opposed in advance what was to characterize all German idealism—namely, the constructivist procedure by which objectivity is deduced on the basis of subjectivity; as against this method, which came to be emblematic of the so-called "metaphysics of subjectivity," he held that theoretical objectivity is *found*, or *given*, in the form of a precomprehension. The situation is no different in the case of the ethical precomprehension: just as it *happens* that we can know an object only under these conditions of experience, so it *happens* that it is only within a horizon of meaning defined by the idea of autonomy that we can think about ends. With regard to ethics, the consequence is essential: the *absolute* foundation of value judgments breaks down—since nothing any longer prevents us from imagining ourselves able to consider ends in terms of other practical categories: but the ethical dimension, for all of that, does not disappear—it remains a necessary point of view, a horizon of meaning, although it can never be transformed into a dogmatic judgment of value.

Third, and finally, because ethical precomprehension must be conceived as a given and not as based on some absolute subjectivity, the result is that the moral vision of the world cannot itself be thought of as *absolute*: it must, if you will, allow for the possibility of erring. To put it in Kantian terms: moral judgment, instead of being dogmatic, becomes *regulative*. More explicitly: if ethical precomprehension is a principle of reflection, the relation between the structure of precomprehension and existence (i.e., the existence of a particular act capable of being made to correspond to precomprehension and of being subsumed under it) is not settled in advance; and their agreement, if any, can only be a matter of supposition, never of deduction or dogmatic assertion.

This threefold reconception of the practical subject, due to the integration of finitude with the principle of autonomy, is by itself sufficient demonstration that the idea of the subject can be reconfigured and deployed in a way that does not lead philosophy back along paths that have now become impassable. It supplies proof that the end of the era of monadologies can indeed be made to lead on to a reappropriation of subjectivity and of the humanistic values from which it is inseparable: beyond the alternative between monad and *Dasein*, the way of the subject remains open.

Notes

PREFACE

1. Surely it was Nietzsche who, in *Schopenhauer als Erzieher* (Schopenhauer as Educator, 1874), gave this cleavage its most caustic expression, stigmatizing the "learned history of the past" as a flawed enterprise that "has never been the business of a true philosopher" (*Untimely Meditations*, translated by R. J. Hollingdale [Cambridge: Cambridge University Press, 1983], 186).

2. It is clear, for example, that no one doing philosophy today would dream of thinking up a new system—a sign that all possible philosophical positions (on objectivity, for example, or on rationality) have already been exhaustively explored in some sense, and that the philosophies developed from Plato to Heidegger form a closed set of axioms. Foucault's distinctive genius (and surely the key to his success) was to have intuitively grasped this closure and to have tried instead to apply one such possible position (say, Nietzscheo-Heideggerian) to fields and to subjects that had hitherto lain outside philosophical discourse. Notwithstanding all the objections that could be brought against the choice of *this* particular philosophical position, and all the reservations that could be expressed about the way in which it is applied, here one encounters a *style* of philosophical activity that incontestably created new opportunities for the future of philosophy.

3. See Michel Foucault, *The Order of Things: An Archeology of the Human Sciences* (New York: Pantheon Books, 1970), 317 (originally published as *Les Mots et les choses: une archeologie des sciences humaines* [Paris: Gallimard, 1966]) on the "analytics of finitude" as "the end of metaphysics."

4. The two arguments are closely connected, moreover, for the affirmation of an unconscious is one way to express human finitude by denouncing any attempt at mastery as illusory: if man cannot be sovereign over himself, how can he be sovereign over nature?

5. I have tried to show elsewhere ("Martin Heidegger: Essais et Conférences, 1954," in François Châtelet et al., eds., *Dictionnaire des oeuvres politiques* [Paris: Presses Universitaires de France, 1986], 319–27), on the basis of an analysis of Heidegger's *Essais et conférences*, how this logic of modernity (whose main arguments the Frankfurt School later helped to popularize through its insistence on the "dialectic of the Enlightenment") made a particularly striking impression on Heidegger by bringing together the metaphysics of subjectivity, the reign of technology, and the appearance of the totalitarian phenomenon. It was also recalled there how Foucault (see *Discipline and Punish: The Birth of the Prison*, translated by Alan Sheridan [New York: Vintage Books, 1977]) made Jeremy Bentham's "panopticon" the symbol prefiguring the camps of a transparent, completely rationalized society.

6. See Claude Lefort, *The Political Forms of Modern Society: Bureaucracy, Democracy, Totalitarianism*, edited by John B. Thompson (Cambridge: MIT Press, 1986), 305.

7. Didier Éribon, *Le Nouvel Observateur*, 18–24 October 1985.

8. The appeal to the idea of the subject is no less obvious when one makes an issue in present day society of the defeat dealt to democratic ideals by the tyranny of the media and the barbarism of advertising: is it really possible to conceive of the argument from "alienation" being redeployed in a way that does not require it to be bolstered by the valorization of self-identity and self-mastery—all constitutive aspects of the subject?

9. In the interest of calming the waters, a few brief reminders will confirm that this is not an ex post facto formulation: "If we cannot today (this is obvious but has to be emphasized in view of the predictable criticism) simply return to the values of the philosophy of the Enlightenment, it is equally impossible not to refer to them, as '68 philosophy tried to do, and to effect a tabula rasa of the tradition" (see Luc Ferry and Alain Renaut, *French Philosophy of the Sixties*, translated by Mary H. S. Cettani [Amherst: University of Massachusetts Press, 1990], xxvii; originally published as *La Pensée 68* [Paris: Gallimard, 1985]); parallel to the "systematic critique of the illusions relative to the subject," there is the question of "thematizing this survival of subjectivity after the critique" (30); "[i]t does not follow that, having established that man is not really (*hic et nunc*) autonomous (that he is open to his other), one has to go to the extreme of withdrawing all meaning and function from the idea of the ideal, in short, from the very Idea of autonomy" (211); and so on.

10. See the review in *L'Événement du jeudi*, 12–18 December 1985, and the commentary by L. Séguin in *Magazine littéraire*, 1–15 January 1986. In this connection see too the articles by Elisabeth de Fontenay and F. Wahl in *Le Nouvel Observateur*, 13–19 June 1986, devoted to "the return to the philosophy of the subject," which is described as "a venture in restoration" that abandons itself to the "narcissism of consciousness," to an "excessive reliance on the cogito" and to the fantasy of a "full, or at least not structurally dissociated, subject."

11. See, for example, Ferry and Renaut, "Le sujet en procès," in H. Nagl-Docekal and H. Vetter, eds., *Tod des Subjekts?* (Vienna/Munich: Oldenbourg, 1987), 119: "No more than it is for us a matter of resuscitating the Cartesian *cogito* can there be any question of considering all our opinions, all our choices, and all our decisions as the products of some autonomous and sovereign freedom, keeping the 'noumenal subject' outside history. Simply this: since everyone must in fact agree that the various discoveries of the unconscious neither can nor should lead to a renunciation ruinous to the *ideal* of autonomy, which interpretation of the subject corresponds to this radically new situation?"

12. See Ferry and Renaut, *68–86: Itinéraires de l'individu* (Paris: Gallimard, 1987).

13. Martin Heidegger, *Chemins qui ne mènent nulle part* (Paris: Gallimard, 1962), 83–84. (Note that this work is reprinted as "The Age of the World Picture" in *The Question Concerning Technology and Other Essays*, translated by William Lovitt [New York: Harper & Row, 1977]; the passage cited is at page 133). In the

same vein see the *Brief über den Humanismus* (Frankfurt: V. Klostermann, 1949), published in English as "The Letter on Humanism" in *Martin Heidegger: Basic Writings*, edited by David Farrell Krell (San Francisco: HarperCollins, 1977): individualism, for the same reason as collectivism, nationalism, or internationalism, is "an anthropologism, and as such subjectivism" (244).

14. Here, again, this was an aspect of our analysis of contemporary antihumanism that was widely misapprehended: when we claimed that French philosophy of the 1960s broke with the values of humanism, we were told that Foucault had not ceased defending humanity against all the systems that were crushing it; when we claimed that in its own way May 1968 involved the same logic, we were told that surely no moment in recent history had more completely glorified the human values of freedom, generosity, or fraternity than this one. The debate would gain enormously in clarity if it were to be admitted that humanism and individualism do not perfectly overlap and that individualistic forms of antihumanism are in fact possible. This would require that the relation between subjectivity and individuality at last be precisely identified—which, in one sense, is the central objective of the present work.

CHAPTER I
HEIDEGGER

1. By way of example: "No matter how our histories may tabulate the concept and course of modernity, no matter which phenomena in the fields of politics, poetry, the natural sciences, and the social order they may appeal to in order to explain modernity, no historical meditation can afford to bypass two mutually related essential determinations within the history of modernity: first, that man installs and secures himself as *subiectum*, as the nodal point for beings as a whole; and secondly that the beingness of beings as a whole is grasped as the representedness of whatever can be produced and explained" (Heidegger, *Nietzsche*, 2 vols. [Pfullingen, 1961], available in English in a four-volume edition edited by David Farrell Krell, *Nietzsche* [San Francisco: Harper & Row, 1979–1987]: the above passage is found at III, 178). That is: the advent of man as subject and the reduction of all reality to what is an object for a subject constitute the two chief moments of modernity.

2. See the "Letter on Humanism," in *Martin Heidegger: Basic Writings*. Humanism for Heidegger "does not set the *humanitas* of man high enough. . . . [T]he essential worth of man does not consist in his being the substance of being, as the 'Subject' among them" (233–34).

3. Heidegger, *The Question Concerning Technology*, 116.

4. Ibid., 100.

5. As early as 1929, during the Davos debate (see Martin Heidegger and Ernst Cassirer, *Débat sur le Kantisme et la Philosophie* (*Davos, mars 1929) et autres textes de 1929–1931* [Paris: Beauchesne, 1973]), Heidegger mentions the absurdity of a situation "in which the sciences, both those of the mind and that of nature, have occupied the totality of what is knowable," to the point that one might sup-

pose "nothing more is left remains (to philosophy) besides scientific knowledge" (28–29).

6. Heidegger, *Nietzsche*, IV, 5.

7. Ibid., III, 87. It is in this sense, for example, that man's *technical* relation to the world may be described as having begun with the Cartesian reduction of nature to the status of an "extended thing"—in which case reality becomes equivalent to calculability and thus to "machinability" for the "master and possessor of nature": see Heidegger, *What is Called Thinking?*, translated by J. Glenn Gray (New York: Harper & Row, 1968), 235 (originally published as *Was heisst Denken?* [Tübingen, 1954]).

8. Heidegger, *Questions*, II (Paris: Gallimard, 1968), 15.

9. Heidegger, *Nietzsche*, IV, 101. Metaphysics, in this sense, is the ground for what later occurs (i.e., "the ground for subsequent thought" [*"Grund für das Nachkommende"*]).

10. Heidegger, *Questions*, II, 160.

11. Heidegger, *Nietzsche*, IV, 86.

12. Ibid., III, 178.

13. Heidegger, *The Principle of Reason*, translated by Reginald Lilly (Bloomington: Indiana University Press, 1991), 33.

14. Ibid.

15. Heidegger, *The End of Philosophy*, translated by Joan Stambaugh (New York: Harper & Row, 1973), 38–39.

16. Heidegger paid particular attention to Leibniz in his courses at Marburg. See *Metaphysische Anfangsgründe der Logik im Ausgang von Leibniz* (1928), II, 26, published in English as *The Metaphysical Foundation of Logic*, translated by Michael Heim (Bloomington: Indiana University Press, 1984).

17. Heidegger, *The Principle of Reason*, 22–23.

18. Ibid., 43–44.

19. Heidegger, *The End of Philosophy*, 57.

20. Ibid., 48.

21. Ibid., 42.

22. Here I rely on a passage from his *Schelling*, stunning for its verve and vigor but nonetheless highly problematic, in which Heidegger attempts in three pages to describe the logic of the path taken by modern philosophy from Descartes to German idealism: see Heidegger, *Schelling's Treatise on the Essence of Human Freedom*, translated by Joan Stambaugh (Athens: Ohio University Press, 1985), 92–94.

23. On this essence of the *cogitare* (hence of the Cartesian "subject" as *res cogitans*), see Heidegger, *Nietzsche*, IV, 104–18.

24. See for example, Heidegger, *The End of Philosophy*: "Every *subiectum* is determined in its *esse* by *vis* (*perceptio—appetitus*)" (38), and thus "hints at the essential realm of the *perceptio*, although in such a way that its fundamental characteristic as effecting (*actio*) first becomes evident, and the essential core of the *actualitas* is determined" (36). Similarly, in Leibniz emerges "the volitional basic trait in re-presentation itself as the *perceptio*" (63).

25. On this aspect of the Heideggerian interpretation of Kant, see for example "Kant's Thesis on Being" in *Questions*, II, 105: Kant "understands Being . . . by

positing [it] as an act of human subjectivity"; see also Heidegger's *Die Frage nach dem Ding* (Tübingen, 1962), available in English as *What Is a Thing?*, translated by W. B. Barton, Jr. and Vera Deutsch (Chicago: Henry Regnery Company, 1967), 142: thought "as representing in concepts . . . must unfold itself from out of itself and bring what is to be represented before itself"—and so "is spontaneous, spontaneity." His *Schelling* provides support for this reading from another angle: "Kant . . . realizes on the path from the *Critique of Pure Reason* to the *Critique of Practical Reason* that the real nature of the 'I' is not the '*I think*' but the '*I act*.' I give myself the law from the basis of my being: 'I am free'" (92).

26. On the (quite classical) interpretation of Fichte, see again Heidegger's *Schelling*: "Every being which is at all has its being in terms of the I which, however, is originally positing, as I think, deed, and as deed a deed of action (*Tathandlung*), freedom" (92).

27. On anthropomorphy, see Heidegger, *Nietzsche*, IV, 83: Metaphysics "must seek the true and the real in the *absolute humanization* of all being. Metaphysics is anthropomorphism—the formation and apprehension of the world according to man's image"; see also *The End of Philosophy*, 35–36. In the 1928 Marburg course already mentioned, Heidegger had not yet worked out this concept of anthropomorphy: see *The Metaphysical Foundations of Logic*, 88, where the monadological interpretation of logic is called "simply anthropomorphism."

28. Heidegger, *Schelling's Treatise*, 92.

29. Heidegger, *The End of Philosophy*, 38.

30. Heidegger, *Nietzsche*, IV, 179. Similarly, the *Schelling* mentions the influence of the *Monadology* on German idealism, locating in Leibniz the decisive gesture: the "change from *hypokeimenon* to subjectivity" (182).

31. See the preface to Hegel, *Phänomenologie des Geistes*, edited by W. Bonsiepn and R. Heede, vol. 9 of *Gesammelte Werke* (Hamburg: Felix Meiner Verlag, 1980), 18; also the new translation into French by G. Jarczyk and P.-J. Labarrière, *Phénoménologie de l'esprit* (Paris: Gallimard, 1993), 80.

32. On the representation of Being, see the two-volume French edition of Nietzsche's *Der Wille zur Macht* translated by G. Bianquis (Paris: Gallimard, 1948) [henceforth "Bianquis edition"], Book II, §8, I, 221; note that the pagination of the recently reissued edition (Gallimard, 1995) differs from that of the original. The remark about will to power is taken from Part II ("Von der Selbstüberwindung") of *Also Sprach Zarathustra* (1891), also translated by Bianquis (Paris: Aubier-Flammarion, 1969), I, 249.

33. Heidegger, *The End of Philosophy*, 38.

34. Heidegger, *Nietzsche*, III, 222. Independently of its use by Hegel and Nietzsche, the monadological and anthropomorphical structure is found by Heidegger in other descendants of Leibniz: "[Schelling] must show that nature also is intrinsically ego-like, not only relative to the absolute ego which posits it: that it is only a yet undeveloped 'ego.' And *there* is the place where Leibniz's doctrine that all being are representing beings is incorporated" (*Schelling's Treatise*, 93); "Immediately and mediately (through Herder), Leibniz's metaphysics shaped German 'humanism' (Goethe) and Idealism (Schelling and Hegel). . . . Schopenhauer's main work, *The World as Will and Representation*, with its altogether superficial

and scanty analysis of Platonic and Kantian philosophy, gathers up in one all the basic directions of the Western interpretation of beings as a whole . . ." (Heidegger, *Nietzsche*, IV, 181).

35. On this theme, which in Descartes would correspond, so to speak, to the taking into account of the nondeducibility of the real (and hence of ontological difference), see in particular the brilliant investigation of Jean-Luc Marion, *Sur le prisme métaphysique de Descartes: Constitution et limites de l'onto-théo-logie dans la pensée cartésienne* (Paris: Presses Universitaires de France, 1986).

36. See the *Monadology*, §40–41. (Originally composed in French in 1714 as a paper entitled "Monodologie," this work first appeared in J. E. Erdmann's two-volume edition of Leibniz's works, *Opera Philosophica* [Berlin, 1840]; numerous versions exist in English, among them the translation by P. G. Lucas and Leslie Grint [Manchester: University of Manchester Press, 1953; reprinted with minor corrections, 1961], based on Henri Lestienne's edition; see too *Monadology and Other Philosophical Essays*, translated by Paul Schrecker and Anne Martin Schrecker [Indianapolis: Bobbs-Merrill, 1965].) Since by virtue of the principle of continuity there can be no absolute distinction between the possible and the real, the possible refers to what *can* exist—not only in the sense that its existence is not impossible (as in the case of its negation), but also in the sense of something that has a *power*, or a *tendency*, to exist; by virtue of this tendency, all possibilities would exist if the requirement of their compossibility with the other possibilities that also exhibit a tendency to exist did not thwart this common impulse toward existence.

37. In his *Nietzsche*, Heidegger analyzes a short undated passage of Leibniz (see *Die Philosophische Schriften von G. W. Leibniz*, edited by C. I. Gerhardt, 7 vols. [Berlin, 1875–1890], IV, 289–91): Leibniz's thinking, he says, here first attains "the culmination of its mysterious lucidity." Inventing a surprising term, Leibniz states that *dici potest omne possibile existiturire*—"Thus every possible can be said to strive to exist" (see *The End of Philosophy*, 42–43): existence thus become a necessary condition of essence itself, so that from the possible to the real there is no more leap to be made.

38. On this question, the parts of his *Schelling* that explain how from Kant to Hegel (and thence to further attempts to advance beyond Kant) philosophy manages to construct systems (14–61) remain among the most stimulating that one can hope to read.

39. The advent of philosophical discourse in the form of a system corresponds in this sense to Leibniz's vision of the world itself as a "system of preestablished harmony." See §59 of *Theodicy* (*Essais de théodicée sur la bonté de Dieu, la liberté de l'homme et l'origine du mal* [1710], available in English in numerous editions, among them E. M. Huggard's translation under the editorship of Austin Farrer [London: Routledge and Kegan Paul, 1951]); *Monadology*, §80–81, and so on. I shall return further on to what seems to me to have made this system necessary in the monadological framework: it is not clear that its meaning is fully grasped if by "preestablished harmony" one merely refers to the process by which the modern subject submits the world to the requirements of reason.

40. Heidegger, *The End of Philosophy*, 57.

41. Heidegger, *Nietzsche*, III, 85–87, 102–3 (on §374 of *The Gay Science*, "Our New Infinite").

42. Heidegger, *The End of Philosophy*, 36.

43. Leibniz, *The Monadology*, §57.

44. Nietzsche, *The Gay Science* [*Die fröhliche Wissenschaft*, 1882], translated by Walter Kaufman (New York: Vintage Books, 1974), §374, 336.

45. Nietzsche, *Beyond Good and Evil: Prelude to a Philosophy of the Future* [*Jenseits von Gut und Böse*, 1886], translated by R. J. Hollingdale (Harmondsworth: Penguin Books, 1973), 31. One is reminded of §109 of *The Gay Science*: "Let us beware of . . . call[ing] the universe an organism. . . . [It] is in all eternity chaos . . ." (167–8).

46. Heidegger, *Nietzsche*, IV, 136.

47. Thus Heidegger could insist on the "essential ground of the historicity of the history of metaphysics" (ibid., 138) and stress the way in which Nietzsche "misapprehends" the real nature of its relation to Descartes (136).

48. Heidegger, *Nietzsche*, IV, 147.

49. The French translation by P. Klossowski appeared only in 1971; the German edition dated from 1961, and throughout the 1960s the teaching of Jean Beaufret took its inspiration, faithfully and honestly, from this.

50. See the French edition of Heidegger's *Vortrage und Aufsatze* (Pfulligen: G. Neske, 1954), published as *Essais et conférences*, translated by A. Préau and J. Beaufret (Paris: Gallimard, 1958), 283ff. "Berkeley's argument . . . rests on Descarte's fundamental metaphysical position and . . . takes the form *esse* = *percipi*: 'being' equals 'represented being.' Being is subordinate to representation in the sense of perception. . . . Being is by virtue of representation. Being is equal to thought inasmuch as the objectivity of objects is composed, is constituted, in the representing consciousness, in the 'I am thinking something' . . ." And Heidegger contrasts Berkeley's formulation with Parmenides' Fragment III, seemingly so similar to it: "Thought and being are both the same," he says, to emphasize the reversal that divides the great Greek epoch from modernity: "Parmenides restricts thought to being. Berkeley restores Being to Thought. To reply to the Greek formula, and in some measure to be identified with it, the modern thesis should be read: *percipi* = *esse*."

51. David Hume, *Treatise on Human Nature*, edited by L. A. Selby-Bigge (Oxford: Clarendon Press, 1888; 2nd edition, 1978), 4.

52. Most recent studies of Hume note with various differences of emphasis the distancing of empiricist philosophy from the Cartesian model of the subject. It had been noted earlier in Gilles Deleuze's interesting study *Empiricisme et subjectivité: Essai sur la nature humaine selon Hume* (Paris: Presses Universitaires de France, 1953), available in English as *Empiricism and Subjectivity: An Essay on Hume's Theory of Human Nature*, translated by Constantin V. Boundas (New York: Columbia University Press, 1991), to which I shall return; in this work attention is concentrated on the way in which empiricism refuses to take subjectivity as self-evident, posing instead the problem of how it came into being: "How does the mind become a subject?" (23). See also Michel Malherbe, *La Philosophie empiriste de David Hume* (Paris: Vrin, 1976): "The self is thus no

more a subject than a thinking thing: it is necessary to give up all the *cogitos*" (161); Yves Michaud, *Hume et la fin de la philosophie* (Paris: Presses Universitaires de France, 1983): with empiricism "there is no more master subject" (32), and to the extent subjectivity remains an issue, "this is subjectivity without a subject: where there is no center, no good point of view, there can no longer be a subject, even if the operations remain assignable to a subjectivity" (220–21). It will be agreed that, under these circumstances, it is hard to imagine writing the history of subjectivity today without trying to bring out the specificity of the empiricist moment.

53. It will of course be necessary in this connection to indicate why the Humean approach to the problem fell short of criticism in the Kantian sense.

54. And not at all, as in the neodogmatism of Heidegger, on the basis of the sudden appearance of Being. On the meaning of this "Copernican revolution," see Luc Ferry's preface to Kant's *Critique of Pure Reason* (Paris: GF-Flammarion, 1987), xivff.

55. Heidegger, *What is a Thing?*, 56. In the same connection compare *Schelling's Treatise*: "Kant comes . . . back to the fundamental meaning of the primary philosophical concepts of the Greeks" (37). We know that the whole conclusion of *Kant und das Problem der Metaphysik* (Bonn, 1929) [the "*Kantbuch*"] was that the transition from Kantianism to German idealism was a kind of relapse, marked by "a growing forgetfulness of what Kant had won"—i.e., a decisive deepening of the "problem of finitude" that would overturn the "supremacy of reason and the understanding" (*Kant and the Problem of Metaphysics*, translated by James S. Churchill [Bloomington: Indiana University Press, 1962], §45, 252–53).

56. See Heidegger, *Kant and the Problem of Metaphysics*, §31; Cassirer and Heidegger, *Débat sur le Kantisme et la Philosophie*, 77–78.

57. Heidegger, *Nietzsche*, III, 222.

58. Martin Heidegger, *What is a Thing?*, 55. Note too Heidegger's view of the Kantian idea of the a priori as determining the "essence of things" on the basis of "what belongs to the subjectivity of the subject" which is thus consistent with the way in which "for modern philosophy the I-principle is the first principle" (166).

59. Heidegger, *Questions*, II, 113.

60. On the Heideggerian interpretation of Fichte, see the introduction to my *Système du droit: Philosophie et droit dans la pensée de Fichte* (Paris: Presses Universitaires de France, 1986).

61. Michel Foucault's relation to Kant is especially significant in this regard. Foucault, whose translation into French of Kant's *Anthropologie in pragmatischer Hinsicht* (1798) (*Anthropology from a Pragmatic Point of View*, translated by Victor Lyle Dowdell [Carbondale: Southern Illinois University Press, 1978]) appeared in 1964, reproduced the main lines of Heidegger's interpretation of the *Critique* two years later in his *The Order of Things* as the "analytics of finitude" (also sometimes referred to as the "analysis of finite reason": see Ferry and Renaut, *French Philosophy of the Sixties*, 101–7), crediting Kant with the first overthrow of the age of representation. While his 1983 seminar on "What Is the Enlightenment?" gave fresh evidence of an abiding interest in Kant, the point of it was to insist on the necessity (as against that "analytics of truth" which, in proceeding along the path opened by Kant in the *Critique of Pure Reason*, in effect summa-

rized the critical tradition) of opting for another critical ideal, nearer to the spirit of Kant himself in works like the one on the *Aufklärung*: the ideal of a "philosophical inquiry into what we are in our actuality" (*Magazine Littéraire* [May 1984]: 35–39). In falling back from an "analytics of finitude" upon an "analytics of truth," the later Kant of the major works therefore would keep the promise he had made earlier. This analysis, and the kind of interest/disinterest to which it testifies, brings together all the elements that drove Foucault to embrace a Heideggerian reading of Kant.

62. See *Disputatio metaphysica de principio individui* (1663), in J. E. Erdmann, ed. *God. Guil. Leibnitii Opera philosophica quae estant latina, gallica, germanica omnia* (Berlin: G. Eichleri, 1839–1840), 1–5. A brief analysis of this text can be found in Y. Belaval's *Leibniz* (Paris: Vrin, 1970), 36ff. In it Leibniz asserts the thesis that "each individual is individuated in the totality of his being (*sua tota entitate*)." In §9 he clearly states the problem of the status of "human nature," asking whether or not "Plato's humanity" and "Socrates's humanity" were intrinsically different.

63. See Gerhardt, ed. *Die philosophische Schriften von G. W. Leibniz*, VII, 393; also IV, 433: "It is not true that two substances [that] are entirely similar may be different *solo numero*."

64. Bertrand Russell, *A Critical Exposition of the Philosophy of Leibniz* (2nd edition, Cambridge: Cambridge University Press, 1967), 343.

65. The two determinants of monadic individuality are inseparable: for if substance were not simple, but made up of parts, a monad could differ from other monads only in respect of the internal fitting together of its parts, the elements of all of them being intrinsically identical. On this view it would therefore follow that each substance is individuated "in the totality of its being," though two indiscernible realities exist at the level of its component parts.

66. One passage to which I shall return, in §13 of the *New System of Nature and of the Communications between Substances, as Well as of the Union of Soul and Body* (originally published in Journal des Sçavans [27 June 1695]; see *Leibniz: Philosophical Writings*, translated by Mary Morris [New York: Dutton, 1956], 104), emphasizes this with sublime clarity: "[In] the strict metaphysical sense there is no influence exerted by one created substance on another. . . ."

67. As evidence of this relationship, which needs to be made more precise, recall that Hegel praises the virtues of Leibniz's *Theodicy*—the most esoteric working out of the theory of preestablished harmony: see for example H. B. Nisbett's translation of Hegel's *Vorlesungen über die Philosophie der Geschichte: Einleitung*, published as *Lectures on the Philosophy of World History: Introduction, Reason in History* (Cambridge: Cambridge University Press, 1975), 42–43.

68. If only to the extent that it subjects to the principle of reason that domain of history that had until then appeared the most resistant to displaying any real rationality. In this sense, Heidegger is right to define Hegelianism—the "height of metaphysics" (*Questions*, II, 52)—by the attempt to "subsume history into the system" ("Letter on Humanism" in *Basic Writings*, 239).

69. In his *Political Philosophy 2: The System of Philosophies of History*, translated by Franklin Philip (Chicago: University of Chicago Press, 1992), Luc Ferry has shown how these criticisms, characteristic of all the variants of contemporary

Heideggerianism (including, notably, its various applications to political philosophy) consist, first, in identifying the very project of the philosophy of history with the specific way in which it was executed by Hegel (in the form of the theory of the "ruse of reason") through a return to Leibniz (rather than to Kant and Fichte); and, second, in attributing the effects of *such* a philosophy of history (the affirmation of a sense of development, the claim to a science of history, the historicist dissolution of any moral view of the world, and so forth) to the passive aspect of the reign of the subject, which calls history to account just as it does nature.

70. See, for example, Foucault's famous article "What Is an Author?" in *Language, Counter-Memory, Practice: Selected Essays and Interviews*, translated by Donald F. Bouchard and Sherry Simon (Ithaca: Cornell University Press, 1977), 113–38.

71. See Michel Villey, "L'Humanisme et le droit," in *Seize essais de philosophie du droit* (Paris: Dalloz, 1969), 60ff., which regards "modern juridical humanism" as applying to law "the tendency to posit *man* as the principle and the end of everything"—as a result of which, for "nearly all modern thinkers about law," "man is the *author* of his law" (emphasis added). Villey summarizes the extent of agreement among the various schools of "contemporary opinion" in juridical matters by Sartre's statement: "Man has no legislator other than himself."

72. On this solidarity between humanism and contractualism, see the chapter by R. Derathé ("The Theory of the Social Contract or of the Purely Human Origin of Sovereignty") in his *Jean-Jacques Rousseau et la science politique de son temps* (2nd edition, Paris: Vrin, 1970), 33ff. The notion of contract resolves the problem of how men came to foreswear the independence of a state of nature in which they were not subject to any political authority: the birth of civil power results from the transition from this situation of independence to another form of freedom, now conceived as auto-nomy, as subjection to a power of "human institution" that one has given to oneself.

73. Witness the fact that he imagined nonregressive remedies for the excesses of individualism aimed not at restoring the structures of traditional societies but at developing civic morality, either by strengthening communal institutions or by creating new intermediate bodies (on these "safety valves" of individualism, see Jean-Claude Lamberti, *L'Individualisme chez Tocqueville* [Paris: Presses Universitaires de France, 1970], 71–75).

74. "The Liberty of the Ancients Compared with That of the Moderns," in *Benjamin Constant: Political Writings*, translated by Biancamaria Fontana (Cambridge: Cambridge University Press, 1988), 309–28.

75. Ibid., 311. In this passage, as in the ones that follow, the emphasis on the discriminating appeal to independence is mine.

76. Ibid., 312.

77. Ibid., 316.

78. Ibid., 316–17. The theme is a veritable leitmotif of the speech: "For the ancients when they sacrificed that independence to their political rights, sacrificed less to obtain more; while in making the same sacrifice, we would give more to obtain less" (317). The edifice of the ancients, which some revolutionaries—too much imbued with Rousseau and Mably—tried to restore by sacrificing individual

rights to a new "participation in social power," "collapsed" because "the social power injured the individual *independence* in every possible way, without destroying the need for it" (320); "Individual independence is the first need of the moderns" (321); "The danger of modern liberty is that, absorbed in the enjoyment of our private *independence*, and in the pursuit of our particular interests, we should surrender our right to share in political power too easily" (326).

79. Ibid., 310. Throughout this quite remarkable passage, Constant describes the freedom of the moderns in the double sense of autonomy: (". . . it is everyone's right to exercise some influence on the administration of the government, either by electing all or particular officials, or through representations, petitions, demands to which the authorities are more or less compelled to take heed") and of independence (the right of everyone "to dispose of property, and even to abuse it; to come and go . . . without having to account for their motives or undertakings," to lead a life "compatible with their inclinations or whims" [311]).

80. From this point of view, Constant's proposed description of the freedom of the ancients is very incomplete: we see it clearly in Aristotle, where the citizen's right to share collectively in sovereignty is based not on recognition of a principle of autonomy or self-establishment (in which case this right should be shared by every man insofar as he is a man) but in the purposeful organization of nature, according to which "some are made to command and others to obey." The ultimate foundation of sovereignty in this sense is the hierarchy of natures within the cosmos and not the human will, as such, creating its own laws and submitting to an authority it recognizes.

81. Ernst Cassirer, *The Individual and the Cosmos in Renaissance Philosophy*, translated by Mario Domandi (New York: Harper & Row, 1963), 123.

82. Ibid., 123.

83. Ibid., 84.

84. Ibid., 128.

85. Ibid., 91.

86. Ibid., 119.

87. Ibid., 98.

88. Ibid., 85.

89. Cassirer well expresses (ibid., 84) the turning point marked by the philosophy of the Renaissance in this regard: in opposition to the old scholastic adage that "doing follows from being," Pico Della Mirandola asserted that "the being of man follows from his doing."

90. See §48 of Husserl, *Cartesianische Meditationen*, based on lectures given in Paris in 1929 and published as vol. 1 of *Husserliana: Edmund Husserl, Gesammelte Werke* (The Hague: Martinus Nijhoff, 1950); cf. the English edition, *Cartesian Meditations: An Introduction to Phenomenology*, translated by Dorion Cairns (The Hague: Martinus Nijhoff, 1960; 2nd edition, 1977), 105–6.

91. See Marcel Gauchet, *Le Désenchantement du monde: une histoire politique de la religion* (Paris: Gallimard, 1985); an English edition is forthcoming shortly from Princeton University Press.

92. See Ferry and Renaut, *Système et critique* (Brussels: Ousia, 1984), 198ff, 216ff; *French Philosophy of the Sixties*, 41–47, xxviii-xxix; and Ferry, *Political Phi-*

losophy 3: From the Rights of Man to the Republican Idea, translated by Franklin Philip (Chicago: University of Chicago Press, 1992).

93. Concerning this antinomy see Ferry, *Political Philosophy 2: The System of Philosophies of History*; and Ferry and Renaut, *Système et critique*.

94. S. Mesure, in a thoughtful article ("Raymond Aron et le problème de l'objectivité historique," *Commentaire*, no. 35 [Fall 1986]), rightly suggests that the *Critique of Judgement* could provide a more effective model than the *Critique of Pure Reason* for thinking about historical objectivity. He underestimates, however, what such a project would involve: while it surely accords well with the spirit of the third *Critique*, it is not authorized by a literal reading of this text. It therefore calls for a renewal rather than a repetition of Kant's critical philosophy.

CHAPTER II
DUMONT

1. Max Weber, *The Protestant Ethic and the Spirit of Capitalism*, translated by Talcott Parsons (New York: Scribner's, 1958), 222.

2. The brief summary that follows is taken from the paper "Sur l'individualisme" presented by Gauchet at the Collège de Philosophie in May 1987. He developed this analysis further over the course of the 1986–1987 academic year in a seminar sponsored by the Fondation Saint-Simon (in collaboration with Gilles Lipovetsky); see also note 4 below.

3. Prosper Enfantin, *Doctrine of Saint-Simon: An Exposition*, translated by Georg G. Igger (New York: Schocken Books, 1958).

4. Gauchet has shown how during the same period the term also emerged in the quite different ideological context of counterrevolutionary thinking: he thus points out that as early as 1820, in a work by Joseph de Maistre that remained unpublished for a number of years but which later appeared in his *Oeuvres complètes*, the word refers to the modern ignorance of the way in which political unity preexists the individual will and imposes itself on it.

5. Published in English as *From Mandeville to Marx: The Genesis and Triumph of Economic Ideology* (Chicago: University of Chicago Press, 1977).

6. Published in English as *Essays on Individualism: Modern Ideology in Anthropological Perspective* (Chicago: University of Chicago Press, 1986).

7. In Dumont, "ideology" is understood as a "social set of representations," or the "set of the ideas and values that are common in a society." For this definition (as for the ones that follow) I refer to the glossary at the end of his *Essays on Individualism*, 279–80.

8. Ibid., 16.

9. For Dumont, Nazism constituted an attempt of this kind: see his "The Totalitarian Disease: Individualism and Racism in Adolf Hitler's Representations," in *Essays*, 149–79. This important argument effectively puts an end to the hopes of some authors for an integration of the two systems of values.

10. Ibid., 25 (emphasis added).

11. Ibid., 56.

12. See Dumont, "World Renunciation in Indian Religions," Appendix B of *Homo Hierarchicus: The Caste System and Its Implications*, translated by Mark Sainsbury, Louis Dumont, and Basia Gulati (complete revised edition, Chicago: University of Chicago Press, 1980), 265ff.

13. Ibid., 272–73.

14. Ibid., 274–75.

15. Dumont, *Essays*, 25–26. Also: "The man who is after ultimate truth foregoes social life and its constraints to devote himself to his own progress and destiny," and in this sense "the discovery of the self is for him coterminus . . . with liberation from the fetters of life as commonly experienced in the world": "[T]he renouncer is self-sufficient" (25–26).

16. Ibid., 26.

17. Dumont, *Homo Hierarchicus*, 273. Dumont concedes that in an earlier study (in *Contributions to Indian Sociology*, no. 1, 1957, 23–41) he was "a bit hasty" in supposing he could write "that every man has the right to become *sannyasi*."

18. Dumont, *Essays*, 26, 30.

19. Ibid., 30. Dumont also analyzes some Hellenistic prefigurations of this Christian dualism, notably by evoking the Stoic definition of wisdom as detachment from the world (27–29, 32).

20. Ibid., 30. "Christians meet in Christ, whose members they are." Hence Dumont adopts the formula of Ernst Troeltsch (his "main guide" on the subject) characterizing early Christianity as "absolute individualism and absolute universalism" (29–30).

21. Ibid., 31.

22. Ibid., 32. The term "contaminate" carries certain connotations, here as elsewhere.

23. Ibid., 58ff. Here again Dumont follows Troeltsch and his great two-volume work *Social Teaching of the Christian Churches*, translated by Olive Wyon (London: Allen & Unwin, 1950), first published in 1911: the Calvinistic theory of predestination reverses the relation between the individual and the church, for if the elect are so for all eternity, the individual no longer depends on the church for his salvation; the church thus becomes the instrument of the elect, thanks to which they "must rule over the reprobate and . . . carry out their task for the glory of God" (*Essays*, 58). The church as such therefore springs, in Troeltsch's phrase, "from the same principle which appears to give independence to the individual, namely, from the ethical duty of the preservation and making effective of election" (ibid., 58; Troeltsch, *Social Teaching*, II, 591).

24. Relying this time on the monumental work of Otto von Gierke, *Das deutsche Genossenschaftsrecht* (1868–1881; abridged in English as *Natural Law and the Theory of Society, 1500 to 1800*, 2 vols., translated by Ernest Barker [Cambridge: Cambridge University Press, 1934]), Dumont shows how the conception of the community as *universitas*—as the totality of which men are only parts—was gradually replaced by a concept based on the revolutionary nominalism of William of Ockham. On Ockham's view, the community is a *societas*, an association of individuals in whom the individual wills are the basis and foundation of the political order that is constructed from them. While man, for the ancients, was a social

being, and nature a model for the sociopolitical order, the theorists of modern natural law made man not a social but an individual being, whose individuality and self-sufficiency constitute a "state of nature" that is logically prior to social and political life.

25. Dumont, *Essays*, 89. In the assertion of a right to property Dumont also sees an implication of individualism, viewing property as that without which the individual could not be self-sufficient: every attack made on private property is thus condemned for the threat that it constitutes to the very individuality of the individual. Hence the central theme of *Homo aequalis*: while in holistic societies the major philosophical problem is one of hierarchy, of subordination—and thus of *relations between men*—individualistic societies think of individuals as self-sufficient atoms, on which account the relation between one man and another (which is not held to be constitutive of their humanity) recedes into the background, giving way to *man's relation to things*. Henceforth the main problem became how to preserve and guarantee the self-sufficiency of individuals; and so the decisive question became one having to do with the appropriation of things, their production, and their distribution. This gave rise to an approach in which strictly political categories faded away, yielding to a series of questions about "economies" that came to a head in 1776 (which marked the close of a vast period of development with Adam Smith's *An Inquiry into the Nature and Causes of the Wealth of Nations*).

26. See Dumont, "The Totalitarian Disease," in *Essays*, 149–79.

27. Ibid., 89.

28. Ibid., 16–17.

29. Dumont, *From Mandeville to Marx*, 8; see also *Essays*, 25–26, 62, 73. I emphasize the two determinants confounded here.

30. Dumont, *Essays*, 25–26.

31. Ibid., 59, 61, 62, 75–76.

32. Ibid., 25–26. Concerning independence, see also pages 57, 61. Dumont contrasts the independence of the moderns with the interdependence characteristic of holistic societies based on the principle of hierarchy (60).

33. Ibid., 73.

34. Ibid., 61 n. 2.

35. Ibid., 73. Rousseau describes the state of nature as characterized by "this perfect independence, this unchartered freedom," and, in calling attention to the dangers of individualism, stresses all that is "fatal to the growth of our highest faculties" which would have come about had they in fact occurred; see *The Social Contract* (Amsterdam, 1762), in *The Political Writings of Jean-Jacques Rousseau*, edited by C. E. Vaughn, vol. 1 (Cambridge: Cambridge University Press, 1915), 27.

36. Dumont, *Essays*, 261. Dumont borrows the concepts *Naturwille* and *Kürwille* from Ferdinand Tönnies to designate this "unchartered freedom."

37. Ibid., 56.

38. Ibid., 261–62. Note there too that beginning with Descartes, "*subject and object are absolutely distinguished*," and the world becomes "a world without man, a world from which man has deliberately removed himself and on which he thus able to impose his will"; for "this transformation has been made possible only by the devaluation of the relations between men, relations which generally [i.e., in holistic societies] commanded the relation to things."

39. Gilles Lipovetsky, *L'Empire de l'éphémère: La mode et son destin dans les sociétés modernes* (Paris: Gallimard, 1987), available in English as *The Empire of Fashion: Dressing Modern Democracy*, translated by Catherine Porter (Princeton: Princeton University Press, 1994).

40. Ibid.; see, for example, 6–7, 60–61, 71–72, 235–41. Among the many persuasive arguments and facts Lipovetsky uses to support his thesis, one stands out: as against "the age-old power of the traditional past," democracy is a society organized in relation to the present and in openness to the new—and what phenomenon is characterized more than fashion by the celebration of the present and by the worship of the new (see, for example, 4–5, 18–19, 152–55, 231)?

41. Ibid., 240.

42. Ibid., 241.

43. See ibid., 8. The fine statement there suggests a far more nuanced position: "Pessimism about the present, optimism about the future."

44. See, for example, ibid., 238, where within a few lines contemporary French social movements are said to be characterized both by the "demand for the freedom to live as one pleases *right now*" and by "social explosions provoked by individual motivations and demands."

45. Ibid., 6, 239; also see 240–41.

46. Ibid., 221.

47. Ibid., 221–22.

48. Ibid., 223–24.

49. In Part Two of this book I attempt to show, by analyzing the Leibnizian monadological model, that the valorization of independence only apparently radicalizes the demand for freedom that is constitutive of the valorization of autonomy—that it is, to the contrary, perfectly consistent with the perspective according to which freedom is only the "freedom of the turnspit."

50. Ibid., 8–9; on the "antimodern attitude," see also 127.

51. See Allan Bloom, *The Closing of the American Mind: How Higher Education Has Failed Democracy and Impoverished the Souls of Today's Students* (New York: Simon and Schuster, 1987); Alain Finkielkraut, *La Défaite de la pensée* (Paris: Gallimard, 1987); Michel Henry, *La Barbarie* (Paris: Grasset, 1986).

52. Dumont, *Essays*, 267: "I must confess my irenic preference for [hierarchy]." (In the same sense, see 73–74, 77, 81–82, 85.) Hence it is that one may speak of "dramatic change" (52) and describe "the destruction of the hierarchy of values" as the destruction of "'human ends' by equalitarian individualism" (173).

53. See ibid., 221; and *From Mandeville to Marx* on totalitarianism as the frantic will to reunify the social—as against individualism which, by undermining tradition, destroyed every social convention that had grounded this unity (108).

54. See Dumont, "The Totalitarian Disease," in *Essays*, 149–79: "Hitler projected onto the Jew the individualist tendency he felt within himself as threatening his 'Aryan' devotion to the community" (168); in Hitler, "the idea of domination as resting only on itself, without any other ideological basis than the affirmation that 'nature' wished things to be so, is *nothing but* the result of the destruction of the hierarchy of values, that is to say of human ends, by equalitarian individualism" (173, emphasis added); "Racism *results* here from the holistic representation of community disintegrating under the action of individualism" (175, emphasis

added). In the same vein, in American society, "the abolition of slavery gave rise after a short time to racism," which thus is one "of the involuntary consequences of equalitarianism" (*From Mandeville to Marx*, 12).

55. In the interesting February 1978 issue devoted by the journal *Esprit* to Dumont's work, P. Thibaud avers that despite its "pessimistic" outlook, "it should be understood not as a condemnation of the ideals of equality and communication, but as a reminder that not every goal can be achieved under any conditions" whatsoever (i.e., the unity of the social cannot be founded on the basis of the individual). I fear that this is an "optimistic" reading of Dumont, and that a doctrine regarding racially-based domination as "nothing other than" the effect of the destruction of hierarchy by the principle of equality in fact condemns this principle. See Dumont himself on the transition from hierarchy to individualism: "The moment hierarchy is eliminated, subordination has to be explained as the mechanical result of interaction between individuals, and authority degrades itself into power, power into influence, and so on"—leading finally to the "devastating attempt of the Nazis to base power on itself alone" (*From Mandeville to Marx*, 10, emphasis added).

56. For example: "I never said, as some seemed to believe, that hierarchy is better than equality" (*From Mandeville to Marx*, 12). See also the preface to the revised French edition of *Homo Hierarchicus*, xxi-xxii (originally published as "Questions à Louis Dumont sur la modernité," *Esprit* [September-November 1979]: 67).

57. Dumont, *Essays*, 74.

58. Ibid., 81.

59. The reader will recall the definition of the individualistic ideology as valorizing "the independent, autonomous, essentially nonsocial being."

60. Kant, *Grounding for the Metaphysics of Morals*, translated by James W. Ellington (3rd edition, Indianapolis: Hackett, 1993), 54.

61. See Dumont on Locke in *From Mandeville to Marx*, 54–55.

62. See particularly Philonenko's preface to his translation into French of Kant's *Kritik der Urteilskraft*, published as *Critique de la faculté de juger* (Paris: Vrin, 1965).

63. The conclusion of Lipovetsky's *Empire of Fashion* (see pages 240–41) reminds us of some formidable realities in this connection.

64. Alongside Kant, it is necessary to mention also Fichte's deduction of intersubjectivity as a condition of subjectivity. One of Dumont's essays (see *Essays* 113–32), devotes a few pages to Fichte, mistaking him as one of those for whom modernity attempted (to its misfortune) to reconceive the notion of totality (in this case, the national totality) on an individualistic basis. No one, of course, can be expected to keep up with the most recent scholarship on an author as little-known as Fichte (in the light of which Dumont's analysis of the *Wissenschaftslehre* [Science of Knowledge, 1794] is, however, particularly underinformed), but today we know that in Fichte the relation between individualism and universalism was far more complex than previously assumed, and that it was clearly different in the *Speech to the German Nation* of 1807 from what it had been in 1796, when Fichte wrote in the *Grundlage des Naturrechts* (Foundation

of Natural Right): "The individual, as such, does not exist, the concept of man is not that of an individual, but that of a species"—in short, "man becomes man only among men" (*Fondement du droit naturel*, translated by Alain Renaut [Paris: Presses Universitaires de France, 1984], 54–55). Surely this is an example of the human desocialization that would come to define modernity. See my *Système du droit*, 181ff.

65. Dumont, *Essays*, 60.

66. Ibid., 267. See also page 266 ("[. . .] such recognition [of *alter qua alter*] can only be hierarchical") and *From Mandeville to Marx*, 106 ("[. . .] we are those who have, with Locke, enthroned private property in the place of subordination, or, for that matter, have chosen to be possessing and producing individuals and have turned our backs on the social whole, because of the subordination it entails, and on our neighbor, at least insofar as he would be superior or inferior to us").

67. Once again I must refer the reader to Gauchet's valuable analysis (with G. Swain), *La Pratique de l'esprit humain: L'institution asilaire et la révolution démocratique* (Paris: Gallimard, 1980).

68. Considering, for example, the development of the new categories of economic thinking (in which individualism masterfully prevails via liberalism as "possessive individualism"), Dumont does not for a moment call for a "turning back": "To downgrade the economy would really be to invite a resurgence of subordination, as a consequence of which fearful complications would await us," for "subordination in its normal form, as a value, is excluded in the most complete way from our ideology" and "it could only be reintroduced in a shameful, pathological—indeed oppressive—form" (*From Mandeville to Marx*, 107–8).

69. The interview already cited ("Questions à Louis Dumont sur la modernité"), in arguing against any attempt to return to traditional societies, calls for us to accept ("like Tocqueville") that "we are dedicated to the dignity of man, and thus to equality." The only prospect that this interview holds forth, therefore, is of being attentive to the ways in which even in modern democratic societies traces of hierarchy persist: "The fundamental value is maintained, but subject to constraints." Whether present or absent, or only vanishingly present, hierarchy as a value thus remains the only pole of meaning.

70. Dumont, *Essays*, 116, 207–13, 251–52; see also *From Mandeville to Marx*, 42.

71. Dumont, *Essays*, 210.

72. Ibid., 207.

73. Ibid., 210–11.

74. This is obvious for Herder, and even for Hegel (if only insofar as one thinks of the celebration of the idea of "theodicy" in *Reason in History*); in the case of Marx, the link indicated by Dumont involves conceiving history in terms of the Leibnizian scheme, according to which the universal is the result of particular wills.

75. Ibid., 211.

76. Ibid.

77. Ibid., 215.

78. Ibid., 211. This essential specification thus profoundly relativizes the potentially unitary character of the "Leibnizian model."

79. See Dumont, *From Mandeville to Marx*, 21.

80. Dumont, *Essays*, 213.

81. Ibid., 251 n. 25.

82. The point of view corresponding to a real reconciliation having been rejected, how—between the two poles of an analytic contradiction—could any third one fail to be excluded?

83. Ibid., 213.

84. That is, in the sense of a regulating ideal.

85. Leibniz's insularity is underscored by Dumont's very comparison of the monadological system with other moments of modernity. See, for example, his remark regarding Leibniz and Quesnay (who also tried to occupy an "intermediate position between pure and simple holism and modern individualism"): "As a *distant* but striking parallel, one would think of the metaphysics of Leibniz" (*From Mandeville to Marx*, 42, emphasis added).

86. Leibniz, *Monadology*, §57, 544. I return to this theme at the beginning of Part Two below.

87. The extraordinary final page of Kant's reply to Eberhard is in this regard a model of strategic proficiency: if Kant presented his own arguments for the agreement (required by Reason) between nature and freedom as the "true opinion of Leibniz," this was obviously meant in the sense that for him the truth of the theory of preestablished harmony was to be found in its *transformation* into a principle of reflection; see *The Kant-Eberhard Controversy*, translated by Henry E. Allison (Baltimore: Johns Hopkins University Press, 1973), 160.

88. For the moment I reserve judgment on the matter vis-à-vis *contemporary* (post-Hegelian) individualism.

89. §109 of the *Gay Science* ("Let us be wary") constitutes a systematic critique of all possible theodicies: the world must be thought of neither as a living being nor as a machine, nor as having order, law, beauty, end, or meaning; once "dedivinized," it appears as "everlasting chaos" (167–69).

90. On this point consult the fine analysis of Michel Villey, *La Formation de la pensée juridique moderne: Cours d'histoire de la philosophie du droit, 1961–1966* (4th edition, Paris: Montchrétien, 1975), 199ff; also 206ff, with regard to the anti-Aristotelian (and above all anti-Thomistic) thesis that "individuals alone exist."

91. This *necessary* condition is fulfilled in Ockham without requiring him to be seen, as Dumont insists, as "the herald of the modern turn of mind" and the originator of "a tremendous inroad of individualism" (*Essays*, 62–66).

92. I am thinking here especially of the contribution of Duns Scotus concerning the theory of individuation by form: see Geneviève Rodis-Lewis, *L'Individualité selon Descartes* (Paris: Vrin, 1950), 27ff.

93. Rodis-Lewis's excellent study captures this ambiguity perfectly. I also wish to point out that here I am thoroughly indebted to Frédéric de Buzon, whose fine paper "L'Individu et le sujet" (delivered at Cerisy in July 1986 and subsequently published in E. Guibert and J.-L. Vieillard-Baron, eds., *Penser le sujet aujourd'hui* (Paris: Méridiens-Klincksieck, 1988) called my attention to this point. I endorse most, but not all, of his analysis, and claim responsibility here only for those conclusions that seem to me warranted.

94. This insight is due to de Buzon, ibid.

95. René Descartes, *The Philosophical Writings*, translated by J. Cottingham, R. Stoothoff, and D. Murdoch, 3 vols. (Cambridge: Cambridge University Press, 1984–1991), III, 302–4.

96. See Étienne Gilson, *The Spirit of Mediaeval Philosophy* (New York: Scribner's, 1940), 209–28. See also Rodis-Lewis, *L'Individualité selon Descartes*, 12ff, where moreover it is recalled how ambiguous Aristotle's writings were in this regard.

97. See, for example, Rodis-Lewis, *L'Individualité selon Descartes*, 68.

98. See ibid., 67ff.

99. Descartes, *Philosophical Writings*, III, 243–44.

100. Ibid., III, 179; see too Rodis-Lewis, *L'Individualité selon Descartes*, 83.

101. Recalling that for St. Thomas "specifically identical souls are individualized by their very incarnation," Rodis-Lewis notes the difficulties to which the school was thus exposed (18ff), and explains why, in view of these difficulties, no scholastic at the start of the seventeenth century accepted the whole of the Thomistic solution by matter (34); on Suarez, see 31ff.

102. See, for example, F. W. J. von Schelling, *On the History of Modern Philosophy*, translated by Andrew Bowie (Cambridge: Cambridge University Press, 1994), 42–63.

103. Quoted by Rodis-Lewis, *L'Individualité selon Descartes*, 98.

104. Maine de Biran, *Oeuvres choisies* (Paris: Aubier, 1942), 143. Heidegger himself seems to subscribe to the second interpretative logic: "Descartes above all obviously thinks of his own 'ego' as the individual person (*res cogitans* as *substantia finita*). Kant, on the other hand, "thinks [of] 'consciousness in general'" (*The End of Philosophy*, 98).

CHAPTER III
LEIBNIZ

1. The *Theoria motus abstracti* and the *Theoria motus concretis* make up the *Hypothesis physica nova* of 1670.

2. Heidegger, *Schelling's Treatise*, 92: "Idealism is the interpretation of the essence of Being as "Idea," as the being represented of beings in general. . . . With Leibniz, [. . .] every being, insofar as it is, is intrinsically representing in various stages and degrees from the muted confusion of the lowest living creature up to the absolute luminosity of the divine ego itself and its representing. Representing, *idea* now becomes the essential constituent of every being as such."

3. Hegel, *La philosophie moderne*, vol. 6 of *Leçons sur l'histoire de la philosophie*, translated by P. Garniron (Paris: Vrin, 1985), 1606–1607; published in English as *Modern Philosophy*, in *Lectures on the History of Philosophy*, translated by R. F. Brown and J. M. Stewart with H. S. Harris, 3 vols. (Berkeley and Los Angeles: University of California Press, 1990–).

4. Charles Renouvier, *Manuel de philosophie moderne* (Paris: Paulin, 1842), 420.

5. Charles Renouvier and Louis Prat, *La Nouvelle monadologie* (Paris: Colin, 1899), 5.

6. In Rodis-Lewis's *L'Individualité selon Descartes* (see 74ff) we find the main features of the Cartesian theory of the relation between the mind and the body mentioned in her discussion of the formidable problems that conceiving the unity of the individual involves.

7. It should obviously be made clear that the appeal to preestablished harmony also occurs in connection with those relations that are internal to the body itself or to the mind itself, in the restricted sense of the term. It can easily be understood by reference to the second thesis that constitutes the monadological idea: the fragmentation of substance.

8. See for example, as against Descartes, Leibniz's pamphlet "On the Improvement of Metaphysics, and on the Concept of Substance" (1694): "[T]he concept of *force* . . . sheds much light on the understanding of the true *concept of substance*. . . . This force of action, I affirm, is inherent in all substance, and always engenders some action; that is, corporeal substance itself—and the same is true of spiritual substance—is never inactive" (in *Monadology and Other Philosophical Essays*, 82–83).

9. It will be understood that, *stricto sensu*, for Leibniz the "mind" designates those centers of energy to which reality reduces (and which he calls monads) that are endowed with reflection. Thus in §19 of the *Monadology* he distinguishes three levels among the forces constituting reality. The most elementary monads (physical forces, plants) experience only a succession of internal states and possess the power to modify these states. Above them there is the sphere of *souls*. The souls of animals are endowed with memory; but only souls that are also capable of thinking by reflection (and not, like animals, by the mere association of ideas) qualify as "minds"—the third level—in the restricted (and traditional) sense of the term. It is, however, no less true that all monads are minds in the broad (and revived) sense of the term, since, matter not existing in and of itself, reality is made up of immaterial forces. See in this context the famous passage from the *Monadology* (§66–67): "There is a world of creatures, of living beings, of animals, of entelechies, of souls, in the smallest particle of matter. Each portion of matter may be conceived of as a garden full of plants, and as a pond full of fishes" (547). Note, in the same sense, how the *New Essays* ground the notion of an "analogy between bodies and spirits" on the principle of continuity, such that "From us right down to the lowest things, 'the descent is by easy steps, and a continued series of things, that in each remove, differ very little one from the other . . . the several species are linked together, and differ but in almost insensible degrees . . .'" (see Book III, chapter VI, §12 of the *New Essays on Human Understanding*, translated by and edited by Peter Remnant and Jonathan Bennett [Cambridge: Cambridge University Press, 1981]).

10. For a more exact study of this work, see the valuable annotated translation by Jeanine Quillet, "Disputation métaphysique sur le principe d'individuation de G. W. Leibniz" in *Études philosophiques* (January–March 1979): 79–105.

11. St. Thomas Aquinas, *On Being and Essence*, translated by Armand Maurer (2nd revised edition, Toronto: Pontifical Institute of Mediaeval Studies, 1968), 69.

12. Ibid., 36–37: "What we must realize is that the matter which is the principle of individuation is not just any matter, but only designated matter. By designated matter I mean that which is considered under determined dimensions." The "non-designated matter" is primary undifferentiated matter; the "designated matter" is

"this [latter] kind of matter" (i.e., that part of sensible matter that is capable of being, as it were, pointed out by a finger).

13. The problem is taken up in *On Being and Essence*, 51–59.

14. See Étienne Gilson, *History of Christian Philosophy in the Middle Ages* (New York: Random House, 1955), 375: " [. . .] each angel is less an individual than a species, forming by himself alone an irreducible degree in the descending scale that leads to the body."

15. On the Aristotelian antecedents (in connection with the immaterial substances that move the stars) of this Thomistic exception to the principle of individuation by matter, see Quillet, "Disputation métaphysique," 83.

16. A sketch of this argument is found ibid., 84–85.

17. Ibid., 80.

18. Ibid., 84: "Leibniz's definition of the individual substance hardly changed"—even if in 1663 it still remained to construct the purely mathematical determination of individuality as a monad. Quillet shows that at the time Leibniz conceived individuality in a physical way, as a real entity, and not as a metaphysical point.

19. Such differences as are admitted in the *Monadology* can only be qualitative: if, as is established in §1, the monads are simple, they cannot differ from each other quantitatively (i.e., by the way in which their parts were arranged).

20. P. F. Strawson, *Individuals: An Essay in Descriptive Metaphysics* (London: Methuen, 1959), 125–26.

21. Note that the first thesis constituting the monadological idea prevents us even from escaping Eleaticism by reintroducing a difference between things as a function of their existing in different places in space: since space can no longer be taken as real, spatial differentiation cannot affect identity.

22. This is contradiction of the reflexive or "performative" kind, in the sense that the subject of an utterance (in this case the utterance that there is no change) cannot apply the content of the utterance to itself (since there is no *cogitatio* without a succession of *cogitata*).

23. First by Kant, in the "Note to Amphiboly of Concepts of Reflection" in the *Critique of Pure Reason*, translated by Norman Kemp Smith (New York: St. Martin's Press, 1965). Kant sees in the wholly deductive and logical Leibnizian method a model for dogmatism, in the sense that the whole of the system is claimed to be deducible on the basis of purely logical principles, without seeking to determine whether what is deduced in fact corresponds effectively to an experience previously devalorized as a "confused mode of representation" (282). This method set the philosophical tone, in any case, that German idealism was to inherit from Leibniz.

24. Leibniz, *Monadology*, 534.

25. The following remarks are taken from Jacques Rivelaygue's luminous discussion of the *Monadology* a few years ago in one of his seminars. I cannot say how indebted the present analysis is to his reading of this work: both Luc Ferry and I were pleased to be able to acknowledge his influence upon our current research in the first volume of our edition of his collected papers, *J. Rivelaygue: Leçons de la métaphysique allemande* (Paris: Grasset, 1990).

26. See ibid., 18.

27. Leibniz, *Monadology*, 535

28. Ibid.

29. Strawson, *Individuals*, 121.

30. Leibniz, *Monadology*, 535.

31. On account of this fact, contrary to what René Sève has argued in his unpublished doctoral dissertation *La Philosophie du droit de Leibniz*, and subsequently in *Les Fins et les règles: Leibniz et l'École moderne du droit naturel* (Paris: Presses Universitaires de France, 1989), I fear that it is necessary to relativize substantially Leibniz's contribution to an authentic *philosophy* of law.

32. The reader will recall the familiar formula of the *Critique of Practical Reason*: "[the] freedom of a turnspit, which when once wound up also carries out its motions of itself" (see the translation by Lewis White Beck [3rd edition, New York: Macmillan, 1956], 101).

33. Leibniz, *New System of Nature*, §16, in *Philosophical Writings*, 107. The emphasis on some particularly significant expressions of the emergence of individualism is, of course, mine.

34. In 1705 Bernard Mandeville published a poem of some 400 lines entitled "The Grumbling Hive: Or, Knaves Turn'd Honest." It was only in 1714, with the addition of a long commentary in the form of remarks, that the whole work appeared under the title *The Fable of the Bees: Or Private Vices, Public Benefits*. It was still further augmented by the editions of 1723 and 1729. Regarding the English edition, see n. 37 below.

35. On this point see the impressive works of P. Carrive, *La Philosophie des passions chez Bernard Mandeville* (Lille: Publications de l'Université de Lille-III, 1978) and *Bernard Mandeville: Passions, vices, vertus* (Paris: Vrin, 1980).

36. Adam Smith was to formulate this theory in 1776 in his *Wealth of Nations*.

37. Mandeville, *Fable of the Bees* (London: Wishart & Co., 1934), 27–38.

38. Ibid., 35–37.

39. Ibid., 38.

40. Dumont, *From Mandeville to Marx*, 75.

41. Mandeville, *Fable of the Bees*, 46, 64.

42. Ibid., 31.

43. Ibid., 156.

44. Dumont, *From Mandeville to Marx*, 70. See the discussion there of Mandeville's "philosophy of individualism," which Dumont takes to show that "the idea that the passions are so arranged that 'their apparent discords harmonize to the public good' does represent a step further in the emancipation of the Individual."

45. I pass over the tricky problems posed by the formulation of the theory of "the invisible hand" and its relation (coherent or not) to the *Theory of Moral Sentiments* (1759), which seemed to found the social connection less on self-interest than on a "sympathy" often confounded by interpreters with "benevolence." On these questions note the valuable updating by Jean-Pierre Dupuy, "De l'émancipation de l'individu: Retour sur "Das Adam Smith Problem" (unpublished paper delivered at the conference on "L'Individu" held at Royaumont, 22–24 October 1985) and "L'Individu libéral, cet inconnu: d'Adam Smith à Freidrich Hayek"

(originally published as a paper of the Centre de Recherche en Épistémologie Appliquée [CREA] at the École Polytechnique in Paris and later incorporated in his *Le Sacrifice et l'envie: Le libéralisme aux prises avec la justice sociale* [Paris: Calmann-Lévy, 1992] as the first chapter of the book). In a subtle discussion of Dumont's arguments, Dupuy shows that Smith's model "obviously has a 'ruse of reason' structure" and "cuts a Leibnizian figure" (see *Le Sacrifice et l'envie*, 30ff).

46. I take these formulations from Manfred Frank, *Die Unhintergebarkeit von Individualität: Reflexionen über Subjekt, Person und Indivduum* (Frankfurt: Suhrkamp, 1986); see the French edition, *L'Ultime raison du sujet*, translated by V. Zanetti (Paris: Actes Sud, 1988), 9–14. See also his *What Is Neostructuralism?*, translated by Sabine Wilke and Richard Gray (Minneapolis: University of Minnesota Press, 1989), and "Subjekt, Person, Individuum" in Nagl-Docekal and Vetter, eds., *Tod des Subjekts?*

47. Frank, *L'Ultime raison du sujet*, 81.

48. Quoted ibid., 24.

49. Ibid., 89.

50. Ibid., 81: i.e., in relation to the scholasticism of Saint Thomas and Nicholas de Cusa.

51. Ibid., 90.

CHAPTER IV
BERKELEY AND HUME

1. David Hume, *An Abstract of the Treatise on Human Nature* (London, 1740), reprinted in L. A. Selby-Bigge, ed., *A Treatise of Human Nature*, 646–47.

2. Kant, *Critique of Pure Reason*, 667–68.

3. Fichte, *Nachgelassene Schriften*, edited by H. Jacob (Berlin: Junker and Dunnhaupt, 1937), II, 248. This passage is quoted by Alexis Philonenko in his *La Liberté humaine dans la philosophie de Fichte* (Paris: Vrin, 1966), 29.

4. Fichte, *Nachgelassene Schriften*, II, 248.

5. Berkeley, *Philosophical Commentaries (Generally Called the Commonplace Book)*, edited by A. A. Luce (London: Thomas Nelson and Sons, 1944), 7, 156.

6. See Martial Guéroult, *Berkeley: Quatre études sur la perception et sur Dieu* (Paris: Aubier, 1956), 23ff.

7. Heidegger discusses this meaning of idealism in his *Schelling*: "For Descartes, *idea* means representation. . . . But all representing is I represent, I think, and all kinds of the ego's behavior, feeling, too, are representation in the broad sense, thinking. . . .[T]hinking as 'I think' becomes the court of judgement over Being: thinking—the *idea*. This doctrine of Being, namely, that Being is definable in its nature in terms of thinking is thus an Idealism" (92).

8. See Guéroult, *Berkeley*, 25ff., which well lays out the role played by Descartes, Locke, and Malebranche. I present them here as being related in a clearly different way, emphasizing their central place within the fertile tradition inaugurated by Descartes (in which the primacy of the *subject* is affirmed within the framework of an idea of being).

9. Descartes, *Selected Philosophical Writings*, translated by J. Cottingham, R. Stoothoff, and D. Murdoch (Cambridge: Cambridge University Press, 1988), 73, 84.

10. See the valuable chapter by Ferdinand Alquié, "La vision in Dieu et la critique de l'innéisme" in *Le Cartésianisme de Malebranche* (Paris: Vrin, 1974), 194ff, particularly this passage: "But, wonders Malebranche, is it likely that God created so many ideas in the mind of each man? Certainly it is not impossible. His power is such that He might have produced an infinity of ideas in each of us. But He could have achieved the same result much more simply. It can be concluded that He did so, and this in the name of the principle of the simplicity of means: God would offend against a kind of requirement of economy, or aesthetics, if He actualized in a complicated way what He could do simply. Instead of creating an infinite number of ideas in each mind, it is enough for Him to disclose to every mind the ideas that are in Him" (196).

11. This point is strongly emphasized by Joseph Moreau in his edition of Malebranche's *Correspondence avec J.-J. Dourtous de Mairan* (Paris: Vrin, 1947), 98. See also Alquié, *Le Cartésianisme de Malebranche*, 410.

12. Malebranche emphatically insisted on the difficulties posed for reason by a Creation that, as the source of an imperfect world, seems incompatible with divine perfection: "The world is unworthy of God. . . . Thus God cannot form the plan of producing it" (*Oeuvres complètes* [Paris: Vrin, 1958–1970], v, 11); even more radically, how "[c]an God will that we are, He who has no need of us? How can a Being in whom nothing is lacking and who is fully self-sufficient, will something?" (*Oeuvres complètes*, XII, 200).

13. On the experience of insomnia, I can only refer the reader to Emmanuel Lévinas's admirable *De l'existence à l'existant* (1978): see the English edition, *Existence and Existents*, translated by Alphonso Lingis (Dordrecht: Kluwer, 1988), 65ff, for a superbly apt description of the way in which "the vigilance of insomnia which keeps our eyes open has no subject." Whoever has not experienced this dispersion of the insomniac self ("swept away by the fatality of being") cannot have a sense of what is meant by the dissolution of subjectivity. On the philosophical meaning of this Lévinassian analysis of insomnia, see the third section of Chapter 6 ("Fragment of a Phenomenology of Eros") of the present work.

14. Berkeley, *Philosophical Commentaries*, (§427a, 808), 166.

15. Berkeley was surely the first to have noted what is absurd in theories of knowledge that posit an object-in-itself as the cause of representation: in the name of exactly what is something to be posited as an "in-itself" (since if we are the ones doing the positing, it is not an in-itself but something that already constitutes an object for us, thus falling into the area of representation)? In objecting to this dimension of the in-itself, by which being is thus reduced to representation, Berkeley made an important step forward in modern philosophy—without which a critical approach to the problem of objectivity (as a problem to be resolved without stepping outside the subject) would have been impossible. Hence Kant could legitimately, at the end of the "General Observations on Transcendental Aesthetic" (*Critique of Pure Reason*, 89), praise the "good Berkeley"—without prejudice to the highly unsympathetic discussion of empiricist idealism (that "dogmatic ideal-

ism" which denies the existence of matter) in the *Critique*. The importance of the Berkeleyan objection to the in-itself in the genesis of the critical tradition also raises the question why Kant despite everything looked favorably upon what he called the "thing-in-itself." I do not propose to work out this question here: at least one ought to credit the *Critique* for employing this notion (unless, of course, in doing so it sowed the seeds of incoherence) in a sense compatible with the undeniable contributions of the "good Berkeley."

16. See *Siris: A Chain of Philosophical Reflexions and Inquiries Concerning the Virtues of Tar-Water, and divers other Subjects connected together and arising from one another* (Dublin, 1744), particularly §251ff, in A. A. Luce and T. E. Jessop, eds., *The Works of George Berkeley, Bishop of Cloyne*, 9 vols. (London and New York: T. Nelson, 1948–1957).

17. For a detailed treatment of these questions, see the fine work of Geneviève Brykman, *Philosophie et apologétique chez Berkeley* (Paris: Vrin, 1986).

18. See Berkeley, *Principles*, §27: "A Spirit is one simple, undivided, active being—as it perceives ideas it is called the *understanding*, and as it produces or otherwise operates about them, it is called the *will*"; also §28: "I find I can excite ideas in my mind at pleasure, and vary and shift the scene as oft as I think fit. It is no more than *willing*, and straightaway this or that idea arises in my fancy. . . ."

19. On the revival by German idealism of this definition of activity as a limitation of activity (i.e., diminished activity), see Cassirer's commentary on Maimon in *Les Systèmes post-Kantiens*, translated by S. Bonnet et al. (Lille: Presses Universitaires de Lille, 1983), 67ff.

20. Berkeley, *Principles*, §26. See especially §29: "Whatever power I may have over my own thoughts, I find the ideas actually perceived by Sense have not a like dependence of *my* will. When in broad daylight I open my eyes, it is not in my power to choose whether I shall see or no, or to determine what particular objects shall present themselves to my view; and so likewise as to the hearing and other senses; the ideas imprinted on them are not creatures of *my* will. *There is therefore some other Will or Spirit that produces them.*"

21. For a detailed study of the Fichtean solution, see my *Système du droit*.

22. In his *Grundlage der gesamten Wissenschaftslehre* (1794), Fichte gave a fine definition of criticism as a philosophy of immanence, thus recognizing Berkeley's unimpeachable contribution: "In the critical system, a thing is what is posited in the self; in the dogmatic, it is that wherein the self is itself posited: critical philosophy is thus *immanent*, since it posits everything in the self; dogmatism is *transcendent*, since it goes on beyond the self" (*Foundations of the Entire Science of Knowledge*, translated by P. Heath and J. Lachs [Cambridge: Cambridge University Press, 1982], 117).

23. Fichte, *Nachgelassene Schriften*, II, 248.

24. On the comparison with Berkeley as it was made during Fichte's time, see Philonenko, *La Liberté humaine*, 78 n. 7.

25. Alexis Philonenko was the first to draw attention to Fichte's transposition of the Leibnizian monadology to the realm of practical philosophy. This transposition can only be fully understood, however, by seeing how it destroys the monadicity of the "freedoms."

26. Fichte, *Nachgelassene Schriften*, II, 247.

27. Luc Ferry, in the first two volumes of his *Political Philosophy*, has systematized the arguments in favor of the reading proposed by Alexis Philonenko on this point.

28. On the extraordinary Fichtean promotion of philosophy of law, see my "De la philosophie comme philosophie du droit," *Bulletin de la Société Française de Philosophie* (July-September 1986).

29. See my translation of Fichte's *Grundlage des Naturrechts* (*Fondement du droit naturel*, 54).

30. Ibid., 62. In the same sense, see the letter to Reinhold of 29 August 1795 ("There is no individual, but there are not at least two of them") in the first volume of *J. G. Fichte im Gespräch: Berichte der Zeitgenossen*, edited by Erich Fuchs (Stuttgart/Bad Canstatt: Frommann-Holzboog, 1978–1991); "No Thou, no I: no I, no Thou" (*Foundations of the Entire Science of Knowledge*, 172–73); "It is man's *destiny* to live in society; he *ought* to live in society. One who lives in isolation is not a complete human being. He contradicts his own self" ("Some Lectures Concerning the Scholar's Vocation" in *Fichte: Early Philosophical Writings*, translated by Daniel Breazeale [Ithaca: Cornell University Press, 1988], 156); "Only the human species exists" (ibid., 184). It is obviously the whole deduction of intersubjectivity (see Part I of the *Grundlage des Naturrechts*) that establishes how reflection on the juridical relation between freedoms reciprocally limiting each other provides the critical solution to the problem of objectivity: see Renaut, *Système du droit*, 162–89.

31. See particularly *Siris*, §254: "[T]he phaenomena of nature, which strike on the senses and are understood by the mind, do form not only a magnificent spectacle, but also a most coherent, entertaining, and instructive Discourse. . . . As the natural connexion of *signs* with *the things signified* is regular and constant, it forms a sort of rational discourse, and is therefore the immediate effect of an Intelligent Cause."

32. For a very detailed examination of this linguistic paradigm, see Brykman's *Philosophie et apologétique chez Berkeley*.

33. Hume, *A Treatise of Human Nature*, xvi: "There is no question of importance, whose decision is not compriz'd in the science of man; and there is none, which can be decided with any certainty, before we become acquainted with that science. In pretending therefore to explain the principles of human nature, we in effect propose a compleat system of the sciences, built on a foundation almost entirely new, and the only one upon which they can stand with any security."

34. Ibid., 43.

35. The formula is Michel Malherbe's in *La Philosophie empiriste de David Hume*, 51–52.

36. This question appeared, of course, in Kant's 21 February 1772 letter to Marcus Herz, which asks "What is the ground of the relation of that in us which we call 'representation' to the object?" (in *Philosophical Correspondence, 1759–99*, translated by Arnulf Zweig [Chicago: University of Chicago Press, 1967], 71).

37. See Chapter I of Deleuze, *Empiricism and Subjectivity*.

38. Ibid., 22.

39. Malherbe, *La Philosophie empiriste de David Hume*, 63.

40. Michaud, *Hume et la fin de la philosophie*, 257, 259.

41. On this "atomism" of impressions, see Malherbe, *La Philosophie empiriste de David Hume*, 91; also Deleuze, *Empiricism and Subjectivity*, 27 ("the mind is in itself a collection of atoms").

42. Malherbe, *La Philosophie empiriste de David Hume*, 91.

43. Hume, *Treatise*, 2–4.

44. Ibid., 252.

45. Ibid., 5–6. The very argument by which Hume justifies this principle of differentiation is thoroughly Leibnizian and explicitly employs the principle of continuity: "[I]f this shou'd be deny'd, 'tis possible, by the continual gradation of shades, to run a colour insensibly into what is most remote from it; and if you will not allow any of the means to be different, you cannot without absurdity deny the extremes to be the same." In short, Hume holds, there cannot be the least gap between the gradations of the same color.

46. Ibid., 252.

47. Malherbe, *La Philosophie empiriste de David Hume*, 93.

48. Quite obviously, the empiricist transposition of the monadologies also involves other important adjustments. Because the monads are impressions, they cannot be "without birth or death," for example, as in Leibniz. Their immediacy and simplicity makes it indeed possible to think them as unalterable and without duration, but because they "succeed each other with an inconceivable rapidity" and are "in a perpetual flux and movement" (252), they are, of course, perishable.

49. Malherbe, *La Philosophie empiriste de David Hume*, 92. All the perceptions experienced include totalities and result from an association that is always already based on simple sense-data that do not correspond to any particular experience. The example, mentioned earlier, of the simple impression produced by the burst of sunlight is obviously metaphorical—the experienced impression of light is always accompanied by various connotations (heat, pain, or pleasure, and so forth) that already combine a multiplicity of simple elements.

50. Ibid., 96. "Because the whole reality of the complex is contained in the simple elements . . . the atomic difference is always effective[;] it is even the effective presence of the mind."

51. Hume, *Treatise*, 251–52.

52. Ibid., 635. For this genesis of the Self see the excellent analysis by Malherbe in *La Philosophie empiriste de David Hume* (at 103ff and 159ff). Note particularly the splendid formula "The for-itself is an accident" (105).

53. Hume, *Treatise*, 252–53.

54. Hume, *Enquiries Concerning the Human Understanding and Concerning the Principles of Morals*, edited by L. A. Selby-Bigge (3rd edition, Oxford: Clarendon Press, 1975), 54: cited in Deleuze, *Empiricisme et Subjectivité*, 138.

55. Deleuze, *Empiricism and Subjectivity*, 26; on impressional atomism, see also 27–28, 105–7.

56. Ibid., 119.

57. Ibid., 132.

58. Deleuze, *Anti-Oedipus: Capitalism and Schizophrenia*, translated by Robert Hurley, Mark Seem, and Helen R. Lane (Minneapolis: University of Minnesota Press, 1983), 16.

59. Ibid., 20.

60. Ibid., 40–41.

CHAPTER V
HEGEL AND NIETZSCHE

1. This is not the place to reexamine the complex but hackneyed question of the continuity and/or discontinuity that characterize the relation between Hegel and Nietzsche. In this connection see particularly Karl Löwith's important book *From Hegel to Nietzsche: The Revolution in Nineteenth-Century Thought*, translated by David E. Green (New York: Holt, Rinehart and Winston, 1964). For studies of Nietzsche see, for example, J. Granier, *Le Problème de la vérité dans la philosophie de Nietzsche* (Paris: Seuil, 1966), 43ff; and G. Morel, *Nietzsche: Introduction à une première lecture* (Paris: Aubier, 1985), 241ff.

2. Heidegger, *Essais et conférences*, 132.

3. Nietzsche, *Beyond Good and Evil*, 31.

4. Nietzsche, *The Gay Science*, 305.

5. Nietzsche, *Human, All Too Human: A Book for Free Spirits [Menschliches, Allzumenschliches* 1878], translated by Marion Faber with Stephen Lehmann (Lincoln: University of Nebraska Press, 1984), 14.

6. Nietzsche, "Zur Philosophie und ihrer Geschichte," §621, in *Die Unschuld des Werdens: Der Nachlass*, edited by Alfred Baeumler, vol. XI (Stuttgart: Alfred Kröner Verlag, 1913), 237.

7. Nietzsche, *The Gay Science*, 305–6.

8. Max Horkheimer, *Between Philosophy and Social Science: Selected Early Writings*, translated by G. Frederick Hunter, Matthew S. Kramer, and John Torpey (Cambridge: MIT Press, 1993), 335, 375.

9. Ibid., 375.

10. Ibid.

11. See, for example, Ernst Cassirer, *The Philosophy of the Enlightenment*, translated by Fritz C. A. Koelln and James P. Pettegrove (Princeton: Princeton University Press, 1968), 209: ". . . [the] *Principles of a New Science of the Common Nature of Nations* is the first systematic delineation of [a philosophy of history]."

12. Horkheimer, *Between Philosophy and Social Science*, 376.

13. A discussion of the obstacles presented by Cartesian philosophy to the development of a philosophy of history and its emergence with Leibniz can be found in Yvon Belaval's *Leibniz critique Descartes* (Paris: Gallimard, 1960), 88–129.

14. Cassirer, *Philosophy of the Enlightenment*, 228–33.

15. Here again I am indebted to Jacques Rivelaygue for drawing my attention to this problem.

16. Leibniz, *De rerum originatione* (On the Origin of Things), in *Leibniz: Philosophical Writings*, 41.

17. This passage from *De rerum originatione* is discussed by Michel Serres in *Le Système de Leibniz et ses modèles mathématiques: Étoiles, schémas, points*, vol. I (Paris: Presses Universitaires de France, 1968), 255. All of Chapter 2 ("Les multiplicités historiques: Le progrès") of Part I of the first volume (213–87) discusses the way in which Leibniz approaches the question of history: "What can be said of the universe and its plan for progress? Created maximally by God, is it conceivable that He maximizes His perfection over the course of temporal sequences? Is the best getting better?"

18. In his translation of Herder's *Auch eine Philosophie der Geschichte zur Bildung der Menschheit* (*Une autre philosophie de l'histoire* [Paris: Aubier, 1964]), Max Rouché recalls Herder's argument, as against Voltaire, that humanity's virtues are constant and that every period of the past, every culture—provided that it has not been divested of "its national character, of what is specific in its mind and language" (*Sämtliche Werke*, edited by Bernhard Suphan, vol. I [Hildesheim: Georg Olms, 1967], 366)—expresses humanity in its own way. The debate between these two major figures of the Enlightenment was extended (notwithstanding the differences between the two works) by the *Ideen sur Philosophie der Geschichte der Menschheit* [4 vols., 1784–1791] (first published in English as *Outlines of a Philosophy of the History of Man*, translated by T. O. Churchill [London, 1800]), in which Herder (in Part II) argued against Kant. Kant, in his essay "Idee zu einer allgemeinen Geschichte in Weltbürglicher Absichte" ("Idea of a Universal History from a Cosmopolitan Point of View," 1784), had urged that all epochs be considered as so many stages in the infinite process that leads to the republican constitution. Herder objected that every culture is a self-sufficient end in itself and must be valued on its own terms.

19. For example, see Alain Finkielkraut, *La Défaite de la pensée*, 14ff (published in English as *The Defeat of the Mind*, translated by Judith Friedlander [New York: Columbia University Press, 1995]). With Herder, universal principles ceased to transcend "the plurality of collective souls" and "all supranational values" were "deprived of their sovereignty."

20. Isaiah Berlin, "Herder and the Enlightenment," in *Vico and Herder* (London: Hogarth Press, 1976), 143ff.

21. Ibid., 157–58.

22. On this point, see the pertinent discussion by Alexis Philonenko in his *La Théorie kantienne de l'histoire* (Paris: Vrin, 1986), 128. Independently of Herder's *Briefe zu Beförderung der Humanität* (Letters for the Advancement of Humanity [10 vols., 1793–1797]), which Philonenko mentions, it should be recalled that he wrote important discussions of the Leibnizien system: see *Wahrheiten aus Leibniz* and *Über Leibnizens Grundsätze von der Natur und Gnade*, in *Sämtliche Werke*, II, 211–27. We know that Herder read and annotated the *New Essays*, the *Theodicy*, and the *Monadology*: on the importance of these readings of Leibniz, see Max Rouché, *La Philosophie de l'histoire de Herder* (Paris: Les Belles Lettres, 1940).

23. Herder also took from Leibniz the role of the principle of continuity. In addition to the fact that this principle implies an ontological monism, which Herder adopted as its own (on this point see Max Rouché's introduction to his translation of the *Ideen* [*Idées pour la philosophie de l'histoire de l'humanité* (Paris: Aubier-Montaigne, 1964), 21ff]), he argued in favor of conceiving history

(at least the history of a given civilization) as a continuous progression among nation-epochs, often compared in *Auch eine Philosophie* to the course of a river or the growth of a tree—images that emphasize, together with the unfolding of a divine plan of development (i.e., preestablished harmony), the equal necessity of all historical moments and the perfect continuity they display. On the status of various civilizations in relation to each other, see too Rouché's introduction to his translation of this work, *Une autre philosophie de l'histoire*, 62ff.

24. In this connection see Chapter 4 ("German Identity: Herder's *Volk* and Fichte's *Nation*") in Dumont's *Essays on Individualism*. Dumont, while he realizes that "Herder . . . uses the individualist principle by transferring it to the level of . . . collective entities that before him were unacknowledged or subordinated" (118), interprets this transfer too one-sidedly as having an antiuniversalist and antirationalistic significance.

25. Herder, *Sämtliche Werke*, II, 225.

26. Ibid., II, 215.

27. The role played by the Herderian reprise of Leibniz is superbly analyzed by Philippe Raynaud in his article on *Auch eine Philosophie* in Châtelet et al., eds., *Dictionnaire des oeuvres politiques*.

28. Hegel, *Lectures on the Philosophy of World History: Introduction: Reason in History* [henceforth *Reason in History*], 30–31).

29. Ibid., 77.

30. Ibid., 79.

31. Ibid., 80.

32. Ibid., 91.

33. Ibid., 33.

34. Ibid., 27. There is a direct line of descent from Leibniz's "*nihil est sine ratione*" to Hegel's definition of philosophical thinking as having "no other goal but to eliminate chance."

35. Ibid., 34.

36. Ibid., 35–36.

37. Ibid., 42.

38. Ibid.

39. Ibid.

40. Ibid., 42–43.

41. Ibid., 43.

42. On this point, see Alexis Philonenko's preface to his French translation of Kant's *What is Orientation in Thinking?* (*Qu'est-ce que s'orienter dans la pensée?* [Paris: Vrin, 1978]).

43. Mendelssohn, a favorite whipping boy of Jacobi, had defended the claims of reason in praising Leibniz's philosophy as the highest expression of rationalism (see Philonenko, *La théorie kantienne de l'histoire*, 17).

44. Note in this connection Jacobi's statement in *David Hume über den Glauben, oder, Idealismus und Realismus* [1787] that "I scarcely see a thinker who was more distinctly vigilant than our Leibniz"; he goes on to say, "I am attached with all my soul to the theory of monads." See the French translation by L. Guillermit, *David Hume ou la croyance: Idéalisme et réalisme*, in his *Le Réalisme de F. H.*

Jacobi: Dialogue sur l'idéalisme et le réalisme (Provence: Publications de l'Université de Provence, 1982), 332–43. An English translation was published under the Garland imprint in New York in 1983.

45. Jacobi, *David Hume ou la croyance*, 342. On the idea of "matter" as "life," see the *Monadology*, §63ff.

46. Jacobi, *David Hume ou la croyance*, 335. Jacobi relies here on §62 of the *Monadology*.

47. Quoted in Guillermit, *Le Réalisme de F. H. Jacobi*, 92.

48. On this antirationalist extension of the concept of reason (which Jacobi gets at by comparing *Vernunft* [reason] to *vernehmen* [to perceive]), see Cassirer, *Les systèmes post-Kantiens*, 34.

49. Paradoxical, but not absolutely impossible: in this sense, it is fair to say (and here I fully endorse Philippe Raynaud's shrewd judgment in his article on Herder's *Auch eine Philosophie*) that "Leibniz is at the origin of *all* the streams of German idealism"—including those that exploit it in the interests of irrationalism.

50. This twofold criticism of Jacobi is ably discussed by Robert Legros, *Le Jeune Hegel et la naissance de la pensée romantique* (Brussels: Ousia, 1981), 97.

51. In the *Über die Lehre des Spinozas, in Briefen an Herrn Moses Mendelssohn* (Breslau, 1785), Jacobi argued that causal thought, by making the principle of reason its supreme law, always relates what is given to an already understood condition that it conceives to be its cause: in this sense, it reduces becoming to the deployment of an identity and rules out any role for novelty.

52. Hegel, *Reason in History*, 27.

53. On Spirit as Life see, for example, ibid., 47ff.

54. Hegel, *Phenomenology of Spirit*, translated by A. V. Miller (Oxford: Oxford University Press, 1977), 10.

55. Ibid., 10. Hegel goes on to elaborate: "[T]he living Substance is being which is in truth *Subject* . . . insofar as it is the movement of positing itself, or is the mediation of its self-othering with itself."

56. The characteristics of the "ruse of reason" have been analyzed by Luc Ferry in his *Political Philosophy* 2, 37–40.

57. Hegel, *Reason in History*, 67.

58. Ibid., 43.

59. Nietzsche, *The Will to Power*, translated by Walter Kaufman and R. J. Hollingdale (New York: Random House, 1967), §725, III, 380.

60. Ibid., §1067, IV, 549–50.

61. Nietzsche, *The Gay Science*, §374, 336.

62. Nietzsche, *Will to Power*, §481, III, 267.

63. Nietzsche, *La Volonté de puissance* (Bianquis edition [1995]), Book IV, §493, II, 425.

64. Ibid., Book III, §581, II, 215; and similarly, Book III, §493, II, 425: to see "by a hundred eyes, through *various* persons . . . to see by a multitude of eyes and by very *personal* eyes."

65. It might also be mentioned that the Leibnizian principle of continuity became radicalized through Nietzsche's insistence on "seeing transitions" where

metaphysics saw antinomies and an established dualism: instead of "contrasts," one should grasp "degrees" (Ibid., Book II, §421, I, 374).

66. Nietzsche, *The Gay Science*, §109, 168.

67. On the valorization of independence see, for example, Nietzsche, *Beyond Good and Evil*, §41, 70.

68. Nietzsche, *Will to Power*, §681, III, 360–61.

69. Nietzsche, *Beyond Good and Evil*, §268, 205–6.

70. Nietzsche, *The Gay Science*, §354 ("On the 'genius of the species'"), 297–300.

71. Ibid., 299–300: " . . . the world of which we can become conscious is only a surface-and-sign world, a world that is made common and meaner [since] . . . all becoming conscious involves a . . . reduction to superficialities, and generalization."

72. Nietzsche, *Will to Power*, §786, III, 414; cf. *La Volonté de puissance*, translated by H. Albert (15th edition, Paris: Mercure de France 1923), II, 138.

73. Nietzsche, *Will to Power*, §521, III, 282.

74. Ibid., §552, III, 299.

75. Nietzsche, *Twilight of the Idols* [*Die Götzen-Dämmerung*, 1889], translated by R. J. Hollingdale (Harmondsworth: Penguin Books, 1968), §33, 97.

76. Nietzsche, *La Volonté de puissance* (Bianquis edition), Book I, §268, I, 121 and Book I, §286, I, 130; cf. *Will to Power*, §379, II, 204.

77. Nietzsche, *Will to Power*, §786, III, 413–14.

78. Ibid., §715, III, 380.

79. Ibid., §636, III, 339.

80. Ibid., §784, III, 412.

81. Ibid., §287, II, 162.

82. Ibid., §765, III, 401.

83. Ibid., §783, III, 410.

84. Ibid., §783, III, 410–11.

85. Ibid., §784, III, 411.

86. Nietzsche associates democratic individualism and socialism in a way rather similar to Toqueville in regarding the welfare state as the limit of a modern individualism that creates and exploits it to allow equal access to the greatest possible happiness.

87. Nietzsche, *Will to Power*, §784, III, 412.

88. Note that Nietzsche also sometimes mentions the great figures of the Renaissance, such as Dante and Michelangelo: see *Will to Power*, §1018, IV, 526; on the contrast between the Italian Renaissance and the Northern Reformation, see, e.g., §93, I, 57.

89. See Nietzsche, *La Volonté de puissance* (Bianquis edition), Book III, §49, II, 34.

90. Ibid., Book IV, §469, II, 348–49 (II, 416 in the 1995 edition).

91. This culmination is the subject of Ferry's and my analysis in *French Philosophy of the Sixties*, the archaeology of which I have attempted to give here.

92. See Nietzsche, *La Volonté de puissance* (Bianquis edition), Book II, §55, I, 238.

PART THREE
PREAMBLE

1. The adversarial aspect of this dialogue is analyzed in Chapter 4 of Luc Ferry's and my *Heidegger et les Modernes* (Paris: Grasset, 1988), available in English as *Heidegger and Modernity*, translated by Franklin Philip (Chicago: University of Chicago Press, 1990).

CHAPTER VI
LÉVINAS

1. Emmanuel Lévinas, *Humanisme de l'autre homme* (Montpellier: Fata Morgana, 1972). The passages cited are to be found on pages 73 and 80 of the 1987 "Livre de Poche" edition: pages 65–82 of this edition reprint an article originally published in the *Revue Internationale de Philosophie* in 1968, and published in English as Chapter 8 ("Humanism and An-Archy") of *Emmanuel Lévinas: Collected Philosophical Papers*, translated by Alphonso Lingis (The Hague: Martinus Nijhoff, 1987), 127–40. The two pages cited above correspond to pages 127 and 131 of the English language edition.
2. Lévinas, *Collected Philosophical Papers*, 133.
3. This expression provides the title for Part I of Lévinas's *De Dieu qui vient à l'idée* (Paris: Vrin, 1982); see also page 198 of this work.
4. Lévinas, *Collected Philosophical Papers*, 144. Chapter 9 of the *Papers* ("No Identity," 141–51) is a translation of a 1970 article originally published in *Ephémère* and subsequently reprinted in *Humanisme de l'autre homme*, 83–101.
5. Ibid., 141.
6. Ibid., 142–43.
7. Ibid., 127.
8. Ibid., 128.
9. Lévinas, *Transcendance et intelligibilité* (Geneva: Labor et Fides, 1984), 12ff.
10. Lévinas, *De Dieu qui vient à l'idée*, 31.
11. Ibid., 212–14.
12. Lévinas, *Collected Philosophical Papers*, 145.
13. On the notion of transcendence, see Lévinas, *Transcendance et intelligibilité*, 17, 21, 53; *De Dieu que vient à l'idée*, 130; and *Totalité et infini* (The Hague: Martinus Nijhoff, 1965), 5ff, or the corresponding pages in the English language edition of this work, *Totality and Infinity: An Essay on Exteriority*, translated by Alphonso Lingis (Pittsburgh: Duquesne University Press, 1979), 34–40.
14. Lévinas, *De Dieu qui vient à l'idée*, 130.
15. Lévinas, *Collected Philosophical Papers*, 130 n. 5.
16. Ibid., 151.
17. Lévinas, *De Dieu qui vient à l'idée*, 47.

18. Ibid., 48–50.

19. Ibid., 54–55. Note that the *Cartesian Meditations*, though first published in 1950, were based on lectures given more than twenty years earlier; see Chapter I, n. 90, above.

20. Ibid., 50.

21. For example, see Lévinas, *Transcendance et intelligibilité*, 40.

22. Lévinas, *De Dieu qui vient à l'idée*, 33.

23. Lévinas, *Collected Philosophical Papers*, 94.

24. Husserl, *Cartesian Meditations*, §44, 92.

25. Ibid., §49, 107–8.

26. Note that Fichte contributed to this shift by casting the monadology as a practical monadology.

27. Husserl, *La Crise des sciences européennes et la phénoménologie transcendentale*, translated by G. Granel (Paris: Gallimard, 1976), 460; an English edition of *Die Krisis der europäischen wissenschaften und die transcendentale Phänomenologie* (Belgrade, 1936) appeared previously under the title *The Crisis of European Sciences and Transcendental Phenomenology: An Introduction to Phenomenological Philosophy*, translated by David Carr (Evanston: Northwestern University Press, 1970). I am indebted to the excellent lecture (already cited) given by Frédéric de Buzon, who drew my attention to this passage.

28. Lévinas, *Collected Philosophical Papers*, 95.

29. Ibid., 94.

30. See Lévinas, *Totality and Infinity*, 251–85.

31. Lévinas, *De Dieu qui vient à l'idée*, 192.

32. Lévinas, *Totality and Infinity*, 34.

33. Ibid., 27.

34. Lévinas, *En découvrant l'existence avec Husserl et Heidegger* (Paris: Vrin, 1949).

35. Husserl, *Logische Untersuchungen*, 2 vols. (Halle, 1900–1901). A French version translated by Hubert Elie appeared as *Recherches logiques* (Paris: Presses Universitaires de France, 1959–1964).

36. See Lévinas, *En découvrant l'existence*, 7–52.

37. Lévinas, *Totality and Infinity*, 256–66.

38. See Jean-Paul Sartre, *L'Être et le néant: Essai d'ontologie phénoménologique* (Paris: Gallimard, 1943), Part II, Chapter 3, §1 ("La première attitude envers l'autri: l'amour, le langage, le masochisme"); an English edition appeared as *Being and Nothingness: A Phenomenological Essay on Ontology*, translated by Hazel E. Barnes (New York: Washington Square Press, 1956).

39. Lévinas, *Totality and Infinity*, 257.

40. Plato, *The Symposium*, in *The Collected Dialogues of Plato*, edited by Edith Hamilton and Huntington Cairns. Bollingen Series LXXI (Princeton: Princeton University Press, 1963), 210e, 562.

41. Ibid., 210e-211b, 562.

42. Lévinas, *Totality and Infinity*, 257.

43. Lévinas, ibid., 117. More specifically, he says, the correlate of need is pleasure (*jouissance*) in its ultimate form ("the independence of happiness" [115]):

"Happiness, in its relation with the 'other' of nutrients, suffices to itself" (118). In this sense, need does not destroy the monad's immanence to itself: it is merely a "movement of the same" (116), "the very eddy of the same" (115).

44. Ibid., 257–58.

45. Ibid., 258.

46. Plato, *The Republic*, translated by Benjamin Jowett [3rd edition, Oxford: Clarendon Press, 1888] (New York: Vintage Books, 1991), 279.

47. Lévinas, *Totality and Infinity*, 258.

48. Ibid.

49. Such is the interpretation sketched by Derrida in "Violence et métaphysique: Essai sur la pensée d'Emmanuel Lévinas," in *L'Écriture et la différence* (Paris: Seuil, 1967); see *Writing and Difference*, translated by Alan Bass (Chicago: University of Chicago Press, 1978), 321 n. 92. Of this passage he writes, "[I]t seems to us impossible, essentially impossible, that it could have been written by a woman. Its philosophical subject is man (*vir*)"—in the sense that "perhaps metaphysical desire is essentially virile . . .": to the extent that *logos*, as an act of reducing a thing to itself, is essentially phallic. From the same perspective, see B. Forthomme, *Une philosophie de la transcendance: la métaphysique d'Emmanuel Lévinas* (Paris: Vrin, 1979), 332: the Lévinassian analysis of subjectivity does not refer "interchangeably to the masculine and the feminine"—the subject being "clearly man as *vir* and not as *homo*."

50. Lévinas, *Totality and Infinity*, 258.

51. Sartre, *Being and Nothingness*, 476–77.

52. Ibid., 477–78.

53. Ibid., 506–7.

54. Lévinas, *Totality and Infinity*, 258.

55. Ibid., 258. Lévinas denies as well that the object of the caress is what he calls "the body-expression" (that is, the body as the face of others who confront me)—a denial that also partakes in the rejection of the Sartrean approach, according to which (see *Being and Nothingness*, 476–77) being-in-the-presence-of-others as freedom amounts at bottom to the revelation of others as gaze, as the expression of a face that reveals to me the presence of a freedom, helps this freedom to manifest itself.

56. Lévinas, *Totality and Infinity*, 258.

57. Ibid.

58. Lévinas, *Le Temps et l'Autre* (Paris: Presses Universitaires de France, 1983), 78–79; see *Time and the Other, and Additional Essays*, translated by Richard A. Cohen (Pittsburgh: Duquesne University Press, 1987), 86–87.

59. Ibid., 87.

60. Ibid., 88. Similarly, see page 36 on the feminine as the "very quality of difference."

61. Lévinas, *Totality and Infinity*, 258–59.

62. See particularly the first section ("Insomnia") of Chapter V of Lévinas, *Existence and Existents*, 65–67.

63. Ibid., 67.

64. Ibid., 65.

65. Ibid., 65–66.

66. Ibid., 66.

67. See for example, *Existence and Existents*, 60: "*an impersonal vigilance*"; also 58, where it is described as a "depersonalized."

68. Ibid., 68.

69. Lévinas, *Time and the Other*, 88–89.

70. As intentionality, but also as ipseity—since in principle, in the erotic relationship, we are not *equally* demanded by the other, but only insofar as we are *ourselves*.

71. Lévinas, *Time and the Other*, 94.

72. Lévinas, *Transcendance et intelligibilité*, 21.

73. *Totality and Infinity*, 115–21.

74. Ibid., 94.

75. Lévinas, *De Dieu que vient à l'idée*, 33.

76. Lévinas, *Totality and Infinity*, 259. On the transition from the erotic to the ethical, see Lévinas, *Collected Philosophical Papers*, 146: "[O]penness is the denuding of the skin exposed to wounds and outrage. This openness is the vulnerability of a skin exposed, in wounds and outrage. . . . In the sensibility is 'uncovered,' is exposed a nakedness more naked than that of the skin which, as form and beauty, inspires the plastic arts, the nakedness of a skin presented to contact, to the caress, which always—even, equivocally, in voluptuousness—is suffering for the suffering of the other."

77. Lévinas, *Collected Philosophical Papers*, 133–34.

78. Ibid., 145.

79. Ibid.

80. Ibid., 149.

81. Ibid.; see also 150: "Man . . . has to be conceived on the basis of the condition or uncondition of being hostage, hostage for all the others who, precisely qua others, do not belong to the same [species] as I, since I am responsible even for their responsibility. It is by virtue of this supplementary responsibility that subjectivity is not the ego, but me."

82. On this point see the discussion of the Fichtean deduction of intersubjectivity in my book *Système du droit*.

83. Lévinas, *Humanisme de l'autre homme*, 8–9. In the same sense, see *De Dieu qui vient à l'idée*, 36–37, 101. On errors regarding the transcendental subject, see my book with Luc Ferry, *Système et critique*.

84. Lévinas, *Transcendance et intelligibilité*, 20.

85. Lévinas, *De Dieu que vient à l'idée*, 37.

86. Ibid.

87. See Lévinas, *Humanisme de l'autre homme*, 9: "[T]he man of classical humanism placed his dignity" in "the free subject."

88. On the value and limits of Husserl's contribution to this understanding of the "subjective" as "passive," see ibid.

89. Lévinas, *Collected Philosophical Papers*, 135.

90. Ibid., 132.

91. Lévinas, *De Dieu qui vient à l'idée*, 48. In a similar vein, see *Totality and Infinity*, 88, on the "presence of the Other [as] a privileged heteronomy."

92. *Totality and Infinity*, 115–18.

93. For a somewhat different view of this cleavage, see the fourth chapter of my and Luc Ferry's *Heidegger and Modernity*.

94. Note that Kant's "pre-phenomenological" description of experiencing the law in the form of the categorical imperative corresponds to this moment.

CHAPTER VII
KANT

1. See Kant, *Critique of Pure Reason* (2nd edition), §17, 155–57; §25, 168–69, and, particularly, in the second version of the chapter on the paralogisms, the note on page 378.

2. Heidegger, *Kant and the Problem of Metaphysics*, 48–61.

3. See Marcel Gauchet, *Le Désenchantement du monde*.

4. See G. Lebrun, *Kant et la mort de la métaphysique: Essai sur la Critique de la faculté de juger* (Paris: Colin, 1970).

5. See Luc Ferry and Alain Renaut, "D'un retour à Kant," in *Système et critique*.

6. Here I set aside the question whether in doing this Kant was being unfair to Descartes.

7. On the subject of the schematism, see the final chapter of Ferry and Renaut, *French Philosophy of the Sixties*.

8. Kant, *Logic*, translated by Robert S. Hartman and Wolfgang Schwarz (New York: Dover, 1988), 96.

9. Kant, *Critique of Pure Reason*, 21 (from the Preface to the second edition [1787]).

10. Cassirer and Heidegger, *Débat sur le Kantisme et la Philosophie*. The part of this debate that concerns the theoretical subject has already been analyzed in the final chapter of *French Philosophy of the Sixties*. Here I am dealing primarily with practical reason, which was not treated in our earlier work.

11. Note Kant's original formulation in the first edition (1781) of the *Critique of Pure Reason* "[I]ntuition takes place only insofar as the object is given to us. This again is only possible, insofar as the mind is affected in a certain way." Cf. the revised formulation of the second edition cited at n. 30 below.

12. Heidegger, *Kant and the Problem of Metaphysics*, 162: "[F]inite reason is receptive even in its spontaneity. . . ."

13. See ibid., 162: "But if finite reason is receptive even in its spontaneity and, therefore, arises from the transcendental imagination, then practical reason must also be based on the latter"—through the feeling of respect.

14. Ibid., 163.

15. Kant, *Religion within the Limits of Reason Alone*, translated by Theodore M. Greene and Hoyt H. Hudson (Chicago: Open Court, 1934), 22ff.

16. Heidegger, *Kant and the Problem of Metaphysics*, 163, 165.

17. Kant, *Critique of Practical Reason*, Part 1, Book 1, Chapter 3, 79.

18. The essential document in this regard is Cassirer's account of the "*Kantbuch*" that appeared in 1931: see the French translation of his commentary

on Heidegger's interpretation of *Kant and the Problem of Metaphysics* in their *Débat sur le Kantisme*, 53ff.

19. Witness his presentation of the principle that motivates Heidegger's reading: "This elevation of knowledge that seems to occur when one rises from sensibility to understanding, and from understanding to reason, cannot in any case be taken to mean that we in the least escape finitude or that we can ever be finished with it once and for all. The foundational link with intuition can never be broken, and the dependence that it implies can never be shaken off" (ibid., 61).

20. Ibid.

21. Ibid., 62ff.

22. Ibid., 65.

23. Kant, *Critique of Pure Reason*, §26, 170ff. See also *The Kant-Eberhard Controversy*, 136.

24. The proof that the two spaces must not be confounded is that space as intuition is an "infinite given magnitude," while mathematical space is always limited and can be thought of as infinite only by abstraction from these limits.

25. Cassirer and Heidegger, *Débat sur le Kantisme*, 72.

26. Kant, *Critique of Pure Reason*, 382–83.

27. See ibid., 533 on the theory of the *focus imaginarius*.

28. On the conditions under which concepts can have meaning, see Philonenko's translation of Kant, *Qu'est-ce que s'orienter dans la pensée*, 75.

29. Cassirer and Heidegger, *Débat sur le Kantisme*, 70ff.

30. Kant, *Critique of Pure Reason* (2nd edition), 65 (my emphasis); cf. n. 11 above.

31. Kant, *Grounding for the Metaphysics of Morals*, 20.

32. Ibid., 20.

33. Cassirer and Heidegger, *Débat sur le Kantisme*, 72.

34. Jean-François Lyotard, "La Police de la pensée," *L'Autre Journal* (December 1985): 27–35.

35. Note, moreover, that in the final formula of the imperative the notion of man is explicitly mentioned.

36. Lyotard, "La Police de la pensée."

37. Kant, *Critique of Pure Reason*, 472.

38. Kant, *The Metaphysics of Morals*, translated by Mary Gregor (Cambridge: Cambridge University Press, 1991), §35, III. In the same sense, see Kant, *The Metaphysical Principles of Virtue*, translated by James Ellington (Indianapolis: Bobbs-Merrill, 1964), 78, 84, 91, 97.

39. See Cassirer and Heidegger, *Débat sur le Kantisme*, 225.

40. Ibid., 226.

41. Heidegger, "Letter on Humanism," in *Basic Writings*, 251.

42. Alexis Philonenko, *L'Oeuvre de Kant* (Paris: Vrin, 1969), I, 176, and *Études kantiennes*, 12ff.

43. Quite to the contrary, the theory of the schematism—intended as a reply to Berkeley's objections regarding the representability of general concepts—saves both their representability and their applicability: in this sense, the schematism guarantees the functioning of theoretical reason. Thus there was no need to modify this chapter to protect reason against some potentially disabling weakness.

44. I take these formulas from Cassirer's remarks in the *Débat sur le Kantisme*, 80.

45. Ibid., 78ff.

46. Kant, *Critique of Pure Reason*, 12. It is indeed on the *objective* deduction that the solution of the problem of the limitation of knowledge depends: if the categories are categories of experience, their transcendent usage is illegitimate.

47. In the translation cited of the *Critique* (the second edition), §15–23 correspond to the objective deduction and §24–25 to the subjective deduction.

48. Cassirer and Heidegger, *Débat sur le Kantisme*, 72; see too n. 31 above.

49. Heidegger, "Letter on Humanism," in *Basic Writings*, 255, 259. On this point see Ferry and Renaut, "La question de l'éthique après Heidegger," in *Système et critique*.

50. The disappearance of the very term "subject" (outside of its critical uses) from Heidegger's post-1930s vocabulary testifies to this.

51. On this interpretation of Heidegger's involvement with the Nazis and his gradual "disengagement," see Ferry and Renaut, *Heidegger and Modernity*.

52. On the prospects for a "transformation of transcendental philosophy," see K. O. Apel, *Transformation der Philosophie*, 2 vols. (Frankfurt: Suhrkamp, 1973). Apel's project is masterfully analyzed by Jean-Marc Ferry, *Habermas: L'éthique de la communication* (Paris: Presses Universitaires de France, 1987), 475ff.

53. Apel insists in particular on the necessity of taking account of the lessons of the linguistic and hermeneutic turn.

54. See Fichte, *Fondement du droit naturel*, Part 1, Section 1. On that which, with respect to its meaning, differentiates the Fichtean appearance of this structure from the function that it possesses in speculative philosophies like that of Maimon, see my *Système du droit*, 177 n. 36.

55. See Luc Ferry's excellent discussion of these complex passages in his *Political Philosophy* 2, 151ff.

56. For the sake of truth and of friendship, I must acknowledge that Luc Ferry formulated this hypothesis in seminars that we have been conducting for a number of years now at the Collège de Philosophie.

57. On this point see Cassirer and Heidegger, *Débat sur le Kantisme*, 69.

58. In what follows I repeat explicitly the conclusion of my article (written in collaboration with Luc Ferry) "La dimension éthique chez Heidegger," in U. Guzzoni, ed., *Nachdenken über Heidegger* (Hildesheim: Gerstenberg, 1980).

59. Kant, *Critique of Pure Reason*, 98.

Bibliography

Alquié, Ferdinand. *Le Cartésianisme de Malebranche*. Paris: Vrin, 1974.

Apel, Karl Otto. *Transformation der Philosophie*. 2 vols. Frankfurt: Suhrkamp Verlag, 1973.

Aquinas, Thomas. *On Being and Essence*, translated by Armand Maurer. 2nd revised edition. Toronto: Pontifical Institute of Mediaeval Studies, 1968; originally published 1949.

Belaval, Yvon. *Leibniz: critique de Descartes*. Paris: Gallimard, 1960.

———. *Leibniz: initiation à sa philosophie*. Paris: Vrin, 1970; originally published 1962.

Berkeley, George. *Philosophical Commentaries (Generally Called the Commonplace Book)*, edited by A. A. Luce. London: Thomas Nelson and Sons, 1944.

———. *Siris: A Chain of Philosophical Reflexions and Inquiries Concerning the Virtues of Tar-Water, and divers other Subjects connected together and arising from one another*. Dublin, 1744. In *The Works of George Berkeley*, edited by Luce and Jessop.

———. *The Works of George Berkeley, Bishop of Cloyne*, edited by A. A. Luce and T. E. Jessop. 9 vols. London and New York: T. Nelson, 1948–1957.

Berlin, Isaiah. *Vico and Herder*. London: Hogarth Press, 1976.

Biran, Maine de. *Oeuvres choisies*. Paris: Aubier, 1942.

Bloom, Allan. *The Closing of the American Mind: How Higher Education Has Failed Democracy and Impoverished the Souls of Today's Students*. New York: Simon and Schuster, 1987.

Brykman, Geneviève. *Philosophie et apologétique chez Berkeley*. Paris: Vrin, 1986.

Buzon, Frédéric de. "L'Individu et le sujet." In Guibert and Vieillard-Baron, eds., *Penser le sujet aujourd'hui*.

Carrive, Paulette. *Bernard Mandeville: Passions, vices, vertus*. Paris: Vrin, 1980.

———. *La Philosophie des passions chez Bernard Mandeville*. Lille: Publications de l'Université de Lille-III, 1978.

Cassirer, Ernst. *Les Systèmes post-Kantiens*. Translated by S. Bonnet et al. Lille: Presses Universitaires de Lille, 1983.

———. *The Individual and the Cosmos in Renaissance Philosophy*. Translated by Mario Domandi. New York: Harper & Row, 1963.

———. *The Philosophy of the Enlightenment*. Translated by Fritz C. A. Koelln and James P. Pettegrove. Princeton: Princeton University Press, 1968.

Châtelet, François, Olivier Duhamel, and Evelyne Pisier, eds. *Dictionnaire des oeuvres politiques*. Paris: Presses Universitaires de France, 1986.

Constant, Benjamin. *Benjamin Constant: Political Writings*. Translated by Biancamaria Fontana. Cambridge: Cambridge University Press, 1988.

Deleuze, Gilles. *Anti-Oedipus: Capitalism and Schizophrenia*. Translated by Robert Hurley, Mark Seem, and Helen R. Lane. Minneapolis: University of Minnesota Press, 1983.

———. *Empiricism and Subjectivity: An Essay on Hume's Theory of Human Nature*. Translated by Constantin V. Boundas. New York: Columbia University Press, 1991.

Derathé, Robert. *Jean-Jacques Rousseau et la science politique de son temps*. 2nd edition. Paris: Vrin, 1970; originally published 1950.

Derrida, Jacques. *Writing and Difference*. Translated by Alan Bass. Chicago: University of Chicago Press, 1978.

Descartes, René. *Selected Philosophical Writings*. Translated by J. Cottingham, R. Stoothoff, and D. Murdoch. Cambridge: Cambridge University Press, 1988.

———. *The Philosophical Writings*. Translated by J. Cottingham, R. Stoothoff, and D. Murdoch. 3 vols. Cambridge: Cambridge University Press, 1984–1991.

Dumont, Louis. *Essays on Individualism: Modern Ideology in Anthropological Perspective*. Chicago: University of Chicago Press, 1986.

———. *From Mandeville to Marx: The Genesis and Triumph of Economic Ideology*. Chicago: University of Chicago Press, 1977.

———. *Homo Hierarchicus: The Caste System and Its Implications*. Translated by Mark Sainsbury, Louis Dumont, and Basia Gulati. Complete revised edition Chicago: University of Chicago Press, 1980.

———. *La Tarasque: Essai de description d'un fait local d'un point de vue éthnographique*. Paris: Gallimard, 1951.

Dupuy, Jean-Pierre. *Le Sacrifice et l'envie: Le libéralisme aux prises avec la justice sociale*. Paris: Calmann-Lévy, 1992.

Enfantin, Prosper. *Doctrine of Saint-Simon: An Exposition*. Translated by Georg G. Igger. New York: Schocken, 1958.

Ferry, Jean-Marc. *Habermas: L'éthique de la communication*. Paris: Presses Universitaires de France, 1987.

Ferry, Luc. *Political Philosophy 1: Rights: The New Quarrel between the Ancients and the Moderns*. Translated by Franklin Philip. Chicago: University of Chicago Press, 1990.

———. *Political Philosophy 2: The System of Philosophies of History*. Translated by Franklin Philip. Chicago: University of Chicago Press, 1992.

Ferry, Luc, and Alain Renaut. *French Philosophy of the Sixties*. Translated by Mary H. S. Cettani. Amherst: University of Massachusetts Press, 1990.

———. *Heidegger and Modernity*. Translated by Franklin Philip. Chicago: University of Chicago Press, 1990.

———. "La Dimension éthique chez Heidegger." In *Nachdenken über Heidegger*, edited by Guzzoni.

———. *Political Philosophy 3: From the Rights of Man to the Republican Idea*. Translated by Franklin Philip. Chicago: University of Chicago Press, 1992.

———. *68–86: Itinéraires de l'individu*. Paris: Gallimard, 1987.

———. *Système et critique*. Brussels: Ousia, 1984.

———. "Le Sujet en procès." In Nagl-Docekal and Vetter, eds., *Tod des Subjekts?*

Ferry, Luc, and Alain Renaut, eds. *J. Rivelaygue: Leçons de la metaphysique allemande*. Paris: Grasset, 1990.

Fichte, Johann Gottlieb. *Fichte: Early Philosophical Writings*. Translated by Daniel Breazeale. Ithaca: Cornell University Press, 1988.

———. *Fondement du droit naturel*. Translated by Alain Renaut. Paris: Presses Universitaires de France, 1984.

———. *Foundations of the Entire Science of Knowledge*. Translated by P. Heath and J. Lachs. Cambridge: Cambridge University Press, 1982.

———. *J. G. Fichte im Gespräch: Berichte der Zeitgenossen*. Edited by Erich Fuchs. Stuttgart/Bad Canstatt: Frommann-Holzboog, 1978–1991.

———. *Nachgelassene Schriften*. Edited by H. Jacob. 2 vols. Berlin: Junker and Dunnhaupt, 1937.

Finkielkraut, Alain. *La Défaite de la pensée*. Paris: Gallimard, 1987.

Forthomme, Bernard. *Une Philosophie de la transcendance: La métaphysique d'Emmanuel Lévinas*. Paris: Vrin, 1979

Foucault, Michel. *Language, Counter-Memory, Practice: Selected Essays and Interviews*. Translated by Donald F. Bouchard and Sherry Simon. Ithaca: Cornell University Press, 1977.

———. *The Order of Things: An Archeology of the Human Sciences*. New York: Pantheon Books, 1970.

———. *Discipline and Punish: The Birth of the Prison*. Translated by Alan Sheridan. New York: Vintage Books, 1977.

Frank, Manfred. *Die Unhintergebarkeit von Individualität: Reflexionen über Subjekt, Person und Indivduum*. Frankfurt: Suhrkamp, 1986.

———. *L'Ultime raison du sujet*. Translated by V. Zanetti. Paris: Actes Sud, 1988.

———. "Subjekt, Person, Individuum." In Nagl-Docekal and Vetter, eds., *Tod des Subjekts?*

———. *What Is Neostructuralism?* Translated by Sabine Wilke and Richard Gray. Minneapolis: University of Minnesota Press, 1989.

Gauchet, Marcel. *Le Désenchantement du Monde: une histoire politique de la religion*. Paris: Gallimard, 1985.

Gauchet, Marcel, and Gladys Swain. *La Pratique de l'esprit humain: L'institution asilaire et la révolution démocratique*. Paris: Gallimard, 1980.

Guéroult, Martial. *Berkeley: Quatre études sur la perception et sur Dieu*. Paris: Aubier, 1956.

Gierke, Otto von. *Das deutsche Genossenschaftsrecht*. 4 vols. Berlin, 1868–1881; abridged as *Natural Law and the Theory of Society, 1500–1800*.

———. *Natural Law and the Theory of Society, 1500–1800*. Translated by Ernest Barker. 2 vols. Cambridge: Cambridge University Press, 1934.

Gilson, Étienne. *History of Christian Philosophy in the Middle Ages*. New York: Random House, 1955.

———. *The Spirit of Mediaeval Philosophy*. New York: Scribner's, 1940.

Granier, Jean. *Le Problème de la vérité dans la philosophie de Nietzsche*. Paris: Seuil, 1966.

Guibert, Elisabeth, and Jean-Louis Vieillard-Baron, eds. *Penser le sujet aujourd'hui*. Paris: Méridiens-Klincksieck, 1988.

Guillermit, Louis. *Le Réalisme de F. H. Jacobi: Dialogue sur l'idéalisme et le réalisme*. Provence: Publications de l'Université de Provence, 1982.

Guzzoni, Ute, ed. *Nachdenken über Heidegger*. Hildesheim: Gerstenberg, 1980.

Hegel, Georg Wilhelm Friedrich. *Lectures on the History of Philosophy*. Translated by R. F. Brown and J. M. Stewart with H. S. Harris. 3 vols. Berkeley and Los Angeles: University of California Press, 1990–.

———. *Gesammelte Werke*. Edited by W. Bonsiepn and R. Heede. 21 vols. Hamburg: Felix Meiner Verlag, 1968–.

———. *Lectures on the Philosophy of World History: Introduction: Reason in History*. Translated by H. B. Nisbett. Cambridge: Cambridge University Press, 1975.

———. *Phänomenologie des Geistes*. Vol. 9 of *Gesammelte Werke*.

———. *Phénoménologie de l'esprit*. Translated by Gwendoline Jarczyk and Pierre-Jean Labarrière. Paris: Gallimard, 1993.

———. *Phenomenology of Spirit*. Translated by A. V. Miller. Oxford: Oxford University Press, 1977.

Heidegger, Martin. *Brief über den Humanismus*. Frankfurt: V. Klostermann, 1949.

———. *Chemins qui ne mènent nulle part*. Paris: Gallimard, 1962.

———. *Essais et conférences*. Translated by André Préau and Jean Beaufret. Paris: Gallimard, 1958.

———. *Kant and the Problem of Metaphysics*. Translated by James S. Churchill. Bloomington: Indiana University Press, 1962.

———. *Martin Heidegger: Basic Writings*. Edited by David Farrell Krell. San Francisco: HarperCollins, 1977.

———. *Nietzsche*. Translated by Pierre Klossowski. 2 vols. Paris: Gallimard, 1971.

———. *Nietzsche*. Translated by David Farrell Krell. 4 vols. San Francisco: Harper & Row, 1979–1987.

———. *Questions* I. Paris: Gallimard, 1968.

———. *Schelling's Treatise on the Essence of Human Freedom*. Translated by Joan Stambaugh. Athens: Ohio University Press, 1985.

———. *The End of Philosophy*. Translated by Joan Stambaugh. New York: Harper & Row, 1973.

———. *The Metaphysical Foundation of Logic*. Translated by Michael Heim. Bloomington: Indiana University Press, 1984.

———. *The Principle of Reason*. Translated by Reginald Lilly. Bloomington: Indiana University Press, 1991.

———. *The Question Concerning Technology and Other Essays*. Translated by William Lovitt. New York: Harper & Row, 1977.

———. *What Is a Thing?* Translated by W. B. Barton, Jr. and Vera Deutsch. Chicago: Henry Regnery, 1967.

———. *What Is Called Thinking?* Translated by J. Glenn Gray. New York: Harper & Row, 1968.

Heidegger, Martin, and Ernst Cassirer. *Débat sur le Kantisme et la philosophie (Davos, mars 1929) et autres textes de 1929–1931*. Paris: Beauchesne, 1973.

Henry, Michel. *La Barbarie*. Paris: Grasset, 1986.

Herder, Johann Gottfried. *Ideen sur Philosophie der Geschichte der Menschheit*. 4 vols. Riga, 1784–1791.

———. *Idées pour la philosophie de l'histoire de l'humanité*. Translated by Max Rouché. Paris: Aubier-Montaigne, 1964.

———. *Sämtliche Werke*. Edited by Bernhard Suphan. 33 vols. Hildesheim: Georg Olms, 1967–1968.

———. *Une Autre philosophie de l'histoire*. Translated by Max Rouché. Paris: Aubier, 1964.

Horkheimer, Max. *Between Philosophy and Social Science: Selected Early Writings*. Translated by G. Frederick Hunter, Matthew S. Kramer, and John Torpey. Cambridge: MIT Press, 1993.

Hume, David. *Enquiries Concerning the Human Understanding and Concerning the Principles of Morals*. Edited by L. A. Selby-Bigge. 3rd edition. Oxford: Clarendon Press, 1975; originally published 1894.

———. *Treatise on Human Nature*. Edited by L. A. Selby-Bigge. 2nd edition. Oxford: Clarendon Press, 1978; originally published 1888.

Husserl, Edmund. *Cartesian Meditations: An Introduction to Phenomenology*. Translated by Dorion Cairns. The Hague: Martinus Nijhoff, 1960; 2nd edition, 1977.

———. *Husserliana: Edmund Husserl, Gesammelte Werke*. 29 vols. The Hague: Martinus Nijhoff, 1950–1987; Dordrecht: Kluwer, 1988–1993.

———. *La Crise des sciences européennes et la phénoménologie transcendentale*. Translated by Gérard Granel. Paris: Gallimard, 1976.

———. *Logische Untersuchungen*. 2 vols. Halle, 1900–1901.

———. *The Crisis of European Sciences and Transcendental Phenonomenology: An Introduction to Phenonomenological Philosophy*. Translated by David Carr. Evanston: Northwestern University Press, 1970.

Jacobi, Friedrich Heinrich. *David Hume ou la croyance: Idéalisme et réalisme*. Translated by Louis Guillermit. In Guillermit, *Le Réalisme de F. H. Jacobi*.

———. *Über die Lehre des Spinozas, in Briefen an Herrn Moses Mendelssohn*. Breslau, 1785.

Kant, Immanuel. *Anthropologie du point de vue pragmatique*. Translated by Michel Foucault. Paris: Vrin, 1964.

———. *Anthropology from a Pragmatic Point of View*. Translated by Victor Lyle Dowdell. Carbondale: Southern Illinois University Press, 1978.

———. *Critique de la faculté de juger*. Translated by Alexis Philonenko. Paris: Vrin, 1965.

———. *Critique of Practical Reason*. Translated by Lewis White Beck. 3rd edition. New York: Macmillan, 1956; originally published 1949.

———. *Critique of Pure Reason*. Translated by Norman Kemp Smith. New York: St. Martin's Press, 1965; originally published 1929.

———. *Critique de la raison pure*. Paris: GF-Flammarion, 1987.

———. *Grounding for the Metaphysics of Morals*. Translated by James W. Ellington. 3rd edition. Indianapolis: Hackett, 1993; originally published 1981.

———. *Logic*. Translated by Robert S. Hartman and Wolfgang Schwarz. New York: Dover, 1988.

———. *Philosophical Correspondence, 1759–99*. Translated by Arnulf Zweig. Chicago: University of Chicago Press, 1967.

Kant, Immanuel. *Qu'est-ce que s'orienter dans la pensée?* Translated by Alexis Philonenko. Paris: Vrin, 1978.

———. *Religion within the Limits of Reason Alone.* Translated by Theodore M. Greene and Hoyt H. Hudson. Chicago: Open Court, 1934.

———. *The Kant-Eberhard Controversy.* Translated by Henry E. Allison. Baltimore: Johns Hopkins University Press, 1973.

———. *The Metaphysical Principles of Virtue.* Translated by James Ellington. Indianapolis: Bobbs-Merrill, 1964.

———. *The Metaphysics of Morals.* Translated by Mary Gregor. Cambridge: Cambridge University Press, 1991.

Lamberti, Jean-Claude. *L'Individualisme chez Tocqueville.* Paris: Presses Universitaires de France, 1970.

Lebrun, Gérard. *Kant et la mort de la métaphysique: Essai sur la Critique de la faculté de juger.* Paris: Colin, 1970.

Lefort, Claude. *The Political Forms of Modern Society: Bureaucracy, Democracy, Totalitarianism.* Edited by John B. Thompson. Cambridge: MIT Press, 1986.

Legros, Robert. *Le Jeune Hegel et la naissance de la pensée romantique.* Brussels: Ousia, 1981.

Leibniz, Gottfried Wilhelm. *De rerum originatione* (1697). In *Leibniz: Philosophical Writings.*

———. *Die Philosophische Schriften von G. W. Leibniz.* Edited by C. I. Gerhardt. 7 vols. Berlin, 1875–1890.

———. *Disputatio metaphysica de principio individui.* Leipzig, 1663. In *God. Guil. Leibnitii Opera philosophica.*

———. *God. Guil. Leibnitii Opera philosophica quae estant latina, gallica, germanica oianm.* Edited by J. E. Erdmann. Berlin: G. Eichleri, 1839–1840.

———. *Leibniz: Philosophical Writings.* Translated by Mary Morris. New York: Dutton, 1956.

———. *Monadology.* Translated by P. G. Lucas and Leslie Grint. Manchester: University of Manchester Press, 1953; reprinted with minor corrections, 1961.

———. *Monadology and Other Essays.* Translated by Paul Schrecker and Anne Martin Schrecker. Indianapolis: Bobbs-Merrill, 1965.

———. *New Essays on Human Understanding.* Edited and translated by Peter Remnant and Jonathan Bennett. Cambridge: Cambridge University Press, 1981.

———. *New System of Nature and of the Communications between Substances, as Well as of the Union of Soul and Body.* Paris, 1695. In *Leibniz: Philosophical Writings.*

———. *Opera Philosophica.* 2 vols. Edited by J. E. Erdmann. Berlin, 1840.

———. *Theodicy.* Translated by E. M. Huggard. London: Routledge and Kegan Paul, 1951.

Lévinas, Emannuel. *De Dieu qui vient à l'idée.* Paris: Vrin, 1982.

———. *Emmanuel Lévinas: Collected Philosophical Papers.* Translated by Alphonso Lingis. The Hague: Martinus Nijhoff, 1987.

———. *En découvrant l'existence avec Husserl et Heidegger.* Paris: Vrin, 1949.

———. *Existence and Existents.* Translated by Alphonso Lingis. Dordrecht: Kluwer, 1988.

———. *Humanisme de l'autre homme*. Montpellier: Fata Morgana, 1972.
———. *Time and the Other, and Additional Essays*. Translated by Richard A. Cohen. Pittsburgh: Duquesne University Press, 1987.
———. *Totality and Infinity: An Essay on Exteriority*. Translated by Alphonso Lingis. Pittsburgh: Duquesne University Press, 1979.
———. *Transcendance et intelligibilité*. Geneva: Labor and Fides, 1984.
Lipovetsky, Gilles. *The Empire of Fashion: Dressing Modern Democracy*. Translated by Catherine Porter. Princeton: Princeton University Press, 1994.
Löwith, Karl. *From Hegel to Nietzsche: The Revolution in Nineteenth-Century Thought*. Translated by David E. Green. New York: Holt, Rinehart and Winston, 1964.
Lyotard, Jean-François. "La Police de la pensée." *L'Autre Journal* (December 1985): 27–35.
Malebranche, Nicolas. *Correspondence avec J.-J. Dourtous de Mairan*. Edited by Joseph Moreau. Paris: Vrin, 1947.
———. *Oeuvres complètes*. 21 vols. Paris: Vrin, 1958–1970.
Malherbe, Michel. *La Philosophie empiriste de David Hume*. Paris: Vrin, 1976.
Mandeville, Bernard. *The Fable of the Bees: Or Private Vices, Public Benefits*. London, 1714.
———. *Fable of the Bees*. London: Wishart & Co., 1934.
Marion, Jean-Luc. *Sur le prisme métaphysique de Descartes: Constitution et limites de l'onto-théo-logie dans la pensée cartésienne*. Paris: Presses Universitaires de France, 1986.
Mesure, Sylvie. "Raymond Aron et le problème de l'objectivité historique." *Commentaire*, no. 35 (Fall 1986).
Michaud, Yves. *Hume et la fin de la philosophie*. Paris: Presses Universitaires de France, 1983.
Morel, Georges. *Nietzsche: Introduction à une première lecture*. 3 vols. Paris: Aubier-Montaigne, 1985.
Nagl-Docekal, Herta, and Helmuth Vetter, eds. *Tod des Subjekts?* Vienna/Munich: Oldenbourg, 1987.
Nietzsche, Friedrich. *Ainsi parlait Zarathoustra*. Translated by Geneviève Bianquis. Paris: Aubier-Flammarion, 1969.
———. *Beyond Good and Evil: Prelude to a Philosophy of the Future*. Translated by R. J. Hollingdale. Harmondsworth: Penguin Books, 1973.
———. *Human, All Too Human: A Book for Free Spirits*. Translated by Marion Faber with Stephen Lehmann. Lincoln: University of Nebraska Press, 1984.
———. *La Volonté de puissance*. Translated by Henri Albert. 15th edition. Paris: Mercure de France, 1923; originally published 1903.
———. *La Volonté de puissance*. 2 vols. Translated by Geneviève Bianquis. Paris: Gallimard, 1948.
———. *The Gay Science*. Translated by Walter Kaufman. New York: Vintage Books, 1974.
———. *The Will to Power*. Translated by Walter Kaufman and R. J. Hollingdale. New York: Random House, 1967.
———. *Twilight of the Idols*. Translated by R. J. Hollingdale. Harmondsworth: Penguin Books, 1968.

Nietzsche, Friedrich. *Untimely Meditations*. Translated by R. J. Hollingdale. Cambridge: Cambridge University Press, 1983.

———. "Zur Philosophie und ihrer Geschichte." In *Die Unschuld des Werdens: Der Nachlass*, edited by Alfred Baeumler. Vol. II. Stuttgart: Alfred Kröner Verlag, 1913.

Philonenko, Alexis. *La Liberté humaine dans la philosophie de Fichte*. Paris: Vrin, 1966.

Philonenko, Alexis. *L'Oeuvre de Kant*. Paris: Vrin, 1969.

———. *La Théorie kantienne de l'histoire*. Paris: Vrin, 1986.

Plato. *The Collected Dialogues of Plato*. Edited by Edith Hamilton and Huntington Cairns. Bollingen Series LXXI. Princeton: Princeton University Press, 1963.

———. *The Republic*. Translated by Benjamin Jowett. 3rd edition. Oxford: Clarendon Press, 1888; reprinted New York: Vintage Books, 1991.

Quillet, Jeanine. "Disputation métaphysique sur le principe d'individuation de G. W. Leibniz." *Études philosophiques* (January–March 1979): 79–105.

Raynaud, Philippe. "*Auch eine Philosophie*." In Châtelet, Duhamel, and Pisier, eds. *Dictionnaire des oeuvres politiques*.

Renaut, Alain. "De la philosophie comme philosophie du droit." *Bulletin de la Société Française de Philosophie* (July–September 1986).

———. "Martin Heidegger: Essais et conférences, 1954." In Châtelet, Duhamel, and Pisier, eds. *Dictionnaire des oeuvres politiques*.

———. *Système du droit: Philosophie et droit dans la pensée de Fichte*. Paris: Presses Universitaires de France, 1986.

Renouvier, Charles. *Manuel de philosophie moderne*. Paris: Paulin, 1842.

Renouvier, Charles, and Louis Prat. *La Nouvelle monadologie*. Paris: Colin, 1899.

Rodis-Lewis, Geneviève. *L'Individualité selon Descartes*. Paris: Vrin, 1950.

Rouché, Max. *La Philosophie de l'histoire de Herder*. Paris: Les Belles Lettres, 1940.

Rousseau, Jean-Jacques. *The Political Writings of Jean-Jacques Rousseau*. Edited by C. E. Vaughn. 2 vols. Cambridge: Cambridge University Press, 1915.

———. *The Social Contract*. Amsterdam, 1762. In *The Political Writings of Jean-Jacques Rousseau*, vol. I.

Russell, Bertrand. *A Critical Exposition of the Philosophy of Leibniz*. 2nd edition. Cambridge: Cambridge University Press, 1967; originally published 1900.

Sartre, Jean-Paul. *Being and Nothingness: A Phenomenological Essay on Ontology*. Translated by Hazel E. Barnes. New York: Washington Square Press, 1956.

Schelling, F. W. J. von. *On the History of Modern Philosophy*. Translated by Andrew Bowie. Cambridge: Cambridge University Press, 1994.

Serres, Michel. *Le Système de Leibniz et ses modèles mathématiques: Étoiles, schémas, points*. 2 vols. Paris: Presses Universitaires de France, 1968.

Sève, René. *Les Fins et les règles: Leibniz et l'école moderne du droit naturel*. Paris: Presses Universitaires de France, 1989.

Strawson, P. F. *Individuals: An Essay in Descriptive Metaphysics*. London: Methuen, 1959.

Troeltsch, Ernst. *Social Teaching of the Christian Churches*. Translated by Olive Wyon. 2 vols. London: Allen & Unwin, 1950.

Villey, Michel. *La Formation de la pensée juridique moderne: Cours d'histoire de la philosophie du droit, 1961–1966*. 4th edition. Paris: Montchrétien, 1975; originally published 1968.

———. *Seize essais de philosophie du droit*. Paris: Dalloz, 1969.

Weber, Max. *The Protestant Ethic and the Spirit of Capitalism*. Translated by Talcott Parsons. New York: Scribner's, 1958.

Index

About the author

Alain Renaut, Professor of Philosophy at the University of Caen and cofounder of the Collège de Philosophie, is among the foremost representatives of liberal humanism in France today. He is the author of *Philosophie et droit dans la Pensée de Fichte*, and, with Luc Ferry, has coauthored many controversial books, including *French Philosophy of the Sixties* and *Heidegger and the Moderns*.